THE
LIVING LIGHT
DIALOGUE

Volume 15

Reproduction of the cover image of the
1972 edition of *The Living Light*

[See the appendix for a discussion of the image's symbolism.]

THE LIVING LIGHT DIALOGUE

Volume 15

Through the mediumship of
Richard P. Goodwin

Living Light Books

The Living Light Dialogue Volume 15
Copyright © 2021 Serenity Association
Through the mediumship of Richard P. Goodwin.

All rights reserved. No portion of this book may be reproduced—electronically, mechanically, or via internet transmission—without advance, express written permission of the publisher except in the case of brief quotations embodied in critical articles and reviews. No derivative work—games, supplemental material, video—may be created without advance, express written permission of the publisher. For information address Living Light Books, P.O. Box 4187, San Rafael, CA 94913-4187.

Cover design copyright © 2021 by Serenity Association.
Cover photograph by Serenity Association, 2021; copyright © 2021 by Serenity Association. Reproduction of cover image of the 1972 edition of *The Living Light* copyright © 2021 by Serenity Association.

www.livinglight.org

Library of Congress Control Number 2007929762
ISBN: 978-1-947199-28-6

FIRST EDITION

This volume of teachings is dedicated to the spirit friends who brought to Earth the Living Light Philosophy. With eternal gratitude, we pray that we may demonstrate these principles and continue to bring to publication these teachings.

CONTENTS

Acknowledgment ix
Preface xi
Introduction xv
A/V Class Private 16 3
A/V Class Private 17 45
A/V Class Private 18 85
A/V Class Private 19 119
A/V Class Private 20 151
A/V Class Private 21 179
A/V Class Private 22 211
A/V Class Private 23 241
A/V Class Private 24 265
A/V Class Private 25 285
A/V Class Private 26 307
A/V Class Private 27 327
A/V Class Private 28 343
A/V Class Private 29 365
A/V Class Private 30 383
A/V Class Private 31 405
A/V Class Private 32 429
A/V Class Private 33 447
A/V Class Private 34 459
A/V Class Private 35 481
Appendix..503

ACKNOWLEDGMENT

Grateful acknowledgement is made to the many friends and associates for invaluable aid in compiling this book, for their helpful suggestions, for their loyal interest and encouragement.

Special acknowledgement is due to those who painstakingly and selflessly transcribed and proofread the text.

PREFACE

It was through the mediumship of the Serenity Association founder, Mr. Richard P. Goodwin, that a philosophy known as the Living Light was given in more than 700 classes over a twenty-five-year period.

To be specific, the philosophy was imparted through Mr. Goodwin by a magistrate who had lived on Earth some 8,000 years ago. The former magistrate is known to Living Light students as "the Wise One," and he narrated the journey of his soul on the other side of life, the experiences—especially the difficulties—he encountered in having to face himself, as well as the teachings he earned to help himself through the realms in which he traveled. It was his decision to share the teachings with souls on both sides of "the curtain."

Prior to the advent of the Wise One, Mr. Goodwin had prayed for a teacher from the realms of light. Mr. Goodwin, since age fourteen, had been the instrument through which spirit was able to communicate with those seeking help. But he saw that his mediumship brought only temporary solace, because the people he was trying to help soon became fascinated with the phenomena and ignored the help that spirit was imparting. He prayed for someone who would bring forth teachings that would benefit any soul seeking a path to a greater awareness of himself and of God.

His prayers were answered in 1964 when the Wise One came through for the first time. Mr. Goodwin, at first apprehensive about what this new teacher would impart, was taken into deep trance and not able to control what was being revealed through him. Upon hearing the recorded classes afterward, however, he became convinced of the goodness of the teacher and of the value of the simple, beautiful teachings. This, then, was the beginning of the Living Light Philosophy given to Earth through the mediumship of Richard P. Goodwin.

In carrying out the request of the Wise One and Mr. Goodwin, students of the Serenity Association transcribed from audiotape the classes that had been brought through. Because most are in the form of teacher-student interaction, the classes became known as *The Living Light Dialogue*; and the students were instructed to publish the classes as a multi-volume set of the Living Light Philosophy. *Volume 1* was published in the autumn of 2007.

The present book, *Volume 15,* continues the A/V Class Private series. As their name suggests, these classes were originally given as private classes and were to be shared and discussed only with those who were in attendance. The guidance Mr. Goodwin gave to his students requested that all classes be published after he had passed on to the higher life; and so, these private classes are now becoming more widely available. In many ways, these classes are of a more personal nature. The teacher frequently addressed the students by name and the students would often interact with each other. Many of the teacher's responses include references to the individual experiences of the questioner, and although this helps the student to better relate to the teaching, his responses also reveal the principle involved. Thus, in this series the names of the students are included, but have been replaced with more generic terms of identification in order to respect their privacy.

These classes were held Sunday mornings at the Serenity temple. This particular volume includes nineteen classes, from A/V Class Private 16 through A/V Class Private 35, and cover the period of time from September 29, 1985, until February 16, 1986.

The foundation of the classes—the foundation of the Living Light Philosophy itself—is the Law of Personal Responsibility which states, in part, that we are responsible for all our experiences, and that our experiences are the return of the laws that we have established with our thoughts, acts, and deeds. Through greater awareness of our thoughts and by exercising our divine right of choice, we may choose to establish laws of greater harmony and goodness.

The Living Light Dialogue teaches that we have come to Earth to learn the lessons that are necessary to free us from the dictates and limits of our own thoughts and judgments, which are the mental patterns that we follow through our own lack of awareness and are so very potent, forceful, and limiting. These teachings guide us in making the necessary changes in our thinking in order to free ourselves from those patterns and to express our soul consciousness.

The choice of guiding the direction of our life, as stated by the Wise One when he speaks of being with a person, place, or thing, is, in essence, of being in this world and not a part of this world. He further explains that no matter what experiences we encounter, no matter what we do or do not do, we—our spirit—may view the experience in objectivity from a soul level of consciousness where peace reigns supreme.

The teachings of this volume help us to restore harmony or balance in our life by flooding the consciousness with spiritual affirmations and prayers, a few of which can be found in the appendix. When reason is restored, by balancing our sense functions with our soul faculties, we will consciously experience peace. Without annihilating our ego or our sense functions, we will find a pathway of expression for our soul. Where there was once disturbance, now there is acceptance. Where there was disease, now there is poise. And where there was hopelessness and despair, now there is reason, divine neutrality; and peace shows the way.

If you make the effort to apply these laws, such as, "If man is a law unto himself, what are you doing with the law that you are?", and demonstrate the wisdom of patience, the truth of this philosophy will be your living demonstration.

As the teacher states in CC 130, "My journey of many centuries and much experience has brought me here to Earth to share with you these simple teachings that have come as the effect of a long, long, long journey. Let not *your* journey be so long in the realms of illusion. For it is not necessary for you. For in your evolution, you have earned an awakening. But it is up to you to do something that is constructive and worthwhile."

INTRODUCTION

[This introduction was written by Mr. Goodwin and originally appeared in *The Living Light*, which were the first teachings of the Living Light Philosophy published in book form. The entire text of *The Living Light* was republished in *The Living Light Dialogue*, Volume 1.]

"Think, children. Think more often and think more deeply."

The teachings in this book were given as a progressive series of lessons to a group of four students who were sitting for spiritual unfoldment with me beginning in January of 1964. The communications were regular until October of that year, when nearly a seven-year silence ensued, and resumed in 1971 to the present. They were received in three ways by me as a channel. The main text was taped from a direct control of my voice in deep trance at special sittings of our group, during which I had no experience of the voice or what was being transmitted. A few scattered verses were given independently when I was privileged to see and hear our teacher clairvoyantly. I have also been a channel for this communicant when speaking from the podium at church and in answering difficult questions at our public seminars.

Nearly all we know about our teacher is contained in the lectures. He reports that he had tried for sixteen years to break through an interference barrier that the channel had to deep trance. When our conditions were in resonance with his patient wisdom, he came through ready to teach his understanding. I have seen him as an old man dressed in white with long flowing white hair. He has blue eyes, slightly smiling and deeply compassionate. I have always called him the Old Man. The students liked to call him the Wise One. He is surely one of those often called a Teacher of Light. I do not know his country, although he indicated at one time that he was from 6000 B.C., and a form of a judge in his time.

The text is often difficult, but it is complete, having been transcribed word for word from the original tapes recording the trance voice. It is presented with a minimum of punctuation to be freer for the individual interpretation of each reader. The lessons given before the long silence are phrased with many allegories often paradoxical. There are repetitions and renewals of theme, but it is explained that if an understanding is not perceived, compassion dictates that it be said again. Some of the topics have but a simple mention with little development but all are revealed, we are told, according to merit.

The Old Man is a fine teacher. He has in a hundred ways intertwined his allegory, progressive explanations, unfolding exercises, and timely references to reach a multitude of levels of individual understanding. A notable change is his more direct style of presentation beginning in 1971.

There is an endearing intimacy of person that can be felt through his lectures, a meaningful and loving encounter with a wise friend. Like an old man, he makes a mistake and conscientiously corrects himself a few paragraphs later. He listens often and carefully to our earnest discussions of his words. He consults with a group of experts on evolution and cites their learning in his lesson. His use of the direct address "children" or "my children" is not patronizing but infinitely loving and supportive.

A word must be said about the teachings. The Old Man makes clear that his lessons are not dogma, a creed or a narrow way, but simply his own understanding offered to us as a form of instruction to aid us in our own individual progression. When he speaks of Laws, he does not refer to man-made rules or moral traditions but to the cosmic and atomic way-things-are, the natural world of what-is, the universal laws of life, part of the original creative design and through which creation is fulfilled. These laws are beyond the possibility of being changed, suspended, transcended, or destroyed but they are ever a tool of mankind, not his master. First, through our awareness of the universal laws and then slowly through our developed understanding, the powers of creation are accessible to us. Not power over men's minds or circumstances, but power over whatever is selfish and imperfect in ourselves is the way up the eternal ladder of progression. When the Old Man cautions us concerning the Law of Responsibility or gives us a thinking exercise to explore the Law of Identity in a dynamic manner, he prepares us to take another step. And all move in accordance with the Law of What Can Be Borne.

Our teacher shows us how the two worlds are drawn together. In his realm, he describes, there is a great diversity of thought, many schools of understanding; but the Light is always known by the Light. Because of the interdependence of the two realms, listening to our discussions helped to clarify his teaching to others on his side of the curtain. His love and gratitude he humbly equates with ours.

The lessons to be perceived are not new, they are very old, but they are new to certain levels of our being. I would personally advise the reader, after reading this volume of discourses in full, to make a daily habit (or when there is a feeling or need) to sit quietly with the book. Open it at random and be guided to the Light by the passage that is there for the day. This technique is still used by the original students who were given the lessons and by many students after them who have studied in unfolding classes with me through these teachings.

Go beyond the words into feeling, into the immediate meanings for you. Touch into the inspiration that flows into the form of this book. It is from the Divine.

RICHARD P. GOODWIN
San Geronimo, California
June, 1972

A/V Class Private

A/V Class Private 16

Good morning, students.

For today we'll discuss, for a time, the word of power and its loss to mankind on the planet Earth.

As most of you are aware: to speak the word forth into the universe knowing that it shall not return to you void, but accomplish that which you send it to do. Well, as the covering slowly but surely begins to believe that it is the content which it covers, man loses the power of the word. And so it is that through our evolution we are often tempted to believe that we are the covering at the cost of forgetting the content which we are. Whoever awakens to the content that they are has once again awakened to the power of the word and shall not speak it without its just and due return.

Also, several years ago with some of you students that are still with me here, I discussed the great benefit of what is known in your world as acupressure. I spoke to you of its benefit for your health, your wealth, and your happiness.

And we're moving onward with these classes. And your homework, which is critical as part of the class and [for] a student thereof, must and shall be done. And so in the coming weeks, as you share, students, with the other students here at these classes what you understand of what has been given on the spiritual meaning of the various parts of the human anatomy, for we shall not [proceed] until you have, of course, done your part in study, application, and understanding what the various parts of the human body represent spiritually.

Now today—and our cameraman has benefited greatly from the awakening of what color vibrations create warmth and what color vibrations and combinations thereof create a cool or cold vibration. Now some of you are aware, as you look out at the world and you see in nature a predominant color that you call green. You find security in the color vibration of green, though it may not be a personal preference for your apparel. However, what you understand and view as green is in truth what is known as yellow or gold. Now those of you who recall what has already been given to you in reference to the meaning of color or vibration are well aware that gold or yellow, the vibration of divine wisdom, wears the cloak or covering of what you look and see as green. And so man feels secure with the vibration of divine wisdom.

Now psychologically, mentally, to your minds, colors bring forth from you various feelings, attitudes, and emotions. However, in thorough study you will quickly learn that the vibration known as green, you will always feel more secure in, whether it is the green of a leaf, a tree, a blade of grass, or a piece of paper. Now there's a part of you inside of you that responds, and that response you experience as an emotional security.

In your daily efforts when you experience these emotional upheavals, there are ways of quickly redirecting the energy that is being utilized for realms of consciousness that are in truth most detrimental.

However, as in any study, without application, it is worthless. So as you as a student body, the majority of the student body apply the cleansing breath to free yourselves from those disturbing and diseased realms of consciousness and that becomes a demonstration of the student body, we will then at that time move forward to the application of redirecting the energy going to those realms of consciousness within you by application of gentle pressure on certain parts of your physical anatomy. However, first you must—those who have received the meaning of the different parts of the anatomy—you must first, in these classes you will be asked what the meaning of the different parts of the body are, only those students who have already been given that understanding. Once that has [been] done and you once again have refreshed your memory, then we will move on to the application of gentle pressure to bring about spontaneous change and freedom from those realms of consciousness.

Now it's time for you to ask your questions as part of your responsibility in study and your homework so that we can move on with our classes. So we'll take this moment for you to raise your hands. *[After a short pause, the teacher continues.]* The moment has passed. Yes, [Student S], please.

In what ways can we increase our rate of spin to reverse it to go inside?

Increasing the rapidity of that to enter inward will be brought up in certain applications of pressure after the daily application of the student body to the cleansing breath, which has already been given.

Thank you.

Yes, go ahead with your other questions.

What is the spiritual cause behind the so-called natural disasters the world is presently experiencing?

All form, all forms are links in an eternal chain of which we are all connected. Therefore, when 51 percent of the human species is in a state of discord or out of harmony with nature, all forms, when through over-identification with self, a person tempts to separate themselves from the chain of life of which they are an inseparable part, and when 51 percent of the human species do that, the forms and the nature spirits respond. And it responds in ways that we understand are disastrous to us. It is ever in keeping with the just law and the basic instinct of survival. Did that help with your question? Yes?

I'd also like to ask, At this time what does the majority of the people seem to be into? What are they so discordant about? And I'd also like to ask, Why at this time are there more airplane crashes than, say, boat problems or train problems?

Very good question. First of all, the cause of the discord and the upset is what you know in your world as frustration or the inability to fulfill their judgments. And that inability is caused by depending on something that, by divine law, they have no right to control. And the final result of that type of thinking is frustration and discord. And so it reveals to you, by the experiences of so-called disasters, by the nature spirits of the air, of the earth, and of the various elements as they fight for survival, their basic instinct.

Now why, seemingly, in reference to your question, are there so many seeming disasters concerning the element air? The element air represents what part of the being?

The mental?

The mental world. Absolutely correct. And so it is the mental world that is disturbed and upset. And so the experiences of upset and discord are taking place in that element and, in revealing to mankind, you have many air so-called disasters. Yes.

Thank you.

You're welcome. Now [Student H] had a question here, please.

Thank you. The Living Light speaks of guarding and protecting one's beginnings until they're strong to weather the forces of adversity. In reference to the class discussion on dependence, where does one draw the line between guarding one's beginnings and living in a state of dependence on one's beliefs and judgments of childhood?

Where does one draw the line?

Yes.

By a conscious choice of whether they are experiencing through a conscious awakening to the eternal moment where they create their beginnings. See, whatever began a moment ago is not a beginning. That's something that has happened. It may not be completed. You see, what happens with people who begin things, you see, and do not complete them is they remain in their consciousness as shadows to haunt them.

And so if you have something to do, wisdom reveals to do it and to do it quickly. Now a person may say, "Well, it could take me 10 or 20 years to do what I want to do." But that's an ignorant way of looking at anything. For, you see, if—first of all, you say that it may take 10 or 20 years to accomplish what it is you wish to accomplish. In that 10 or 20 years there are a multitude of beginning steps to the final accomplishment. Do you understand?

Yes.

And so whenever we permit our self to think of our self, we open up this Pandora's box, so to speak, to all of the loose ends, all of the things we began. Because, you see, when we think of doing something, that *is* the beginning. And so man thinks of doing many things and accomplishing many things. And so man has many unfulfilled desires; many beginnings that have not been completed to haunt him constantly.

Now when you think of beginning a project or a change in your life, at that moment you face all of these beginnings that never got completed in your life. This is why a wise man cherishes and guards his beginnings. First of all, he has to work diligently to complete the beginning he's presently thinking of for he has all of the other beginnings of past years that are in the consciousness that rise up for their completion. Do you understand? So— *[The teacher coughs.]* Excuse me. If he speaks forth physically, the word, to anyone, they also have all of these beginnings that are waiting to be completed; so he adds unto himself by the spoken word, you understand, to the listening ear, he adds not only his beginnings that haven't been completed yet for a lifetime but he adds all of those to the person to whom he is speaking. Do you understand?

Yes.

Does that help with your question?

Thank you very much.

You're welcome.

Now what I'm going to do because we've had to make changes in the lighting, as you notice, we have several colors in here, is for you to raise your hand and then to speak your name so that we can get identification here. Yes. Yes.

[Student O].

Yes, [Student O].

Yes, sir. OK. What is our responsibility or what is one's responsibility to an individual or individuals that they have been instrumental in introducing of the Living Light to them?

First of all, has the Law of Solicitation been established prior to the introduction of the Light?

Through the, through the Law of Presence in conversation, yes.

Yes, I see. Well, one's responsibility in the world is to give what one has to give and to care less what the person does with it. Do you understand that?

Yes, sir.

For one to concern oneself with what one is doing with what they have given to them reveals, of course, to anyone they gave them nothing; they made a loan. Do you understand that?

I understand that.

And loans, of course, we understand is debts, would you not agree?

Yes, sir.

Well, none of us wants debts, do we?

No, sir.

Thank you. I hope that's helped with your question.

Yes, sir. [After a pause, the student continues.] *Shall I continue?*

Yes, if you have another question, go right ahead. I don't see any other hands.

OK. Has—is—has, has Earth always been of, in the dimension of duality, of creation?

Earth?

Yes, sir.

Why, yes. Earth has always, always had and is creation, that is, form. In reference—if you're speaking of the awakening of the consciousness while in form, has it always been dual? No, it has not.

In . . .

Yes.

Is, is Earth the only planet that, that has this duality, dimension of duality?

It is not the only planet of evolution that has it at this time. No, it is not. You try to understand there was a time on your planet when there was the singular, the awakening. And in keeping with the Law of Creation, it descended only to rise again to descend again. Yes. As you have a day and a night, so you have an ascent and a descent.

One more.

Yes, certainly.

Could you speak on the phenomena of, the so-called phenomena of Big Foot?

I'm happy that you spoke on the so-called phenomena of Big Foot for phenomenon is nothing more and nothing less than a lack of our understanding of the laws through which it is accomplished. Now if you're speaking of this so-called what you, I guess you call "creature" that seems to appear and disappear, try to understand that there's very little that your mind knows of the planet on which you presently reside. And there are other forms on your planet. And just because you're not familiar with them does not in any way deny the existence of them.

Yes, sir.

What did you want to know about what you call Big Foot that he doesn't feel is any of your business? Pardon? *[Many students laugh.]*

Well, the, the . . .

He doesn't need you to feed him or to care for him. They do quite well. And he's not wanting. And I think that is certainly sufficient to give you some thought, wouldn't you say?

Yes, sir.

He's not domesticated. And [they] don't need the human species to care for them. All right?

Yes, sir.

Thank you. Someone else have a question? Yes?

Yes. [Student L].

Yes, [Student L], please speak up. Good morning.

Good morning. You mentioned in our last class that if we have accomplished over 51 percent of our spiritual contract in the Great Rotunda—

Yes.

—we can move to another expression. Do we not have to work off the other 49 percent in the lower realms prior to the next incarnation?

Not if you have accomplished fifty-one. Fifty-one percent is a majority of your consciousness.

Oh.

That's what you're working off. So when you rise to 51 percent, the other is a shadow.

I see.

Yes.

Thank you.

You're welcome.

May I ask another?

Certainly.

You stated that when we have come full circle, the form consumes itself, having learned the lesson.

Correct.

How do we discern whether we have passed the lesson, or that it is now quiet and will return another time?

Well, it's quite simple, [Student L]. What you understand as concern no longer exists for you when you've passed it.

I see.

It doesn't exist. So if we want to know if we've passed it, all we have to do is be aware of our thoughts and see if we're concerned about it.

Yes.

Pardon?

I see.

See, we're concerned about it while we're working towards it because we want it to hurry up.

That's right.

Yes. It's understandable, you know.

May I ask another?

Certainly.

Are you permitted to inform us, sometimes, during these classes of where our percentages are at this time?

If the Light which I serve reveals to me that it would be beneficial and an inspiration for more of the students to do their homework, then I'm sure it would be revealed. Thank you.

Thank you.

You're welcome. Did you have another question?

Well, I do have one more.

Oh, certainly. I like students with questions because it reveals the law that they are making some effort, even if it's only a moment. Yes, go right ahead.

Thank you. Often people who are married develop mannerisms of the other one. If one discovers after years of separation that he still retains one or more of the mannerisms, does that indicate that they have not surrendered the individual in consciousness?

It most certainly does. They're still identified. They don't have to be.

Yes.

But the demonstration, of course, is the revelation. But one does not have identification with another, only in service to their judgments, which are denials and create needs.

Thank you.

Yes. You see how denial is destiny, [Student L]?

I certainly do.

And that the intensity of density is measured by acceptance?

Yes.

Yes.

Thank you.

You're welcome. *[After a pause during which only the ticking of a clock is heard on the class recording, the teacher continues.]* Clock sounds lovely on the video. Yes, who is back—you just speak your name. Go right ahead.

[Student A].

Yes, [Student A]. Please speak up.

Good morning.

Good morning.

Numbers—the universe is numbers. And I would like to know if our birth number coincides with the numbers of letters in the greatest lesson we must pass in this incarnation?

You would like to know if your birth number coincides with what?

With the number of letters in the greatest lesson we must pass in this incarnation.

Well, now, [Student A], are you inspired by that thought that you've been thinking about those numbers? Are you encouraged or discouraged?

It depends on which numbers I'm thinking about. [Many students laugh.] If I'm thinking about five, I'm encouraged. If I'm thinking about four, I'm not.

Why, four's stability and security, [Student A].

My mind didn't remember that.

Well, I'm reminding you. That's why I'm reminding you.

Thank you very much. So would you have to purify and evolve through those tapes in order to pass that particular lesson?

You are already passing through the lessons you need to pass through, [Student A].

Thank you.

And because one is actually passing through the lessons that they have created in their evolution, that they're already passing through them, that's most encouraging. It becomes discouraging, [Student A], when we want it to hurry up and we are not moving fast enough. Wouldn't you agree?

Yes.

That's when it becomes discouraging: when we judge that we're moving too slowly. Hmm?

Thank you.

Would you rather move slowly and get there or move fast and be constantly distracted?

I'd rather move slowly and get there.

Then your patience has grown in wisdom.

Thank you.

Do you have any other question?

How can we harmonize our lives and accept the true being waiting to serve?

The best way that we can bring about harmony in our life is to encourage our self in our endeavor and not to judge that our endeavor is nonexistent or anything that is discouraging. One encourages themselves through a lessening of dependence on what they cannot control. *[After a pause, the teacher continues.]* [Student A]? *[After another short pause, the teacher continues.]* Hello?

OK.

So you have things in your life that you can control. [Student A]?

That's right.

You can control the way you brush your teeth. Is that correct?

Yes.

You can control the way you comb your hair. Is that correct?

That's right.

And you can and do control what you decide to wear for the day. Is that correct?

That's true.

So take stock of all of the things that you can and do control. Do you understand that?

Yes, I do.

And forget about the things that are not your divine right to control. Do you understand?

I certainly do.

And if you do that, [Student A], you will, from that experience, encourage yourself and move on in peace and harmony and abundant good.

Thank you very much.

Isn't that making a better day for you?

Yes.

Well, it'd make a better day for anyone.

That's right.

You see? You see, you have a responsibility to take care of yourself. You understand that, don't you?

Yes.

Now if you have any left over, you can fill your temptations to take care of somebody else. But usually a person, when they take stock, they find they just about [have] enough to take care of themselves and there's not much or anything left over to be taking care of someone else they're tempted to take care of. Hmm? We do have a tendency to mother the universe—don't we?—when she's such a great mother; she doesn't need another one. Pardon?

Thank you.

You're welcome. Any other questions there?

In Class 8 [CC 8, which was published in *The Living Light Dialogue* Volume 1] *of the Living Light Philosophy—*

Yes.

—there was an explanation of three minds: the conscious, subconscious, and superconscious.

Correct.

The first two create thought forms, while the superconscious mind does not, for it is the channel through which the energy flows.

That's correct.

My channel is—my question is this . . .

Yes?

When do the river of life exercise—when we do the river of life exercise correctly—

Yes?

—is this the area of our minds where we visit?

We go to where we really are, to what we are. That is correct.

Thank you.

Free from all forms and freed from all disturbance. Was there any other question, [Student A]?

What foods are most beneficial to the balance of our form?

What is most beneficial?

Yes.

To the balance of our form?

Yes.

What is most beneficial to the balance of our form is to pause and to thank the Source that is for the opportunity of expressing it. You hear?

Yes, I do.

You see, as I started this class, and the lost, so-called lost word, the wrapper believes it is the content that it is wrapping. And that's the problem in old creation. Do you understand?

Yes, I do.

You see, that would be like your nose telling you it's your whole body and your whole being and if something happened to your nose, that you would die. Do you understand?

Yes.

Well, isn't that kind of ridiculous?

It certainly is.

That's what we're discussing. Thank you very much.

Thank you.

Do you have any other questions to speak forth? But I have [Student M] and [Student B] and [Student D] and [Student Y] and all the others and [Student N] back there and [Student J] is over there. You raise your hands. Now if I left anyone out—is that [Student B]?

[Student B].

Speak right up, [Student B].

Since God works in silence, how does that coincide with what you talked about earlier in class here?

In reference to what?

In reference to speaking a word forth.

God works in silence for God *is* silence. Now, that silence, you understand, that silence is what you are. What you believe you are is the expression of that silence. And that's the problem in life, [Student B]. You see, we *believe* we are the expression instead of the stillness that sustains it. You hear?

Yes.

It is our belief that is the problem. You see, we believe we are the expression. And we believe that, forgetting what we are. Now that does not mean that we should not express; it does mean that we should not permit our mind to convince us that we are the expression when we know in truth what we are: the stillness and the silence and the sustaining power. That's how it works, [Student B]. Pardon?

Well, I, I guess I think of expression as there's the content and then there's also the—

No. Expression is the wrapper. It's not the content. The stillness, the silence, the God, the Truth, that is the content. The expression of that content is the covering of it. See, you are covered in what you believe is a human being. The dog is covered in what we believe is a dog. Now he doesn't believe he's a dog. That's a, that's a belief and that's a creation that we gave to him. Do you understand that, [Student B]?

Yes.

So the silence and the stillness, the power through which this, this wrapper which we call a dog, is moving and expressing itself is identically the same that we truly are. You see?

Is it the vibration of the expression, then?

The vibration of the expression is dependent upon the density of the form which is obstructing the flow, [Student B]. You see, form is an obstruction to the flow or the stream of consciousness. And as it obstructs the flow or the stream of consciousness, depending on how little or how much of an obstruction the form is, is the expression. Pardon?

Thank you.

So you take a form that is very, what you would say, very light, that form is a less obstruction to the Light. It is not as dense, you hear?

Yes.

And in that sense the stream is flowing more freely through that form. It's not as dense. For example, the same law of the physical is the same law of the mental. If one has a thought, the thought does not become gross or solidified until we convince our self that it is us. When we convince our self it is us, it forms a judgment and the obstruction to the flow of the Divine Consciousness, then, is a greater obstruction. You hear?

Yes.

And so a person can have many thoughts. And that is the design of the human mind. But when a person believes they are one of the thoughts or many of the thoughts that they have, then they create a judgment. They solidify the form. They make it more gross. This is why a wise person may have many thoughts, believe that he is none of them and, therefore, ever remain free.

You see? So we should have thoughts. It is necessary for the form. That's the way—that's the form that the Light is flowing through. But not to be so foolhardy as to convince our self that we are any one of them. That way, we'll always be open and we will fly, so to speak, freely in the fresh air of reason, which will transfigure us. Did you have another question, [Student B]?

Yes.

Yes. Go right ahead.

It's about Halley's Comet coming next year.

It is coming next year. It's returning.

Yes.

Yes. It will always return to your planet.

Does it have a spiritual meaning?

Indeed, it does. You're going to find—not just because it is coming; it is coming in keeping with laws established in the planetary system—you will find a great change in reference to the many years you have been experiencing this phenomenal fear of nuclear warfare. After its arrival and its passing, within ninety days, your world will begin to become aware of changes made in the mental worlds of the powers, so-called, to be in your world, in a mental world. And change, definitely for the better, shall come from it.

Good.

Yes.

Thank you.

And your history of your planet will reveal whenever Halley's visited your planet, there was a change in the civilizations in reference to their awakening for a time. Pardon? Yes. Any other question, [Student B]?

Not, not at this time.

Fine. Now try to understand with the vibrations of the green light—did you ever try to see with green, blue, and white lights [shining in your eyes]? Hmm? Well, I want to save the energy to use for his mouth rather just his eyesight for the class. Now who's back there, please?

[Student Y].

Very well, [Student Y], speak right up.

OK. Does—when you speak of going inside or within oneself, does that mean within the parameter of the physical body?

Yes, if you understand your physical body is the shape of an egg.

OK. And does that extend out and around or—I'm trying to get—

Yes, it does. And if you've got an extension of up to five feet, then I want you to come and sit here next to me so that we can both work on these students out there. [Many students laugh.]

OK.

Pardon?

All right. I've been trying to find that place and I get, my mind does something with that. So I, I want—

Yes, but isn't that a wonderful experience, considering it's your mind and it's responsible to do what you tell it to do?

Yes.

Isn't that wonderful?

Yes.

Yes. And you see how unruly it's become.

Yes.

Well, you put it right in its place. It's a child.

OK.

And without you, it wouldn't exist, [Student Y].

OK.

Don't ever forget that.

Thank you.

You see? You see, it's run wild only because it hasn't had anyone telling it, "That's it. You've done enough." You see?

Yes.

That's the only reason. You see, it's like a very little child. And if you're not there to care for them and say, "Now this is what you do and that's what you don't do," and you constantly monitor them—you're experiencing what happens to them, aren't you, [Student Y]?

Yes.

And is that [a] wonderful step?

It is. Thank you.

Any other questions?

I had another.

You go right ahead.

How does one go about finding out what your job is here?

What your job is?

Yes.

By doing what you have to do and knowing what you have to do, by an acceptance of that light of reason that is within you. And I think our cameraman is taking a morning nap. And did our cameraman pawn—pan out here? Pawn is more like it. *[The teacher and many students laugh.]* Did you pan out there?

I did.

Hmm. Now I may have to set you up as one of my student examples here, [Student R], to show you where to put some pressure to stay awake. Anyone else have a question? Hmm.

[Student U].

Speak right up, [Student U].

Are there nature spirits associated with the higher centers of consciousness?

Why, certainly. Why, certainly. You see, there are angels. Would you consider them lower or higher? Well, of course, there's all kinds of them.

Higher, sir.

Pardon?

Higher.

Well—

Do, do they—
Without nature spirits, there is no form, you know.
Yes, sir.
Yes.
Do they have eternal life, those, those . . .
That which is eternal is formless and free; therefore, it is not limited. You are formless. You are free. Your belief limits you, like anything. So that which you truly are cannot be contained. That which you believe you are is extremely contained.

Now in evolution you have less and less containment because you have less and less dependence, you see, on that which you can't control. People who rely upon that which they can control have less dependence, you see. Do you understand that?
Yes, sir.
You see, it is people who depend on what, by the Law of Life, they cannot control that are restricted and frustrated. A person who relies on that which they are is not a person that is frustrated, is not a person that is discordant and upset and [has] struggle and suffering. Hmm? Those who believe in limit establish the Law of Limit and, therefore, shall experience limit. Pardon?
Thank you.
So if you enjoy limit, then just keep believing in it. You'll have plenty of it. You don't enjoy limit, do you?
No, sir.
Then don't believe in it and you won't have it. It is through belief. Now, it isn't that your mind says, "Oh, I believe in limit." No, no, no. When the mind believes that it is the thought that it is entertaining, which, in turn, solidifies it into a judgment, and then a person, by the form they have created, is convinced by the form that that is them, then that type of a person believes in limit and, therefore, experiences plenty of limit. Pardon?
Yes, sir.

Because they're a very dependent person on that which they cannot control. They may not like it, and if they dislike it enough, they'll stop being dependent upon it. Hmm?

Yes.

Yes, go ahead with your questions, [Student U]. One of my students said he'd rather have the cash. Pardon? Yes. Go ahead.

There was, in, in our text, there was a division of states of, of the nine states of—or there was reference to the nine states of con—

Nine states, yes.

I was wondering how that related to the centers of consciousness that we are.

Why, certainly. There are nine spheres. And what is your question?

How, how do the states like the superconscious, the consciousness and the subconscious; the solar, celestial, and terrestrial; the infinite, cosmic, and universal—

Oh, I see. Well, why don't you go to the very top and [start] with the superconscious? Pardon?

OK.

And then I don't think you'll have any problem if you understand that manifestation is triune and, therefore, inseparable.

But let's get to the question perhaps in some ways that we can relate that you'll have greater understanding of exactly what you want to know. You're speaking of the superconscious, the conscious, and the subconscious, correct?

Correct.

All right. So the energy, that which we are, expressing through the superconscious, a person directs it more to the, to the conscious or to the subconscious, dependent upon their over-identification with self and their service to that which has passed. Now, for example, [Student H] asked a question earlier about beginnings and about the past experiences, is that not correct, [Student H]? Well, see, [Student H], as a student here, asked an honest question, was revealing to you, [Student U], and to everyone else, that the energy he had been experiencing, that which he is, the energy, was being directed to the subconscious for that's where the shadows of the past exist. Do you understand that?

Yes.

So he doesn't have to direct it to the subconscious, where he's torn up with frustration and emotion. You understand? For those forms are all waiting to be fulfilled. All those beginnings are all loose ends, waiting for their fulfillment, which he did not do for them. You see, it's like a child. You give it birth and stick it over there on the shelf; and it cries. It wants to eat. Well, if you end at just giving it birth, you [have] got a real problem, and it keeps right on crying. Do you understand that, [Student U]?

Yes, sir.

So, you see, that's when you choose, through ignorance, to direct this intelligent Energy which you are to the subconscious. Do you understand?

Yes, sir.

Now you can direct it to the conscious mind. That's where the faculty of reason is available for you. And make an intelligent choice and say, "No, no, no. I'm starting a new beginning. I'm not going to feed all that has passed. It is now a shadow of my ignorance." You see. An obstruction to the light of reason. So when you work with the conscious mind, that's where the light of reason is. The shadows cannot exist there. Do you understand? There's no obstruction. Pardon?

Thank you.

There is no obstruction to anyone who takes control of their mind into the eternal moment. That's where truth is. You can make a decision this instant, moment by moment. Say, "I choose to establish this," and do it. The sadness is when your mind, you decide to do something, seemingly instantaneously there's a great flood of the shadows which exist in the subconscious mind. It does not have to be. You are the director of that energy. Go ahead, [Student U], with your questions.

There is another question on—

Well, let me say one thing. Just a moment, excuse me. You see, that happens because when a person thinks of doing something, at the moment they think of doing it, they start down the slide of self. In other words, they'll have an idea; they'll be inspired to do something. The mind immediately says, though they may not want to admit it, "What's in it for me personally?" Well, when they say what's in it for me, what they are really doing, are all of these things of yesteryear rise up and say, "I want this, that, that, that, that, that." And they don't agree, you know. Go ahead.

We, we cannot have a thought that we do not experience its opposite. How is it that—

That's correct. Where do you think the opposite comes from?

The subconscious.

Uh-huh. Yes, the ones you did before you did them in and in their thinking, you've done them in. You created them and left them out to freeze in the cold. Go ahead, [Student U].

But if we direct it to a level of conscious or superconscious level, then that is not necessarily so.

That is absolutely correct. It isn't so at all. All you do is keep it in the conscious mind and, as I've tried to teach you, give it to God, the Principle of Goodness or speak the word. You see, speak the word and let it rise to where the power really is that sustains it and, and so be it. Hmm?

Thank you.

However, that isn't usually what happens. Man tempts to speak the word and send it to the Power that sustains it, and in an instant there's all of these forms of yesteryear come up and rise in and say all these different things in the mind, if a person does not take control of their mind. Yes. Any other questions?

That's all the questions that I have at this time.

Very good.

[Student M].

Yes, you speak up, [Student M], please.

OK. I have a question. The first one was, the natural signs are known as the music of the spheres, it was stated in our last class. And I would like to know a little bit about what the natural signs were.

Are you saying *sounds*?

No. Signs was what my interpretation of it was.

Well—

Was the natural—

Well, I don't have the record immediately before me. Let's ask [Student S] here. Do you understand what [Student M]'s referring to?

No. I always thought it was sounds.

The natural sounds of the universe are the music of the spheres. This is why I would like clarification with the students. We do have a recorded tape that we could play. You see, [Student M], to, to say that—you see, I'm glad that you're bringing this up, [Student M], because to say that it was stated "the natural signs" of the universe, well, I have to understand if that supposedly came out of my channel's mouth for which I am responsible for in these classes, then I would like to know what these signs are because I don't have any teachings of signs.

It was probably "sounds." The natural sounds of the—the natural sounds are known as the music of the spheres. That makes more sense.

That is correct. However, if I did say natural signs, I would like to [have] your understanding of what that means because I don't know what it means. I don't have any signs. Pardon?

I don't either. I, I don't know what it meant. That's what I was...

Did you check with the secretary when you prepared that question?

No, I did not.

Did you have a question on signs?

Yes.

Did you think possibly you had not heard clearly the word?

Well, I listened to it many times and that's what I kept getting. Maybe that's—

You were satisfied that it was signs?

Yes, I was.

Oh, then that's fine. This is very, very important because I do not honestly recall speaking to any of my students at any time since I've been visiting your planet about signs. I know there are many superstitions about signs. There's many rabbit's foot and all kinds of things that'll do all kinds of whammies, I think they call them.

Now let's go on with the natural sounds of the universe is the music of the spheres. Yes. Yes, [Student M].

Yes. Then I would like you to speak on the natural sounds, the natural—

What would you like to know about the natural sounds? Have you listened to the tree?

Yes.

And how does it sound?

Woooo. [The student makes a sound in an attempt to imitate the sound of a tree.]

Which tree did you listen to? Perhaps you heard one that was a low sound and you're fond of high sounds.

OK.

Which one did you listen to? Did you listen to the maple tree over there? Or did you listen to the willow? Or was it the oak?

OK. So you're talking about the natural sounds of all the, the animals, the plants, the plants and the trees and . . .

Yes.

And that's the music of the spheres.

That *is* the music of the spheres. Not what we speak forth, but our being emanates a color, which is a sound. Pardon?

Yes, yes.

And so if a person has thoughts that are discordant, they emanate colors that are objectionable to animals, trees, flowers, plants that are in harmony with all the others. You see, it's like a great orchestra.

Yes.

And if you're off-key, then you're just off-key. And the orchestra has to pay the price.

Yes.

Pardon?

Yes.

Do you understand?

Yes, I do.

And the orchestra as a whole and collectively, as individuals, don't appreciate it at all. The tree, the flower does not appreciate its exposure to anyone who is discordant.

Yes.

Now here you have a flower with what you call a limited intelligence. Well, it doesn't get up and walk around. Unfortunately, most people on earth cannot see its smile and its joy and its happiness. You see?

Uh-huh.

Yet it has enough intelligence to object to any form around it that is discordant and not happy. Understand?

Yes, I do.

And in fact, it reacts in the only way it can react to show you how displeased it is with your vibration: it wilts and dies long before its time. Pardon?

Yes.

You see, it's like the trees in the temple gardens, and the flowers. A person goes around them, how many times my channel has heard the tree say, "What does that have to do with happiness and joy? What are they thinking about? Why do you allow them around me?" They don't appreciate it, you see?

Uh-huh.

Because, you see, then what we offer to these beautiful, intelligent forms, what we offer to them, you see, is need, need, need, need, need. Then, by offering them need, they suffer, along with the ones who offer them the need. Then, the next thing you know, they don't smile. They're not happy. They start to feel sorry for themselves and they just die off. Do you understand that?

Yes.

Well, [a] discordant note in the orchestra. Go ahead with your questions.

OK. I had another question about when we have a thought form plaguing us and—

You mean when we choose to plague our self with a thought form, is that what you're saying, [Student M]? Yes, because, see, we make the choice, you know—

Yes.

—for them to plague us or not to plague us by our lack of effort. Go ahead, [Student M].

And we're trying to—I'm trying to differentiate the denial of that thought form and the redirecting of the attention away from the thought form.

Yes.

Yes. There seems to be a fine line from denying it: denying its existence and just—to redirecting away the energy from it.

You seem to have difficulty there?

Well, sometimes it feels like a denial. A denial of it.

It depends on how you're handling it, [Student M].

Uh-huh. That's—

Well, for example, say that you choose to have one of your children come in and scream and go through tantrums and after you've opened the door and let them in, you're tired of listening to them. You want them out of your head. Is that the idea?

Right.

Well—

Yes.

First of all, to deny them is like to deny the child you gave birth to.

Right.

Now how could you do that without being plagued with the thought of it?

You can't.

All right. So you have created these children—

Right.

—that now you choose to open the door and you don't like the way they're acting, is that correct?

That's correct.

Well, you see, first of all, you're doing right by not denying they're your children because, first of all, you created them and in second place you opened the door to your house and let them do those tantrums in your head. You understand that, [Student M]?

Yes, I do.

Well, fine. Now you say, "All right, now listen. I'm responsible. I created you. I'm responsible; I opened the door and let you in. Now I'm telling you, you go sit over there in the corner and behave yourself. Don't open your mouth, because if you do, I'm kicking you out." Do you understand that?

Yes, I do.

And then go on about your business. What—that's all right. What—that's all right, Mr. Red. *[The teacher addresses the church's dog.]* He's just off having a nice time there. And what's wrong with that?

There's nothing wrong. That's, that's good.

You do understand that, don't you?

Oh, I do. I definitely do.

Yes. Now you go ahead with any other questions.

Thank you.

You see, that's known as taking control of what we're responsible for.

Yes.

You see. Now you wouldn't want someone else to come in and brush your teeth for you, would you?

No.

You wouldn't like to have their fist in your mouth scrubbing at your teeth, would you?

No.

On a daily basis anyway?

No.

Well, then do it yourself.

Right.

Or someone's going to come with a fist and do it.

That's true.

That's the alternative, my dear. Yes. That's the alternative.

Thank you.

Anyone else have a question?

[Student N].

Yes.

I was wondering, when you educate a denial, does that mean that you no longer have the need or the desire?

No, no, no. No. [Student N]?

Yes.

Yes, now I must get these words—words are so important, you see. When we educate a denial—I don't recall teaching the education of a denial.

Oh.

Does someone else recall that I've taught to educate a denial? [Student H]?

No.

[Student S]?

No.

Now we must understand each other or we can't relate to each other. Isn't that true, [Student N]?

Yes.

Now let us investigate that particular statement there. It's very important. We work to educate our ego for our ego is uneducated because we believe we are the thoughts of our mind instead of the creator of the thoughts through which they are passing on a stream of consciousness. All right?

Yes.

Now, you're speaking about a denial that you have. Is that correct?

Yes.

Now, what does one do with the denial?

Oh—

In other words, you deny the right of the existence of a thought that you've created in your mind. Is that what you're talking about?

Yes.

Now try to understand. Now take a look at destiny here. We deny this and deny that. We deny many things, all right?

Yes.

But, my dear, stop and think: we create the form of the denial in our consciousness. How can you deny your own child? You see, it's a house divided. It is a house divided. It is your mind that creates the denial. And because it's your mind that creates the denial, you are destined to experience it because you have created it. So wisdom reveals the principle of good is the Law of Total Acceptance. Go ahead, [Student N].

Thank you very much.

Did that help with that question?

A lot. Yes.

Yes. Because, you see, whatever we create we're responsible for. We create our denials in our mind. They are our children. They will haunt us and guarantee the destiny of the denial, which is total acceptance of the very thing we have denied because it is a child we have created, and a child shall ever return to the parent. You understand?

So you educate the child? You, you educate the, the children or you or just use total acceptance of it, of the denial?

No. Total acceptance, the principle of good. You have created the form of denial in your mind. It is now your child. You understand that?

Yes.

Now how or not how—because you already know how you've created it: with your own mind. Why have you created the denial? What is the motivation for the denial? Is it based on something you can control? Oh, no, it's not based on something you can control. It's based upon something you've accepted that someone else controls!

I see.

Pardon?

Thank you.

That helps you, doesn't it, [Student N]?

Yes, it does.

So, you see, only a fool denies because he lives to see the day when what he has denied he is now experiencing through acceptance and not by conscious choice.

Right.

In his mind.

Right.

No. It's by the law that was first conscious that he established and those shadows move in. And that's all there is to it. In other words, it's known as our chickens come home to roost. Why not? We're the roost from whence they flew. Pardon?

Thank you very much.

You're welcome. Someone else have a question now? Time is marching on.

Could I ask another one?

Certainly.

I would like to know what the purpose of a relationship is other than having children.

Need. Denial of the truth. There is no other purpose. Denial of what you are in believing in what you are not, and that's what you call relationships.

Is that bad?

Are you speaking of meaningful relationship?

I'm just speaking of—

They're all meaningful.

I'm just speaking of relationships period.

They're all meaningful. They're all the effects of denial of what you are.

Right.

Which creates a need for what you are not and never can be. Hmm?

Thank you.

You see, that's like saying that you have entered, your eternal being, through a soul, you've entered form on Earth. And you're incomplete and, therefore, in constant need because there's another half of you someplace. In other words, that's like believing that you're half there. You don't believe you're half there, do you, [Student N]?

No.

Do you believe you're complete and can accomplish what you want to accomplish in life?

Yes.

And you are not dependent on another half running loose someplace?

No.

Well, you have no problem with relationships, then, do you?
I do, but I—
Well, how could you? If you've accepted that you're whole and complete and you have no need, because that which is complete does not experience need, [Student N].
Yes.
Then how could you have a problem?
Well, what do we do with, with, I mean—
What do you mean "What do you do"?
There are other people on the planet. What do you—
There are other people on the planet? Oh, indeed, there are.
Yes. [The student laughs.]
Some intelligences don't even call them people, but anyway it's the name that humanity's given. Yes.
What would you call, you know, a business relationship or any other kind of . . . I—
Well, now, are you speaking of an exchange of services or are you speaking of involvements? Now if you are speaking of exchange of service, you have no problem.
OK.
Now if you're speaking of involvements, you [have] got nothing but problems.
All right. I understand. Thank you.
Creation, [Student N], is a playpen and only children should play therein. "I have this little, red fire engine. I will let you have it, if you will let me play with your dolly." *[Many students laugh.]* And then make the agreement and that's exchange of service. Right? Pardon?
Thank you.
That's what children do, isn't it?
Yes.
Well, why don't you try being a child for a change, and you'll be freed from all these problems.
OK.

Yes. Any other question? Well, we'll move right along now. [Student L].

[Student L]? You speak up, [Student L], please.

Yes. I have one more. Do the believers in reincarnation perceive their former lives as being on the earth realm through recognition of similar places on other planets or is there another explanation?

The belief in your world of a return to a particular planet is an effect of an over-identification with limit or self. All of nature everywhere, throughout the universes, reveals, to an intelligent being, evolution and evolutionary incarnation. The forms are constantly being refined as the being that you truly are is moving through them. And so it is an effect; what you call return or reincarnation is a living demonstration and an effect of need, which is an effect of denial. Do you understand that?

Yes, I do.

In other words, a person who feels or believes that they are half there lives in the memories of what used to be: the good old days, I think your world calls it. And so our purpose is to help people to awaken, you students to awaken that you're whole and complete; that you're not half there; that you don't have to go searching for another half because everything that you could possibly desire, the joy of living, the happiness, the abundant good is inside of you. You don't have to go to the past or the future to experience the totality of goodness which you are. Yes.

Yes. Thank you.

You're welcome. And is that—someone who hasn't had a question yet. Is that [Student P]?

Yes, I've got a question.

Oh, yes, I thought that I saw your arm, even though it didn't physically get up there. Did you have your Wheaties this morning or—

Yes, I did.

What are you having now?

I have a question—

Perhaps we should change the breakfast menu. Go ahead.

I have a question about when we're working with wood or soil, I feel extremely good. And I was wondering if there's a chemical reaction or . . .

Well, I think that you should feel extremely good, don't you?

Uh-huh.

You feel really good. And if you understand that Law of Association—and I think you have always known that you're a very earthy person.

Yes.

You would have full understanding.

Uh-huh.

So work with earth and work with the trees.

OK.

You see? You see, an earthy person should associate with, of course, the element earth, you see?

Yes.

Try to understand, no matter how much you dig, there's no gold of wisdom down there, and you won't have any problem.

OK. Thank you very much.

Yes, does that help with that question? Now what other questions do you have in revealing your homework?

I was wondering, the element of salt, How does it work with preserving something positive in our universe? I know that it works in preserving.

The principle of preserving preserves. Good, bad, or indifferent, it will preserve. What is it you'd like to preserve? A thought?

Well, I, yes—

A judgment? Don't have any problems with judgments, they have a—they're very salty. All judgments are salty. Haven't you ever noticed how preserved they are?

Right. Well, I was, I was thinking more along the lines of, like if, something positive, like enthusiasm or encouragement.

Oh, that you have to keep seasoned. You have to keep salt in that.

OK. And—

Tell me something, enthusiasm, when you say enthusiasm, that principle, enthusiasm, has no limit, does it?

No, it doesn't.

Well, see, that that doesn't have limit hasn't any salt; you [have] got to season it.

Oh.

You see, now, take a judgment.

Right.

That's quite limited, isn't it?

Yes, it is.

It has limits. It has boundaries.

Yes.

Correct?

Yes.

Very salty. And they certainly have no problem preserving themselves in the consciousness, do they?

Nope.

So try to understand, the functions are very salty.

OK.

The faculties require seasoning. And I think that'll help you.

OK. Thank you.

Yes. And time is running quickly. Yes, who do we have back there?

[Student D].

Has [Student D] had a question yet?

Yes.

Is that you [Student D]?

Yes, it is.

Well, you speak your name and speak right up.

I would like to know, there's a lot of negativity with the, the understanding that two is duality. Is there a positive side to that that we can focus on so that—

Why, certainly! You have two eyes and you're grateful that you have two, aren't you?

Yes!

You have two feet. Are you not grateful for that?

Definitely.

You have two hands. Are you not grateful for that?

Yes.

Let's be positive with two.

OK.

The two that we can control.

Oh.

You see, my friends, if you want two and you want, you have these desires for relationships, say, "OK, hand number 1 and hand number 2." *[Almost all the students laugh.]* Have a relationship. Time's running quickly. Yes, [Student S].

Would you please explain how the odic power is transmitted through water?

The odic power? The odic force?

Yes.

Ah. And you want to know how it is transmitted through water?

Yes. Or, or why is it through water and not through one of the other elements?

For this element that you call water, without it there is no form on your planet. And so in order to stabilize form, you must use the element through which the odic force can do so. Do you understand?

And how's our timing here, cameraman?

About fifteen.

Well, that's very nice. Yes, go right ahead, [Student S].

The other weeks you were discussing, like, the higher benefits of the fire cen—fire, the element fire, as opposed to the lower . . .

Yes?

. . . aspects of it. And so could you please discuss those higher and lower aspects of the water, element water?

Well, water, as you well know, is used to drown a person. That's a negative aspect, isn't it?

Right.

It's also used to quench the thirst and restore a person who's dehydrated. That's a positive aspect, isn't it?

Right.

And so when we look at all of these things, as [Student D] just said, there's so much negativity over two or duality. And yet I don't find anything negative at all about two hands to use instead of one or two eyes or two nostrils through which to breathe. Have you ever noticed in your house that there's only certain things that aren't duplicated?

Yes.

You have more than one thumb. You have more than one forefinger. You have more than one big toe. You have more than one little toe. Go down the list of your little house and look at the parts of your anatomy that are not dual. And then you'll have a greater understanding of what you think is need and why you believe in need, for you have the support of looking at form. You see?

Thank you.

So be grateful that whatever you have that is dual, like two hands, they're yours. You can do something with them. They're not dependent on anything you can't control. Only place your attention in life upon what you can control, for by so doing you'll grow in personal responsibility. And that's where the joy of living truly is. Do you understand that?

Yes.

See, what someone else does or doesn't do denies you of the joy of personal responsibility. By placing thought and attention to what you are not, in the divine law, able to control, you deny yourself of the goodness that exists within you. Hmm?

Yes.

Any other questions there?

Yes, I do. In regard to [Student P's] question, you spoke of her good feeling and identification with things of the earth—

Yes.

That she's an earthy person.

Yes, for she has spent much time in identifying with earth. Yes.

If a person seems to have a great identification and affinity with the water—

Yes.

—although their sign, their basic incarnation comes under, like, say an earth center or a fire center, how is that explained?

Well, it's quite simple: it's because a person is identifying with, through belief and experience, with that particular center of consciousness, through the laws of association. You see, for example, early in life in your earth experiences you—if a child has registered a very good feeling while exposed to water, the years pass, the awareness of the experience disappears; it dims and disappears, and yet they have a great, good feeling when they're in water. Do you understand that?

Uh-huh.

So you have, as I have shared with you over these many years, you have the hereditary impact in the consciousness; you have the environmental impact in the consciousness. And through the laws of association, these are all interwoven.

OK. Thank you.

Does that help you? You see? You see—and also don't limit the experience to after you're born. You see, at the moment of conception—and if you check with the mother, you'll find there were many experiences that she went through and made a great impact upon your consciousness while you were still in the womb.

Dealing with the water center?

Yes.

Thank you.

That's a fondness that you have.

Uh-huh.

So that fondness, you see—I'm telling you that that fondness was an environmental impact while you were still in the womb.

OK. Thank you.

You see? When you understand the cause of something, you have the cure of it.

Uh-huh.

You see. So if you understand that when you're in water, you feel real good—are you following me?

Yes.

The next step is to understand that it's been created by experience, environmental impact—

Uh-huh.

You understand that? And that if it's water, you can have it wherever you want. Now, the principle is water. You can have it in a glass or in an ocean. It should make no difference when you understand the principle.

OK.

Do you understand that?

Yes.

You see, because it is through the Law of Association that it is happening, you see?

Uh-huh.

Only judgment stands in the way of how it's going to happen. You can let it happen with a goldfish bowl. It doesn't matter. Water is water. You hear?

Yes.

Now I hope that's helped with your question, [Student S].

Thank you.

And it's also freedom. Yes. Now who is that? [Student O] has a question?

Yes, sir.

Go right ahead, [Student O].

Could you speak on the origin of the word never?

You like *never*?

No, sir, but it kind of perplexed me when I think about the word.

Yes. Well, it should perplex everyone. Whoever rises supreme in the universe to say *never* guarantees soon. That help with your question?

That's, that's just the word period, not making a reference to anything—

The word means something to who—to the speaker. *Never* means something to you, doesn't it? *[After a pause, the teacher continues.]* Pardon?

Yes, it does.

Have you not said in your life you would never do certain things?

I have.

And have you not lived to do some of them?

I certainly have.

We all live to do all of them. A wise man does not use that word. Those words are used by fools. That's their language. That's not the language of an intelligent being. No. Hmm?

Thank you.

For you do nothing but feed the adversity you have created by an uneducated and ignorant ego. You only guarantee it. The adversity, therefore, then by the very Law of Creation, becomes the attachment.

Thank you.

You're welcome. Yes, now, [Student J]. I'm happy that you're here today.

[Student J]. Good morning, sir.

Morning.

What other words are used by fools?

Well, *limit* is used by fools. *Never* is their top choice from that realm down below. And *"I will not"* is also used by them. In fact, they have their own dictionary. Would you like their dictionary?

I'd like to know what's in it so I can avoid it.

Oh, there's so many words. So put those in your dictionary.

Yes, sir.

And when you say *avoid*, delete that and [in its] place [use] *caution*, for that's the word of the Light. You see, there are two dictionaries in the universe: there's a dictionary of Light and the dictionary of darkness, [Student J]. We just got a few minutes on that little magnetic tape, he says. But as you students evolve and we get into the pressure and the changing in the consciousness and we start doing more homework, we will reveal that dictionary to you. And you'll be amazed of the benefit by refraining from using those words because there's great force that's used in those forms. Hmm?

Yes. Thank you.

And there's a lot of things we'd like not to experience. And if we'd like not to experience [those things], we should certainly refrain from the word *never*.

Now I must say good day. I [will] keep this thing here because I'm always getting corrected that—I hear my channel gets corrected—I take it off too soon. *[The teacher refers to his pattern of removing his microphone before he finishes speaking.]* So thank you very much.

SEPTEMBER 29, 1985

A/V Class Private 17

Good morning, class. A very fine day to go sailing in consciousness to new horizons and new shores of experience.

Your world is entering the element air, as your planet Earth has been now for some time. And so you will have more and more experiences in your world with all factors that are governed and controlled by that element. And because the element air is the element through which the Light of eternal truth is more fully expressed, you will find more and more experiences in your material world of things being governed by the Light.

Now ofttimes in these classes with you, wisdom dictates a review and repetition of the teachings that you have already been given in order that you may broaden your horizons and, in so doing, gain a greater understanding as the effect of your efforts.

And so, as I have spoken to you many times, the destiny of denial, I'm sure at least some of you realize what that destiny truly is. The destiny of denial is the totality of dependence on what, by the law, you cannot control. And so a wise man does not deny, knowing that by so doing he is destined to depend and to serve what he cannot, by the law, control. And so we consider, in those attitudes of mind, acceptance and its effect, the joy of living, the abundant good of life. So let us spend a few moments this morning, before getting to your questions that you have prepared, on how that works in the consciousness. Whoever denies anything in consciousness does so by serving a created form that they are not and, through directing energy to the form of their creation in mental substance, becomes dependent upon it. They cannot control what they have created for they have created it as an effect of the denial of what they are. So to deny the right of existence of anything is not only to become dependent by it but it is also to be controlled by it.

When we permit ourselves to believe that what we have created we are, rather than to accept the demonstrable truth that what we have created we are responsible for, and through the Law of Responsibility and by the Law of Beginning or creating we can end within our consciousness, that offers to us, that truth, the goodness of life, the joy of living.

Now in reference to that particular sharing with you of understanding, I'm going to give you a moment to ask questions in respect to that particular discussion here this morning. If you'll be so kind as to raise your hands at this time. *[After a pause, the teacher continues.]* Well, I'm happy to see all my students are in total acceptance. The totality of acceptance sometimes overwhelms us, doesn't it? Is that [Student B]?

Yes.

Yes, speak right up, [Student B].

Whenever we do—

Good morning.

Whenever we do accept, isn't there a rejection or a denial of what we've formerly denied?

When we accept, the question is, When we accept, are we denying what, [Student B]?

What we formerly denied. Once we accept something—

No. No, once we accept in consciousness the responsibility of all that we are responsible for, once we accept that, it no longer controls us. It is when we deny it that it controls us. Not when we accept. Whenever we accept anything, we place our self in the position, through personal responsibility, of that which, by the law, we do control. When we accept it is when we control it. When we deny it is when it controls us.

The question, I think, perhaps you're referring to what may have been denied in the past by accepting in the present, is that not a denial of what already has been. Was that the question?

Yes. Yes, it was.

No. When we accept, we accept wholly in the moment in which we are. All of the shadows which have been and which only exist through a denial in the present, that's the only way they can control us, [Student B]. You see, the true being is an eternal being. In the present moment is the—the true being controls the present moment. Through the control of the present moment we are freed from all that has been and whatever may yet be. Did that help with the question, [Student B]?

Yes.

So it is a matter of the control of the mind: to remain in the consciousness of the eternal moment. For it is the eternal moment, that is what we are. And what we are is the Law of Controlling what we are. We are not what has been. That is not what we are. It is when we permit our mind to believe that we are what has been that we are controlled by what has been and, therefore, are not experiencing the joy or the fullness of life, for we are divided in consciousness. And through that division, we are in a process of self-destruction. Does that help with that question, [Student B]?

[Thank you.]

Yes, you're welcome. Anyone else have any questions in reference to that particular subject this morning?

[Student U].

Yes, [Student U], good morning.

Good morning. [The telephone rings.] *When we deny something . . .*

Yes?

. . . I'm a little confused about how it is that we are destined to serve that.

When you—when we deny anything in consciousness—you understand that?

Yes.

When we deny anything in our consciousness, we deny the right to its existence. When we deny the right to its existence within our consciousness—that which we truly are is the consciousness of God or good—when we deny that, we become the servant of the angel who fell from the grace of God through that very same principle. Do you understand that, [Student U]?

Yes.

For at that moment we become greater than what we are by believing what we are not, as Lucifer became greater than what he truly is, the Principle of Good, he became what he is not. And in that becoming is in control of the realms of form. Do you understand that, [Student U]?

Yes. Thank you.

All right. Now is there any further question in reference to that principle?

Then when we accept something, we absorb that and thereby control it or control it within ourselves?

That's the only place you can ever control it, is within yourself. When you accept, you move in the will of goodness. The will of good—goodness is what you are. When you accept within your consciousness, you move within the will of goodness. You see, you deny because you believe what you are not. That is the only incentive to deny. For example, by denial you believe that you are that, that, that, and that. Slowly but surely, through an evolutionary process, you gradually evolve from believing you are that and believing you are that and believing you are something else. Now one moment you believe you are materially poor; the next moment you believe that you are materially quite well off. Is that not correct?

That is correct.

Well, the same principle is at stake in these beliefs and denials. That is not what you are. You are not poor. You are not wealthy. You are not this. You are not that. That is created in a mental world. What you are is *everything*. Do you understand that? And because you are everything and in that realm of truth you are a part of everything, you need not be concerned about absorbing anything because you cannot absorb what you already are. Now what else do you have to say there, [Student U], in reference to that fear of yours?

That pretty much covers it right now.

Pardon?

That pretty much covers it right now, sir. Thank you.

Yes. Try to remember that fear is the mind's control over the—temporary control over that which you are. However, it is only a temporary control. Hmm?

Thank you.

You're welcome. Yes.

[Student M].

Yes, good morning, [Student M].

Good morning, Mr. Goodwin. Yes. Through acceptance, and we're moving up through this river of, the river of life in the will of God, is it not so that through total acceptance we watch the shores, which are our beliefs and our judgments, and we just watch them like a movie.

Yes?

And we see them much more clear as we're moving. The faster we move, the more clarity because there's less identification.

That is correct. That is correct. Let us not forget in viewing the movie of our own creations, our own beliefs, let us not forget we are responsible for them though we are not them.

Yes.

Yes. Was there something else, [Student M]?

No, I was just—the, the question was—I was just trying to understand that it was like—it seems, like, the faster we move up through that river and the movie is going by—all our thoughts, our judgments, all our beliefs—it, it just makes it almost impossible to really get stuck in the mud.

Indeed, it does. You see, that is in keeping with the teaching that work is God's love made manifest, for that in truth is what it is. When you are active, when you are working, that is, constructive—constructive results from your efforts, which is freedom from [being] dependent upon your results—when you are actively moving in constructive good, you are not tempted and not attached to what you are not. Therefore, you free yourself from the bondage of belief for you are too active in constructive good and experiencing the joy of living. It is when a person or persons are not active and they think about all these forms of their creation—they think they are thinking about the forms of creation. The truth of the matter is the forms that have been created are knocking at the door of their conscious[ness] demanding, demanding to be fed. And so the mind is filled by these many forms. And they disagree and you have discord and disease and destruction, self-destruction. Do you understand, [Student M]?

Yes, I do.

And so a person who sincerely seeks to experience the abundant good of living is a person who finds themselves active, accomplishing constructive good, and not ever thinking about what they do not have for they are extremely active in producing and constructing the good of living and experiencing the joy of life. It is only when we permit ourselves to be the victim of the forms we have created, by our thought patterns and judgments, that we experience a lack of goodness, a lack of abundant flow, a lack of the wealth and health and happiness that is our birthright.

Thank you very much.

And so I have recommended over so much time and to so many students in many, many realms, if you have only one job in life and you are not happy, then get two jobs. And if you have two jobs in life and you still find that you are not happy and fulfilled, then get three jobs. Because I know if you work on three eight-hour jobs that you would have little time or energy to think and, therefore, to be a victim of and servant to the forms of your judgments that are not healthy nor beneficial. Did that help, [Student M]?

Yes. Very much. Thank you.

You're welcome. Yes.

[Student D].

Good morning, [Student D].

Good morning. Does a judgment precede denial and then is the suspension of judgment, does that create acceptance?

The creation of a judgment—first of all, we must [have] denied what we are. We must first deny what we are to experience a need. We cannot experience a need until we have first denied what we are.

Now we deny that we are happiness. When we deny that we are happy, we experience a need to be happy. When we experience a need to be happy, we look at the world through eyes of comparison, the ribbon of comparison, and we make a judgment. So we make a judgment that we will be happy if we have something that we do not have. So if we are able to accomplish that and to get something that we don't have, which is already the effect of our denial, and it has to be something that we, by the very law, cannot control—for if it were something that we could control, we would already awaken that we have it, for man is well aware of what he can control and he is also sometimes aware of what he cannot control. And so we make the judgment that is what will make us happy. Even though it is a denial of the law and we cannot control it, we seek to experience it, and we suffer the consequences of our attempts, our temptations, and our effort to control what, by the law, we cannot control.

Now the opposite of that, of course, is the experiencing of the abundant good of what we are, [Student D]. Do you understand, [Student D]?

Yes.

And so remember that it takes a glorification of the self to rise sufficiently high in the universe of consciousness to deny the Power that sustains us. And, you see, we do not experience that denial until we have reached a point in our consciousness where we truly believe we are greater than that which sustains us. That's known as an uneducated ego, [Student D]. So it's a matter of educating the ego so it is not tempted to make such a foolish step in evolution. That help you?

Yes. Thank you.

Yes. All right. And is that [Student N]?

Yes.

Yes. Speak right up, [Student N], please.

If you're trying, if you're creating, attempting to create something in the present that in the past, when you tried to do it, it was nothing but frustration, how in the pres—is it little by little in the present that you, you break through everything to, to create freely or ...

There's only one way: the moment you permit yourself concern, you are the victim and the servant of those forms that have passed that offered you the frustration before. So if you permit yourself to be concerned of what the results will be from your efforts and, therefore, become attached to the fruits of action, then you will serve and repeat the experience of the past. Yes, does that help you, [Student N]?

Yes.

Yes. So, you see, if you do what you have to do because you know it's right and good to do it and you just do it, you have no interest nor concern of what the result is, then you are freed from the suffering of the attachment to the fruits of action. You know what you're doing and you are not concerned what someone else will do or what the results will be from it. Do you understand that, [Student N]?

Yes.

Then you will not be the servant of the shadows which are from the experiences of your past years. So if you are—if you enjoy suffering—some people think they do enjoy suffering and they like to repeat past experiences that offered them frustration and suffering, then, of course, it's the path that one has chosen. However, one will get through it in time. Hmm?

Thank you. Thank you very much.

Yes. I find that most encouraging. Truth, I've always found, is encouraging, not only to myself but I've witnessed students who feel it's greatly encouraging. Hmm? Because, you see, then we can clearly take a look and see, "All right, I'm going to be concerned of how this is going to turn out. I remember ten years ago, I was concerned about how something very similar was going to turn out and I was totally frustrated for ten years of my life." Now if you do like frustration and you like the sensation from it, then you have no problem because [you] just repeat what has already been. Hmm?

Yes.

But if you don't want the frustration, then change the judgment. Stop being concerned about what's going to happen with your efforts. And whoever is not concerned about what's happening with their efforts in their service to that which they are is freed from the mental realms of frustration. Yes.

But it would seem that—

That's the problem, my dear, is the buts. Go right ahead.

OK.

The buts seem to be a terrible problem. Perhaps we should all stand for class. Yes. *[Many students laugh.]*

It seems that it doesn't even get finished most of the time.

What doesn't get finished?

Well, say, for instance, writing a song or, or . . .

Who decides when it's finished? *[After a pause, the teacher continues.]* Who decides when it begins and who decides when it ends? *[After another pause, the teacher again continues.]* Who makes that decision?

Well, I thought I did.

I see. So do you, when—you say that you get started but you never finish, is that correct?

A lot of times.

A lot of times.

Uh-huh.

Not all the time.

No. Sometimes it just comes all the way through in twenty minutes or so.

Isn't that lovely. But it won't respond to your dictates of your mind. Is that correct?

Excuse me?

It will not respond, the inspiration won't respond to the dictates of your mind.

Right.

Well, isn't that wonderful?

Yes!

What kind of song do you want, an inspired one or one that your ego can control?

An inspired one.

Then there you are. There's no problem at all. Tell that part of your ego, the uneducated part, "Look, this is not what you do. And look, each time you attempt to do it, you never finish. You barely get started." Do you understand that?

So . . .

It's known as discernment. When you're able to sit down and tell the universe, "This is the song I'm going to write. I will take a half hour—I'll allow you a half hour. Now finish this song." And your experience is that you end up with a song half-finished or never finished—do you understand?—ever finished.

Yes.

Do you understand that?

Yes.

Well, place your attention upon the songs that are completed. Do you understand?

Yes.

And take your attention, which is your concern, which is attachment to the fruits of your action, off of the ones that aren't completed.

Thank you.

Because they're only completed according to your own judgments. Pardon?

Yes. Thank you.

Who tells you that the song is complete or not complete? You might take the song to a publisher and they say, "Bring it back when it's completed." And you've judged it's already completed. Is that not correct?

Yes.

Well, you see? That's based upon the forms that are in control at the time. Hmm?

Thank you.

I do hope that's helped you, [Student N].

Very much. Thank you.

Yes. Good morning, [Student O].

Good morning. [Student L speaks.]

And [Student L]. You're right next to [Student O], aren't you? Good morning.

Yes. It's [Student L].

Yes, she is. [Student O responds.]

Is anxiety a form of anger? [Student L asks.]

Well, the effect of anxiety, sooner or later, is anger. One does get weary of the experience of diddling in what you call anxiety. You know, when a child doesn't get what they want and they've decided that they've had enough of energy released through jumping on one foot after the other through anxiety, ofttimes, yes, the result thereof is anger. [It] doesn't have to be. Ofttimes the result is momentary anxiety and a wonderful experience of reason. Pardon?

Thank you.

Yes. And what is one anxious about in life, [Student L]?

Their denials?

Their denials? Does it help them to be freed from them? Or does it help them—what does it help feed, a faculty or a function?

A function.

Well, which function?

Well, anger is one of them.

Well, I think if we take a look, we'll quickly see it's self-pity. So we have to ask our self what we experience that we like from self-pity.

That we like?

That we like! You know, we all realize that we only do what we really want to do. And ofttimes we say, "Why, I never wanted that experience." Well, no, that's the effect of the law established. We wanted something else, we thought. We always get what we really want, [Student L]. We don't ofttimes like it, but we do get it. When a person is honest with their desires inside, they soon find out, "I have this experience. I'm anxious, I'm this, I'm that. I'm concerned about my denials. Yet I'm doing exactly what I want to do and I know very well that I am. Now let me make more intelligent choices." Would you not agree, [Student L]?

Yes.

So, you see, there really is no problem. We put our attention upon what we want to become. And stop being so concerned, which feeds the pity of our self, in what we're trying to overcome. What has gone has gone. What has passed has passed. That's not what life is. If we do not wish, for some strange, strange type of thinking, to experience the joy of living, then all we [have] got to do is concern our self with what has been. It's an absolute guarantee to be miserable. And I would say that anxiety is well placed under the umbrella of misery. Wouldn't you?

Of Misery?
Misery! Miserable.
Oh.
Do you feel joyous when you are anxious?
No!
Pardon?
No, it's miserable.
Yes. So, you see, with such a beautiful life waiting, ever available, moment by moment, why would we want to choose to be miserable by being anxious over how something's going to turn out?
Well, we wouldn't.
Pardon.
We wouldn't if we, if we realized we were choosing it, right? [The student speaks softly.]
If we realized what, [Student L]?
If we were choosing it.
We're always choosing it.
Yes.
Yes. You see, it's [about] growth. That's why we're here in school, isn't it? So we can say, "Well, this is my experience. I don't like this experience. Now let me see, which of the laws have I been applying that guarantee that experience? Well, now let me do a little more study. Let me be a bit more honest with myself because I don't care to have those experiences anymore, be it in divine order. May it ever be in divine order." Because we don't want to speak to the universe and say, "I'll never have those experiences again!" God forbid, we guarantee it. Hmm?

Yes. You know, there's one thing—it's passing through the universe this morning. I've heard so many of my students [say they are] looking forward to their retirement in life. And I was thinking, I was thinking as many centuries as it's been, there must be something wrong with me that I don't consider retiring. But then I look again and I say, What will I retire to? And I look down there and I see that great big mouth just waiting to gobble me up. And oh, it doesn't—[I] have no more interest in retirement. Hmm? So many people think of retirement. What does it mean? I think it's so important, you see, that—not just because I—well, I can't say I never had the chance to retire. I retired from my wife eons ago. *[The teacher laughs.]* If you call that retirement.

I prefer to say that we chose our own path, you understand. You see, things come into our life in keeping with the law. We have our experiences and then we move on, you see, to many, many other experiences. But if changing from one experience to another means retirement in the consciousness of my students, then I bless you all in your retirement, if it was possible for me to bless you, but I'm not particularly that kind of a teacher.

Now who else has a question here? Any blessing, I need [to] bless myself, if possible. It's not. Yes, [Student B].

Is the center that we make our denials in the air center, that you spoke of earlier?

Yes, it is. It is. It is. And it is the direct opposite of the faculty of reason, [Student B].

OK.

It is the direct opposite. We only deny, we only deny in life what is serving a lack of understanding and an absence of reason.

Then is acceptance—do we make our acceptance in, in the reason center or between the air and electric?

We most certainly do.

Oh.

That is the only place that it can be made.

Thank you.

Yes. You're welcome. For, you see, if we try to accept in any of those other realms, then we're going to be controlled by what we understand is our emotions. Do you understand that, [Student B]?

Yes.

And we will not accept. Emotion offers only denial. It is the mechanism that the mind use[s] to serve its own judgments. And so you will find when a person is confronted with their judgments, you will hear the excuses, the justifications. And if that is not enough defense, you'll find them get extremely emotional. And what I've shared with you over the years, it's known as the forces. Wouldn't you not agree, [Student B]?

Well, you see, if we're honest with our self, we'll say, "Why am I so emotional? Well now, this is ridiculous! I'm at the last stages of protecting my judgments." Hmm? You see?

Yes.

And through that awakening and through that honesty one can say, "Now that's it. That's it. This is a total waste of my energy, to defend these judgments, these denials in my life." Does that help, [Student B]?

Thank you.

You're welcome. Does someone else have a question this morning? *[After a pause, the teacher continues.]* You know, you promised me very short classes if you don't do your homework, didn't you? So I don't know, perhaps it's time for me to finish. Hmm? Were we overworked this last week, that we don't have questions? No questions, you know, no answers. Yes, [Student J].

Are you asking regarding questions regarding the subject of this morning or—

No.

—questions generally, sir?

Questions that are in respect to the spiritual classes. You can go through all of the many years, [Student J].

Fine.

Yes.

Should I ask a question?

Oh, yes, indeed.

Thank you, sir.

Because I know you have some.

Yes, sir. I guess I do. Thank you. The first question, sir, would be, What are the most effective procedures to obtain answers to the question, and the question is, In what way can I truly fulfill the purpose of my life?

Yes. Well, to the latter question, you're already doing that. Now I want to speak first to the latter question. It is very important for everyone. You're already accomplishing—and if you want to know how you are accomplishing don't look outside. Take a look and see how, over the years of effort, you are not as dependent upon what you cannot control in life. Now that's where, when you go into the Rotunda and you're asked, "What have you accomplished?" that's where the scales are balanced. "I'm not dependent on that or that or that. I am not dependent on what by the very law I cannot control." You can control your hand; therefore, you serve your hand. Correct?

Yes, sir.

For you can control it. So when you look at what have you accomplished in life, you look inside and you see the areas in your life that you are no longer dependent upon that you don't have control over. Hmm? That's accomplishment. That is the true accomplishment.

Now in reference to asking the question, one should ask the question before they come to class. Each question should be written down. You see? Then the person, the student, should look at their question and ask it inside of themselves. Do you understand that?

Yes, sir.

Now they will come up with many things. That experience is very important for all of us. I would suggest that in the questions that are prepared that a person ask themselves that question, after they have written it down, and be aware of the answers that rise in their consciousness, for that's inner awakening, [Student J]. Did that help with that questions that you have?

Indeed, yes, sir. Thank you.

So accomplishment, you can just make your little chart. You can say, "Oh, yes. I remember five years ago, I was dependent upon that. I was not able to control that. And I am very grateful because I am no longer dependent upon that." For anything you are dependent upon and by the Law of the Universe you cannot control is a lack of accomplishment to return to what you truly are. Hmm?

Thank you.

You can comb the brushing of your hair. You can control your foot. You can control your arm. You can control your hand. You can control your own little universe, you see. It's only when, through momentary errors of ignorance, we step outside of our universe and are, therefore, tempted to control something that is not within the divine law for us to control that we do not accomplish the growth that is what we are responsible for in the Rotunda, [Student J].

Thank you.

Thank you. And did someone else have a question there? Is that [Student L]?

Yes.

Yes, speak right up, [Student L], please.

Thank you. What causes the great changes in awakening of which you spoke whenever Halley's Comet returns to Earth?

Well, if you will study a bit of astronomy and a bit of science, you will understand that the comet, as it passes closer to your particular planet, has a direct effect upon the element air. Does that help with your question?

It does.

And if you will make your effort in study, you will gain a greater understanding of what happens to the Light, which must use the element air, in order to express itself. And now [Student S] has a question, please.

Oh.

[Student S].

Thank you. My first question dealt with the same subject. I'd like to ask, When did Halley's' Comet originate? And what was happening in man's consciousness at that time that there would be such a correlation?

Well, first of all, it was eons and eons ago, its origin. Your astronomers have their own understanding of its beginnings. And you want to know what happened at that time of the people on the planet Earth when it first appeared across this planet?

Well, wherever—I'm not sure—was there an Earth then?

It appears in the sky and it has an effect upon the element air, as it always did have. You do understand that it is separated from a planet, don't you? I mean, everyone does understand that, don't they, [Student B]?

Yes. [Student B responds.]

Pardon?

Yes.

Yes. It's, it's cast off from a planet. Do you understand which planet? *[After a short pause, the teacher continues.]* You don't. All right. That's fine. Now what is it you wanted to know about the people that were on your planet, Earth, when it first passed across the skies and had its effect upon the planet Earth?

Yes.

Yes. Well, you understand that the people on the Earth planet, they are under the control of the Law of Duality and that their purpose of being on the planet Earth is for an awakening of faith. Hmm?

Yes.

Now you have the balance of creation or the senses and the faculties, of what you are and what you are not. And so it is only your faith that will lead you on the path of what you truly are, and your belief, which is the creation, which will maintain the illusion and delusion of what you are not. And so there we have those experiences on the planet Earth.

Now what you call Halley's Comet, which is, perhaps, in your words, you would say, a symbol of an awakening on your planet. When it first appeared, there was an awakening of the masses who were at the depths of the descent into creation and what they are not. Now it is a symbol, so to speak, a sign, you might say, in the sky; although it's not a superstition. It has repeated itself, and each time it does, there is an awakening for your planet. It is sent to your world as you would send a message to a distant relative who you found was in great need. So [to] the masses of your planet, having been so long in great need, an effect of their service to what they are not, to beliefs, you see, it comes as a message, once again, as a help to the planet for the awakening of the people.

Now you will find that these many years of terrible fears and everything of holocaust and nuclear disaster and all the great needs that people on your planet have judged that they have, there will begin a healing balm with those many fears and needs. And, of course, you, as earthlings, a part of the race upon your planet, have the benefit of flowing with the awakening. Perhaps you would call it a more positive attitude, but what it truly is: an acceptance of what is; a refraining from denial and being tempted to be what, by the law, you shall not be. And does that help with that question of yours?

Yes.

Yes.

May I ask, please, What planet it did come from and what that planet represents?

Well, first of all, you may ask what it represents and then you can do your part, as a student and a private student of many years, to do your studies, which you already have, to find out from which planet it comes. And perhaps before I finish answering your question, you will already know for you've already had those teachings. You asked what it represents. It represents and is the light of wisdom. And now you already know what planet it—now someone else have a question, please? Did you have another question, [Student S]?

On a different subject. But that's . . .

That's fine. Go through your different subjects.

Why are the emotions affected with our cyclic change each month? And how can we better control this?

Over-identification to the change of the body through an attachment to it. Now if a person does not want to experience what they consider inconveniences—ladies, especially, I'm sure, consider them inconveniences; they are not designed by nature to be an inconvenience—all they have to do is to refrain from over-identification in form with the flesh, which they are not. It's only a house that they're using. That help with your question?

Yes. Thank you.

Stop thinking about it. Stop identifying with it. Stop allowing it to take control of your mind, and you'll hardly be aware there's anything happening. See, when a person has a change—you see, when there's any change in a person's body, a person that has an upset and an emotion because there's a change, perhaps there's a new freckle. "It just appeared. I just saw it right there, right there in my hand there. A little freckle there. How did that get there? What's going to happen to my skin?" You see, that's an attachment to the form. And then it's understandable when the cycle comes once a month, if a freckle does that, can you imagine what a little flow does? *[Student S laughs.]* Yes, go on with the next one.

In the cloud exercise—

Yes?

—if you are already in a very joyous state and ask what makes us happy, as part of that exercise, is it then accurate, when we just experience the scene that we are viewing, like the landscape and the clouds, or is this just a new device of the mind not to do the exercise correctly?

Well, the thing is, if I'm understanding you correctly, is when you are feeling good and you do the cloud exercise and you experience certain scenes—Is that correct?

Ah . . .

Yes?

My understanding [is], as part of the exercise, we ask what makes us happy.

Yes.

And the cloud takes that form.

Yes. That's correct.

Well, if we're already very happy in—

Are you happier when the cloud takes that form?

Well, it was the first time when I asked and nothing happened. It was just as it was.

When you were happy, it took the form.

No, it didn't take any form. It just stayed as beautiful as the whole scene. It didn't take on anything.

I see. Now, in reference to your feeling good and being happy at that time, were you dependent on anything that you could not control?

No.

As long as you're not dependent on anything that you cannot control and you have no fear of any moment when you cannot control it, for you are controlling only that which is the law for you to control, then there's no problem whatsoever; and there's not a device of the mind.

Oh, good.

Yes.

Thank you.

Go ahead with your other question.

What is the meaning of the wedding ring we wear in our custom and that some countries wear it on the left and some on the right hand?

And others, on the ear.
Oh!
Yes.
And in connection with this, you've often stated—and I'd like to ask what is meant by it—"Love is a simple thing, just like a silver ring."
Not gold?
Right.
Hmm. All right. Now you want to know in reference to the placement of this band of gold? Is that what you asked? *[After a short pause, the teacher continues.]* First of all, you've already had that teaching, and you know what that finger on which your particular civilization places that—
Yes.
—that band. You know what it represents, that finger.
Uh-huh.
All right. Prior to the use upon the finger—there's also, some wear it on a different hand. Prior to that, the ring was worn in the ear. Understand?
Yes.
Now that was a symbol, you see. Long, long ago a man wore it in his right ear and his wife wore it in her left ear. It was a symbol—and you also know what the ears represent, don't you?
Yes.
It was a symbol of the bondage of the human ego amalgamating to become one, for the glory of creation. [Does] that answer your question? *[After a pause, the teacher continues.]* For the glory of creation.

Now marriages, indeed, they say are made in heaven. Why, certainly, if creation is heaven in the consciousness of a human being, then, indeed, they are made in heaven.
Could you repeat that, please?
I say—and I'll be happy to repeat it for all of you. Your world says that marriages are made in heaven. I say that if the minds

of men judge that creation is heaven, then, indeed, it is made in the heaven of which they are aware. For, you see, a person [who] without, without question binds themselves to need and says they experience fulfillment has already denied what they are. And so in the ancient civilizations, the man wore the ring on his right ear; his wife wore the same ring on her left ear. There was no question whose ego was controlled by whose ego. There was no question for everyone knew.

Now as long as a person believes that they are only half there, until they have the other half, which is someplace else supposedly, and the other half that is supposedly someplace else truly believes that only through them can the other person be fulfilled and vice versa, then you have the heaven of creation. Yes, indeed. And the effects of those they call the bundles of joy. *[Several students laugh.]*

Yes, marriage is a wonderful institution, which I, speaking for me personally, do not recommend. I do not find it necessary in order to grow. Thank you. However, for those who, in keeping with the laws of evolution, find it necessary as a part of their process of freedom, then it certainly serves a fine purpose, that institution. Yes. Any other questions? Is that [Student L] or [Student Y] that has a question?

Yes, it's [Student L].

Oh, yes, [Student L].

I had a question—

Speak right up.

I had a question along those lines. Current—

Along those lines? Oh, I thought you were going to ask me a question about money.

I—

Yes, go ahead, [Student L], please. Yes.

Current—

Is it on marriage?

Well, it's about, it's to do with marriage, but not specifically marriage.

Well, marriage and money are very similar. They swim in the same pool. *[Many students laugh.]* Yes, go right ahead.

It's regarding a law.

Pardon? The law, yes, the law does govern the pond, too. Yes. And the pool. Lovely day.

Current statistics indicate that women outlive their husbands, and I'm interested in the law involved. Could it be due to the traditional dependence upon the spouse that they are given the opportunity to grow stronger and discover their own potential?

Well, no, let us, let us, I think, come down a little bit to *terra firma*, down here to earth here. One person judges they're not fulfilled unless they have a husband. Don't you find that most of the people on your planet make that judgment?

They seem to, yes.

They seem to?

Yes.

It's all seeming anyway. It's all delusion and illusion. And so they judge that without a man, they're not fulfilled. And so they get a man, and he has judged without him, she's not fulfilled. So he works like a beaver to keep her fulfilled. And so it's understandable: she stays on earth and he goes someplace else out of the flesh. That's understandable. Hmm? He's working like a beaver to keep up her conviction and judgment that he's an instrument through which she is fulfilled. And so he has to keep fulfilling her. And plus, how many bundles of joy come along? It's something else. It's understandable. Of course, they would go on sooner than the ladies. That's understandable. Yes.

Oh, I see.

Pardon?

I thought there was a spiritual law involved besides.

A spiritual law?

Yes.

Not all men pass on before their wives. Only the majority of them do, [Student L]. *[After a short pause, the teacher continues.]* Pardon?

Yes. Thank you.

And some men who are bachelors, why, they out distance all of them. Pardon?

I understand that.

Yes. Now I don't want you to understand [or] my students to think that I'm anti-institution. I spent and served my time there eons ago. It was short. Thank God. *[Some students laugh.]* It was like having what you call a repetitive phonograph record. *[More students laugh.]* For me. You see, of course, it's different for everyone.

Are there any questions from the men here this morning? There's [Student H] there, yes.

In terms of color temperature, do we feel emotionally secure with the color green because it is a balance of the warm color yellow with the cool color blue?

Well, now before I answer your question, I would like some of my students in class here present—I think it is very important. I don't want them to misunderstand that I felt like a henpecked person. And I would like to have that feeling from some of my students—a little understanding now. When you have a belief that a man fulfills your life, it's quite a job to get it fulfilled. He's got his own to take care of. And when he's got to fill somebody else's, it just does, sometimes, I guess, seem like a person is henpecked. Now, of course, I admit sometimes, you know, I've seen, many times, the roles are reversed, you know. And there are many men, especially in your world nowadays, who feel it's the women's job to fulfill his life.

Now let's have your question on green, please. Oh, definitely green! It's the proper color. I'm glad you asked that question. Green. Well, we can go to this morning's experience, for example.

My assistant, you know, he said, informed me that it was time that our cameraman grew up and had an opportunity to set up the filters and the colors here in keeping with these many weeks that our cameraman has been helped in understanding. Is it a golden day in the atmosphere? Is it more of a blue day in the atmosphere? And so they told him that he would have that opportunity this morning.

So my assistant reported to me, well, yes, it was quite an experience. [My assistant] came down here, [and] there was a blue filter on that one. And there was a white one on that one over there. Well, [we] have moved our equipment here so that we have an actual color monitor so that we can see everything that is taking place on our little monitor, which we brought up from downstairs, there, in our audio-video room. And set it up here so that we could see exactly what everything looks like before these classes, for your films. You're asking about green, you see, and emotional security.

Well, taking a look at that, my assistant informed me, almost made him sick. This was blue. And that was white. And that was white. And so our cameraman decided to change it to a darker blue. Well, there was little, if any, improvement. Strange-looking color to the skin, you know, and the room. And so my assistant recommended to your cameraman here that it would be in the best interest to put a green filter over there, instead of the white one. Well, our cameraman said, "No, green will make it too yellow. It's already yellow." Quite an interesting experience, my assistant tells me. So he put a blue one up there. Looked more yellow than ever before. Finally got it changed to a green one. There was an improvement. But he had to change this blue one over here.

Now what is interesting is this: you see, you cannot grow in a world of creation, you understand, wherever there's form, you can't grow until you have the opportunity to have your experiences. You see, a teaching can be shared with you. The laws can be shared with you. You must personally, from your own experiences, apply or not apply the laws so that you can discern.

Now green, the vibration of green, as I have explained to you, represents a warm and a secure feeling. It is a combination of the wisdom of the universe, of the Light itself (gold) and of the spirituality that we truly are. So as you well know or should know that blue and yellow is a perfect balancing in which a person feels secure. Now, for example, you want to feel secure temperature-wise, then you say that "Well, around 70 [degrees] I'm very comfortable." Is that not correct?

Yes.

Or 72 [degrees]? Hmm?

Correct.

All right. But what you don't see—you sense that with your feelings and your senses that you're warm and comfortable. What you do not make the effort to see is the color in the atmosphere. There is a perfect blending of the yellow and the blue. And you experience that at what you consider a comfortable temperature. But you don't look into the atmosphere to see what color it is, you see? You see, on the cold winter's day with the light so golden—and on some days the lights are very blue. You see? Like our cameraman was trying to correct a yellow day or a blue day, which he judged which was in the atmosphere, and the truth of the matter is—what color day is it, [Student R]?

Well, it was a little blue. And now it's getting more yellow.

Yes, but your monitor's not yellow.

No.

That's because you have a balancing factor. Now that balancing factor, you look in this room and you'll see is green, you see? So that balances the color temperature.

But what you should try to understand is as far as your own temperature is considered—you know, you have winter coming on and you say, "Oh, I'm cold and I'm freezing," your state of consciousness is too blue. You want to brighten it up with a little yellow. You brighten up your consciousness and you will be amazed at the changing in what you consider is your body temperature. For, you see, that's your environment. And by the divine law *you* not only can control your environment but you are responsible for it no matter where you are. So, you see, you have to make those changes within your consciousness. You have to learn how to do that. And then perceive what color is in the atmosphere. And if you want to be warm, then you make those adjustments. After all, you must make the mental adjustments and then, of course, there are certain pressure points in which you balance the color or vibration of your body. One side is blue; the other side is gold. And you apply the proper pressuring in those certain points and you bring about the physical balance. But you must first bring about the mental balance. Does that help with your question?

Yes. Thank you. [Student H responds.]

You're welcome. Yes, [Student J] has a question.

Could you—

And [Student S], too.

Could you please elaborate on the, which side is blue, which side is gold, and the pressure points to adjust for the adjustment, please?

Yes. Now would you consider, with all the studies that you've had, [Student J], would you consider that divine wisdom is an action, a positive action?

Yes.

Then you know where your positive side is, don't you, [Student J]?

Yes, sir.

And spirituality is a total acceptance?

Yes, sir.

That's true spirituality.

Yes, sir.

You [have] got the answer to that one. Did you have another question?

Thank you. What about the pressure points?

Now the pressure points are coming up as soon as my students get their homework done. Oh, yes, there's many different points on the body. And, well, I think I spoke to you years ago about pressure points, didn't I?

Yes, sir.

Many years ago.

Yes, sir.

Many, many years ago. Well, the time is getting closer, depending on the 51 percent of the student body. Perhaps within three weeks, as it starts turning colder, you know, that some of the pressure points that you could personally apply for warming up your little body and changing your attitudes will be given to you. All right?

Thank you.

Because, you know, those private students who have been with me for so many years, it would certainly well behoove you to get out your little diagrams of the human anatomy and the various colors, the representations of the functions and the faculties, and then you'll see what's really happening when you get a few pressure points. You know, in your world it is very accurate, very, very accurate what I spoke to you many years ago about acupressure. Do you recall, aren't you the student—certainly, you are—that asked me about acupuncture?

Yes, sir, indeed.

No, no, no. Acupuncture pierces the skin. You don't want anything like that. But acupressure, which is a very ancient—comes way down from what you consider your Lemurians and your Atlanteans, you know, you don't—you just have to touch the right spot. In just the right spot. And we're going to get to that. It's been many years for you, hasn't it, that you've waited for those points?

Yes.

Oh, yes, yes. Well, we'll—within three weeks, if the class continues to do its study and for your own information because it is not something that one treats lightly. And it is also very important that the pressure be done in a certain way, for if it is not—not that it is extremely detrimental, but it's just not beneficial; it's a waste of time. You must reach—you see, when you get a pressure—you see, on your finger there—try to visualize—I can give you this much—you try to visualize that it's coming to a very sharp point. *[The teacher extends the middle finger of his right hand and points to the tip of it with the index finger of his left hand.]* Hmm? On the finger. And when the pressure is applied, it's like inserting that point into a receptacle. You have to learn to find that. Then you'll see what—you'll see the change. We'll get there. At least to the temperature part within three weeks.

And [Student S] had a question. Do you have another question, [Student J]?

Well, I was just curious as to why you used the index finger instead of the power finger in your demonstration right now.

[The teacher laughs joyously.] Well, what does this finger represent? *[The teacher extends his middle finger of his right hand.]*

Ah, I don't have . . . [Student J responds.]

Do you remember, [Student S]?

Yes.

What does that represent?

Awareness. [Student S responds.]

All right?

Why not the power finger, sir? [Student J asks.]

But the power is no good without the awareness, [Student J]. The power is worthless without the awareness. You see, it's self-healing. Do you understand?

Yes, sir.

So the physician must be aware of what's taking place. And you are the physician at the time. Hmm?

Oh.

It isn't something that someone else has to do. It's something you do yourself. Now if you don't have the awareness of that fitting properly, do you understand that?

Yes, sir.

Then all the power in the world is worthless if it's going to the wrong thing, right? Hmm?

Right.

You see, if you direct the power and you are not aware and the power is not serving the purpose of its design, do you know what happens to the power?

No, sir.

It returns unto itself. Hmm? Yes. You see? So it's very important that you have awareness. Hmm?

Yes, sir.

Especially being the physician who is healing yourself or will be very soon in that respect. Hmm?

Thank you.

You see? Now I have one of my students here, [Student R], who I have been working with—is that not correct, [Student R]?—who has been interested in pressure for many, many years. Many, many years. And so it's coming along. You'll see. But the thing is that it is the attitude of mind along with the proper application of the pressure. The awareness, you see—if you don't have the awareness, you don't have the proper attitude of mind and you don't have the right color combination, it's imbalanced, you see. You see? You're either too blue or you're too yellow. One or the other. But if you take the two together and you have the perfect balance of the blue and the gold or yellow, then you have that beautiful expression of green. And you don't have to go around the universe, as some of my students do, crying for green because, you see, it's a matter of balancing this vibration inside. You see, if you put the blue with the yellow into perfect balance, you're going to have all the green you could possibly ever desire in creation. But you must do that inside your consciousness. And, you see, I have found, over these many years, you know, whenever, whenever there's a shortage of the green, I know very well the person's too yellow, you see. There's not enough blue, the combination in the consciousness is way off, you see. Hmm? You see? There's too much yellow and not enough blue. Now you know that blue is spirituality. Well, what is faith, child? You see?

You see, you've got to learn to work with these things, to understand them, to be aware of them and bring about this balance within your universe. Because the outward manifestations are revelations of the inner attitude of mind, and it shows that the inner attitude of mind is out of balance, you see? It's out of balance. And the coloring is off, you see. And so we don't have enough green. Hmm? You see? Now a person could say, "Well, there's not enough green of the kind of green I want." Well, green is green. Whether it's the green leaf that you see or it's green paper or it's green anything, you see. You create that green within the conscious[ness]. Look, like attracts like and becomes the Law of Attachment. If you have a balanced universe in the consciousness, that balance is green. You understand? You experience the abundant good of life. There can be no need. There can be no shortage. So, you see, you must learn to balance in the consciousness the yellow with the green. *[The teacher may have misspoken: he may have intended to say "with the blue." Earlier in this class, he stated that green was "a combination of the wisdom of the universe, of the Light itself (gold) and of the spirituality that we truly are." That said, he may not have misspoken.]*

Now, try to take a look at these things. You see, a person who is blue, you say is a person who's despondent. But they have something to be despondent or discouraged over. They make the effort, right? But a person who is yellow, that's something else. They're not doing anything. Right? So, you see, you've got to take a blending of this yellow and this blue and this yellow, you see? You want to be cautious in your endeavors, in your efforts, which, of course, yellow offers to all of us. Yellow, gold, divine wisdom offers us caution. And you want to be blue and determined, you know. Spirit vibration is a determining vibration. So you [have] got to bring about a balance with that in the attitude in the consciousness. Hmm? See?

Now any other questions here? Does [Student S] have a question? Yes.

I'd like to ask, Is that one of the reasons why we get so cold during and after our spiritual classes because of the, the spiritual blue?

Why, certainly. You will experience it, of course, as a changing in the atmosphere. Absolutely. Absolutely. Ask my channel after I leave. He freezes to death. But not as long as he used to. But there has to be a readjustment, you understand. Try to understand when I'm using his little house, I have a blue and yellow combination that's different than his, you understand?

Yes.

Might be a little more blue. Might be a little more yellow. Do you understand? And so then I go, and then his form has to readjust to another coloring imbalance. Hmm? Yes.

Now are there any other questions, as my good student here is enjoying his morning nap. Only the four-legged one is allowed that. Yes. Is that [Student B]?

No. [Student B responds.]

No. Who's right there? [Student A]?

[Student A].

Oh, speak up, [Student A], please.

How may we sustain and maintain the spirit of enthusiasm and joy and become more childlike?

How may we maintain the spiritual vibration of enthusiasm? By accepting, [Student A]. Accepting. Accepting that it's happening. Do you understand that?

Yes.

Accept that it's happening; you guarantee the experience. Deny it, and you guarantee that experience. Hmm?

Thank you.

Accepting, [Student A]. Accept it.

All right.

Go ahead with the other questions.

When we do the cloud exercise and look to the left and see the shape of a form . . .

Yes?

. . . and we also look to the right and look directly in front of us at different times when we're doing the cloud exercise, can you give me the names of those directions?

Well, the thing is, you see, one is what you are receiving the other is what you're creating, [Student A].

I see.

And the other is what you are.

Thank you.

All right, [Student A].

Why do some sounds and colors have a more soothing effect on us than others?

Well, that's most understandable [that] they have a more soothing effect. Now there's two different ways. There's a way—there's a soothing effect because of your attitude and the color that you're into. It mixes and blends beautifully. Then there's the basic vibration of your aura, which is another color. And you have exposed yourself to harmonizing colors. Hmm?

Yes.

You see?

Yes, I do. Thank you.

And this is why sometimes a person doesn't have to say a word; they only have to see their face [and] you don't feel right. Well, your colorings are way off. The two of you are not going to mix at all until somebody makes a change in their consciousness. That's when you pause before you open your mouth, right, [Student A]?

Yes. [The student laughs.]

Because you can feel it.

Yes.

Go ahead with your questions, [Student A].

In [Consciousness] Class 160 there is a breathing technique on inhaling and exhaling peace.

Yes?

Do we do this with our mouth, our nose, or a combination of both?

What did it say in reference to the many years of your study—Oh, I see. You speak with the secretary here right after class. All right?

I . . .

Because you do know. And I want her to refresh your memory. You owe that to yourself, [Student A].

Yes. Thank you.

All right? Yes, go ahead.

When there is harmony within and without one's being, is one free?

That is freedom, [Student A]. Whenever there's harmony within, without is totally under control, see, if you consider without the area of your own universe.

Thank you very much.

You're more than welcome. Now did [Student D] have a question there?

Yes, I did.

You speak right up, [Student D].

I would like some information on the color red. Now I understand that red is action. And the hands are action, The Living Light *[textbook] says that. But the color of the hands is yellow. And you mentioned that—*

What do they control?

—wisdom is action. So could you clarify that a little bit?

Certainly. What do the hands control in your world?

Well, they manipulate things.

Indeed, they do. And that which is manipulated is a victim or controlled by the manipulator, would you not agree, [Student D]?

Yes.

And the hands are yellow. Their action is red. And what color is that?

Orange. Creation.

That's correct. Does that help with your question, [Student D]?

Yes.

Yes.

May I ask another one?

Oh, certainly.

Is gratitude, is it located in the heart?

Gratitude?

Yes.

The heart is the voice of the soul, [Student D]. And gratitude is a triune soul faculty thereof. Does that help with your question?

Yes. Thank you.

You're welcome. Do you have another?

The Living Light *[textbook] speaks of universal love.*

Yes?

And I wondered if you could speak a little on what universal love is in comparison with the earth loves that we know.

Oh, yes, certainly. Well, universal love, nothing is exempt, including the rosebud or the dandelion. Now when you can look at a dandelion and you can feel the same feeling and experience that you have when you look at something you judge you're in love with, then you have attained universal love.

Thank you. [The student speaks very quietly.]

Pardon?

Thank you.

Does that help you feel better?

Yes. Yes, it does.

Yes.

I have one more question.

Go right ahead, please.

When babies are asleep, where do they go, especially the small infants?

The angels are working when the baby sleeps to your world.

And why do so many of them cry when they awaken? Is it because they have to come back?

They don't want to come back into that form here. It's a very heavy form, the human body.

Oh.

And once you leave it, you don't want to come back into it, you know.

Right.

And so they awaken to, "Oh. Here I am again. Yes." [The teacher speaks as though he were dejected and some students laugh.] Because the soul knows that [it's] back in school.

What, what is the best approach to help them out of that space when they awaken and are crying?

Music.

Oh.

It calms the animal beast. Music.

Oh, thank you.

You see, in the recovery realms of consciousness there and when many of the souls come over, music is played constantly for the harmony and the healing. It's very important. Whether you sleep or are awake, the proper type of harmony of music, it's critical.

Then is that a good practice in the hospitals? You know, they play music in the nurseries.

Should always have music.

Ah.

The music should never stop where there's healing being done.

Oh, thank you.

Should never ever stop. You see, for example, because the sounds of unfulfilled desires leave our universe [and] go out into the atmosphere—and they are extremely discordant. Do you understand?

Yes.

Even though some people, well, most of your people do not hear them as audible sounds, try to understand they are registering within the consciousness. And therefore, to counteract that constant bombardment, it is critical and extremely important that you have the healing harmony of good music. Hmm. Yes, I know. *[The teacher acknowledges the signal from the cameraman that the tape is about to run out.]* Thank you.

Thank you.

You're welcome. Yes, [Student N] has a question.

In The Living Light *text it talks about the, the form while it's still in the womb passes through all stages of evolution.*

That's correct.

What, what are all—what—I guess it's a big question, but what are all the stages of evolution? And do we pass through them again once we've been born and, and grow, grow up?

On another planet?

No, on this planet.

No, no, no. The embryo is going [through] and showing to you the various stages of evolution of the forms on your planet in the nine-month process, [Student N].

Yes.

Do you understand?

Yes, I do. Thanks.

Now, when you, in evolution, enter one of the other planets, there, to express in physical form in time yet to be for you, then that form you pass through and that embryo goes through all the evolutionary processes of *that* particular planet, which are different than your planet. Do you understand?

Thank you.

You're welcome. Well, they tell me the time is up. I'm getting better at this. We've got two and a half minutes. Do you have a question, anyone else? I have right here—who is that? [Student M]?

Yes, it was said that to be poor, many centuries ago, was a sin against God.

Was a what?

A sin against God. To be poor.

Oh, yes. Definitely! Absolutely! It's a denial of the Law of the Principle of Goodness. Of course, it would be considered a sin. Yes, an error is considered a sin. Yes.

Yes.

Yes.

Now why, when did the change happen where, you know, in some religious sects they have the vow of poverty and denial and . . .

To—I'm taking this off and I shouldn't. *[The teacher refers to his microphone.]* To justify their own lack of effort and understanding, you see? You see, it's one thing to place your attention on a material substance until that becomes your god, and then you've transgressed a natural law. But the natural law is the abundant good of living [and] is the divine birthright of all beings. And when you do not experience the abundant good of living, then you are going against the Divine Law or the Principle of Good, known as God. And in that respect, it is a sin. Indeed, it is for it is a mistake and an error. Did that help with your question?

Yes.

I must say good day for the timing has passed. Thank you.

OCTOBER 6, 1985

A/V Class Private 18

Good afternoon, students.

I see that you have had a most interesting, perhaps, unusual day today. However, it has offered to you a wonderful opportunity in understanding what is known as vibrations and color and sound. So it is important for each of you to have these wonderful experiences in order that you may gain even greater understanding. Now the, of course, temptation of the mind is to look out at what it judges it cannot control and, in so doing, to blame outside for the opportunity. However, we're going to have our class here today. We're having our class. And whenever we feel in life that something is just not working out, remember that only fools quit before the victory.

Now in reference to your questions, it is of the utmost importance that you have your questions for your classes, for it is only through the opportunity of asking your questions, submitting them, and writing them down that you can awaken to what is of value and of interest to you on your spiritual path up the mountain of truth and freedom. In reference to that, there are many paths up the same mountain, and that which is your path is different, in a sense, than anyone else's path. And so when you are peaceful, you are inspired to ask certain questions, and in so doing, you receive answers to those questions and that helps you in understanding your interest and the particular path that you are on. So your questions reveal to you the seeming detours and pits along your path as you ponder the questions and the answers.

Now we're going to go right ahead this afternoon. It is rare that we have classes in what you call the afternoon. Before getting to those questions, I feel very good that you have had the opportunity to see what various frequencies of color can do and what you can to do correct them and to understand that with an attitude of mind of joyful acceptance of good, you emanate certain colors from your aura. And they mix with other people's auras and colors, and your filming reveals what is truly going on.

Now the secretary will kindly read the questions that have been prepared.

It was said that good music is helpful in the healing process. What type of music would be considered good?

Yes. In reference to good music: now try to understand that good music is ever subject to the censorship of our past experiences. And so for us as individuals in a mental world, you see, what we judge is good music is dependent upon our feelings of good, which are experiences which have passed. Now, for example, when the judgments of the human mind are satisfied, at that moment we experience what we understand as God or a good feeling.

And so it is with music. From past experiences, when our judgments were satisfied, we then became receptive—for no censorship of mental substance was in the way—we became receptive to the Principle of Good, known as God. Now when we do not feel good, we, of course, realize that judgments that we believe that we are, are unhappy. And because we believe we are the thought of the mind, instead of the true being which uses the mind, and because the mind is the vehicle through which the judgments express themselves that we have created, when the judgments are not satisfied, they inhibit our experience of what we truly are.

And so good music, good music is music that a person is receptive to and feels good. Now some people, they like slow music. Some people like fast music. Some people like hard rock music. Some people like soft rock music. Well, what you should try to understand, in reference to that question, that what is taking place is the judgments of the mind are satisfied; they lay down and take a nap and you experience at that moment who you truly are, and that's good. However, that's good because the judgments have been satisfied.

Now what is good music? That that I have discussed is good music subject to censorship of the human ego, the uneducated ego. Good music is music that is harmonious and pleasant, peaceful, enjoyable, and is instrumental, consistently, not dependent upon the satisfaction of judgments, is instrumental in strengthening the true being to once again experience God, the Principle of Good. Does that help with your question?

Yes. Thank you.

Yes. Certainly.

Why is salt necessary for the existence of darkness?

Why is the mineral salt necessary for the existence of the darkness?

Yes.

It's their food. It's their sustenance. Well, I see, I see that that is not clear or is not satisfactory to the minds of the questioner. Salt, a mineral—the refinement of the minerals of creation—you hear?—

Yes.

—is the very substance that is necessary for the lesser light to have control over, temporarily, the Light that you are. Now when you, for example, consume a meal, if the meal contains no salt or what you call salt substitute, it is not desirable to the taste buds. Would you not agree?

Correct.

What controls the taste buds?

The jud—

Past experiences, would you not agree?

Yes.

What controls past experiences?

Judgments.

And who is the king of judgment?

Lucifer.

And so you will find that the salt mines are ever in need of workers in order to supply the substance required by the lesser light. Go right ahead with your question.

Thank you. What are the most effective procedures to obtain the answer to the question: What is one's greatest responsibility?

In reference to what is one's greatest responsibility, one's greatest responsibility is experiencing that which they are. For that which they are, freed from dependence on anything they can't control, that which they are is personal responsibility. Now man's greatest responsibility is his personal responsibility: the ability to respond to what he is rather than to respond to the temptations of what he is not. So man's greatest responsibility is the responsibility to his true being. And in the effort to face and to apply one's responsibility to their true being, man is freed from all of these seeming needs, all of these disturbances, and no longer is a servant of that which he is not. Yes.

Thank you. What planet did the missing link of man come from? And is this the same planet that Halley's Comet came from?

Yes.

Thank you.

Next question.

What is the purpose of an embryo going through all of the evolutionary processes of the planet it is entering?

To reveal the soul's evolutionary journey. Yes.

Thank you. Recently there was mention of the power finger and the awareness finger. Will you please give us the fingers and their meaning?

The fingers and their meanings have already been given to some of my private students and, as secretary, those now in private class may ask you for those, for they've already been given and you already have them, correct?

Yes. Thank you. Middle C is the color white on the musical scale and is the balance point on the scale of sound. Number five is faith, the number of balance. Is middle C, the color white, and the number five one and the same?

Is middle C, the color white, the number five, and what else?
And balance.
And balance? Yes, it is. You just speak right up there.
OK. What takes place when our channel performs rescue work?
What takes place in what respect? Do you—is—I see. You just have the question, What takes place when my channel is working in his rescue work? *[In previous classes, students raised their hands or spoke their names to ask their questions, but in this particular class, questions were written down in advance and submitted to the secretary, who then read them to the teacher. This arrangement makes it difficult for the teacher to get clarification of a question.]*
Yes.
Well, first of all, what takes place, there are many sinking, what you would call, sinking souls in the universe, sinking only in the sense that they are firmly convinced that they are the temptation and the weakness that they are temporarily identifying with. So in that respect, what takes place: you can only offer to another what one has first offered unto themselves. And therefore, a channel or anyone must first offer to themselves the absolute awakening that they are not dependent on anything they cannot control; they are not the weakness or the temptation or the need or the denial. And then they are qualified to be a rescue worker by rescuing themselves. They are, therefore, in a position to be an instrument through which others are rescued or helped. Yes.
Thank you. Would you please discuss the silence and lack of spoken words practiced by certain Eastern religions and various sects in the United States?
Silence and the lack of the spoken word?
Yes.

Why, in reference to that particular question, it's most understandable: they're terribly fearful of contamination. You see, as I've spoken before, in your evolution, a mouth you have earned to use. Now the contamination or pollution is ofttimes, to many people, something that they fear, which only reveals that mental substance, not God, [and] belief, not faith, they are still serving, for in the midst of the Philistines thou shalt be delivered. In the very midst of the pollution, with faith one shall rise free and clear. Now one uses discretion when they are awake and they see clearly and they know beyond a shadow of any doubt that there is such poisonous gas in the atmosphere they will not long endure in the form in which they are presently identifying. So one takes corrective measures in consciousness, and the wisdom and the Light within will reveal that the person physically remove themselves by first removing themselves in consciousness. Thank you.

Thank you. During contemplation time, why do the hands fall asleep?

Well, there can be several factors involved in reference to that; it's most interesting. Usually the seeming problem is that the flow of the energy through the physical body is being obstructed at that time, and they awaken and their feet or their hands have, what you say, gone to sleep. They are receiving insufficient energy. Yes.

Thank you. Is truth ever the covering or content of an expression?

Is truth ever the content or covering of expression?

Yes.

Well, truth is perceived. Truth is perceived. Truth cannot cover. Truth uncovers. Truth is never a covering. It's an uncovering. It's a revelation. For example, the Light dispels the lesser light for it uncovers it; it does not cover it. And so one in their seeking and searching in life works to uncover within the various layers that have covered up the Light that they are.

Now, for example, a student asks questions. It is important: as a student asks a question they uncover or reveal to the Light that they are and to anyone else who is truly in the Light, they uncover and reveal unto their true Light the areas in consciousness that require more effort. Yes.

Thank you. When a thought form or a group of thought forms do not receive energy from their creator so that they go to someone else, are they attracted to a receiver by their covering or subject matter or by the vibration contained within? And how can we help the receiver of our forms?

In order to help the receiver of the negative forms of which you speak, which are only given birth from denial of what one is—that's how negative forms are given birth: by denial of what one is and believing therefore what one is not. How can we help another who is receiving our forms as a receiving set? We can help them most by helping our self. For as we help our self, we free our self from the denial of what we are and, therefore, emanate what we truly are and not what we temporarily believe that we are. Otherwise, there is something else working, known as need. The need to mother or to control another being as we look and believe we are being compassionate when in truth we are covered with the judgment of compassion as we are feeling pity within our self from the denial of what we are. Yes.

Thank you.

You're welcome.

Does everyone have the same contract in the Rotunda, like to separate truth from creation? Or does each individual also have a specific personal service contract?

Oh, yes. The principle is that everyone, in evolution, will grow and accept what they are and free themselves from the covering of what they believe that they are. So one enters into the Rotunda with many coverings, and in principle, all shall awaken to what they are by refraining from believing in the levels that cover what they truly are.

Thank you. [Does] the beating of the heart and the rhythmic cleansing breath coincide?

Yes, it does.

Thank you. Could you please speak further on the parts of the body that are not dual and why they show us about the understanding of need?

Well, yes, yes, indeed, it's a most interesting question. Well, all we have to do is look at the human anatomy and we can see the parts of the anatomy that are not dual. For a mixed class, it does seem a bit difficult, for some, for me to discuss, but you only have one part of the body to relieve yourself, to relieve your bladder; for either sex, man or woman, you only have one. And that reveals [for] people who believe that they are the body, it is understandable when they see that they have two hands, two ears, two nostrils, they have two eyes—only one mouth and only one part of their body in which to relieve their bladder, etc.—it is understandable that when they look at those parts in their consciousness that they would believe that they're only half there. Because, you see, they look and see the duality of their form: two feet, more than one toe. And they see that everything is duplicated except that particular part, you see. And so it is, indeed, understandable for anyone who believes that they are the form—and by believing they are the form, are addicted to and controlled by all other forms [and] from their own belief, they offer that to the world—it is understandable, with that phase of evolution, that a person would say, "I only have one of this. Someone else has the other part." Does that help with the question?

Yes. Thank you.

You're welcome.

Is it advisable for the same room to be used for meditation for two people?

Well, of course, that's dependent, if the two people want to become each other, yes.

Thank you.

I mean, if the two people in question have a need to become one, if the two people feel they're only half there, then it would be, of course, in keeping with that. Yes.

Thank you.

You're welcome.

[I] would also like to ask if the same room is used at two different, separate times by two different people, would it also apply?

Yes, indeed, it would because, you see, sooner or later, and usually sooner, one says they had a very terrible meditation because of the terrible vibrations that the other person was in there before them.

Thank you.

Yes, in other words, mental substance reigns supreme while in an effort of spiritual awakening. Yes.

Yes.

Try to understand that spirituality is not dependent in any way upon the mind [or] the body. It is just the reverse. The body, the mind, the thoughts, the judgments are wholly and completely dependent upon the Light in order to even exist. Yes.

Thank you. How can we use our hindsight to become our foresight so we have more insight?

Oh, such a beautiful question. One word only need be applied: honesty. The application of honesty. Some people call it sincerity. Honesty is all that is required. Yes.

Thank you. Through the intercourse of divine will (electric) and divine love (magnetic) we reach the balance or neutrality. Could you please speak more on this principle of electromagnetic?

Yes, indeed, the divine love and the will of goodness or God. Yes, if you will look at divine love and the divine will of God, you will find it is absent of need for it is absent of denial. You will also find in all forms, including the blade of grass, they are in truth electromagnetic. And so it is an amalgamation;

it is an intercourse within the consciousness of the electric and the magnetic within the domain and the divine right of the individual. Freed from all dependence on anything that one cannot control, the will of God and goodness amalgamates in the beautiful divine love of God's expression within the consciousness, freed from all need, dependence, denials, and judgments. Yes.

Thank you.

You're welcome.

As we consume what we believe we are, we become what we are. How may we consciously consume what we believe we are?

How may we constantly consume what we believe that we are?

Yes.

Oh, there's no problem at all. My students are doing it constantly. There's no problem. There's a constant consummation of believing they are what they believe that they are. They're absolutely convinced at times. You see, the effort, you see, is to be made in refraining from believing that you are the forms of your creation. The effort is to be made in accepting what you are by refraining from what you believe that you are. For beliefs are in a constant process of change, depending on the judgments, which are the forms [that are] ever creation, from the denials of the divine truth and goodness and love and joy and happiness that we are. Yes.

Thank you. During the rhythmic cleansing breath at times I experience a vibration in rapport with the vibration of the note. What is occurring at those moments?

With the vibration of the what?

Of the note.

Well, in reference to the question, which is most important, in becoming receptive to the vibration of the note, be it in Divine order, the student feels good and is inspired to work harder, which is God's love made manifest, then it is the thing to do. It is definitely, positively the thing to do. Yes. Thank you.

How may we cultivate universality?

By accepting what we are and [to] stop believing the obstructions that we create are us. It has—you see, to believe requires conviction. To be convinced requires judgment. To create a judgment requires denial. To [deny] is the destiny down. Yes.

Could you please speak on the dangers involved in piercing the skin?

Skin represents sensitivity. It is where sensitivity is registered by the form. Sensitivity in reference to physical substance. Now when a person pierces their own sensitivity, when they do that or when they permit that to be done to them, they come under the control of whoever is doing the piercing. Therefore, if you find a need to pierce your skin, make the intelligent decision to do it to yourself. So when the experience from the piercing is registered in the consciousness, you can say intelligently, "I didn't care for that experience I did to myself. I'm not going to do it again." Yes. Thank you.

Thank you. When, after having chosen a course of action, doubts arise, what does that indicate and how best may we work with them to be free?

Yes, indeed, it reveals an identification with belief, which we are not about to let go of. And they come up and are known as doubts. That's known as quitting, fools, just before the victories in life. Yes.

Thank you. Everything exists within us. How may we recognize and accept this simple truth?

By refraining from believing in what you are not.

When we be in the moment of now, we are using the power of concentration by directing our attention fully and totally on what we are doing and freed from the thought of I. When we feel uncomfortable within, should we ask for an account of all bodies before rising in consciousness to a better rate of vibration?

Absolutely. Definitely. All bodies are vehicles that, without you, can go nowhere. So it is your divine right and responsibility not to ask but to demand an accounting of your vehicles.

Thank you. When we emanate harmonious thoughts, are we able to help the nature spirits with the energy they use to do their work here on earth? Which centers are drawn from? Air, ethereal, celestial, or what?

Well, in reference to that question, when we emanate harmonious thoughts, it's so nice that they are emanated at times. However, it's rare that we are aware that we are emanating harmonious thoughts. However, you want to know which of the centers is being used?

Yes.

Which is the center—I shall ask you, as secretary, the question—which is the center that frees you from the bondage of belief? Which faculty?

Reason.

It's located between two centers.

Yes, the reason.

Yes?

Located between the air and the electric.

Yes? Now you have an answer to that question.

Thank you.

You're welcome.

What is the difference between the astral world and the magnetic field that surrounds our earthly planet?

What is the difference between the astral world and the magnetic field that surrounds our planet?

Yes.

Well, that is the astral world. That's where they live in the magnet. That's why they're in the astral—they're earth-bound. They cannot free themselves from the magnet.

Thank you.

Listen carefully, children. Belief is a magnet that binds us. Faith is an electric power, the Light itself that frees us. Yes.

Thank you.

You're welcome.

If we are drawn to that which we vibrate to in color, sound, and shape—

Yes.

—is that how the souls on earth come to this particular place? And is it the same elsewhere for all beings?

Yes.

Thank you.

That is correct.

Are the higher planes set up, so to speak— [The clock begins to chime as this question is read.]

I think it would be advisable if you would consider pausing during the chiming of the clock. And will my cameraman see that's taken care of? *[After one clock stops chiming, another is heard in the background.]* Yes?

I will pause.

Did we not speak on this just the last class? *[The teacher refers to class A/V Seminar 7, which was given three days before this class.]*

Yes.

Was there some problem there?

I don't know where this question comes from.

That is not what I asked. I asked, Was there some problem in reference to asking the question while your little clocks are chiming?

I'm sorry. I didn't—

Did I not ask at the last class that while the clocks are chiming to please refrain from asking the question?

Yes, you did mention it. And I apologize.

I accept your apology. Would you make effort to remember for your good?

Yes, I will.

Very well. Go ahead now with the question.

Thank you.

You're welcome.

If we are drawn to that which we vibrate to in color, sound, and shape, is that how the souls on Earth come to this particular planet? And is it the same elsewhere for all beings?

Yes, that question I had answered and that is correct. It was the next question that you were reading while your clocks were chiming.

Are the higher planes set up, so to speak, like our government here in the form of a hierarchy?

There is a hierarchy wherever there is form. Yes, that is correct.

Thank you. Is my understanding correct, that the entire universe of beings, no matter what level of being they are at, is in constant process of learning so that there is no end to the process of growth?

There is no end to the process of growth of limit. Expansion of limit is growth of form. God cannot, does not grow. You, soul, goodness, the spiritual good that you are, that which you truly are does not grow. What would it grow to? What would God grow to? There's nothing to grow to. You are good. That good *is*. You are covered with the limit by belief. And from belief—beliefs change, expand, and grow. Forms limit, change, evolve, and grow. Your service, that Light that you are, is in your identification with mental substance to the Light that you are. The forms in which the Light is expressing itself, they expand, they grow. And the purpose of your journey through form is served and your responsibility is well done. Yes.

Thank you. Do you know of your existence before your earth form?

Yes. Everyone, everyone is aware of their existence prior to the entrance into any form the moment they refrain from believing what they are not.

Thank you. If a man is helping another and he leaves his form while doing so, does that act or good deed help him in the same way if he has been in great difficulty at that time prior to leaving?

Kindly reread your question.

If a man is helping another and he leaves his form while doing so, does that act or good deed help him in some way if he has been in great difficulty at that time prior to leaving?

Well, first of all, we don't know, in this particular case that's being referred to, if in helping another there was great good done. Many people help another to help themselves, and there's no good done. So in reference to questions of that nature, it is a matter of working with the responsibility within oneself: what motivated a person to be an instrument through which another is benefited. There are many varying factors in reference to the question, and it would require one that's more specific.

OK. Thank you.

Yes.

Expand, please, on the theory of nightmares.

The theory or the experiencing of nightmares?

The question says "the theory of nightmares."

Well, it's not theoretical. It just is. In your world of, of dream state, of course, there are nightmares. They express in many different ways, ever in keeping with your beliefs of who you are. [When] you believe that you are the limit of the experiences of the day, [if] you're not satisfied, your judgments, in expressing themselves, you can prepare yourself for some type of a nightmare or dream. Of course, everyone dreams. Unfortunately, too many dream while their eyes are open. But in reference to nightmares, unfulfilled desires express themselves, and frustration expresses itself. Emotional upheavals express themselves. And the judgments have a field day while you're out to dinner. Yes.

Is all form actually the color yellow or golden?

Well, I haven't taught that. I have taught that the leaves, the trees, the green that you see, in truth, is gold. However, now that the question has been brought up here in these private classes, that which you call the essence of a thing, that is what *is*. That's what is. And so the essence, the true being, the Light itself is gold. It's gold. And, like the size of a pinhead, it sustains whatever form covers it. Yes.

Thank you. When you are listening to music and you get chills, is that being registered in the functions or faculties?

Well, first of all, if you're aware of the chill in mental substance, it's registering in the functions. However, try to understand whatever the faculties are receptive to, the functions waste no time in grabbing ahold of. And that's called registration in the functions. Yes.

Thank you.

You're welcome.

Does the celestial center connect with the center between the air and electric, and then form our outer shell of our egg or universe?

Yes.

Thank you.

You're welcome.

What are the four planets corresponding to the earth, fire, water, and air, and the four corresponding with the electric, magnetic, odic, ethereal, and the planet with the celestial?

I will start you off with one: Mars and the fire.

Thank you.

And we'll get to the others as time progresses.

OK. Is character a composite of principles that we live by?

Indeed, it is.

Could you give us a greater understanding, please, of the fountain exercise?

The fountain exercise, given to some of you some time ago, contains all of the colors or frequencies that are. Now when you gain control through an exercise with the fountain exercise, you will have control, to an ever-increasing degree, over your mind, which was designed to serve you. Yes.

Please discuss the meaning of the different colors of hair and the spiritual lessons they represent.

The hair, a part of the covering of the temple, the covering of the roof of the temple, God's temple, and the coloring of the eyes, the skin or complexion, the size, the sex, and the experiences, of course, in life are all a part of experiences in evolution. They are composed and designed in such a way as to reveal to the awakened soul, awakened in the sense that they've peeled off the layers and coverings which they had believed that they were, reveals to the awakened soul the lessons that they have to study, to apply, and to pass in their evolution.

And this is why it is so very important, in spiritual classes especially, to ask your questions, to write them down so that you may identify and awaken with the path that you are walking upon spiritually. And so it is, indeed, of more value to awaken to the principle and to perceive why your little house, your temple of God, is short or tall or thin or brown or yellow or red or black. And to awaken to that through an awakening of the laws by your interest and effort to apply them.

You see, ofttimes in questions of this nature, they can be, indeed, detrimental and not serve their true purpose of the Light in the sense that one learns that this color is such and such, and that color is such and such. Therefore, they are this color hair; therefore, they are more evolved than that one who has that color hair. And so it is not in the best interest to be specific about what this particular skin coloring represents and doesn't represent, when you have been given already the principle of the laws and the colors and their meanings. And so it's a matter of personal inner awakening to understand, which will be instrumental in keeping a person free from the pit of judgments. Go right ahead with your questions.

Thank you. Please discuss ways—

Yes. Kindly, would you reread that, please?

Yes. Please discuss ways of generating energy to help in a particular situation.

Through an acceptance of that which you are by refraining from believing that you, your mind, can do anything, that only the Divine Goodness that you are can inspire you to do something. And when that goes to work, there is no concern over the results. And from no concern over the results, there is no attachment, there is no bondage. And no attachment to the fruits of action and no possibility for the human mind, in its cunningness, to do things other than the true spiritual motivation of the moment.

Thank you.

You're welcome.

Are there any questions or requests of the Light that we are advised to make to prepare for transition or for our next work assignment?

Well, especially in reference to transition, it is very important to make the effort daily to refrain from believing in the judgments that try to control your life. For when you leave at transition and these forms you clearly see, and they order you to do certain things and you find yourself, indeed, upset, for they order you to do many things. *[The clock starts chiming.]* You see—we'll pause a moment. *[After the clock stops chiming, the teacher continues.]* Well, don't be concerned about shutting off the clocks. The vibration is beautiful. And time passes so quickly. They tell us in your world every fifteen minutes; I think that's what they're telling you.

Now transition and believing that you're the forms. For example, you leave the physical world and these many forms that you see because they've been with you for so long. And you find them order you to do things you don't want to do. And they're very, very definite about you doing it. Well, try to understand that they were created at a time in your life when you did [serve them]; you created them and you served them. But you moved on. And expanding your consciousness and you don't want to serve them anymore. Well, that did not annihilate them. Not at all. And so they wait for you.

Well, if you believe you are the limit, if you permit yourself to believe by an over-identification with your little physical and mental form, then, of course, you are one of their victims. And especially is it difficult for those who believe that that's someone outside when it's a child you have created, and therefore you are greater than what you've created. And it is extremely detrimental not to awaken and to make the effort daily to understand, "That is not me. It is something I have created," for when you pass on at transition, they all rush in, very hungry. Yes.

Thank you.

You're welcome.

How long a period in our time passes after transition before we experience another incarnation on another planet?

Well, that is very individual. And it is dependent on the willingness of the being to accept, to grow, and to expand in the form in which they are identified with. For example, if a person, having a shorter stay in between incarnations into their next step and their next planet—a person who has truly made the effort and has applied the truth that they are *in* form; they are not a part of form; they are using form and shall not be used by form, that person has a much, much shorter stay in between incarnations and their ever-evolving school of life.

Thank you. When you are at the beginning of a project and you are facing all your incomplete beginnings, crying for fulfillment, how do you decide which of these should be completed?

By first accepting that they are forms you have created and by accepting they are forms you have created, you start on the path of gaining control over them. Now once you have gained control over them, you make the effort to keep control over them. And after you've done that, you give birth to the project and what you want to do. And you don't let the door open up in your consciousness for them to get back in. Yes.

Thank you.

And you do not quit before the victory no matter how long something takes, as long as it is within your divine right and control.

Thank you.

Yes.

When we choose our obstructions, is there a dominant motive or need common to all of us that dictates our choice?

Indeed, there is. And *need* is the proper word.

Would a person be able to effectively arbitrate a dispute by considering each party's motives through the teaching: What am I? Who am I? Where am I?

Yes. And they would have had reached a state of illumination in order to discern that, yes.

What is the Living Light's definition of an arbitrator?

What is the Living Light's . . .

Definition of an arbitrator?

An arbitrator?

Correct.

One who recognizes their own needs. And whoever recognizes their own needs and demonstrates the truth that they are not those needs is therefore qualified to view, to see, to understand the needs of others involved, which create discord and disturbance where you would consider an arbitrator is necessary. Well, what does an arbitrator do? An arbitrator makes no judgments. That's an arbitrator. An arbitrator works to communicate with two opposing forces. An arbitrator works to reveal to the opposing forces, through communication and awakening, that it is in their own personal selfish interest not to battle anymore.

Thank you.

You're welcome.

If a person, through neglect, harmed other people or other species and before he left earth, he made a 51 percent change in consciousness in considering others, would it be necessary to have to face all whom he had harmed on the other side?

I see. Now your question involves many realms of consciousness. A person, you say, has made a 51 percent change in reference to someone that they have hurt?

In his whole state of consciousness.

Well, first of all, let's go to the basic principle: he who lives to hurt another shall live to see the day when all his selfish motives pain shall take away. Now only pain can take away the selfishness that one believes, for a time, that they are. And so pain, which is—you see, let us understand what pain is. Pain is an identification with limit or form: at which time one is identified with limit and form, and the limit and form is not satisfied with the experiences that it is having. And that is registered as pain or painful. Now for a person who believes, that is great suffering. For a person who knows who they are, what they are, and why they are, they are able to endure whatever registration of the form there may be, for they are sufficiently separated in consciousness so that they are able to go through the various struggles and to go through them graciously.

Now a person who gripes and complains about everything in their life is a person who is dependent on something outside they can't control. A person who accepts, "This is my life. I can do with it as I choose to do with it. My thoughts [and] experiences of this moment are subject to my decisions," is a person who is free. Yes.

Thank you. Is a person's motivation to live in the past his dependence on what he judges he had in the past as compared to what he judges he has now? Does the belief in the past control a person because he denies the truth that it's a shadow?

The belief in the past controls a person; indeed, it does, for they deny the truth of which they are. And anyone who over-identifies with themselves very quickly finds themselves drifting to past experiences and feeding intelligent energy to shadows which have not had, to their satisfaction, the energy that they want. Yes.

Could you please explain the saying the guest will not quest? [The saying from The Serenity Game is, "The guest will never quest."]

Yes. Only the owner experiences quest and thirst. The guest shall never quest. You hear?

Yes.

For one who is a guest not only recognizes [but] also accepts, "All that I see, all that I feel, all that I experience is loaned to me for a time for I am a guest." And one who has that awakening and demonstrates that is one who is freed. And therefore, the guest shall never quest; the guest shall never thirst for they know that they are a guest in the universe and everything they believe they are is only loaned to them for a time. Yes, I hope that's helped with your question.

Yes. Thank you.

You're welcome.

Please explain how we create a mental block.

A mental block?

Yes.

A mental block is created by creating a judgment. All, all judgments—by believing we are a thought passing through our mind, we create a judgment. And a judgment is a mental block. It's a mental block to something. Yes.

Thank you.

You're welcome.

If a person reasons about things that are good in their life, but does not have an inner feeling they understand as gratitude, what can they do to help themselves feel gratitude?

Well, just speak forth those first words of that sentence. Speak right into the microphone.

If a person reasons about the things that are good in their life . . .

Yes.

. . . but does not have an inner feeling they understand as gratitude, what can they do to help themselves feel gratitude?

The only way to feel gratitude is to demonstrate gratitude. Now a person doesn't feel gratitude but they believe in gratitude. Is that correct?

Yes.

They state they want gratitude?

That, that's correct.

I see. Well, we always get what we really want. So if we really want gratitude, there is no problem. Life will respond through experience. And sooner or later we will find we feel the very deepest of gratitude. Yes.

Thank you.

You want to know how to feel it? There is no painless cure. There is no painless way. A person, like, says they believe in gratitude; they know it's beneficial, but they don't feel it. Well, life will offer to them the necessary experiences so they will very soon feel it. Just a matter of time and patience. Yes.

Thank you.

You're welcome.

If a person wants to give up something, a judgment or a habit, consciously, but cannot let it go, how can they work with what it is preventing them when they cannot see what it is?

Well, the only way that one can see what is preventing them from making a change in their life is through honesty with oneself. Honesty requires communication. Honesty requires the acceptance that you are not the form, you are not the limit, you are more than just the physical bones and flesh that you see. Yes.

Thank you.

You're welcome.

Have we been told what the spine represents? May we, if not?

Well, that question is incomplete. You may have that resubmitted. May we ask what the spine represents? And of what benefit will it be [to] you to know unless you state your reason for knowing. What will you do with that awakening? So that question is to be resubmitted.

Thank you.

You're welcome. *[The clock begins to chime and the secretary pauses in reading the questions submitted by the students.]* Is that all your questions now?

I was just pausing for that one chime. Thank you.

Pardon? Oh, you—the one chime. One chime doesn't do it. It's when you have all these multiple chimes. Thank you. Go right ahead.

OK. Thank you. I can see a judgment when I see its results. But I can't seem to recognize it in its formative stages. How can I see them sooner?

Well, in order to see a judgment being given birth, all one has to do is to ask themselves: "Where am I in consciousness? What am I in consciousness? Who am I in consciousness?" And they'll very quickly see inside whether or not a judgment is being given birth. Yes.

Thank you.

You're welcome.

From things I have said and things said to others, I get the impression, sometimes, after passing over, they dwell in houses or buildings, like cabins. Do we go through such a time? What are we doing when we are there? And can we help another, such as contributions of energy to help something like flowers be there?

Well, we can certainly help another as soon as we help our self. And how we help our self is to feel in the abundant energy of life and become a living demonstration of that. And those are the greatest flowers that you could ever share with anyone in life. Yes. Now we have time for one more question. I have a few things to say. And class is a bit, what you might consider, late today. Yes.

Thank you. What are the detriments of the consumption of real cold or—I'm sorry, I can't read it—beverage to an individual being physically, mentally, and spiritually?

Well, physically—you mean drinking beverages that are really cold, like ice?

Yes.

Is that what you're referring to?

Yes, I believe it is.

Well, first of all, your little house that you have earned in evolution has not been designed for—well, how would you best say [it]—has not been designed for, for drastic temperature changes. Now, first of all, a person believes that they have a thirst. Then they believe that they have a thirst that [can] only be quenched by a certain temperature of a fluid. And then they believe that it's not hot enough, it's not cold enough, and they go to extremes. And so whatever we consume in life that is the effect of our extremes, then, of course, our body and our minds must pay the price.

Thank you very much. And you had a few questions left, did you?

There's only one and I will need some help interpreting it at another time.

Well, then you had no questions left because you're not able to read that one. Is that correct?

That's correct.

Well, then that's just fine. You send that back for resubmitting. And so I'll go back here because I said we were finishing up and you have finished up: you've asked the last question that could be intelligently read. Is that correct?

That's correct. Thank you.

Well, fine. We'll just send it back for, for resubmitting.

Now I have a few things here to say before I leave. We have a few moments [of tape] left there, do we?

Yes. [The recording technician responds.]

[We] have a few moments there. This day is so important. [It] is very important to all of you. It is not frequent that you have the opportunity to demonstrate your value for the spiritual Light that you are. This is one of the rare occasions, one might say, that you have had this opportunity to serve the judgments that have flooded your consciousness this day and to serve the darkness that only belief, only belief could bind you there or to serve that which you are. And so although there are many little opportunities in the course of a day, it is rare that there is such an opportunity with such a great impact that offers so many, so many armies of judgments and so many judgment generals to come in and for you to experience within your brain and within your head. And so this day marks a most positive and important day.

I'm happy to say, from the reports that I had received over this day here in your world, that my channel had no problem whatsoever recognizing the general judgments, the judgments with their great authority, trying to take over his little mind today as he worked and worked and did *not* quit, did not quit regardless of the judgments.

I find our cameraman here. I look over and see my different students. I find the judgments trying to peek up out of the basement, but I'm going step on those little fingers, those claws right now with my own foot and have none of that foolishness around my channel.

Now I have taught you over these years, look for the good and the good you shall experience. And so my channel was told regardless of what happens, class shall be given this day. Even [if it] is to be given to my little four-legged friend who finally, I guess you'd call it, gave up the ghost and went and laid down on the couch over there. He waited so long for class. Now, so, you see—although he still, he still hears me out there, but he decided he needed a place that was a bit cooler. *[The teacher refers to the church's dog.]* And I'll tell you right now, if any of you would like to spend an hour in here or an hour and a half, you'll find out. I won't hear—you won't hear anything about being cold this winter if you sit here in this room. *[The spotlights used in recording the class quickly heated the small room.]*

Now what I want to say to you is look at the mountain of things of emotions that rose up into your mind this day and instead of feeling bad and sad and pity yourself over it, you haven't had a nap or you haven't had this or haven't had something else, look and see, "Thank you, God, I was able for a time to grow up and be a man. I was able to grow up and be an adult. I was able to keep my eyes open. I was able to make it to the gate of victory."

Now what happens with a person when they're faced with changes? All the judgments rise up. I know what they say to your mind, some of you. They say, "Well, I won't have time to do this. I won't get my afternoon rest today. I still have this master tape and all these audios and videos that I've got to do. And I'm just so totally tired and exhausted." Wouldn't you agree, my cameraman over here? *[After a short pause, the teacher continues.]* I couldn't hear you.

No.

Oh, you don't agree with me. You managed—you crawled up out of that so you won't have that experience today, is that what you're telling me?

Uh-huh.

Well, I'm happy to hear that. Did you get a little help?

Yes.

Oh, yes. Are you grateful to the students that worked with you?

Uh-huh.

Did they irritate you?

Some.

Well, irritation wakes the soul. It's the soul we're considering today—isn't it?—in class and every day. I'm so happy that you got yourself irritated. I think you'll get a bit more irritated before you get to leave today, along with a few others. But that's good because irritation wakes the soul.

Now the question is—oh, this lovely room here and everything. You had all of these experiences this morning. What is important, what is truly important to you as students, private students, is, "What is there in these experiences that I can take within my consciousness and grow? For I became aware of many judgments. I became aware of, Why don't those people out there do differently? I became aware of all of that. What can I do with this in my mind that's taking place to offer to my life greater good?" You see? That's what's really important.

Are you awake there, [Student R]? *[Student R served as the cameraman and the recording technician.]*

Yes, sir.

Yes. Do you feel a little bit—would you like a glass of water or something?

No, thank you.

I see. All right. Very well. Otherwise, you could come sit over here if you require a little more light.

No, thank you.

Very well. And so this is very, very important for none of my students to feel or to believe, first, to believe that they are the cause of causing this class to be so many hours in what the mind would consider late. For, after all, none of us in life are that great. I know there are times when we'd like to believe we're that great, but none of us are really that great. No, no, no, no.

Now, my assistants have reported to me several factors that came about that brought us all this wonderful experience today. Several factors.

When you want the assistance of the Light in any project you are doing, then you must learn to ask, and you must learn to ask each time. Now our cameraman here, he has been very consistent in asking for the assistant that, in keeping with the laws, he had earned to come in and help with the lighting. Is that correct, [Student R]?

Yes, sir.

Now no one in creation is perfect. And is it not correct that this was the first morning that you did not ask for that fine assistant of mine, that technician, Albert, to come and help you?

Yes.

And was this not the first day that you did not ask that fine technician what type of a day was it, color-wise, in the atmosphere?

Yes.

Yes. Well, now it's important that we take what few minutes we have left here to understand these laws. Now what do you feel tempted you not to ask?

I didn't feel there was enough time. Things were a little bit too rushed.

And so there wasn't enough time to ask the technician who I sent to your world to help you over these many weeks with all of this to ask, is that correct? Is that your feeling?

Well, I thought that I had asked, in a way that I had, I had asked, "Are—Is this acceptable?" or "Is this all right?" And the answer that I got was yes.

Do you mean at the time the monitor was checked?

This is earlier. Yes.

Why, it was most acceptable. My assistant told me it was most acceptable. That was not where the problem—you had done your part there. That is correct. And that was acceptable. You had asked if that was approved. Is that correct—that's what my assistant tells me.

I believe that—

And the coloring was excellent. Do you recall how nice the color was?

It seems to me it was nice, yes.

Now the problem came with your audio, didn't it?

Yes.

Now after your audio and your video wasn't getting to your monitor, did not all the color frequencies change?

Everything went to, ah . . . yeah.

Well, this is the good news! You all got to see what the minds can do color-wise. This is very important. This is why I'm staying here these few moments to help you all. You see, my good students, what you must understand, that when the assistant, the technicians I sent to you this morning, approved the lighting, which [the] color was just absolutely excellent, one of the finest we had had—is that not correct, [Student R]?

Yes.

It was excellent. Wasn't too yellow, and it certainly wasn't blue.

That's correct.

I see. Then your problem was, of course—and there's a lesson to learn—that because you had connected, he tells me, your video line to your audio line, you had a problem with, with your currents.

Yeah, I misconnected the cables.

Yes. What do they call it in your world? You had AC/DC problems?

No. It had to do with . . . video. [It is difficult to accurately transcribe the student's complete response; a few words are missing.]

Well, AC/DC, A and V. You had A/V problems.

Yes.

But, you see, also I [had] reported to me that you had, you had AC/DC problems with those cables. They tell me. Did you choose the fat one, where the fat one belonged on the thin one?

Yes.

And was that not based upon shadows?

That's what I'm told, yes.

What do you base it upon, because I must leave here soon? Yes.

Yeah.

What do *you* base it upon? I don't want you to tell me what you were told. I know what you were told. I have a full report.

I don't know.

Did you base it upon presuming that it was like everything else?

Yeah. Just past experience.

I see. And how do you feel about that?

I messed it up.

Well, do you feel good about seeing how color in the atmosphere changes according to the emotions and the upset of people?

I'm grateful we're finally getting the class done.

That is not my question, child. That is not my question. *[After a short pause, the teacher repeats himself.]* That is not my question. Are you grateful for the awakening, physically, to see what mental-emotional upset will do with color that is literally, physically recorded on tape?

Uh-huh.

Were you able to see the difference?

Well, yeah, [it was a] difficult time. I wasn't aware of the cause. I was aware of the effect.

That's what I'm interested in. Were you or were you not, as a student of mine, aware that the approval was given to you as the color was checked on that monitor prior to class?

Yes.

And that when my channel was sent down and I was prepared to come to class that the video line had not been checked by responsible directors?

That's right.

And that there was no problem with the coloring and the filming.

No.

Until after the upheaval and the upset.

That's correct.

And are you aware, you students, that there was great difficulty after the upset?

Uh-huh.

And as long as the upset continued, the coloring had a problem until we passed the noon hour, which created even a greater problem?

Yes.

I see. All right. Now it's time—Do you have any questions before I go? *[The teacher now addresses the secretary; he had been addressing the vice president who also served as the recording technician.]*

No. Thank you very much. [The secretary responds.]

And does this vice president and the cameraman have any questions here?

No, I haven't. [The vice president responds.]

Do you have any statements?

No, sir.

I see. No questions and no statements. I see. Do you understand what took place?

Yes.

And would you kindly speak it to me so I can assure you that we have communicated? Do you believe it was all your fault?

No.

Yes, go right ahead.

Well, it was due to emotional upset that the color balance was all lopsided and—

Well—

—we had a difficult time getting it back into balance.

That's correct. Now what is important here, for all of my students here today, what color did the emotional upset create in the atmosphere?

We started out with a gold and ended up blue.

And the test was made, and it wasn't gold and it wasn't blue. It was one of the finest tests.

It was very harmonious.

And after the emotional upset, what color did the atmosphere turn to?

It went yellow.

It went to very yellow.

Yes.

And as the upset continued what color did it turn to?

Blue.

There's your answer, students. Start studying and applying the laws. You've had a wonderful, beneficial day. And thank you so much. And I look forward to seeing you and saying, "Good morning," instead of "Good afternoon."

OCTOBER 13, 1985

A/V Class Private 19

[The audio portion of the first twenty seconds of this class seems not to have been recorded on the videotape.]

We believe in life what we deny. We do so by transgressing its right of existence, and in so doing we then believe that it is us. However, whatever we accept in life we recognize the right of its existence and, in so doing, grant it its right to fulfill a good purpose in our life.

We have discussed over these many years to be in a world and never a part of it. Being a part of anything in life is when we deny its right of existence, for in accepting the right of existence of anything we are freed from becoming it.

My children, look at what we ever seek to become. What we seek in life to become is what we have first denied that we are. And by denying that we are what we seek to become, we transgress the law of what we are. By refusing to accept what we are, we fill our lives with needs, we fill our lives with struggle and with strife. And that is ever the payment of denying the divine right of existence of all forms in a world of form. This happens to us through a lack of effort of understanding what we are, of understanding the purpose of our being, of a lack of accepting what we understand, for we, in time, shall learn, through the many worlds of experiences, that we are everything, and yet, we are in truth no thing. When we reach that point in evolution, we will no longer experience need; we will no longer seek; we will no longer search, for we will have finally accepted what we are, who we are, and know beyond a shadow of all doubt where we are.

And so this fulfillment of life and this joy of living waits for everyone in the moment of accepting everything, for when we accept everything, we know we are no thing, and we move in evolution beyond all things, which represent, of course, limits. And all limits represent restrictions. And all restrictions represent a lack of understanding.

Now my assistant, who came here to your world just yesterday and again this morning, revealed to you students, who were present, what happens in a world of things, a world of images. How color changes. How vibrations and frequencies change. How sounds change.

For some time, my channel has shared with you the great importance of everything in a world of things in its place and a place for everything in a world of things. And when the effort is not made to put everything in a world of things in its place, then you have an effect: a vibration of discord and disturbance. For example, [for] some of you who were not present here in this temple yesterday, I'll share, for a few moments, those experiences reported to me. The lighting here that you see in this room has gone through a few trials and tribulations. The changing of the color frequencies is not only subject to and dependent upon the attitudes of people present but that attitude of people present is reflected in the objects that surround you. When they are not properly cared for by a place for everything in a world of things, they create a disturbance in the atmosphere and the coloring changes. Here yesterday, we moved from a condition of blue to a drastic change in a condition of a yellowish-orange. There were no changes in these lovely lights that you have placed here. The only change that took place was a change in putting everything in the room in its proper place. Then we moved from a coloring of orange-yellow into a natural coloring.

Now I know that you will note this morning that the coloring is more of what you would consider a natural coloring. Would you not agree, cameraman?

Yes, sir.

Now this is not just dependent on certain filters. This is subject to and depending upon the vibrations present at the time. And if you could view this lovely room at this moment, you would note that everything that is possible to be put in its place is put in its place, what you call in your world, neat and clean.

Try to understand, when you expose your life to a place where you have what is known as clutter, the light available to the room, to the home, and here to the temple reaches the objects that are in their place. If you have many objects and you put them in the corner or you put them someplace where some of the objects do not receive and are not surrounded by the light, that is where you have shadows. Now shadows are where the realm of shadows live. Those are known as demons. They live in the lesser light. And whatever is not surrounded by the light is controlled by the lesser light. Now whatever is controlled by the lesser light experiences what you know in your world as need, for need only exists where the light does not reveal the path clearly in front of anything. And so if you have and are exposed to any place where you spend any time where everything that your eyes view is not surrounded by light, that part of the object or the person or the thing that is not surrounded by light is in need, and need are the shadows of denial.

We deny what we do not see. We deny what we believe we do not know, for we deny that which sustains us when a part of us is not being sustained sufficiently by it. Now when you have, your mind, flooded with the Light, you are freed from denial, for denial can only exist with those who do not see. And those who do not see are those who expose themselves to insufficient Light in order to see. For one does not see where Light is insufficient for that which does the seeing is dependent upon the Light in order to serve the purpose of its design.

And so we find whenever we have objects in a world of creation just thrown into a corner or piled one upon the other, the only one that is receiving the light is the one in front or the one on top. Now no one likes to be the last in line, and no one likes to be at the bottom of a pile. And so when we permit ourselves to demonstrate that we are on the bottom of the pile, then we are the last in the line. And we demonstrate that by not making the effort to put everything in its place within our consciousness, and our living quarters reflect that truth to us. They not only reflect that truth to us, they offer to our mind the natural defense mechanism of our judgments.

Now the natural defense mechanism of our judgments is what is known as justification. The expression of justification is what is known as a lack of control of the human mind or an emotional explosion. Now when you recognize that that is what it truly is—an expression of the defense mechanism of a judgment made by the mind which is denying the Light of eternal truth which the person truly is—then you will have no problem, as you look around your world and your home, and you see that there are many objects that are not receiving sufficient Light for there are too many of them. The effort is not made to put them in their place that they may be surrounded with Light. Then you can understand your state of mind at any given moment.

Whoever accepts their ability to live life fully, wholly, and completely demonstrates it with that which surrounds them, for outward manifestations in life are revelations of inner attitudes of mind.

Our life, indeed, is the way we make it. We always have the moment of choice to make it the way that we want to make it: filled with the joy of life by accepting what we are and making the simple and the small, little changes. Begin with daily effort. Don't wait until it becomes a monumental job. Whatever is done consistently, repeatedly, as a daily effort, soon becomes a natural way, a harmonious way. And so to procrastinate and to finally do it with emotional upheaval, to do it with justification, does not serve you well. It serves something else for it is a retaliation that is motivating you to make the changes. And whoever in life makes changes motivated by retaliation of past experiences, whatever we do to the shadows we believe that we are, they return tenfold on another day at another time.

So when you have something to do, do it quickly, do it daily, and do it step-by-step. Be patient with yourself and express the wisdom of a soul faculty.

And now it's time for your questions that you have prepared. And so if our secretary will speak up, I'll be happy to, once again, share with you whatever I may have to share.

Thank you. It is stated in The Living Light *[textbook] that all our experiences work through the steps of love, belief, desire, will, creation. Would directed energy have to be equal among these five steps in order to have a harmonious experience?*

In order to have a harmonious experience one must not permit themselves dependence, for dependence is subject to denial. One depends on things. One relies on the Light. Now there's a vast difference between dependence, which reveals need, and reliance, which reveals a return to what we truly are.

Thank you. Does belief have its own color or does it absorb the color of that which it creates?

Belief absorbs the original color of its own judgment. For example, a person first makes a judgment. They make a judgment and experience a denial. Now whoever believes that they are part and not whole and complete, whoever believes that they are not [a] whole and complete being is destined to experience need. Whoever permits their mind to believe that there is something that someone else has that they need in order to experience what they judge they want to experience, that person has denied the truth that they are what they truly are. And that person, from that denial, has only accepted a part of what they are; that part being an ever-changing limit or form.

Now in reference to the color vibration of belief, it is the color of bondage. And so if you will pause for a few moments and you will ask yourself the question, How do you feel when you are dependent on something you can't control? How do you feel when you believe you are experiencing the effects of denial, which are need? How do you feel when you believe that? You will very quickly come to an understanding of the color of dependence, belief, judgment, and bondage. And we'll get back to the question later in the class.

Thank you. The Living Light also states [in Discourse 49], "When the bird flies, the motion is not the air nor is it the bird; but it is the essence, the true essence, of creation herself." Is this saying that the bird in this case is a servant freed from self and attachment to creation?

Is it saying, Is the bird freed from self and attachment to creation?

Correct.

No, it is not saying that, for, you see, the bird still has belief.

Thank you.

Now when the bird no longer has belief, the wings will not move. The bird will just be free.

Thank you.

You're welcome.

Do some whales deliberately choose to leave their ocean habitat and travel within a land's waterway in order to communicate by demonstration a plea of ecology to man?

Well, that would be a very nice thought to entertain. And a lot of us would prefer to see it that way. However, if you will look at the records of the two-legged animal, the records of the four-legged, the records of all the creatures of your planet, you will find there are those with what you know as suicidal tendencies. And so we have, in your world of creation—there are many forms that from their own over self-identification enter the realms of consciousness of self-destruction, and you know that as suicidal. Yes.

Thank you. Will there be a day on our planet when man communicates with and includes the viewpoints of animals in his governmental decisions? And has there ever been such a day on earth?

First of all, there certainly has been such a day on your planet. And second, yes, that day shall return.

And I would like to say one thing more: in reference to people and forms who have suicidal tendencies, there is ofttimes, out of these seeming disasters, great good and benefit comes. And that is the thing to look for, is the divinity in disaster.

Thank you. Could you please explain the significance of the fingernails on the right hand?

Is this a question from a person who has yet to learn what the fingers represent?

I understand that they were given it a very long time ago. I don't know if they are aware of it.

I see. Well, first of all, I will go by my feelings and say to the questioner, first present yourself with an understanding of the meaning of the fingers. Now once that is settled within the consciousness of the questioner, then resubmit the question so we can have a greater understanding for the benefit of the entire class why certain parts of the anatomy are protected and the cause thereof. Yes.

Thank you. The philosophy teaches that it is not what you put into the mind that frees you but what you must take out of the mind that frees you. Does it follow, then, that putting more and more knowledge into the mind just is more baggage to carry or more clutter?

It is true for those who believe they are their denials, yes.

Thank you. Do we have a duty to acquire knowledge to use our mind as a computer, a tool of endless information?

Yes, we have a responsibility while in our service of the Light that we are to evolve the forms or limits in which the free Light is expressing itself. And in that respect, we not only have a duty but a responsibility to use the anatomy to its full purpose of its design. Yes.

Thank you. Does knowledge that is acquired during our lifetime carry over to our next experience?

Knowledge knows much. And when the knowledge is brought to the Great Rotunda and everything is weighed out and the mountains of knowledge are displayed, there's one small grain of wisdom that makes the final decision. And in reference to does this knowledge carry over, in the sense that the soul and its experiences and the forms, ever evolving, the more refined that the form we are presently in is, [the more] evolved and the more refined that it is, the soul, ever in keeping with the Law of Evolution, enters a form more developed and more refined, yes.

Thank you. Is knowledge of any benefit to our soul or is it only for the benefit of our ego?

Well, knowledge is designed to be a servant of the eternal Light through which limit or form may be evolved. And in this evolutionary process—you see, for example, take knowledge and superstition. Superstition is an instrument of the uncontrolled desires of the human mind, and superstition is an instrument through which the senses express themselves through what you know as emotion. Knowledge, expressing itself through the function of what you understand as logic, is instrumental in bringing about a balance between the realm of emotion and the realm of logic and what you understand as facts. And so it is serving a purpose of its design, when we permit it to do so.

And when a person becomes more knowledgeable in their mental world of why they experience needs, when a person becomes more knowledgeable of why they have emotional reactions in their life that they don't seem to be able, at times, to control them, when they become more knowledgeable of the causes of them, then balance is brought about in the mental world. And when balance is brought about in the mental world, the soul is free to express itself. Yes.

Thank you. With the computer freeing man's mind of many mundane chores he formerly used his mind for, what is man to do with his mind?

Well, in reference to what man should do with his mind, he should use his mind in order to absorb, to gain more knowledge, and to use the knowledge wisely. Now, for example, of what benefit is it to be knowledgeable on anything if, in so being knowledgeable, one does not share that knowledge when it is solicited and, in so doing, be an instrument through which a mental world is slowly but surely brought into balance?

Thank you. It has been stated that green leaves are in truth yellow. Where does the blue come from to make them look green to our human eyes?

Man is both a spiritual and a physical being. And man is not only the spiritual and physical being, so is a plant and so is a tree. And therefore, we look at something and we see it with physical sight as what you call the color green, when it is truth, divine wisdom in expression. And when you look with your spiritual light, you'll see the divine wisdom and not just be blinded by the expression.

Thank you.

Yes.

Does our soul ex—pardon me, I'll wait. [The secretary reading the written question pauses as a clock chimes.]

Yes, go right ahead. *[The teacher speaks after the clock has finished chiming.]*

OK. Does our soul express just once in form on this planet?

Does our soul, the individualized soul, express in one form on *this* planet?

May I correct—

You mean on the Earth planet?

Does our soul express just once in form on this planet?

Our soul is in an evolution journey. Absolutely. And so we move from what your present planet is through the evolution on to the next planet and the next solar system and the next and the next. We have not come out of nothing, and therefore we don't return to nothing in reference to an individualized soul, which is the covering of the form of the Spirit. Yes.

And is there a regular progression from planet to planet or does it vary with the individual?

No, there is a regular progression.

The Living Light [textbook] states that the—

In keeping—Excuse me, please—there is a regular progression in keeping with the law established by the individualized soul in their incarnation, yes.

Thank you.

In other words, there's no guarantee that you move from planet five to planet six. It's ever in keeping with the laws of evolution established by the individual. Yes.

Thank you.

You're welcome.

The Living Light [textbook] states that the solar plexus is our center and circuit, and that from it all things have come and to it all things shall return.

Correct.

To my understanding this is also known as the water center. Does our soul reside there? If not, where? And how does this relate to our emotions and balance?

Well, in reference to the solar plexus, which is the center of the universe in the anatomy in which you find yourself presently encased, for example, you understand that center, sun, is a source of light, a source of heat. Is that not correct?

Correct.

Well, without a source of heat and the substance of what you know as water, you do not have what you understand as expression or steam. So in that respect, yes.

Thank you.

Now you want to know if the soul lies there?

Resides there, yes.

Well, find me a part of the temple of God, the house of goodness, in which the soul is not residing. Otherwise, you'd have to say, "I can do without my foot. I can do without my arm. I can do without my head." You see, the thing is that in your world you have those who believe that the soul is located in the brain. However, you remove the brain and there's still life. So one cannot limit that which they are to some particular part, perhaps the ankle or the toe or something. You may have cause to have more attention directed to a particular part of the house of goodness, the temple of God, but that in no way guarantees that's the only place you are. Yes.

Thank you. Why is it that the mind judges that for it to have a certain expression that it has to eliminate another? And what is and how can we create balance between all of our expressions?

First of all, for the mind to judge, it denies. There's the denial, the judgment. And so when you deny and you judge, and then you experience need. So when you experience need, then you look out in order to fill the need. And the judgment says that someone else has it. Therefore, you have to have it even at the cost of annihilating them. Do you understand that?

Yes.

All right. Go ahead.

The Living Light [textbook] states from love comes belief, desire, will, and creation. Your channel has stated that if we must believe, believe in something beneficial. What other way is there to be here expressing if we are not creating through belief so that we may express our divine love?

Well, of course, you are in a constant process of creating and believing and binding oneself. The thing is to be in it and not a part of it. To use it for what it is designed to be used and not to lose such control that you believe that you are the limit.

Thank you.

You're welcome. When you take a glass of water, do you believe that you are the water?

No.

You do, however, believe a need for it, is that correct?

Yes, we do.

So you believe the thirst, which is a judgment which tells you to quench your thirst you must have whatever you have judged is necessary to quench the thirst. Is that not correct?

Yes.

And is that not something outside upon which your mind permits you to be dependent?

Yes, it is.

Fine. Thank you.

If matter and energy can be neither created nor destroyed, are they one and the same? And what is the process or cause of energy becoming matter as we understand it?

Well, first of all, they're one and the same. Matter is energy; energy is matter. Now it is varying—what would you say—varying frequencies of energy. For example, let's go to the universe that surrounds us, and let us take a look and see. First of all, you look into the air, but you do not see what you call matter. You do not see matter in the air, what you understand as matter. However, it is there in a very fine expression. And it is from that that, through various changes in the energy streams that are passing through the atmosphere at all times, that when they converge in a certain, particular way, you have an experience of, perhaps, some type of a gaseous condition in the atmosphere. And when those streams begin to converge in their own particular, different ways, you then begin to have what you call substance or form or matter; something that you can feel.

Now everything that you see and that you experience, like this table and this chair here and all of this in what you call matter or substance, once the atoms, electrons, and molecules are changed, you no longer see them. Now, they return to their true essence.

The essence of all things is Light. All things. The essence of all things is Light. The essence of all things is the Principle of Good. Now the atoms and the electrons and the molecules that are composing the flower that sits upon the table are identically the same electrons, atoms, and molecules that are composing the table on which the flowers in the vase are standing. Now those identically same electrons, atoms, and molecules compose your flesh and bones. Those same electrons, atoms, and molecules are the same ones that compose your thought and thought form. Now it is the frequency and combinations of these electrons, atoms, and molecules.

They are everywhere in all universes, in all solar systems. When they are changed in varying ways, you experience them as a vase of flowers, a leaf upon a bush, an animal, or a human being. They are only different combinations, so to speak; they're identically the same. And so Light is in everything in varying degree.

Now when you take something and you remove it from the Light which it is a part of, then it begins to make changes and to experience what you understand as need. A person who turns to the Light is a person who is fulfilled. It is like an object, when exposed to the Light, it reveals what it truly is for it is then sustained by the Light.

Now let us go to what you understand as film, what you understand as filming of objects, which are in truth varying degrees of lights, dependent upon their atomic structure. You take a film and you expose it to the light, and it destroys what you understand as the film. And so you preserve the film by placing it in lesser light or what you understand as darkness. The film, however, if you will try to follow me here in this discussion, the film is a recording of shadows. The film records shadows. That's what it does. It is a registration of illusion. It is not genuine. It is not reality. It is, however, a registration of the emanation of an object. It is not the object itself.

Now that which is illusion can only be preserved in lesser light or darkness. And so you find in film, you find in your advancing technologies, an expression of how you, your mental world truly is. When a person believes an illusion, they are controlled by the illusion as long as they identify with it. Now when you cast the Light—and in this philosophy we share with you the light of reason, for Light is fully expressed through the soul faculty of reason—the illusion dissipates. The registration of the film in your mind is therefore destroyed. And then you say, "In that particular situation I saw the Light." And what is meant is that the illusion no longer is in control in their life. I do hope that's helped with your question.

Thank you.

You're welcome.

When we record things on crystal, is it the same principle as you just mentioned on recording on film?

No, it is not. Presently you record things on what you understand as film. You are recording shadows and illusion. Crystal is the only registration that is accurate, that is genuine, and that is true, for it is the only thing (crystal), as a mineral, that reflects the light as it is and not as the illusion that is created by the varying frequencies of light. Yes.

Thank you.

You're welcome.

Are the higher realms of the spirit world on outer dimensions of the Earth or are they part of other universes or do they encompass all universes?

They are all that you have just stated. They encompass all universes.

Thank you.

You're welcome.

Will we, as students, be permitted to continue in the Living Light classes right after transition?

Well, that, of course, is subject to and dependent upon what you do with what you receive. Yes.

Thank you.

You're welcome.

Please explain how to demand an accounting of our vehicles, as was mentioned in a recent class.

Your vehicle is responsible to serve you well. It has a duty and a responsibility to grant unto you an accounting, daily. If it does not grant you an accounting of its service to you—for it is dependent upon you and a servant of you—if it does not account to you and give you an accounting, then it is your responsibility [to] see that it does give you an accounting. Yes.

Thank you. Do the fingers of the right and left hand have the same meaning?

Yes. Receiving and giving. *[A clock begins to chime.]*

Thank you. Please explain the natural Law of Balance—

Yes. Would you like to be patient for a moment?

I'm sorry. Yes. [The clock stops chiming.]

Yes, I know that sometimes you do forget, but now go ahead and speak forth.

Shall I wait 'til they finish? [A clock in another room begins to chime.]

Yes, we have a few more clocks. *[After all the clocks have finished chiming, the teacher continues.]* You see, I would like to say this, though the clocks are at times irritating, irritation, I've taught you before, wakes the soul. And we're not going to remove the clocks in the temple, until all students are freed from the dependence upon the illusion known as time. *[Several students laugh.]* Go ahead with your question.

Thank you. Please explain the natural Law of Balance and how we can be cautious and not fall into the dual laws of creation.

Well, in respect to the natural laws of balance, if you will accept the demonstrable truth that like attracts like and that balance is not what your uneducated ego tells you: you need to be brought into balance and this is what you have to have that you don't have—that's absolutely contrary to what balance truly is. You see, when the human mind dictates what balance is, then nature, that which is natural, doesn't exist, for the human mind has already denied the balance that it is. It's already denied it from its own judgments and belief.

Thank you.

You're welcome.

When we place our attention on what we want to become, are we putting our faith in our true being and are we bringing about the changes necessary to free ourselves from our own bondage?

Yes, to put your attention on what you want to become by accepting the truth of what you are. When you accept the truth of what you are, you move on, on the path of becoming what you desire to become by accepting what you are. It is only from denial of what you are that you have the experience of need.

Thank you. Are the centers in us the same as the centers that are in the earth plane? And may we know what center corresponds to the ozone layer?

Well, in reference to the ozone layer of which we've discussed quite a bit for some time, you understand that the planet Earth is number five?

Yes.

How many centers are you aware of?

Nine.

And what is the fifth center?

Electric.

And what follows it?

Magnetic.

And what balances the electric and the magnetic?

The odic.
Yes? And now you know what the ozone layer is, don't you?
Thank you.
You're welcome.
In a previous class there was an explanation given on the horizontal law, the parallel law, and the upward Law of Continuity.
Yes.
Would you please explain this and how it pertains to the river of life exercise?
Well, in reference to explaining the parallel law and the horizontal law and the vertical law?
Yes.
Well, one first pauses and they ask themselves for an accounting. And the accounting is given by the vehicle through which the person is expressing. And in that accounting, the accounting is revealing clearly to the individual whether or not it is horizontal, is parallel, or it is vertical. Do you understand?
Yes.
And so it is up to the individual to inform the vehicle and the parts thereof that it shall make its changes and move to a vertical consciousness. In other words, when you are identified with the horizontal consciousness, you are ever dependent on what is flowing through you. Do you understand that?
Yes.
And as long as you're dependent on that, you're going to be in that horizontal condition of experiences. Now when you get a full accounting of what your vehicles are doing, in reference to, Are they horizontally working? Are they working parallel? Or are they taking their orders from the vertical? And you, of course, are the vertical. Do you understand?
Yes.

So either you make the effort for them to give you a daily accounting or they continue on to control your life. And in respect to that, you'll have no problem whatsoever understanding the stream of consciousness and your little boat.

Our auras our fields of energy. And may we know how we can demagnetize and purify our aura?

Oh, why, certainly. Auras are, definitely, energy emanations in varying colors. You may change or extend your aura at any time of your choice through a proper control of your mind. And as your aura expands and extends, whatever is within its sphere of action is controlled by your aura in that respect.

Now how to demagnetize and to purify your aura is a matter of taking control of the vehicles through which that which you truly are is expressing itself. And that's subject to your making the daily effort, beginning, of course, with your daily effort of meditation, helping to gain control of your mind, and to definitely get an accounting from your vehicles. Because without you, your vehicles do not exist. They owe you a daily accounting.

Thank you.

And some vehicles have gone into such license and have finally convinced the true person that they are the true person, that it's going to take, of course, a little effort.

Thank you. Is there a difference between the brain and the uneducated ego?

Well, if you're speaking of brain as a substance through which all experiences are recorded, in that respect, yes. But the uneducated ego uses the brain, and it takes a look at what the brain has recorded in your earthly experience and that which has made the greater impact, of course, has the greater ability to convince you that you are it.

Thank you.

You're welcome.

Changes in the physical body affect the spine. Changes in the centers can affect the body, affecting the spine. Some people then get their spines readjusted. May we be told what the spine represents?

The spine is the instrument, physical instrument, through which the river of life is flowing.

Thank you.

In other words, it's the protector.

Thank you.

You're welcome.

Slow steps are sure steps. What are the first steps one can take in beginning to educate an ego?

Well, in respect to our responsibility to guide or to educate the ego, which is our duty and our responsibility that it may serve us well and be an instrument through which great good floweth, we cannot even begin the first step until we accept personal responsibility. Not until we accept that, "This is the hand that I have earned in my evolution at this time. This hand is responsible to what I choose this hand to do. This hand shall not tell me what it's going to do. It is my responsibility to tell it." That is the process of guiding or educating, controlling the human ego. Yes.

Thank you.

You're welcome.

Many healers of old and even the present seem to absorb the disease of another in the healing process. Why do they do that and how do they eliminate it from their own forms?

Well, first of all, why do they absorb the disease of another? Is that the question?

Yes.

Yes. Well, first of all, absorption is the process through which one is healed by a removal of the forms that are the cause of the discord in the being. Do you understand?

Yes.

And so those forms must be removed from the individual, from the patient. Now there are those on your planet who have, in their evolution, earned the awakening and the ability to absorb those forms and, therefore, to free the patient from the control of them. And so it is a part of the healing process for the healer to absorb the forms. The next step, of course, the healer must have qualified themselves in healing themselves by freeing themselves of their own forms when they are controlled by them. And by that demonstration be an instrument through which they may absorb those forms that are causing the discord and disease and cast them off after the absorption. Fortunately or unfortunately, if a healer does not take care of themselves, they find themselves in a weakened or exhausted condition; they will absorb the forms of others and they will suffer the consequences of the discord or the disease. Yes.

Thank you. I have been contemplating the five lower centers and the five physical senses of our Earth. This is what I have considered: that earth correlates to touch, fire with smell, water with taste, air with hearing, electric with seeing. Is that correct? And would you speak on those senses and the centers?

Well, first of all, I do feel that that is encouraging. The student is making the effort to, to make some correlation. However, I would like to advise at this time that we make a little more study and application of the centers within the being, specifically in reference to the fire and the water center. So I would like to say to this student, the questioner, and to all of my students at this time, to make effort to awaken the faculty of the fire center and especially the faculty of the water center, for the centers are not exclusively controlled by the functions, regardless of belief. Yes.

Thank you. Is the purpose of creation our awakening?

[Is] the purpose of creation our awakening? The purpose of creation is to serve [as] a vehicle through which it may be awakened. The purpose of our journey is to awaken creation that it is a vehicle to serve the Light, for without the Light it does not exist.

And I would like to speak in one particular respect on the fire center. If you would awaken the faculty of thrust, and stop believing it's only for one other thing, you would soon find freedom from bondage and so many, many problems that beset some of my students at times. So let's work on thrust, and let it be motivated by wisdom and guided by reason. Then let us thrust ever forward. Yes, go ahead with your question.

Thank you. Would you please share with us the true cause of senility?

The true cause of senility is nothing more and nothing less than an over-identification with what we understand in this philosophy is known as self. It is the final stages of an over-identified, uneducated ego.

Thank you.

And in fact, I think in your world they call that senility "retirement." *[Several students laugh.]*

Would you please share with us the cause and the cure of grinding one's teeth during sleep?

A lack of expressing one's determination in a conscious state in a constructive, positive way; a belief in an obstruction to their own expression. Yes.

Thank you. Frequently, after thunderstorms, where there has been much lightning, there is a certain green coloring to everything. Is this an effect of the light temperature or is it due to another cause?

It is an effect of light temperature, yes.

Thank you.

You're welcome.

Would you please share with us the true meaning of the crescent moon and star symbol?

Well, the crescent moon is the ancient, eternal symbol of the ever increasing and growing. And when it is combined, the crescent, with the star, the single star, then it is an ancient symbol of the increasing and the growing of the consciousness in its service to the Light which it is, in awakening the forms of limit or creation.

Thank you. When one has a stubborn attitude, like, for instance, a donkey which sits on a position and will absolutely not budge, what is the first step in breaking up a pattern of such hard egotism?

Breaking the pattern of what?

Such hard egotism.

Yes. Well, stubbornness, of course, is an expression of the soul faculty of determination in a total identification to the realm known as emotion, where the defenses of a person's judgment are expressed. And so we find people who, at a moment, truly believe they are the judgment or the denial of their mind with a great deal of donkey-consciousness. And so I suppose in your world those would be called donkey-heads. And I think, if you recognize, that at times a person is a donkey-head—but there's one thing about a donkey: sooner or later it gets a desire to eat, and sooner or later it will move. And if you have an understanding of that, then you won't battle a donkey-head. You'll recognize it for what it is, and that there are times when it has to have a swift kick; otherwise, it's not going to move at all. *[Many students laugh.]*

Thank you. When one finds love, the love we seek outside, inside our self, does one then love everything outside oneself equally without partiality?

Well, it depends on what one means by *love*. Now if one means, by *love*, an expression of feeling to the leaf of a tree, the same as a dog, cat, or human being, in that respect, yes. Because, you see, love is an expression of our true being amalgamating with the true being that is in the form of the tree or the flower and [is] an expression in that respect. It does not experience need, for how could it experience a need when it already knows what it is and it knows it's everything? Yes.

Thank you.

You're welcome.

Is there anything wrong with the expression of sexuality, as long as it doesn't interfere with another's divine right or does it always, by its very nature, interfere? And if so, is there a higher expression of this energy and what would that be?

Well, I've discussed that many times. There certainly is a higher expression of that energy. That energy is not designed by the Divine Architect to be locked in the fire center of the senses. It is—it's true and only purpose is for procreation. It serves no other purpose, except to those who deny the truth. And one denies the truth and, in so denying, believes that somebody else has what they have denied. In reference [to], Is it interfering with, with another's divine right? Well, there are two interferences with the divine right. First of all, there is the interference of denying that one is whole and complete and is only half there. And then like attracts like and meets another person that's half there. And so in that respect, you've got two denials of the divine right.

Now when it serves its true and only purpose of its design, exclusively for procreation, then you have two people who intelligently make a decision and, in keeping with the laws of the universe, are instruments through which the negative and positive poles come together, that an intelligent, illumined being may enter ever in keeping with the laws established.

Thank you.

You're welcome.

But try to understand that in keeping with the demonstrable law that like attracts like that whoever has denied the truth and accepted and believe they are half there could only meet another person who's half there. And they shouldn't expect a wholeness from a half—I didn't want to say a half-wit—but from a half person. *[Many students laugh.]* You can't expect—you see, it is very egotistical to think that, first of all, a person has accepted that they are half there and the other half of them is someplace else. But, you see, I've yet to find that two halves make a whole. In that respect nothing appears to be whole, unless you want to call *whole* something that fills a need. And it never does fill a need because it's never identical.

You see, they say our expectations always exceed the results. Well, they always will because there's no one as perfect as we are. So if we believe we're half there, but we're perfect halves, and we establish the law to find another perfect half, the other half-person is never ever up to snuff. Does that help with the question?

Yes. Thank you.

And if we're deluded for a time that they are, we very soon find that we made a mistake. Yes. I think you call that divorce in your world. I call it retirement, myself. *[Again, many students laugh.]*

Why is it that a major part of humanity shows the true representatives of heaven such little respect when to do so is so destructive to oneself?

Because there is—whoever over-identifies with mental substance, with self, is on the path of self-destruction, for they have denied what they are, and by denying what they are, they believe what they are not. And whoever believes what they are not is definitely in a path of self-destruction. Yes.

Thank you.

You're welcome.

What is the root or cause of frivolity in one's nature, the impulse to throw it all away?

Well, a person moves through various expressions from disappointments, discouragements, and etc., whoever over-identifies with that realm and believes that they are that. And so they reach a point where they just throw it all away. Wouldn't you say?

Yes.

And so—however, it doesn't last. In the throwing-away process there's always something: "Oh, I better save that." And then we find what we call clutter bugs, where the demon thrones [are]. Hmm?

Yes, you know a person, when they go to move something out of their life, the more they start to move, they suddenly say, "Oh, I might use that tomorrow." Well, the demons are not going to let their houses go.

Right.

Yes, go ahead, please.

Thank you. Does satisfying our judgments form habit patterns?

Yes, because, you see, for example—and I've spoken many times on that—whenever you feel that you have a desire for something, control it for at least five minutes and grant yourself the opportunity [to ask yourself], "Is that me or is that someone else that wants this? And is that someone else just using me?" and "How long will they use me? And how will they leave me after they're through using me?" You know, when you have something come up in your mind that tells you that you need something, that makes you subject to something outside of yourself, then it's wise for a person to pause and to recognize the truth that there's something that's going to use you. And how long are they going to use you? And what condition will they leave you in when they're through using you? Yes.

Thank you.

And how much use will you get out of them in the process? And is it worth it? That's the question an intelligent person, of course, will ask.

Thank you. Is man's physical body a composition of minerals of this planet?

Yes, indeed, it is. Definitely the planet on which you are, as all forms are composed of the minerals of the planet on which they exist. Yes.

Thank you. Is a gas state one stage of evolution of a mineral?
A gas state?
Yes.

Why, certainly. It's an early stage. Very early. Everything is light; everything is energy. And its composition is in varying degrees. There is no difference. There's only one Light; there's only one energy in all the universes in all your solar systems. Yes.

Thank you. Will you please explain the principles of cleaning our head, also, the principle of demagnification?

Well, yes, I did have a report on my channel and [he] felt that was very important. Reading a little book there, a manual or something in your world on cleaning up your head every nine hours. Well, you know, some people require an every-nine-minute cleaning because nine hours, you see, is just too long. And then it becomes a phenomenal chore, like cleaning one's house. However, yes, to take stock. You see, it's an accounting of your forms that are responsible to you. What have they done in the last nine hours? What have they done in the last nine minutes? What have they been telling you? And how well have they convinced you that you have a need that causes you to be a victim of someone you can't control by divine law? Hmm? So that's cleaning up one's head.

And one's head—an intelligent person makes that effort by getting an accounting from their vehicles. How else are you going to clean up what doesn't give you an accounting, you see? And so you get an accounting and you clean up your head, and you reissue the orders and reinforce your regulations governing your forms. And nine hours later you get another report from them. As I said, ofttimes some people need a nine-minute cleanup on their heads.

And as far as demagnetizing, you see, I think my channel reported to you, you ought to demagnetize every, well, you should demagnetize every seventy-two hours [at a] maximum. What is [demagnetization]? A person who believes that they are a judgment and are so over-identified with that denial of what they are directs the judgment to the water center, the magnetic center, where you know it as emotion—you see, that's the feminine part of form. Magnetic is the feminine, the delicate part of forms. And contrary to the electric, which guides one on, through direction, to thrust and to the light of reason, the feminine part of man—and by "man" I mean humanity—is the magnetic part, and that is the water center of emotion. Now when a person permits their denials, the expression of them, which are their judgments, to enter into the water center, they have, there, created what you understand as the soldiers of justification. Now whoever permits that to happen has placed their vibration into the magnetic and is a victim of the feminine frequencies in the atmosphere. And so a person should be aware of that condition and should therefore demagnetize themselves at least every seventy-two hours. Because, if they don't, they only convince themselves, beyond a shadow of any doubt in mental substance, that everything's wrong outside and the cause of their experiences are ever outside in their life. And therefore, they're a total victim of whoever crosses their path. Yes.

Thank you. Is my understanding right, that within the electric divine will and the magnetic divine love, they each contain a separate self which is the imbalance of both and is known as the soul or covering of the formless, free Spirit?

Well, the soul is the covering, the celestial marriage, the covering of the Divine Spirit which you are. And, of course, that which is the covering or the limit or the formation is always electromagnetic because that is what brings—that's those two opposite poles amalgamated, brought together. You have the celestial marriage and you have the expression thereof. Yes.

Thank you. Why does our formless, free Spirit need a covering? And what purpose does it serve?

I've stated before, the free Spirit, that which you are, doesn't *need* a covering. Need does not exist in what you are. Formation, the coverings, the vehicles, the forms, the limits—limits are the ones that have need. Limitless has no need. Only limit has need. Form has need for it has closed itself from the truth that it truly is and has made a limit. Yes.

Thank you. Is the heart where our soul expresses? And is that like a covering in form?

Yes. The heart—however, most people have a tendency to believe the heart's their water center. The heart is not their water center. The heart's not the emotions. The heart is the vehicle through which the soul expresses. The heart doesn't experience need for the heart—the soul is not denial. Yes.

Thank you. Does the light of reason contain within it a high percentage of motivation?

The light of reason is motivation of wisdom. The movement of wisdom is the light of reason.

Thank you. High noon and midnight give us greater opportunity to view the Light. How does the sun and moon correlate with that? And do the sun and moon within themselves contain the electromagnetic principle?

Yes. The moon is magnetic, and the sun is electric. The sun, exploding a part of itself, has given forth to you your moon and your solar system. It is the same principle in all solar systems.

Thank you.

You're welcome.

When our self-pride is being glorified through the judgments being fed, we are said to have a greater receptivity to the divine infinite flow. How can that be when we are engrossed in self-love?

Well, so [it's] your understanding of self-love. So that question needs to be clarified. Kindly read it again.

When our self-pride is being glorified through the judgments being fed, we are said to have a greater receptivity to the divine infinite flow. How can that be when we are engrossed in self-love?

Because you're off-guard. You're off-guard. *[A few students laugh.]* And when you're off-guard, that's when the Light gets in. Of course, it's no guarantee when you're off-guard that that's the only thing that gets in, but the possibility's there. Pardon?

Thank you.

You're welcome.

Why is the payment in the Light greater than the payment in the darkness?

The Law of Responsibility. You don't get something in life for nothing. When you receive more Light, when you experience more Light, then you have a greater payment, you have a greater duty, you have a greater debt.

Thank you.

Now what is the debt? The debt is that the darkness, that's what you have believed that you are, doesn't have such a hold on you. And to the mind, that's a debt; it's a weight. Yes.

Thank you.

You're welcome.

There are three panes of glass to honesty: care, kindness, and consideration. They are known as spirit, soul, and body. How do each of these correlate with each other? Are the first three soul faculties?

They are soul faculties. Care, kindness, and consideration?

Yes.

Pardon?

Yes.

They are soul faculties.

Thank you.

What is your question?

How do they each correlate with spirit, soul, and body?

The soul faculties express the soul. Spirit and body—soul, spirit, and body is one and the same. *[After a short pause, the teacher continues.]* Now I think you're a little bit stunned at that. But we'll have to pause so you can think a little more. Spirit, once covered, has form or individualization, and you call that soul. Do you understand that?

Yes.

Soul, once covered with limit, has what you understand as body. Do you understand that?

Yes.

And so the covering of a thing is sustained by the thing which it is covered by. Do you understand? In other words, the soul cannot exist without your Spirit, that which you are. Do you understand that?

Yes.

Your body cannot exist without your mind or mental body; that cannot exist without your soul body, etc., etc. Do you understand that?

Yes.

And so in that respect, body, mind, and spirit—body, soul, and spirit is one and the same.

Thank you.

It is only a covering through which that which you are is expressing itself. And that which you are, expressing itself, refines the covering and, therefore, expands its consciousness or its limit. Man does not fly without dependence on some outward object. Man could fly. Man has flown. Man is designed to fly, what you call levitate and to move, but it is man's belief that binds him and grounds him to your planet. It's not the design that grounds man. It's man's own belief in his own denials that does that. Yes, go ahead with your question.

Thank you. That's all the questions at this time.

Fine. Well, it's a lovely [day]. And the time has certainly passed. And a very fine and beautiful day. And I note for those of you who look at your last class here, from last week, you'll get to see a few changes in coloring and different things. And I think today you're going to see quite a difference. And, you know, it is only through—the demonstration is the revelation. Let's look at the good and the positive in these things because when our minds, in our evolution, will only permit us to accept that which is physically demonstrable to us, then that, of course, is what is necessary as we move ever onward and upward.

Thank you very much, and good day.

OCTOBER 20, 1985

A/V Class Private 20

Good morning, class.

Such a fine day to have our little class here. We'll wait a moment for these chimes of time and delusion to cease. *[The clock chimes as the teacher is speaking, and after it stops, he continues.]*

Today, this morning, we're going to speak a bit more on the vibration. As you know and as we've often discussed with you, vibration is color and vibration is sound. And we are all receptive to vibration because we are vibration.

Now to some of you I spoke of the colors of red of action and of white of purity, of the blue of spirituality, which, as you perhaps are noting on your little picture box out there, that the day is filled with this lovely coloring of blue. We've also discussed with you the wonderful color brown, the color of earth, also representative of confusion. And so you note that I have, my channel, dressed today in varying shades of brown. Not that I considered he was confused; however, it is an understanding of why brown represents confusion. You will note that brown is a most difficult color with which to harmonize. And sometimes I can be most difficult, it seems, to get along with.

And so today I have a shade of browns, varying shades. Now why is the color brown so difficult to harmonize with? The only color that you can use to bring about any balance to what you know as brown is white. And so I have taught you over these years that a little brown and a lot of white is known as beige or soul vibration or coloring.

Now you will note, there, on the picture you're viewing at this time that there is much blue, and you will note that is coming through the windows here. You will note, if you look there on my right side here, that where the light is being obstructed, the blue, that the coloring of the room is showing a more natural coloring. Now this is vibration. I spoke to you about the yellow days. I've spoken to you about the blue days. And I've also spoken to you about the coloring of the atmosphere and the changing of the coloring of the atmosphere in keeping with one's attitude of mind.

Often over these many centuries, students have asked, "What is the best color for my aura? What color is my aura?" And the first question that I have asked them, when that question has been asked, [is], "Tell me what your attitude is, and in so doing you will tell me what your color is. And in so doing that you will know beyond a shadow of any doubt when you're green, when you're yellow, when you're blue, when you're brown. You will know when you are a harmonious individual in the natural balance of the universes, and you will know when you are difficult and discordant."

And it takes a great deal of purity to bring about a change in anyone who is difficult, for difficulty is an expression of a lack of honesty with oneself. One does not find life difficult, one does not believe in negative attitudes when one is honest with oneself, for in that honesty one knows why they are, what they are, and who they are. The problem seems to lie in accepting that the experiences, which are color, which are frequencies and vibrations, harmonize with our little universe or they are discordant with our universe.

And so it is of the utmost importance to each and every individual to be aware of their attitude of mind so that they may be aware of the vibration or color that they are emanating. And when one is aware, and through that effort of knowing their attitude at any moment, they begin to see, in the atmosphere in which they move, these various changing colors according to their attitudes of the moment. And so they know their color, and by knowing their own color or vibration, through honesty, they know the colors that are coming into their universe and leaving their universe.

Now many people still believe that their experiences in life are circumstantial; they do not have control over them. And that, indeed, causes a life absent of the happiness and the goodness and the joy which is our responsibility to experience.

Now, for example, this lovely room here, this day, you know—slow steps are sure steps under the guidance of reason and the Light of eternal truth—our technicians could correct easily this very blue day here [that] we have, but it would mean a great expenditure for you, as students, which is really not necessary at this time. But I will share with you how this blue could be corrected more than it is. It is corrected sufficiently for our work. However, it would require a very large, pure white reflector against that wall there, which would reflect back into the room the bright, overpowering blue of the daylight that is coming through this window. Well, as you, as students, know, we're not in the movie production nor filmmaking business. And so in keeping with our evolution, our technicians feel that the color correction, considering the equipment that we have, is certainly a fine job, and it is not necessary at this stage of evolution to go to such a material expense, when a greater balancing and correction can be done through the attitude of the students in attendance at the time of this filming.

I know that some of you have noted a vast change in frequency and in vibration, those of you who have decided to receive our private-class, little [video] cassettes. I know that you have noted a drastic change in the coloring towards the end of our class.

Now, my good student, Isa Goodwin, has ofttimes been credited with being one of the world's best irritators, which I am so happy that she has earned that credit, for irritation awakens the soul, and that's the only purpose of our journey through form. *[Isa Goodwin is Mr. Goodwin's mother. She would regularly instruct, guide, and correct the students through Mr. Goodwin's mediumship.]* And so it was only here at our last class that some of that credit got directed my way. And for the benefit of all of you, I was happy to be instrumental with the technicians that that emanation of emotional determination, known as anger, could be recorded indelibly on the magnetic film so that you may awaken to see what the atmosphere that surrounds anyone, when they're in emotional determination, may look like. You might have noted on your little [videotape] cassette that the colors all started to break up and turn a, a firehouse, I think you would call it, a firehouse or fire engine red. And so you've heard over these years how a person becomes red with anger. I've yet to find one purple with anger, for purple is one of the colors representing understanding. But I have found many people in reddish brown, brick red, and fire engine red when they are expressing emotional determination.

Now all of these experiences and what you may consider demonstrations are essential in your stages of evolution. My channel was most unhappy in reference to the energy being utilized in that way and, of course, that expressed a moment of self-interest, for he first had to make the judgment it was his energy. Well, being human, one does not want to dissipate precious energy when ofttimes one finds great difficulty in being receptive to it, especially if they find, for a moment or two, they must defend their territory.

Now defending one's territory is a basic animal instinct of the human species, and one rises to defend what first one judges is their territory because of a fear registration based upon past experiences in one's own life. And so we find that people who have emotional outbursts, expressing their determination through the water center, are people who are temporarily identified with a territorial type of complex, you might say. And therefore, they rise to defend what they first believe that they, of course, possess.

And so today, we're going to get on with your questions shortly, but to receive the greatest benefit from these private classes—and one should consider that nothing in a world of form is ever guaranteed—one should consider applying and studying what they have already received. And when you have something of value, to use it, for the lack of using it is abusing it. And so as you receive these classes of demonstrable laws, if you don't use them each day in your varied expressions, then you abuse the privilege of receiving them. The law alone, no man and no mind, makes that decision. The law works that way: ever to maintain and to sustain balance of the whole.

Now many people ask, "What is law? What are the laws?" Law, law is an expression of balance. That is what law is: an expression of balance for the good of the whole. That is law. Just. Fair. Without personality. A principle known as consideration. The love of goodness.

And so the law, infallible, ever works to sustain and to maintain balance. The Law of the Universe, that is what you truly are. And whether it is a plant or a tree, a blade of grass or an ant, everything, being law, is of course subject to its being. And so man, no less in the sight of the Principle of Good, known as God, is no less law. Law unto what he is. And in so being, man is therefore receptive to and subject to the law that he is.

And here we have the Law of Vibration. Man *is* law. Man's expression is vibration. Man's receptivity to what he expresses, his own receptivity is fulfillment of law and is known as experiences in life. And so as some of my students have said over these years, what goes around comes around. And so if your emanation, your vibration, your attitude of mind is emanating a coloring that is difficult to harmonize with—after all, my good students, how many pure beings have we found in our experiences in life?

We ever search for purity. We ever look across the worlds of creation for the virgin births. We want the purity without the blemish. And so here we are, these little specks, these little blemishes, ever looking for the purity. Why does the blemish ever seek the purity? Because the blemish must, the blemish must ever seek to blemish anything it judges is not like unto itself. And so the blemish in our consciousness ever seeks to convert everything it judges is pure.

And so here we go through the universes of experiences. The little speck, the little blemish ever working to contaminate. But that is not what we are. That's only what sometimes we believe we are. And so whenever a person experiences need, they can be rest assured, at that time they are the blemish on the universe of divine balance, the balance within their own consciousness.

Here we are, a universe unto our self. And we look out and we look at the sun. And we see, oh, it's way out there, the light. Because we have long ago blinded our self that that sun, moving in a solar system, is inside of our self.

And so we look out and we see, "Oh, full moon tonight. Oh, my." And then we look around at creation and we see, for a moment we see, "Oh, how they're so emotional and so upset." Well, where's the moon in the centers of your consciousness? Why, of course, here you have—what does the moon control? [It] controls the waters of your planet Earth. Of course, it does. It controls the tides of creation. And so anyone who permits themselves to identify with the moon in consciousness is affected by the movement of the waters, the tides of creation in the water center. And yet they could just as well, within our own consciousness, identify with the sun or one of the other various planets, considering you've already been given their understanding so many, many years ago in our private classes. And so [that over-identification will continue] until we come to that stage in evolution where we look out at the universe and we refrain from denying that which is moving in the solar system is moving within your consciousness in the various centers of consciousness.

And so let us look out at the universe and let us see—like my fine technician today recommended, that we place one of these little filters here, the silver one, to help bring about some balance here in the atmosphere—let us look around and see, "That which I see at this moment or at any moment is that which I be for a time. Only for a time. I look out and I want something, I think. I want it because for a moment I have denied its existence." And so we seek as an effect of denial. And yet we pause and then we awaken. "I am all that I seek for I am whole. I am fulfilled. I am complete. That which I truly am is perfect balance. And being perfect balance, I alone choose the law that I am. And this which I choose, this law that I am, to identify with reveals to me in my experiences in life if I have chosen wisely or if I have not. And if I choose wisely, then my experiences in life are harmonious. The law does not fail me, for in truth one cannot fail themselves for they are the law." Therefore, one who believes that there is no good in their life for them—whoever believes that they are not growing, evolving, and expanding is one who has gone to sleep only for a time. And even in going to sleep, the law is fulfilling itself.

And now we'll take a little time here for the questions that you have prepared. And so if the secretary will kindly speak [them] forth at this time, [we will begin].

Thank you. Is self-concern an expression of fear that it may be proven that the mind is not necessary for the accomplishment of the good in life?

Self-concern is an expression of fear in this respect: one identifies with what they judge they do not have. Having so made the judgment and believing they are the judgment of their mind, they look out and make another judgment that what they need someone is or someone has. Now in so doing they experience what is known as self-concern if they permit their mind the thought that they may not be able to control to the satisfaction of their judgment that which they believe that they need, for they have denied that they have it. And so in that respect, fear, of course, is a function guiding the concern of the individual of the possibility they may not be able to control what they believe they must have. Thank you.

Thank you. How would an experience, which reinforces a judgment, become an experience which broadens our horizons through greater acceptance?

Well, in reference to an experience which broadens one's horizons, all experiences in life, effects of the return of the law established by the person experiencing, all experiences broaden or expand the consciousness, regardless of how joyous or sad or disturbed one may think they are at the moment of the return of the law. In that respect, they serve as instruments to awaken the individual who is over-identified with limit from a lack of effort to understand and to apply what they truly are. Yes.

Thank you. In an earlier class it was stated that when we permit ourselves to think of the things we want, we guarantee the obstruction to our desires because the mind is designed to bring about a balance in the mental realm. How do we stay free of the thinking of what we want, while making effort to attain what we want?

Attainment is an effect of changes in the attitude of a person's mind. Now without attitude changes, one does not experience what they desire to attain. Now, for example, it is often said a house divided cannot stand. You ofttimes find in [the] mental world that a person says, "I have worked so hard to attain this, and there's been no change for me at all. And I'm just as far from attaining it as I was the day that I started." That is a person who temporarily believes they are speaking how they feel, when they are in truth being dishonest with what they truly are. They are attaining what they truly were motivated in the beginning to attain. For example, a person may say, "I've tried everything and nothing works for me." Well, of course, nothing works for them for they have attained the satisfaction of the judgment that they believe that they are, and that was the true motivation in the beginning of their efforts.

Now in time in evolution, through the lamp of honesty and the light of reason, they will face that and they will say, "Well, I did attain what I was truly motivated to attain. I have proven now to my satisfaction that nothing works for me no matter how hard I try. Therefore, I somehow have been left out in the universe. I'm a poor, helpless soul. I am a cripple of total self-pity and everyone should pity me because I've worked so hard and nothing works for me." I do hope that's helped with your question.

Thank you.

Yes.

One of our earth dictionaries defines ignorance *as the condition of not being informed, lack of knowledge, or unaware. Would you please give the Living Light's definition of error of ignorance?*

Well, the error of ignorance is to experience without an awakening of the law that one, being a law unto themselves, has established. *[A clock begins to chime.]* Now we'll pause for a moment. We will be ignorant of the chiming clocks and pause for a moment. *[The chiming stops.]* Now if they've satisfied themselves, we can go on. A person— *[Another clock begins to chime.]* They haven't satisfied themselves yet. You know, there's one thing about satisfaction, there's no end to it. But because they're wound up, they're bound to unwind. *[Again, the chiming stops.]* I think, perhaps, that's satisfied itself there. A person who is ignorant or not informed by their own lack of effort, a person experiencing that which they desire not to experience, consciously desire not to experience, and yet they experience it, is a person who, through lack of effort, is far from well-informed. And it is a person's, well, a person's responsibility to study, to educate themselves, and to apply the law that they are in an intelligent, reasonable way. And so when you permit yourself, through distraction and diversions, not to do your part, as a responsible person, to look at the experience and say, "Ah, I do think this is the connection to my attitude just the other day," [you experience what you do not appreciate]. I do hope that's helped with your question.

Thank you.

You're welcome.

Is there a location or special state of mind or preparation that we should do prior to viewing Halley's Comet in order to receive the maximum benefit for which it was sent?

Oh, yes. Definitely. There's a great deal that one can do with, really, not any great effort. [And that] is to refrain, during the time, from the slightest possible identification with self, which offers nothing but need.

Thank you.

You're welcome.

Is the irradiation of food advisable to kill insects, bacteria, and molds or will they only mutate to more tenacious forms?

Well, in reference to that question—and some of your scientists have already feared for a long time, your material science, that the insects will take over your planet—well, man, one of the biggest insects of all, has done [and] is doing a fine job in ever strengthening the immune system of what you call the insects. They have a long record of endurance. And each day, what you call your insects or bugs are getting stronger and stronger because you are introducing into their life a great determination for survival. And whenever—you see, the law that works for man, of course, the bigger insect, works for the little insect. And whenever you work to bring about their destruction and annihilation, you help the Law of Survival to strengthen itself and become more immune to the poisons you introduce into their lives.

Thank you.

You're welcome.

Is there a new planet to be discovered in our solar system and is this what some call Vulcan?

Well, I don't know, I expect you people might call it a new planet. It's been there for a long, long time. It is one of the recent arrivals in, I would suspect you'd call it a recent arrival as far as the other planets that you are aware of, but you can call it whatever you would like. Yes, that's what your world is calling it. But the planet has been there for eons of time.

And—

You are recently suspecting and becoming aware of it, and that is good news, in one respect, for it shows identification with exploration of the world around a person is growing, is increasing. And when a person has finished looking outside for the causes, [their] mind will reach its limit and it will start looking at the universes within. Yes.

And what does this planet represent?

It represents, as the forecomer of what you call Halley's Comet is bringing to you, it represents a broadening horizon, a greater awakening for the civilization of your planet. Yes.

Thank you.

You're welcome.

It is said that honey is the glue of deception, and yet it is also said you catch more bees with honey than vinegar. What, then, is the truth of this?

Well, the truth is quite simple: to the believer, to those who believe they are the forms they create, then it is true, of course, you can catch more flies with honey than you can with vinegar. No one ever said, at least in the Living Light, that you can catch more bees with honey. You catch more flies with honey. And so it is, it is the glue of deception and those who insist on believing the forms they identify with are glued with the honey, the sweetness of their own glory.

Thank you. How and why is curiosity the father of frustration and fascination is the mother?

[A plane passes over the temple and the noise of the engine is readily heard, even though this class was given indoors.]

Well, if you will be so kind to be patient while this little buzz saw goes through the air here, then we will repeat the question. All right?

Yes. Thank you.

And I'm sure you will enjoy, after listening to your classes, a little pause of a little plane going by or something, a few changes. If our cameraman was alert, he might be able to film it. I see it right over the tree, but he'd have to be very quick. But, oh, I think he's going to miss it. It's up there, unless you found another one on the ground. Yes. Now you speak right up [with] the questions so I can hear you, please.

How and why— [The microphone of the secretary, who was reading the questions, was turned down or off, which resulted in the recording level of the question being so low, the teacher had difficulty hearing it.]

No. How and why what?

Is curiosity the father of frustration and fascination the mother?

Well, yes, indeed, how and why. How and why is curiosity the father of frustration, and what is the rest of your statement?

And fascination the mother.

Whenever you permit your mind to be curious of something, you identify with that [which] you are curious with. Would you not agree?

Yes.

And so you father frustration, and in so fathering it, you also mother fascination. For a person is curious over something only to be trapped like the fly in the web of the spider by becoming fascinated with it. And so you father frustration through curiosity, and you mother it through fascinating with yourself, for you are the father of the curiosity, and therefore your fascination is the mother of it. And you are the child or the victim of what you have done. Does that help with your question?

Yes. Thank you.

You're welcome.

Could you please speak on obedience, the Law of Abundance?

Obedience, the Law of Abundance?

Yes.

If one is not obedient to the faculty of gratitude for the crumbs of life, then one does not experience the abundance that is the effect of the continuity of that law.

Thank you. Is it true that all the has-beens live in the water center? And are there no has-beens in the earth, air, or fire center?

Without water, form does not endure in any universe at any time. Water is the element of life. Now you think of water, the element water, you think of it only as you see, perhaps the water in a container, the water of the river, the water of the ocean. But you have not awakened to the water element of the atmosphere. Hmm? Yes.

Thank you. How do the has-beens delete and change under the guise of improvement whatever they fear?

Kindly repeat the question.

What do the has-beens delete and change under the guise of improvement of whatever they fear?

What do the has-beens believe and change?

Delete.

Oh, what do the has-beens delete and change under the guise of improvement?

Right. Of whatever they fear.

Of whatever they fear. Because has-beens are created by individuals who believe they are need. And so they are created by mental substance and contain, within their very being, all these necessary ingredients of deception and temptation. And so under the guise of improvement or change, they tempt you to continue to serve them so that they can continue to survive.

Thank you.

You're welcome.

Some people have said Atlantis was destroyed by nature. Was it the result of too much mental activity?

Some have said that what was destroyed by . . .

Atlantis.

Was destroyed by what?

By nature.

Destroyed by nature? Whenever the laws of nature, whenever there is an imbalance on any planet, then you have what is known as an escape from the imbalance. Now what you understand as an escape from the imbalance is known in your world as a self-destruct; it's a way of getting out. Now when you understand that the human mind and mental substance creates many forms—unfortunately or fortunately, they ofttimes are discordant to the natural, harmonious law of the other species or forms, such as the plants, the flowers, the trees, the animals, the insects, and the mammals, etc., etc., and on down the line, if you want to consider it down. Then, when man's thoughts and emanations and the forms that he creates are discordant by being the, the armies of denial of the Principle of Good, when need-forms flood the atmosphere, they become a battle and destructive to the lilies of the field, whom the Principle of Goodness has so beautifully cloaked. And when that happens, you have what is known as a disturbance with the nature spirits. Now that disturbance, you understand, the expression of that disturbance and discord, you understand that as volcanic eruptions, earthquakes, disasters, and etc. Yes.

Thank you. How can one neutralize the beginnings not finished so that one has power to follow through on a present beginning?

Well, when a person no longer entertains in the mental consciousness that which has passed and takes control over their attention, identification with what they are working on, then one frees themselves from what has been.

Thank you.

In that respect.

I have a difficult time shaking sleep forms as soon as I arrive home and on rising. Is there a way to awaken or reawaken in an alert state of consciousness?

Yes. Well, first of all, in reference to that question, it reveals that the repetition of the form is taking control, and the true being [has] made themselves a victim of that repetitive form. Now you fight fire with fire, and you use repetition with repetition. If one is the victim of a repetitive form, known as a particular—what you would call a habit, that— *[A clock begins to chime.]* We'll pause for a moment. *[After a pause, the teacher continues.]* It's quite lovely to have this little musical interlude of the clocks. We'll see the good in all things. And so one, having chosen to place themselves as a victim of a repetitive pattern, one works to establish an opposite repetitive pattern. And so one says, like the questioner says, [they] go home and they fall asleep, one says, "Wide awake. I'm wide awake. Wide awake." The direct opposite of what the other form that has already been created is saying. Yes.

Thank you.

You're welcome.

If one feels they are not doing their life's work as they see it, how can they feel encouraged if life's situations seem to be blocking advancement?

Well, stop seeing what is negative so that you can experience what is positive. You know, so often in life we have—it's like a yawn, you know. We first have the judgment, and then we have to go— *[The teacher deliberately yawns.]* You see? And [did] you ever see a person yawn in front of several people? The next thing you know everyone is yawning. It shows you how much control that people really have, doesn't it, sometimes? Pardon? Ah, you see. And so it's like a person who wants to do their life's work; well, they, first of all, start with demonstrating the law, the soul faculty of gratitude. They say, "Thank you, God, for whatever it is I'm doing, I am doing for that which I truly am, the goodness that is. I am an inseparable part of that goodness or God. I'm not the whole God. Let me not be tempted to ever think that I am, but I am an inseparable part of that."

And a person therefore, slowly but surely, will start changing their mental substance from believing in a negative attitude to begin to believe in a positive attitude. Remember, whatever you say to yourself reinforces whatever you believe that you are. So if you want to believe that you're a negative being and you keep telling yourself that, you only guarantee it. It's like a person [who] says, "Well, I've studied for thirty years and, you know, I'm just the same as the day I started thirty years ago." It's the farthest thing from the truth. All they [have] got to do is look in the mirror and see all the changes they've gone through. If they don't want to be honest enough to face the truth inside themselves, let them look into a reflection. And they cannot deny the reflection. Yes.

Thank you.

You're welcome. That's how one encourages themselves to refrain from serving the judgment that has offered them no good in life. That's all. Yes.

How can one communicate with a creature in their care who is causing difficulty by things they are doing?

Well, are you speaking of a creature as a, as a two-legged human being or a creature as a four-legged one? Please clarify your question.

I believe the questioner is referring to a four-legged creature.

A four-legged creature, not a two-legged creature.

Right.

I see. Well, first of all, by refraining from the need of controlling them. You see, first of all, if you don't have a need to control someone, you start on the path of wisdom and light to establish the law for yourself. Now if a person has difficulty controlling a creature that they live with, in doing what they want to do, well, all that person has to do is to be honest with themselves and find out what they're doing. And once they find out what they're doing, they can make intelligent choices of how the two creatures will live under the same roof. Yes.

Thank you. Are numbers the creation of man?

Are numbers the creation of man? Numbers are the principle of what you call man, not the creation. You see, as long as the question is expressing the belief that man is flesh, bone, and limit, then it is not mathematic. No. What man is, is mathematic. Yes. But what he believes he is, is the farthest thing from it.

The—

Math, you can balance. What man believes that he is, is so changing it cannot be brought into balance. Yes.

The next question is, Why is man seemingly more receptive spiritually to numbers rather than what is known as handwriting?

Now you'll have to restate your question. I don't know what's the problem with our little system, although we are going to replace that little piece of equipment for one that will even do a little better job. It's rather old. But we've got to be patient with these things. So please restate your question because it's difficult to hear in here, unless we can turn up the volume a bit. Yes, go ahead.

Why is man seemingly more receptive spiritually to numbers rather than what is known as handwriting?

Well, why is—thank you very much. And that was better. I could hear you. Why is man spiritually more receptive to numbers than he is to handwriting? Because what man is, is mathematical. What man sometimes believes that he is, is not mathematical. And so handwriting is dependent upon man's beliefs and is an expression of man's belief. That's not what he is. That's only what he sometimes believes that he is. And if you believe that you are very happy and joyous, your handwriting is going to show certain indications of that.

Thank you.

If you truly believe it.

Is, in truth, intuition a frequency that is nothing more than a constant transmission in the atmosphere?

You'll have to restate your question because our audio man is having difficulty here.

Is, in truth, intuition a frequency that is nothing more than a constant transmission in the atmosphere?

Is truth an intuition?

I think what they mean is—

I would like a clarification on that.

I think what they mean is, Is intuition in truth a frequency that is nothing more than a constant transmission in the atmosphere?

There is a perplexed vibration with the question. Because, you see, it is more than one question and is not separate. So let's separate the questions the sentence contains. Now read it slowly, please.

Is, in truth, intuition a frequency . . .

Is intuition in truth a frequency? Question one, correct?

Yes.

Well, it depends on your understanding. Is intuition—read that first question again.

Is, in truth, intuition a frequency . . .

In other words, the question is asking, Is intuition a frequency?

Yes.

Intuition is a frequency. Truth is not a frequency. Yes, go ahead.

And they want to know, is it a constant transmission in the atmosphere?

It is constant. Yes, it is.

Thank you.

What else [is] the question asking?

I think that is it on that one.

Now read that question again.

Is, in truth, intuition a frequency that is nothing more than a constant transmission in the atmosphere?

All right. Yes, go ahead.

In what direction does the transmissions of man's minds move?

In what direction?

Yes.

Do you mean what is the common direction?

I think so, yes.

Horizontal.

Thank you.

Ofttimes vertical on a downward slant. *[Many students laugh.]* I think you call that a 45-degree angle. Yes, go ahead.

Thank you. Please speak more on so-called time and the relativity of its relation to man's mind.

Well, you see, I've spoken before that time is an illusion created by the minds of men. It is an illusion in your belief. You see, time, Life, Light, Love is all energy. You see, what time really is, not what you believe it is—what you believe it is, is an illusion. You look at a clock and you say, "Well, this much time has passed." That's something you've created. Time, Light, Truth, Life is all energy. That's all that it is.

So you look out at the stars there at night and you say, "Oh, that's so many light-years away." Well, this is all relative, you see. In your present evolution you say it will take, oh, six months to get to that particular planet because you calculate out that it's this many light-years away and etc., etc. And then when you return to your Earth, the people will be forty years older than when you left them. You see, this is all the world of *maya* and illusion. However, as long as you believe in the illusion of the limit of your form, then you're going to understand time as an illusion that it is. It's an illusion. It is an—a person who awakens within their being, that which they are, is no longer limited by forms created by illusion.

You are Light. Light is Life. Love is Light. Time is Light. Energy is Light. You are a light contained by your belief, which is an illusion.

Thank you. Would you please share with us your understanding of the story of Prometheus?

In reference to that question, first of all, it is not fair to my other students to not put it in terms a little bit clearer, you hear?

Yes.

Now I may answer your question, but in so doing I transgress the Law of Consideration of all of my other students. Now I want to speak on that for a moment. I have come and spent much time with you to bring you words that I sincerely accept could be understood by the body, the whole body of the students here. And in so doing I expect that you, as students, bring me questions that would be in keeping with the Law of Consideration that we may maintain and sustain a more receptive vibration to the humbleness of your English language, you hear?

Yes.

For me to enter into the realms of discussion and the laws of entropy, etc. and etc. is not considerate of my student, earthly, body. Kindly resubmit that question next class.

Thank you. Would you please share with us more of your understanding of minerals and their properties, in particular, are there any minerals with beneficial properties, like sea salt?

Well, there are many minerals. Your planet is filled with all the beneficial minerals that you could possibly require for the sustaining of balance in your life in a chemical way. Yes.

Well, I don't find many of you plucking the mint and enjoying the benefits thereof. I don't find too many experiencing the wonderful benefits, when their chemicals are low in iodine, from eating the onion as it comes from the ground. I don't see many of my students eating the beets raw, possibly with a little vinegar on them. I find even fewer of my students eating the raw Swiss chard. I find even less of my students looking out there at this wonderful world here of creation and eating the tops of the carrots. I find them, somehow, experiencing and enjoying the part that was never meant for the two-legged animal; it was reserved for the little bugs and the insects. I find few of my students benefiting from the, what you call the skins of the potatoes. I find even less of you benefiting from the lovely chemical of quinine in the, what you call the skin of the grapefruit. Yes. Next question, please. *[A clock begins to chime.]*

May I pause a minute, please?

I would like to say one thing, as soon as our lovely musical chimes stop. Whatever in creation we have judged we cannot control, we defend and protect the judgment by another judgment which says it is distasteful. Go ahead with your questions, please.

Thank you. Why is it—

Especially the tops of the carrots. Go ahead. *[Many students laugh.]*

Why is it that man fears God when he is close to accepting God?

Why, because man knows what he's doing. And because he knows what he's doing, he's very fearful. He's got to go and face Him. Yes, you see, all men know in truth what they're doing. And they know that they have to pay their debt. And what is their debt? Their denial of what they are. They all know what they're doing. They all know what they're doing. Inside of everyone, they know exactly what they're doing. They know that they have set aside what they are in order to experience what they judge is a sensation of what they are not. Yes.

Thank you.

You're welcome.

Earth scientists have theorized dark stars so dense and with such gravitational fields that no light escapes their pull. If these dark stars exist, could you share with us your understanding of their physical purpose and spiritual meaning?

Yes. Thank you very much. In reference to that lovely question, stars are no different than the so-called minds of men. You know, they all have their personalities, just like a tree has its personality. Now you have in your world, in your species, you look around and you say, "Oh, I [have] got to stay away from that one. They're a real sponge." Well, just like, just like that statement, there are stars there that are sponges, and whatever comes within their gravitational pull, they gobble it up. Yes.

Thank you. Would you please discuss the triune nature of laws?

The triune nature of law or laws?

They have plural. Laws.

I see. Well, let us go to the singular in reference to law and we can grow from there and have as many children as we'd like, lovely bundles of joy there. They want to understand the triune nature of law? I've discussed shortly here, a little while ago, what law is. It is an expression of maintaining and sustaining perfect balance. That's law. For the good of the whole. Now the triune nature of law: there is the expression of it; there is the return of it; and there is the perfect balancing of what's out and what returns. And that is its basic triune nature. In other words, you can say, giving, receiving, and deciding. Yes.

Thank you. What is happening when a person feels a lot of pressure on the very top of the head?

Is the pressure consistent or periodic? Is it of a long duration or a short? Do you have the answers?

No, I don't.

You do not have the—the question is incomplete. Have it resubmitted, please.

OK. Thank you. To my understanding duty, gratitude, and tolerance correspond to the odic center and its counterbalance, money, ego, and sex correspond to the earth center. And faith, poise, and humility correspond to the electric center—

Very good study, yes.

And its counterbalance, self, pity, and friendship, correspond to the fire center.

Encouraging. We're getting there.

Is this correct?

Why, yes, it's correct. Study what you've already received and I don't think you'll have any question on its correct[ness].

If so, what are the triune faculties corresponding to the magnetic and to the counterbalance water centers?

Have the question resubmitted in a statement of what they have tried to understand in reference to what was already given for they've done a fine job so far.

Thank you.

There's no sense in stopping just before the victory. Yes.

Thank you. In The Living Light, *it states that mantras were given to help activate the gland through which our vision peers into your world.*

Yes.

Could you give us those mantras again?

You have lost them, secretary?

To some they were not given.

Have you lost them?

I'm not sure they were ever given to me.

Have you lost them, cameraman?

They were given before I came to this organization. They were given during the 1960s in the Living Light Discourses period.

Ah, where is my friend, [Student J]?

Right here, sir.

Have you lost them?

No, sir.

Good for you. I will speak to you—have my channel speak to you and Isa speak to you after these classes today. You may share them with the secretary. *[Isa Goodwin is Mr. Goodwin's mother. She would regularly instruct, guide, and correct the students through Mr. Goodwin's mediumship.]*

Yes, sir.

And in turn, because there is a little inspiration in the class today of studying and applying and getting something out of these classes, because I know the mantras were given to some of you students on earth, and so I'll speak to you about sharing a certain part there, all right, [Student J]?

Yes, sir.

Thank you very much. Yes, go ahead with your next question, please.

Thank you. When I practice the middle C exercise, I feel like it brings me into balance and clears my aura. Is this its design? And does it also work to purify the forms, like the true rhythmic cleansing breath does? Is there a next step to the middle C exercise?

When you reach perfect balance, there's no place left to go. And you're doing a fine job and I'm so happy that the universe of the questioner is in perfect balance, as they state that it is. When you reach perfect balance, there's no place left to go, except to step off the cliff with a judgment. All right? Yes. Thank you.

Why are we told not to place our attention on our solar plexus? And why would the water center be the center of our universe? And is this the true center for both spiritual and physical?

You have to be patient because my little friend, Boomer, is here and he's disturbing my other friend here. *[Boomer was a frog who lived at the temple and would often sneak into the temple when a student failed to completely close a screen door.]* So just be patient. I've tried to get, you know, you people not to let Boomer into the house because he gets quite disturbing, you know. My channel found him in his closet here just the other week. He was very upset because some of my students down there don't keep the screen doors closed. Now you be careful because Boomer's here. And we don't want any disturbance with all these lights and equipment. So just be at peace for a few moments. And he's just, he's very close, the little frog. Now go ahead. You will have to repeat the question. I'll try to calm down these little creatures here.

OK. Why are we told not to place our attention on our solar plexus?

Well, first of all, have you been able to peer directly at the sunlight? At the sun itself?

No.

Without some protective aid? That answers your question, for the solar plexus is the sun of your universe. Go ahead.

And why would the water center be the center of our universe?

Well, the water center is the center of life. You see, without water and without light, there is no life. Yes.

And is it the center for both spiritual and physical?

It is the center for the manifestation of the Light of the Spirit. Yes.

Thank you. [A small frog croaks in the background.]

Boomer! Yes. *[Boomer croaks several more times.]*

What is the purpose of this school?

What is the purpose of this school right here? This little temple?

It doesn't specify, but . . .

What is the purpose of which school? Are they talking about the high school down the road?

I don't know. It says "this school."

This school. That means this school here that you're attending. You see, you want to be specific here. What is the purpose of this school? Well, the purpose of this school is to be an instrument through which, through your own efforts, you may apply the laws that the Light reveals and, in that application, fulfill the purpose of your journey on earth, and to face the joy, the *joy* of personal responsibility. Not the thrill. Because ofttimes the mind doesn't find it thrilling to face personal responsibility. But joyous, yes! For it is joyous to apply personal responsibility. It brings about a good feeling in all parts of the being. Yes.

What causes the soul to rise?

What causes the soul to rise?

Yes.

Whenever you accept personal responsibility for all your thoughts, acts, and deeds, the soul rises to its heavenly heights [to] return to the home that it truly is. Yes.

What are wings of genius on which the soul is lost?

Wings of genius on which the soul is lost is when one is completely addicted and bound by mental substance.

Thank you. What is a psychic and what center or centers of consciousness do they operate in?

Resubmit the question for obvious reasons.

In reference to what is called a lost soul, what is it lost from?

Lost from its true home and temporarily residing in a workhouse. Yes.

Thank you.

Salt mines are ofttimes referred to as workhouses. Yes.

How may we strengthen our spine, namely the lower area of the spine?

No problem whatsoever: exercise your divine right of the lord of your universe, known as your will power.

Thank you.

The spine is designed to respond to your will power, considering that is where the will flows.

Thank you. What relationship does protoplasm have to the centers we are studying in class at this time?

What relationship does protoplasm have to the centers we're discussing? They do not exist without it.

Thank you. Should the room we use for meditation be totally free from mental substance, such as books and magazines?

Books and magazines are not mental substance, only to the one who has a need for them.

Thank you. The finer, lighter vibratory waves are touched while listening to the flute. Does this instrument bring us into closer harmony to our true being?

It can. It is one of the oldest instruments on your planet. And when properly attuned to the vibration of the person playing it, it can and has ofttimes throughout the ages accomplished that. Yes.

Thank you. What is the purpose of fresh air while doing our exercises?

Without uncontaminated atmospheric conditions—you see, nature's balance is transmitted through what you know as the atmosphere or oxygen. And when a person does not permit themselves to be receptive to that balance of the atmosphere that nature is emanating, then there are difficulties, ofttimes.

Thank you.

You have time for one more question.

When a soul does something of great magnitude here on earth for the good of humanity and they leave before it can manifest, are they allowed to view it from where they are or are they told somehow?

No. They continue on with their work. And they are inseparably a part of it until their job is completed.

Thank you.

You're more than welcome. I see time passes quickly. You have a lovely day. I know that you will. *[The teacher begins to remove his microphone.]* And [it's] been [a] most enjoyable class. And let's have a balanced day. You know, it takes a little wisdom to balance spirituality. And so let's put a little bit of gold into this blue day today. And, as I've spoken before—Oh! You can't hear me, can you? I must remember that that little thing here, [this microphone], is required for you to hear me over there. So I'm going to say good day and thank you all so very much.

OCTOBER 27, 1985

A/V Class Private 21

Is it recording now?
It is now.
Yes. It just stopped itself, did it?
It did.
Well, now, we'll get on to that. *[The teacher laughs joyously.]* I can assure you that my assistants inform me that your fine filming equipment is free from material defects. So we'll go on here with our class on incentive and survival.

Now ofttimes my students will speak out about, oh, discouragement and not being happy. They really don't need to speak about it. You know, the demonstration in life is the revelation. And when I find a wet duck waddling around the temple—or two—no one has to tell me that they're discouraged or unhappy with their life. But I want to encourage you that whenever a person feels like a wet duck and they're discouraged and nothing [is] really worth living for, that there's a divinity in that seeming emotional disaster and irrationality; there is great good for it reveals to anyone who is a little awakened—and we all are a little awakened, hopefully, myself, a little awakened—it reveals to us that we are beginning to experience the incentive for survival.

And so one doesn't run away from home to get home. When one believes they are unhappy with the home that they have created, an intelligent person simply begins a remodeling or redecorating process. Now one doesn't tear up the foundation of a house and expect not to experience the storms when they come, for without the foundation, there's no roof to weather the storms of old creation.

And so we have these lovely classes and these wonderful experiences, and I have something here to discuss with you also on incentive of survival, as you sit there in that lovely room and look up to that lovely, gabled ceiling there and see that there, according to your experiences, something is missing. Yes, something is missing. It's presently out there in the garage. Now it's important for you, as private students, to understand the incentive of survival.

You are in a temple of Light. In a temple of Light, you are exposed to rates of vibration that are different than what you are used to. You are exposed to higher frequencies in the atmosphere. Now while you are exposed in a temple of Light, you swim along with the flow of the river or you struggle to swim against the currents. Now when you struggle to swim against the currents, you ground yourself in the joy and the happiness of living. And so you emanate from your being this electromagnetic energy. Now this energy is used by the forms in the atmosphere who come from the realms of consciousness which you, as a student body, demonstrate by a majority or 51 percent of your presence. Now, for example, if you permit yourselves to entertain in consciousness the denial of the Light while exposed to the Light, what you do in truth, by such a judgment in consciousness while exposed to the Light, you direct, not consciously, but you direct energy, ectoplasm, to mental realms of consciousness. For whoever is exposed in the Light and while exposed in the Light denies the Light by believing in need, which is the demonstration of denial of the Light of truth, directs this energy, which is flowing through their body, through their being, directs this energy to forms in mental worlds.

Now your chandelier that used to be on the ceiling of your dining room in this temple crashed to the floor as a physical demonstration of 51 percent of the student body denying the Light while exposed to the Light.

[The dining room chandelier crashed to the floor the previous Thursday evening while the students were at the temple in the dining room, watching a movie. Fortunately, no one was injured.]

Now I'll try to be a little bit more specific with you on this. It is not survival, it is not happiness, it is not good, when we deny good by a lack of effort to flood our consciousness with the good that we are while exposed to the good which the Light is. Many of you feel, at times, frustrated while exposed to the Light. You feel personally injured. You sometimes feel slighted or not treated [well], not respected for the efforts you believe that you are making. *[A clock begins to chime.]* And we'll pause for a moment. This is an understandable experience for anyone who believes they are the form they create.

And so the real struggle for you, as private students, is to make greater effort to refrain from believing that you are the limit, for whenever you permit yourself to believe you are the limit, which is what you would consider common practice in the jungle of creation, when you permit yourself to believe that you are the limit while exposed to the Limitless, you have a great battle within your consciousness. *[The teacher coughs.]* Excuse me. And as that battle in your consciousness progresses, you are tempted to free yourself from the experiences and effects of the battle. You become battle-worn and bored. You become battle-scarred and frustrated. But I am here to assure you it is only an effect of making the effort to believe that you are limit while you are exposed to the Limitless.

Now whoever exposes themselves to the Light, to the Limitless and whoever walks upon that path and has the opportunity of being exposed, over a period of time, consistently, must make changes in consciousness in order to survive in the Light of truth, which they are. The effect or experiences of not making those changes is so frustrating; it is such a discord, disturbance, and disease of the mental substance in its great effort to remain in control that a student on the path of life goes through the gates that clearly state: grow or go. There is no other choice, for the choice has been made by the student upon their arrival on the path. And so as many prophets have so often spoke, many are called; a few are chosen. Few, few choose to remain upon the path and go through the purification in consciousness that is inevitable.

No one wants to say with their mind, "I don't want to make a change, for I don't know what I will get from the change. What will I be if I give up what I have?" If we insist on believing that we have, then we cannot move along the spiritual path and experience what we are. As long as we believe that we have, then we will not move beyond that point in consciousness to experience what we are, for our minds are dependent upon the forms we have created.

We find our security in what is familiar. And whoever finds their security in what is familiar to them cannot make the changes in a harmonious and joyous way. However, we have every reason to be encourage[d] for we are all making the changes in spite of the mind that believes that it has. Whoever believes that they have is the servant of the have-beens or the good old days or the good old times.

Now we'll go to our secretary with any questions that you have on today's subject matter or any that has already been shared with you.

Thank you. God's angels fulfill the law and man is a law unto himself. Would you please speak more on that beautiful truth that God's angels fulfill the law?

Yes, indeed. God's angels fulfill the law. Man is a law unto himself. God's angels are man, and they are in a state of consciousness beyond the limits of belief. And so God's angels fulfill the law and man is a law unto himself. Man chooses moment by moment in his life to believe he is the forms that speak in his mind or to accept that he is that intelligent Energy which is responsible, responsible for using the vehicles of limit for the purpose of their design. Yes.

Thank you. Comparison seems to be dual in that it can be used by the mind to make intelligent decisions and it can also be used by the mind to discourage us. If it is dual, is comparison limited to creation?

Comparison is our identification, either in a mental world or in a change that we are considering between what has been, what is, and what we desire to be. For example, a person looks out at the world and they see themselves as they look at another. And so that is a comparison of bondage. A person looks out and sees another in order to see themselves. That's a comparison. Another person looks out, sees others, looks inside, sees themselves, sees there is no difference in the true being, only a difference in expression. So people use comparison in the sense of, "That is what that person is. This is what I am based upon my judgment of what they are." Therefore, comparison in that sense and use of the word is a servant of the judgment of mental substance.

Now when a person sees that tree is not the same as that tree. That's a comparison. There is a difference. However, when one looks with the Light and one sees, "That energy, that which I am, is expressing through that form. That same energy is expressing through this form over here. The forms that I see are different, but that which is, is not different. I have comparison for I have two eyes. And two deceives me for truth is single." Yes.

Thank you. It was given in an earlier class that the moon controls the life force of the planet. In a recent class you stated that without water there would be no life on this planet. If it is so, that the life force expresses through water, could you share why this is so?

Why is it so that life force expresses through water? The element water? Is that your question?

Yes.

Well, life force *is* water. It is the light of water. It is, in the sense of life as you know life—you believe that life is form. It is movement, and that is the element water. And the element water (belief) is controlled by the moon which governs the element water of the planet on which you presently reside. That is not what you are; that is what you believe you are. Life force is not light power. It is our interpretation of it.

Thank you. Could you please clarify: is it correct that the water center is located in the solar plexus?

It is not correct. The water center is not the solar plexus. The solar plexus is the center of the universe; it is the sun and it is the light.

Thank you.

It must—you see, if you try to understand that the elements, the centers, the earth, fire, water, electric, magnetic, odic, etc., etc., if you would try to understand that they are inseparable in order that you experience limit or form as you know form.

Thank you.

Yes.

Would you please share with us those pressure points that would allow us to control our own temperature?

I will be more than happy to share with you the pressure points. And we're going to begin on the pressure points as soon as the directors in your Earth planet come into a harmonious agreement, so that I may show you the most important pressure point: the one that controls the water center or the emotional level of consciousness of the directors of our little earthly expression here.

Thank you.

You're welcome.

According to Greek mythology, Prometheus was a god who was moved by the struggles and suffering of man in darkness. Without permission, he took fire from the realm of the gods and gave it to man. For this act he was punished by Zeus.

Correct.

Throughout the many years of his punishment, Prometheus did not despair for he perceived the day when his punishment would end with the fall of Zeus. Would you please share with us your understanding of this story?

Well, in reference to his punishment, which is an effect of his identification with the fruits of action. Now I know it seems lacking in compassion to state that truth; however, one's experiences of punishment is an effect of their attachment to the fruits of their action. And though one may not say, "I consciously am attached to the fruits of my action," one experiences the effects of that attachment through suffering and, of course, through punishment.

Now there is a delicate, a delicate balance between identifying with oneself in order that one may remain in the limit in which the true being is expressing. And so your planet is a planet of limit. It has been discussed before. It is the fifth planet. [We are] here to demonstrate faith, the opposite of belief.

Now, in reference to Zeus, the king below has been called by many names throughout the ages. The fall of that boy down there is when the light of reason shines upon his control of life force. Now limit is the domain, the rightful, just domain of the king of creation. And so that's his realm of consciousness.

Now what man is, is not limit. We all know that. Man is expressing through limit. And so man, moment by moment, has the opportunity to choose what he is and what he is not. And when man chooses what he is not, man is then aware of limit, man is then aware of suffering, man is then aware of temptation and attachment to the fruits of action, for man has done that in keeping with his belief.

How does one move from belief to faith, from bondage to freedom? It is a moment-by-moment effort by any individual. You've been given cleansing breaths. You have been given certain parts of the anatomy to ever help you to awaken in your understanding.

A person who makes effort to help themselves to be free from those limits is a person who works sincerely to help another, for God and goodness enter a person's life in their sincere effort to share that goodness with another. To share is not to loan. To share is to be an instrument through which the goodness flows freed from any return. So God helps those who help themselves by helping others, for when a person makes the sincere effort to help another, they must first help themselves in order to be a qualified instrument through which another may be helped. Yes.

Thank you. The Law of Harmony is expressed through the triune faculty of faith, poise, and humility. And through direct concentration on the Law of Harmony we can express our spirit through more beautiful levels. Please share with us how to concentrate on the Law of Harmony.

By not permitting the mind to experience denial of what you are. That means total freedom from need. Whoever makes effort to control their mind experiences the Law of Harmony, which they are, for there is no discord nor disease created by denying what they are.

Thank you. Within the past several weeks the Russians claim to have visually seen in outer space what appeared to them to be three very large angels. And they also claim to have discovered the lost continent of Atlantis by submarine. Are there three large angels in outer space and what do they do?

Well, if you consider intelligent beings from planets you are yet to be aware of as three large angels, if you consider the particular emanation of their vehicles in space as angelic forms, then in that respect your statement is correct.

The planet has always been monitored. It is the responsibility of the intelligences in the universe that are, in order to relate to you, a step ahead of the Earth planet's intelligence. So as an adult is responsible for a child in their care, so those who have evolved to a more expanded consciousness, whose intelligence is refined and who use it wisely, are responsible for the children in their care. And so the planet Earth and the habitants and all of the creatures upon it are under the care and responsibility of the more evolved beings in the universe.

Now in reference to the statement of a discovery of one of the lost planets *[The teacher seems to have misspoken. He may have intended to say "continents" instead of "planets."]* of your Earth planet, one of the lost areas of civilization from eons ago, it is not the first time they have come across the, what you would call, the discovery. It will not be the last. And in reference to Atlantis or in reference to the other continent, which is rising, it is true that certain evidence is being revealed, and it is true that certain scientists have already discovered it. However, it will create a great deal of controversy, but the evidence, physical evidence, will be available for the masses of Earth to share their controversy and battles over. Yes.

And will it benefit mankind, this discovery?

All discoveries are designed by the Law of Discovery to benefit mankind. Yes.

Is there any significance in the fact that one discovery is below the surface of the earth and the other above the surface? If so, what is the significance?

The significance is very clear: that which is above shall balance that which is below. And that is the evidence of that, as your comet is coming closer to your planet. Yes.

Thank you. Please discuss what is meant by the term psychic, *for there are various interpretations. For example, Edgar Cayce said that he was a psychic, and yet did not appear to have engaged in psychic phenomena in his work, but appears to have practiced mediumship. Then there are people who engage in psychic phenomena and claim they are mediums. How then is one to know the difference unless they are fortunate enough to be in this school?*

Well, one will know the difference ever in keeping with their own needs, which is denial of what they are. Mediums and psychics, we have discussed before. A psychic is not a medium; however, a medium has incorporated in with the many other experiences the talent known as psychic. Psychic is something that can be uncovered without any great, lengthy study or discipline. Mediumship and prophecy is something that may be uncovered over a period of a long time and great discipline. However, a prophet, if they are a prophet, is, through that discipline and through that great effort over a long period of time, is aware of the law of the causes of things. Psychics are able to see into a dimension that reveals many things to happen, usually related to [the] material plane, related to mental and material experiences, for they are in tune with the realm of consciousness of a mental world. And ofttimes are quite accurate in reference to their predictions. And lacking discipline—usually they lack discipline—they do not have the understanding of the causes of these various experiences for the effort has not been made to rise in consciousness to realms where the laws of cause are revealed.

Thank you.

You're welcome.

There is an old saying that when one member of a family dies, that two more family members will follow within a year. Is there any truth to this saying?

Well, it is ofttimes an expression, in many families, in the sense that three is the manifestation of fulfillment of law. The fulfillment of law is the manifestation thereof. And so in keeping with that same Law of Manifestation, unto the third generation shall the law fulfill itself. Yes, in that respect.

Thank you. When we bring our mind back to home to the peace within us, do we touch into the childlike vibration of joyous spontaneity?

Yes, if you understand joyous spontaneity is not sensual excitement, that is correct. Yes.

We are Energy, Light. And as we blend with one another, we are surrendering the levels that no longer serve us.

Yes, when we send the—when we no longer serve the levels that are not serving us well, we go home and come back again to create new levels that may serve us better and serve us well. Yes.

Thank you. How does the magnetic principle, also known as the power of believing, correlate to the cloud exercise?

Well, yes. In the power of believing and creation, you see—for example, the human mind is creating many forms moment by moment. As long as a person insists on remaining in that realm of consciousness through identification, then it, of course, is advisable that they practice constant creation of their forms, instead of just being the victim of the lack of controlling the forms that are being created in their mind. Yes.

Thank you. In perceiving vibrations, which are color and attitudes of mind, how may we neutralize the effects we feel, but are not, at times, consciously aware and alert enough to stand guardian at the portal of our own thought that we may experience the freedom and joy of our eternal soul?

Yes, one cannot experience the joy of our eternal soul, of that which we are, without making the effort to stand guardian at the portal of our thought. You see, you can't get something for nothing. So there's no way that that can be.

If we have lost 51 percent control of our being—

Yes.

—what is the best way to change our attitude or rate of vibration?

To do your cleansing breaths. To do your cleansing breathing religiously. And without the application of what has been given, it's a waste of your time and energy to even be present in the classes. Well, it's not only a waste of your time and energy, it's a waste of many others. You see, you can't go to school to learn something and turn around and not make the effort to learn it and then, even worse, not make the effort to apply some of what you have learned and expect a benefit. Yes.

Thank you.

You're welcome.

When we ask ourselves the answers to the questions we write, are we in rapport with our spirit guides and soul mate, the so-called other half of ourselves?

You are in rapport, when you ask the question and receive the answer, with the true motive and from whence it cometh.

Now I have been—it is my duty and responsibility to monitor you students in private classes on a daily basis. And I have, over these weeks, witnessed and—and also I can't—you know, one isn't everywhere at once, not in the sense of identification anyway. I have had reports from my assistants that some of you have written down questions. You've asked that question to receive an answer within your consciousness. And I've witnessed more than one of you, and so have my assistants, of tearing the question up completely and going to another time and writing another one. So, you see, there is no guarantee that when you ask a spiritual question that it's coming from a spiritual realm of consciousness because some of you students have already had those experiences [and were] not happy at all with your question after you've received your own answer. Hmm? And then there's the other ones who've put their questions down. They've pondered it and they've asked it several times and presented more questions to them—which is very good. So it's coming along very nicely. Yes.

Thank you.

But don't, please don't deceive yourself that when you think of a question to ask in spiritual class that it came from some spirit guide because there are many kinds of guides. There are all kinds of mental guides, you know, and astral guides. And there's also need guides. There's a whole army of need guides, you see. *[A clock begins to chime.]* Now we'll be patient just a moment, my friend. There now. Yes, did you wake up from your snooze? You haven't been out there, have you? There, there. *[The teacher addresses the church's dog as the clocks chime.]* Yes, I think we will all agree that our need guides are more attentive to us than any other guides that we've experienced, would you not agree?

Yes.

Yes, go right ahead, please. They seem to do the most talking. *[After a pause, as clocks continue to chime in the background, the teacher continues.]* Yes, it's all right now that—I can hear you now.

OK. Would the faculties awareness, attention, and appreciation correspond to the magnetic center? And if so, are the corresponding functions hate, fear, and sensitivity? Also, I would like to know how to continue with this study?

Awareness—it's not—in reference to continuing with the study, let's begin with awareness and attention. And let's not limit it to a water center, which is magnetic. Pardon?

Yes.

And so there are several questions there. However, I'm interested in the most important one: How should I consider—how should I continue with this, my study of these classes? All right? Now I want to go to that particular question because we have an answer through which you will grow more harmoniously and enjoy more of the goodness of life: refrain from concern over spiritual efforts in life. For concern over spiritual efforts reveals a mental form demanding to take control of what is spiritual. The Light is not designed to be the victim of limit. The Light is limitless and is not—it is designed and serves as the very essence and the sustenance. Without the Light, form does not exist. So to permit form, which—when a person is concerned, a person is concerned by an identification with mental substance where limit is the ruling principle. And so when you permit concern over that which is limitless, what you do in truth is deceive oneself. One cannot afford the luxury of concern or the imposing of limit over the Limitless. Yes.

Thank you.

You're welcome.

What center does the faculty of respect reside [in] and what are the other two faculties corresponding to it?

In the faculty of respect, kindness, and consideration, hmm, and cooperation. Well, we can take the banner of character and we can ask our self the question, "Am I a character or am I character?" Now there's a difference between the question "Am I a character?" [and] "Am I character?" There is a difference. If one believes that they are a character, they usually believe quite, quite accurately. Yes. The question must be properly directed in the consciousness. "Am I character?" "Yes, I am character."

Now comes the next question: What character? That rises up in the consciousness. Good character, poor character, weak character, strong character. And the mind goes out and starts its comparison. It looks to find support in others for what it judges is weakness in itself. Now if it does not find the weakness that it is looking for, then it creates it in its consciousness. And how does it create it? Through the Law of Temptation.

And so whenever you enter that realm of consciousness, you experience over-identification with self, self-concern, self-interest, and become, in time, self-destructive. Now I do hope that's helped with that question.

Yes. Thank you. Does disassociation correspond to separating truth from creation? And is there any distinction between them?

Yes, it certainly does, separating of truth from creation. The Law of Disassociation. It most certainly does. Yes.

Where is the plane of purification?

Oh, the plane of purification. If you wish to experience the plane of purification, then please apply the pathway to it. And when the student body begins to religiously practice their cleansing breath, their cleansing breath, then they will experience the effect of purification. And that effect is the separation of truth from creation, the harmony, the joy, the good, the peace, the abundance of living. Yes.

Thank you.

You're welcome.

It is stated that when our attention span becomes shortened, the energy moves from one level up to another, causing what is known as short-circuit in our electric body, and energy is released to our magnetic field. Does this short-circuiting occur every time we change levels or is it just when we are not making a conscious change of levels?

It only occurs when a conscious change of levels is not made. It is when levels of consciousness are [changed] and the effort is not made to guide them, that you have a grounding and a short-circuit. And I don't recall ever stating that the energy's moving up, when I find just the opposite to be true. It usually is moving down. Pardon?

Thank you.

Yes. It's nice to do a few cleansing breaths, you know. One can even do their cleansing breath while they're operating the camera, hmm? Yes, go right ahead.

When we are in a certain level, do we keep our focus only there or do we keep in view all the others while we are using that level?

Well, there are two ways. Ofttimes we keep in view all the other levels and we are tempted. And to the wise man who does not look at all the other levels at that time, then he's not tempted and able to remain on that level of consciousness as long as he consciously chooses to do so.

And is our cameraman doing a cleansing breath over there? Pardon? Yes, it's nice to do a cleansing breath. Don't you feel better with a little cleansing breath? It's nice to experience what one is, after having experienced what one is not, wouldn't you say? Pardon? I couldn't hear.

Yes. [*The cameraman responds.*]

Yes. Yes. You go right ahead with your questions, please. [*The teacher addresses the secretary, who is reading the questions that the students prepared.*]

Thank you. Shadows make judgments about themselves being threatened. Can they be educated into not making decisions as we are working on educating ourselves?

Yes. Judgments, the shadows, these forms, are children. And you must offer to them alternatives. You see, as long as you insist on living in the level of consciousness of believing you are the limit, then you have these experiences with the judgments that you have created, and the children. And so you must treat them as you would treat a child. "All right, if you insist on doing that, then you won't have any dinner. If you insist on doing that, then you won't have that." And that's how—it is the educational process, you see. It's the educating of the uneducated ego. You offer it alternatives. That's how you, that's how you train a child. And when you insist on believing that you are that little child within, then you have a great responsibility to educate that child. The only thing is, there are many children in there, doing many things. Yes, that's not only your responsibility, it's in your own best interest to have a talk with them and give them an alternative. "If you insist on doing that, then this is what you're going to have to pay as your payment." Yes.

Thank you. Logic as we know it generally has steps in its process. Is reason the same or different? And if reason has steps, may we be given them?

Reason has no steps. That which are the steps are reserved to the realm of consciousness of steps, where you stumble, and that is along the mental realms and the functions. Reason is a light. It shines on everything. There are no corners in the realms of reason. The Light shines clearly; there are no obstructions to it. And a person may choose to move from what you understand as logic to reason at any moment that they choose to do so. Now a person, when they're irrational and believe that they are these forms that they temporarily are serving, if a person takes a look and says, "Now is this in my best interest? Do I feel better? Is my day a better day from having served and believed that I'm those things?" Then make an intelligent decision. And when they do so, they say, "No, now this just isn't worth it. I'm going to do my cleansing breath. I'm going to move up from serving those forms. And I'm going to experience a beautiful day." Yes.

Thank you.

You're welcome.

If a person commits suicide who is in great agony at the end of a physically, so-called, fatal illness—

Yes?

—is there a difference in the correct or incorrectness of it compared with someone trying to just get away from living because of emotional experiences?

The payment for having over-identified with the body, the vehicle, for having over-identified with what they are not, is still a payment. Yes.

Thank you. Do each of the fingers have a different color or are they red, as is the hand?

No. No. They all have different colors.

Thank you. We are told—

Now perhaps if you understand and make some study, you'll perceive what colors are the fingers in keeping [with] what they're basically used for. Yes. You know, they all have their colors, you see. And you just understand, a little study, what they're used for, what they represent spiritually, and what you do with them mentally and then you'll have greater understanding. Yes.

Thank you.

You're welcome.

We are told the turnabout in treatment of the Earth will be manifest. Some philosophies prophesize that the Indians of America will be very instrumental in protecting the Earth. Will they be?

They already are instrumental in caring for the planet Earth. Yes.

Thank you.

They just don't receive what you call publicity.

If one finds oneself in an unhealthy relationship with another and one feels they have taken personal responsibility for the relationship, but it doesn't heal or change for the good, what can one do that will help the situation?

Well, if one feels they have an unhealthy relationship, meaningful relationship, with another person and they're not happy with the results—is this what I'm hearing?

Yes.

And they've ended the meaningful relationship?

I, I understand if it doesn't change for the good, what can they do to help the situation.

I see. Well, if it doesn't change for the good, they never ended it in their consciousness. You see, if you end a meaningful relationship or a relationship that proves not to be healthy, if you have ended it within your consciousness, then you are free from it. Don't you see that?

Yes.

You see, the relationship, the meaningful relationship hasn't ended yet. Yes.

Thank you.

Because, you see, had it ended, then there would be a healthy situation. The ending of anything is dependent on how much one believes they are the thing that motivated them. For example, if one truly believes they are the motivation, and then one is totally attached to the harvest of that effort of their motive. And it can only end in consciousness by educating that form of motivation, which is born out of the denial of what they are. Yes.

Thank you.

You're welcome.

When you speak of age in relation to returning to the Source, does that mean the age of the soul?

When I speak of age in returning to the Source?

Yes.

Well, in what respect is the question asked?

I'm not sure I understand. Would you like it repeated?

Yes, repeat the question.

When you speak of age in relation to returning to the Source, does that mean the age of the soul?

Well, I think, here, I feel a little bit of confusion over the question. We want to clear that up. When you speak of age of returning to the Source, there is not—you have soul, which is a covering of Spirit. Spirit is what you are. Light, Energy, Intelligent is what you are. Now that Light-Energy is covered with what you understand as soul, as a vehicle of expression. And from that there are the other coverings and bodies of that, of that Energy. Now Light, Energy, Truth, what you are, doesn't age. Form ages. Limit ages. And in that respect, returning to the Source reveals the aging of many forms in the evolutionary path. I do hope that's helped with that question.

Thank you.

Yes.

Is sweetness and joy soul faculties, if the motive is pure?

Sweetness and joy?

Yes.

Sweetness?

That's what they—

Sweetness implies sourness. I see. Well, I would not say that sweetness is joy. Sweetness is dependent upon an opposite. Joy is not. Now you say, well, there's joy and there's sadness. Well, if you place joy, a spiritual faculty, into the mind, then you have opposites. Yes.

Thank you.

You're welcome.

If one has not acquired The Living Light *book, can it be a detriment to one in this philosophy?*

If one has not acquired *The Living Light* book—it is the textbook of the philosophy and it might be advisable that a student, especially a private student, have one.

Thank you.

I'm sure, if they've never had the opportunity or—surely, they've had the opportunity to have one. However, see that you speak to my channel after [class]. If it is a sincere student that for some reason or other has not one, surely, we could find one somewhere. Yes.

Thank you. Would you please explain what the use of marijuana has on the mental, physical, and spiritual bodies?

Dependence.

Thank you.

You're welcome.

How do the angels of Light, here in this temple, fulfill the laws we have established as a student body and as individualized souls?

How do the angels of Light fulfill the law in reference to the student body?

Yes.

There's a school here for your physical bodies to attend. Yes. Without them, there would not be a physical school for your physical bodies to attend.

Thank you.

You're welcome.

There are nine centers of consciousness. There are forty soul faculties and forty sense functions.

Correct.

Does it not mean, then, that within each center of consciousness there are five triune soul faculties and five triune sense functions?

Are you good at math this morning?

No. [The secretary laughs as she responds to the teacher.]

Well, I see some of my students are poorer at math, and I see some are excellent at math. Now I think we should clarify that. There are nine centers of consciousness. Nine spheres of action on which there are nine planes to each sphere. That is eighty-one. Now go ahead with this question on this three times five.

It says there're nine centers of consciousness. There're forty soul faculties and forty sense functions.

That's right.

Does it not mean that within each center of consciousness there are five triune soul faculties and five—

No, it does not. However, with continued faith, which is the number of five, you will perceive the nine there are. Yes. Go ahead.

Thank you.

Pardon.

Thank you.

And I would recommend that the questioner study *The Living Light* textbook and the tapes [of previous classes], please.

Does all form contain within itself nine centers of consciousness?

Yes.

Thank you. It was said in a previous class that law was the expression of balance.

Yes.

And that it was triune.

Correct.

Made of giving, receiving, and deciding. Could you please speak on how that pertains to the Law of Attraction?

How that pertains to like attracts like?

Yes.

Which is the Law of Attraction?

Yes.

Well, how it applies is quite simple: once we identify with the law that we are, we are consciously aware of its own attraction. You see, like attracts like in order to support and sustain itself.

Thank you.

Yes.

It has been said that the eyes are the windows to the soul. And it appears that as our soul expands, our peripheral vision becomes more acute.

It does? *[Many students laugh.]* I'm so happy. Such a lovely day. You know, one can never be, one can never present themselves in any realm of consciousness without learning something. Like I see the spots on the carpet which I want you directors to be sure are cleaned before this day ends. You always learn something. Now what was that I just learned? State the question again, please.

It has been said that the eyes are the windows to the soul. And—

The eyes are the looking glass of the soul. Yes. Yes.

And it appears that as our soul expands, our peripheral vision becomes more acute.

Does that mean I can see more?

I think so.

Well, yes. No, no, no, on the serious side there, a person's a little more aware. Yes, I can see back here. Yes. And over there. And there. No, I'm trying to—let me see here, peripheral vision. Yes, yes. Well, yes, I think that the questioner means that they are becoming aware of more than they were aware. And in that respect, absolutely! Yes, one does see more.

Peripheral. Peripheral. Yes. I find that word interesting. I never had that in my dictionary. However, one should always be receptive to expansion. Peripheral. I like that. No, I do. I do. You know, without humor, then forget—the soul is lost. I like that. I like that. You get to see more. That's very important. I want to, I want to experience that for a few moments. You know, a person, no matter how much you've experienced, there's always something else that's interesting, hmm? Yes. I must tell my channel to get more peripheral. *[All the students laugh loudly.]* Now, seriously. [Student J], is that your question?

No, sir. Thank God. [The teacher and many students laugh.]

I thought you would thank God and have a nice day.

Yes, sir.

Hello?

Yes, sir.

Yes, yes, what a lovely day there. Now I want to pause on that peripheral. I—the, the, that's an interesting vibration to me. Well, [Student R], I think that you should consider being more peripheral.

Yes. [Student R laughs.]

[The teacher laughs joyfully.] A little more peripheral. A little more round. So you can roll with the punches instead of [being] so block-headed square. Yes. All right, go ahead with your question, please. *[The teacher laughs again.]* Well, you know, there's one thing about something that's round, it'll roll, you know. And there are times when a person wants to roll and not just sit, you know. And if you're a square, you're just stuck. Yes.

I don't notice any of your vehicles with square wheels. *[Many students laugh.]* They all roll. They're all round. Let's get more peripheral. Yes, go ahead.

Thank you.

And that questioner, I do know who you are, so don't you dare take it personally or I'll have [Student R] spend his whole evening [to] counsel you [on] not being so sensitive and taking everything personal, as though the world is all wrapped up with your judgments. All right? All right. Go ahead, secretary.

Thank you. We have been taught that there are nine spheres and nine planes of consciousness—

Yes.

—through which we will pass before reaching that from which we came.

Correct.

Are the planes of consciousness the centers which we are studying now? Please explain.

Well, please explain if they are the centers, the answer is yes. What is it you want me to explain? I think I've answered the question. Yes. Read that question again because it's a most interesting forming of a question.

We have been taught that there are nine spheres and nine planes of consciousness—

Correct.

—through which we will pass before reaching that from which we came.

Correct.

Are the planes of consciousness the centers which we are studying now?

Correct.

And then it said, "Please explain."

Well, what do they think I'm here for? I just did.

Thank you.

Go ahead, please. I mean, I don't take it personally, but I wanted to try to understand if "Please explain" is another question. *[Many students laugh.]* Go ahead, please.

Do we express on the spheres alternating back and forth, inward and outward, the way we do in the centers of consciousness?

Well, yes, we do. Why, certainly. Because that's where they are, is a center of consciousness. There's nine of them. Yes. Go ahead with your question.

Thank you.

In and out is absolutely correct. But ofttimes you close a door and pound to get back in. Go ahead, please.

Please explain why in creation love and hate often become one and the same.

Well, in creation, love and hate both express a denial of the truth. For example, you know, I think it's so important here, a meaningful relationship today. Because there's so much interest in meaningful relationships nowadays, it seems. Whenever a person, through over-identification with what they believe that they are—they always find something missing up there. And so they make a judgment they're only half there, you know, like a half-wit. And so they go out into creation ever to fill this vacuum, this half. They know that they're not all there, because they don't have all that they judge they should have. So the judgment is made that somebody else has got the other half. And so they search the universe of old creation to find the right one that will fit. And they find, "This one seems to fit. Therefore, they must be my other half." Well, when they go to control the other half to keep it in harmony with the half that they believe that they are, they have serious problems. And they call that meaningful relationships. Yes.

Thank you.

Offers so-called hate and so-called love. Hate and love. It's attachment, of course, to their fruits of action. I think it'd be nice if they'd call it a bundle of joy, myself. Go ahead.

We live in a youth-orientated society which demonstrates preference to younger people in the workforce. What are the spiritual ramifications if one chooses plastic surgery as long as they remember and demonstrate that they are not their body and work on separating truth from creation?

Waste of time and money unless they change their attitude and become youthful in their consciousness.

Thank you.

Now if covering—if stretching the skin—if one believes by stretching the skin and judges that makes them look nineteen again and in that judgment an attitude change is made in their consciousness, then for them, of course, it could be beneficial in that respect. However, you know, it's kind of like a student cheating. You know, you go to school in your material schools and you [are] supposed to study and to learn your lessons. And then the tests come. And if you haven't been facing your personal responsibilities, you start snitching and finding some shortcut or to pass your exam by stealing it from someone else. Well, when you look into your reflectors, your little ponds and rivers and mirrors and things, you call them, and you see that, "Oh, I don't like the looks of my face. It's a youth-orientated society, and I'm looking very old," you're looking at what you have done with your life. And so if you want to cheat and have cheating experiences, then you start covering up the form that you have created.

You see, you create your age as far as your form is. You create that through your own vibration and attitude. If you want to restore your youth, then you must make effort to restore the inspiration, the joy, [and] the incentive. All of those things you must restore in consciousness. Now when you restore them in consciousness, your form will finally show the results. Does that help with your question?

Yes. Thank you.

Everything else is a matter of covering up. The only one you're deceiving is yourself. Go right ahead.

Please expound on the principle of science versus Spiritualism, and the interworking and correlating relationship in the development of man.

Spiritualism and science is one and the same. Spiritualism is the science of understanding life. That's what Spiritualism in its true meaning is. Yes.

Thank you. Is form a gross manifestation of a transmission on a certain frequency from a particular source?

Now read that slowly. Is what?

Is form . . .

Is form.

. . . a gross manifestation . . .

A gross manifestation.

. . . of a transmission . . .

Of a transmission.

. . . on a certain frequency . . .

On a certain frequency.

. . . from a particular source?

From a particular source. Yes. There's only one particular Source, and that's correct, yes.

Thank you. Are frequencies a property of the upper center of consciousness?

Are frequencies a proper—are frequencies a, a what?

A property of the upper centers of consciousness?

If you consider lower is upper and upper is lower, yes.

Are forms a property of the lower centers of consciousness?

If you consider lower, higher and higher, lower, yes.

And—

In other words, they are properties of all the centers. Yes.

And what is the nature direction of frequencies of the universe?

What is what?

The nature direction of—
What is the nature direction?
Yes.
Or natural direction?
It says "nature," but they may have meant "natural."

I think you, as secretary, have a responsibility to preview those before class so you can get the questions in correctly here—and the wording. Now read that again.
What is the nature direction of frequencies of the universe?

What is the natural direction of frequencies of the universe? By direction do you mean horizontal—well, I see what you're referring to. They're horizontal. In reference to the question that is being asked, they are horizontal. Yes. You're speaking of form, aren't you?
I'm sorry, I don't know for sure.
Read the question again.
What is the nature direction of frequencies of the universe?

Oh, no, you're not speaking of form. That question is to be resubmitted because, you see, you can't just answer a question that has a meaning to one person and a presentation that is another meaning and—no, you resubmit that question. Go ahead, please.

Thank you. Please explain why man is seemingly able to defy, for a time, the nature pull of the frequency.

Please explain why man seems, for a time, to defy the what?
The nature pull of the frequency.
Man only believes that he is. He doesn't at all. Go ahead.

Thank you. Is it advisable to play "The Laws Be" tape during meditation, while sleeping, and during the taped breathing exercise? [Audio cassettes of spiritual affirmations of the Living Light Philosophy were available to the students. Affirmations were repeated for the length of the tape. This particular question refers to an audio cassette tape with "The Laws Be" affirmation, which can be found in the appendix.]

Oh, absolutely, as long as you can tolerate putting up with yourself after. *[Some students laugh.]* [It's] known as payment and attainment. But I would say that you should consider if you're living under a roof with anyone else, including a little dog or a cat. Yes, go ahead. You know, slow steps are sure steps. I wouldn't leap into a pond that I hadn't first tested with my toe. Go ahead.

Thank you. In its discussion of the Law of Harmony, The Living Light [textbook] states that through the faculty of faith, poise, and humility we are enabled to rise to more harmonious levels of consciousness. Would you please explain how to apply this faculty to free ourselves from a tenacious, belligerent level of consciousness?

Faith, poise, and humility? [A] belligerent level of consciousness and those who control belligerent [levels] don't even recognize faith, poise, and humility. So you first have to do your cleansing breath and get out of the thing that's in control. I mean, they do not even recognize faith, poise, and humility. You want to free yourself from belligerence? I think the question the questioner is asking [is], "How can I free myself from my nasty, belligerent attitude and the poison that I spread in my universe and everything that I touch or come in contact with?" Isn't that what—I think it's asking.

Yes.

Well, stop thinking of yourself for a change and you won't experience that belligerent cockiness, so to speak. Yes.

Thank you.

You're welcome.

When we are making continuity of effort in overcoming a belief or a pattern, and the pattern denies that any progress is being made and that our efforts are in vain—

Yes.

—what would we say to the pattern or should we ignore it?

Well, you may ignore it for a time, but those around you, I guarantee you, won't ignore it for long. Well, you do your cleansing breath and start making some effort and stop laying on your duff and start doing your responsibility. You know, you have a responsibility for living. You just don't lay on your duff and expect the world to just come and feed you, you know. I know a lot of people like to lay on their duff and be fed in bed and everything else they want in bed, while they're on their duff. But you face personal responsibility and start growing up. Now read the question again. Same question.

In its discussion of the Law of Harmony—

Yes.

—The Living Light [textbook] states that through the faculty of faith, poise, and humility, we are enabled to rise to more harmonious levels of consciousness. Would you please explain how to apply this faculty to free ourselves from a tenacious, belligerent level of consciousness?

Start growing up and making some effort.

And also, my dear students, I [would] appreciate [it] if you would not dictate how I'm to give my responsibility as a teacher. You really don't have to order me to explain. I'm more than happy to share with you. So I would appreciate your little efforts in life to refrain from ordering me to explain because I don't think that I've had any problems with any of you that you need to order me what to do.

And do have a nice week and refrain from any need for me to explain when you have, perhaps, some explaining that you might work with yourselves. And now I want to see that you have a—I took this off again [the microphone], you know. I am not perfect. I never did tell you I was perfect. But just because I never told you I was perfect doesn't mean I want you to order me to explain. That's my purpose here to share with you. And I would like to know, what my question is, [what] my students mean [by the word] *explain*. I would like to know what that word means. And before I leave you—and I only got a couple of moments left according to the situation here. I want to ask the secretary, What do you mean for me to explain?

I'm sorry, I'd have to check with the person who wrote it.

What does *explain* mean to you? Does *explain* mean—I'll tell you what *explain* means. It means to satisfy your judgment. But that isn't why I've come. So I'm not going to explain. All right?

Thank you.

Have a nice day. Thank you and good day.

NOVEMBER 3, 1985

A/V Class Private 22

Good morning, class.

We'll continue on with our studies on this philosophy of living. And now on this nice, moist, and beautiful day, we are going to begin our class with your questions. And so the secretary will kindly read the questions that have been submitted.

Thank you. Do close personal relationships, including relationships with animals, continue after transition? And if so, do the relationships continue through and beyond the nine planes and spheres into succeeding incarnations in other forms on other planets?

Well, now in speaking on that question in reference to close relationships and how long a duration are they? Do they continue throughout your present earthly experiences or do they not? In reference to that, relationship is ever dependent, as you are speaking on close relationships, dependence on denial of the wholeness that one is. Now in accepting that one is not whole and complete, one experiences a need for something outside of themselves to, what they call, fulfill themselves. And so in that respect, as long as a person is experiencing that level of consciousness, then a person experiences what they know as an attachment or a bond. And for those in those states of evolution, there is, of course, in keeping with the individualized laws of the people or the animal, they continue on with what the questioner refers to as a close relationship.

Now that does not mean if one has evolved to higher levels of consciousness that they do not experience encounters with those they have known in the past. However, the need to experience or to reexperience these close relationships no longer exists in the consciousness of a person who has accepted that they are in truth whole and complete.

Thank you. What is the purpose of this school?

The purpose of this school has been stated before. And I will state it for you once again. The sole purpose of this school is, as a school, being an instrument through which demonstrable laws of life may be revealed to those who are seeking to fulfill the true and only purpose of their journey on the planet Earth.

Thank you. What causes the soul to rise?

Well, in reference to the cause of the soul rising or falling, of the soul expressing itself fully, wholly, and completely or only partially, is ever dependent upon the vehicle through which the soul is expressing itself. For example, if one has chosen to over-identify with the covering of their soul, then their soul, in that respect, does not express itself fully, only partially, for it is subject to the censorship of the covering that, through error of ignorance, one has permitted [oneself] to over-identify with.

Thank you.

You're welcome.

You have spoken of logic and knowledge being a balance for each other. Are they faculties or functions? And is logic located in the air center?

Logic and knowledge—knowledge is a function of the human mind, and logic is a function of the human mind. Both are dependent upon the experiences one has encountered and earned in their life for they are censored by judgments that the mind has made. Though one may declare that something is logical to their mind, to another mind, it is directly the opposite or illogical. One may state their knowledge on any subject, ever dependent upon the experiences they have already identified with and believe that they are. Therefore, the censorship of knowledge and of logic is ever present. Therefore, they are functions of the mental world.

Whereas wisdom is a faculty of the eternal being, and wisdom does not require defense or justification. Knowledge requires the support and defense of past experiences. Logic requires the defense and experiences of the past. However, wisdom, as I have stated, being an expression of the soul, a faculty of the soul, does not require any defense. It stands in the Light that it is.

Thank you. How can we help ourselves be off-guard more to allow the Spirit in to work?

The question is, How can we help our self to be off-guard more?

Yes.

Well, I don't think that you will find any difficulty in being off-guard. The question is, How can one best help themselves to be on guard? For if a person is not on guard, they are not in control. Therefore, they are off-guard and out of control. Now I think the questioner is asking their question in respect to being more receptive to that which they are and less identified to that which they are not. And so it is a matter of making conscious effort. A person must make a conscious effort in order to enter a state of consciousness through which they have control over their beliefs, their judgments, and their thoughts. That requires concentration. So a person who experiences that which they truly are and, therefore, is qualified and able to communicate with the universe as it is, not dependent upon the censorship of mental substance. It requires a conscious effort to be on guard before one enters a state of consciousness to be receptive to what they truly are.

Thank you.

You're welcome.

Why did Jesus say, "You are the salt of the earth. If the salt has lost its savor, of what good is it?" That statement feels positive, but salt seems to be a part of our slavery to the prince of darkness. How can salt be positive, or can it?

There is nothing in the universe that is limit, that is form in any universe, including the Earth planet, that is not a combination of the positive and negative vibration. Therefore, no matter how negative something may appear to our mind, it contains the element of the positive. Salt, used by the lesser light, is also the Light, for the darkness is only a lesser degree of Light. There is no place, there is no form that is not sustained by the Light that is. And so how can something be [positive] that appears to be negative to our mind? Because we quickly judge or quickly enter the negative vibration of consciousness, and in so doing we do not find, unfortunately, many times in our life, we do not find the divinity in disaster.

Thank you.

You're welcome.

You have said without the prince of darkness we would have no flesh. And—

Correct. *[After a short pause, the teacher repeats his response.]* Correct.

Thank you. I understand we choose the earth incarnation to evolve. [A clock begins to chime.] *Should I pause for the clock?*

Yes? *[The teacher asks after the chiming has stopped.]*

OK. How is the prince of darkness connected with the forming of flesh?

What you understand as the prince of darkness is the ruler of the Law of Limit. Now if you find in your experiences that limit has proven to you not to be what you find intelligent, then you make a conscious choice to take control over the mind, your mind that you are responsible for, to refrain from identifying with limit. And so the ruler of limit, known as the prince of darkness, for he has control and is governor over limit, for he chose limit rather than being free to express the intelligent direction of the Light of eternal truth. In other words, the ruler over limit chose the glory of the control of limit rather than the freedom of the expression of the whole. So whenever a person chooses to identify and, therefore, believe that they are limit, they therefore are in the vibration of the governor of the Law of Limit; that is known as the prince of darkness. So whoever chooses the identification with the limit of the form that they are temporarily clothed with is in service to the Law of Limit and, therefore, has already made their choice and has accepted what the Law of Limit has to offer in their life. I do hope that that has helped with your question.

Thank you.

You're welcome.

How can one help educate a desire that has been suppressed when it does not feel that the desire has been suppressed, though indications are it has been?

Well, whenever desire is in control of anyone's mind, of course, it wants to do what it wants to do. And so if a person believes that they are the desire, then of course that is the desire that is in control of their mind. Now that's a person who is expressing an absolute identification with the thought that is in their mind, one that they alone have, by the very Law of Personal Responsibility, created.

Now a desire, a child, that is used to doing what it wants—and it is formed by the very Law of Denial—will deny and justify many things, even to the point of saying that it is suppressed or it is not fulfilled. And so we must separate truth from creation. Creation, in this respect, being the formation of a thought into a form, solidified as a judgment and belief, through over-identification, and limit. So a person in that respect should find the Law of Disassociation not only most helpful but extremely beneficial, for what you permit to entertain in mind sooner or later takes control over what you are, and you experience what you believe you are, which you are not.

Thank you.

You're welcome.

When we are making continuity of effort in overcoming a belief or a pattern and the pattern denies that any progress is being made and that our efforts are in vain, what should we say to the pattern or should we ignore it?

Well, the thing is, in reference to one's efforts in awakening that they are not the pattern or the forms they have created and the form states in their mind that they are making no progress, that is the first indicator that they are about to achieve a victory in taking control over their life. And so it is most understandable that any pattern or any form that one has, in error of ignorance, permitted themselves to once again believe that they are, that as you are gaining control over the forms you have created, that they would tell you that you are making no progress at all, for they appeal to your uneducated ego that another form rises up saying, "It's a waste of time. I've wasted all these years and all this effort. What's the use?" And you find yourself going right back to serve them. So take it as it truly is: an indicator that you are about to succeed. And the forms you have been serving know that you are about to succeed, and therefore they're only alternative, in order to stay in control, is to discourage you so you will stop making the effort.

Thank you. Will it be in our lifetime that man advances his medical technology so that he no longer needs animals for his experiments?

Yes, indeed, it will.

How do we apply the power of love in a selfless way to those beliefs, opinions, and disturbances which we are holding by the power of love?

By refraining from denial of God, which is love. You see, first you must deny the God and the good that you are, the love that you are, in order to experience this need to love another. Love does not contain within its very being what you understand as need, for love—it is not love that denies. It is the opposite of love that denies.

Thank you. Does each planet represent a sphere or are there nine spheres for every planet?

Well, there are nine planes of consciousness and nine spheres. So in that respect, each planet contains the nine planes and each planet is a sphere. Yes.

Thank you. Was transcendentalism, as associated with [Ralph Waldo] Emerson, the beginning of Spiritualism in the United States?

Well, it's your view of what Spiritualism is. If you understand Spiritualism as an organized movement limited to communication with the so-called departed, then in that respect, no. If you understand Spiritualism as an awakening to the spirituality of consciousness, in that respect, then, yes, Emerson was a great contributor. But Spiritualism, in that respect, did not even begin with Emerson.

Thank you. Is it possible to heal oneself from AIDS once it has started in one's system?

Well, in reference to healing oneself from an immune deficiency, to God, good, that which you are, all things are possible. However, unless one qualifies themselves through effort to heal themselves of lesser discords in the being, one cannot expect to be healed from greater discord in one's being. First, make the effort to free yourself from what you understand as the common cold. And after qualifying yourself with that, then move on to pneumonia, double pneumonia, tuberculosis, and I think there's so many diseases that one should first become qualified, in respect to a divine healing, before being tempted into the license of what you understand as AIDS and then expecting the God within you to bring about a cure. Yes.

Thank you.

You're welcome.

Will Halley's Comet be of any help with AIDS or the discovery of a cure since air can kill it?

Yes, it will. Yes, it will. As far as your world is concerned, in reference to taking advantage of natural, divine law, your world is experiencing what you understand as an epidemic. And so as man disregards the natural laws of nature, of the animals and the trees and the plants, you have these experiences and so-called disasters of volcanic eruptions, you have these hurricanes and tornadoes. And as man disregards the natural laws of the balance of a sound mind of a mental world and continues to disregard these laws of nature and these laws of balance, man establishes laws that he experiences what discord or disease have to offer that he may not be so tempted to deny the truth that is.

Thank you. Is AIDS in any other living thing besides humans, like the trees, plants, and insects?

Well, the immune deficiency that your world calls an immune deficiency is not something that's new. It is not—it is an effect of transgression of natural law. Now in reference to, Do the animals contact an immune deficiency? [Does] their system break down? In that respect, yes, they do. Do the trees experience an immune deficiency to disease, discord? Yes, they do. Do the blades of grass and the flowers? Well, yes, they do. For the law that applies to man applies to the cockroach as well as to the bluebird.

Thank you.

You're welcome.

What is the nature of crystal that it so accurately records what it is exposed to?

What is the nature of crystal? The nature of crystal, as far as a material object, is the best possible reflection or honest vibration to the Light that it receives. It reflects more clearly without distortion than any other form on your planet.

And what properties cause it to do this?

What properties? Well, if you can understand that minerals, plants, animals, people all have the ability to reflect the Light that they truly are, then you will understand that what you call the crystal or mineral has less need than most other forms.

Thank you. At what—

Less impurities.

Thank you.

You see, needs are impurities. And so crystal, the mineral, has less impurities than other minerals and other forms. Yes. Has less need.

Thank you. At what stage of our evolution do we begin to work spiritually to help others? Is this something we are inspired to ask to help with or is it assigned to us when we are ready? Or do we primarily have the responsibility to be the living demonstration of what we learn?

We have a personal responsibility to be the living demonstration. That is a personal responsibility. To share that with another one must ever consider the Law of Presence, known as solicitation.

Thank you. In this school what is the principle, for example, the law and principle of belief? [As the secretary reads this question, a clock begins to chime. After a pause to permit the chiming to end, she continues.] *Should I repeat that?*

Were you able to hear it in here? Yes, please do so.

Is this school what—I'm sorry. [Another clock begins to chime.] *It's another clock. In this school what is a principle, for example, the law and principle of belief?*

Kindly repeat your question.

In this school what is a principle, for example, the law and principle of belief?

"For example." In other words, you're giving me an example of the law in principle in belief or is that a question, What is the principle of belief? Or is the question, What is principle?

It seems like their first question is, What is a principle?

What is *a* principle or what is principle?

They said "a."

What is a principle? I want to answer the question not to the satisfaction of the questioner. I want to answer the question—and I have five questions contained in the one question. And so you be patient so that we may share with you what would be, in divine order, beneficial.

First of all, let us ask the question, What is man? Then let us ask the question, What is the principle, man? Well, we seem to have a problem in forming not what is man, but what is principle. So it should be indicative to you that to tempt to form principle, to say, "This is in principle. This here is in personality," we seem to have no problem when we look and we say, "This is personality. I am in principle. You are in personality." So I find with my students ofttimes that the word *principle* appears to be used as a defense mechanism of personality, limit, or form.

Now let us look at it in a little different way, perhaps. The principle and the law is no respecter of form. Therefore, we experience, in what we understand as our experiences, personal responsibility, the experiences thereof, in keeping with principle. For us to defend by limiting what principle is, is to use that which is impartial law as a defense device to support a judgment of our mind that we believe we are. Therefore, I would recommend that the students not be tempted to form that which is principle into personality in order to defend a judgment, a form, which is not principle. And I do hope that's helped all of my students.

Thank you. In the "Where am I?" part of what, who, and where am I? is it wise to begin within oneself and then proceed outward to one's actual position in the universe, as in a particular galaxy?

Yes, there is no other place to begin, except inside of oneself. For if one doesn't begin inside of oneself, one does not begin at all.

Thank you. Is the physical manifestation of ectoplasm in this dimension a primitive stage in the science of Spiritualism, like an infant first opening its eyes?

Read the first part of the question once more, please.

Is the physical manifestation of ectoplasm in this dimension a primitive stage in the science of Spiritualism?

Well, in reference to the physical manifestation of ectoplasm, there is physical manifestation at all times in respect to energy flowing through the forms, through the body. Now one is receptive to intelligent energy at all times. If one does not guide it and control it, something else does guide and control it. And so man has a great responsibility to use it wisely. If he does not, something else will use it and not so wisely. Now in reference to, Is that an early, primitive stage? In respect to the conscious use of it, in that respect, the earthlings and the Earth planet are, in that respect, extremely primitive, yes.

Thank you. I have noticed within myself, while in this school of Light, a tendency for my mind to believe that what one student gets exposed for another student seeming expressing the same level does not. Could you please help me with this belief?

Yes, that's [a] most interesting belief. It's one that has been around for a long time that I've been aware of in teaching school, as a student and as a teacher. First of all, one appears to experience that some people get exposed for doing what they consider certain things, while other people seem to, in the same classes, go scot-free. And it's most understandable. However, one must not deny the Law of Evolution. No one knows themselves so well that they in truth know another, for first one must know oneself in order to qualify themselves to know another. And therefore, people in school, in this school, some seem to get exposure over the slightest thing while others seem to get away with many different things. Those who receive the exposure are revealing, depending on the degree of exposure that they experience, that they are spiritually strong enough to face themselves, to face slipping into belief that they are limit and the things they serve which are discordant and a disease to the Law of Health and Harmony. Then there are always other students who get little or no exposure, it appears. One, however, does not understand the Law of Exposure. Students limit the Law of Exposure to what they see with their senses, to what they hear, and to their functions of their body of limit. They have yet to evolve to the exposure of the Light of eternal truth that is not so demonstrable in a physical and mental world.

And so if you want to help yourself to free yourself from believing in a judgment in your mind that some people get exposure and some people do not, if you want to help yourself, for you can only help yourself—you can never help another until you first help yourself. If you want to help yourself to be freed from that type of a judgment, then take control over the judgment that denies that you are only half there in consciousness; take control over that judgment and you will free yourself from the need to be so attentive to what others are doing and not be so attentive to what you are doing for your own evolution. And when the day comes in your life that through your attention to what you are doing has reached such a state of perfection, then you will graduate from student to teacher. I do hope that's helped with your question.

Thank you.

You're welcome.

Does the soul, after leaving the form, retain its physical characteristic of male or female?

As long as a person believes the form in which they are, then they will continue to experience that limited form, for they still are experiencing denial of what they are and, therefore, are dependent on what they are not. If a person truly believes that their life, no matter how difficult it has been, their only life that they can experience is in the form that they are presently in, then for that person they will continue on in that form until they outgrow the denial of the truth that they are and refrain from depending on what they are not. Yes.

Thank you. It is said in The Living Light *book that when creation, the number two, and faith or balance, the number five, are brought together, you have the great, so-called unseen power that moves all obstructions.*

Yes?

Is not creation belief in form? And how does that mix with faith? It seems to me that we move from belief or creation to faith and not with faith. Also, is this combination the number of seven, of understanding, the great unseen power that moves all obstructions?

Well, now we must be patient here. It's a lovely discourse there that you've read. Now we must take that step-by-step. So let's take it step-by-step in the confusion—and I can understand that—of creation (two), faith (five) and understanding it. So let's go step-by-step, word-by-word, so that we have a clear understanding. Go ahead.

It is said in The Living Light *book that when creation, the number two, and faith or balance, the number five, are brought together, you have this great, so-called unseen power—*

Stop. Now, you see, we must understand what is being stated here. So you read that once more, please. *[After a pause, the teacher continues.]* It is stated in *The Living Light . . .*

That when creation, the number two—

That when creation, the number two. Go ahead.

And faith or balance, the number five—

And faith or balance, the number five. What happens?

This says, "Are brought together, you have this great, so-called unseen power."

When they are brought together. When creation is brought into balance through the power of faith, you have what?

The great unseen power—

You have the great unseen power. Isn't that what it says?

Yes.

Pardon?

Yes.

[A clock begins to chime.] Now you pause a moment, for we now have another unseen power that's quite noticeable: the clock. *[After the chiming stops, the teacher continues.]* All right. We now understand that when balance is brought about in the

world of creation, the duality, by the power of faith, we have this great, so-called unseen power. Is that not correct?

Yes.

And is that not what happens with your experiences in these so-called close relationships, at least for a moment?

Yes.

And everyone else's?

Yes.

All right. Now let's move from that step so we eliminate this confusion on understanding. Yes.

Is not creation belief in form—

Yes. Is not creation belief in form? Certainly, creation is belief and form. It certainly is. And bondage. Now let's move to the next word or two.

And how does that mix with faith?

How does it mix with faith? It doesn't mix with faith at all. When you direct this power, this faith to creation, to bondage, and to belief, when you direct it in that direction, you have what you call a great, unseen power. I've yet to find a honeymoon couple that didn't have this so-called great, unseen power. And I think if you'll study *The Living Light* book again, I did state this so-called unseen power. I didn't say unseen power. I think you will find I stated clearly this so-called unseen power.

Now I have met many people in the universes, and when they're on their honeymoon, they seem to have this great, so-called unseen power. In fact, they often state that they could set the world on fire with no problem; that everything is beautiful, and they've risen to heaven's heights. For they have directed this power of faith to this belief and bondage of creation. Now let's take it a couple of steps farther here. Yes?

It seems to me that we move from belief or creation to faith, and not with faith.

My good friends, you move from creation either up with faith—you move up or down. I've stated before you have faith that when you turn on the switch, the light goes on. You direct the power to the mind, and that's belief. And when you don't experience [that] the light goes on when you flip the switch, then what do you have? You lose your faith. Correct?

Yes.

Well, now, go ahead here. You see, I think what the question is that the questioner is understanding that you simply stop believing and you're free in faith. You have this so-called power available to you moment by moment. Yes. Go ahead.

It says, "Also, is this combination the number of seven, of understanding, the great unseen power that moves all obstructions?"

In all your getting, get understanding. In all your giving, give wisdom. And so that which you understand, you qualify yourself to control by the very Law of Understanding the principle by which it works. Yes? *[After a pause, the teacher continues.]* Is that the, is that the total statement now?

Yes.

All right. Now it's very important here, students, that we work towards some understanding by removing the obstructions in our mind. And we have a tendency to enter these realms where there's no good in the darkness, and yet the darkness is only lesser light. And then we have this tendency to believe that, "Well, I believe this and that. Belief isn't worth anything." That's not true. Belief serves in a world of limit.

Now when you take the power that you are, that which you are, and you direct it to belief in anything, you have and you experience this so-called power. You are the power. You have directed it to the mental world. You've directed it on its return to what you truly are.

So you can look out at the day. You can entertain a belief that, "Oh, it's a beautiful day." And you can direct this great power to that form, to that judgment that your mind has made. And you are temporarily believing that you are your mind; therefore, you experience that. I do hope that's helped with your question.

Thank you. Could you please give us some guidelines how to properly ask a question of the Spirit?

Oh, I wouldn't be so tempted. I do hope I wouldn't be so tempted. For then I would have to carry you on my shoulders, and I have so much I've already earned in these eons to carry. I must rest for a moment. It has been so long since I was a magistrate. I would not like to be tempted again. *[After a pause, the teacher continues.]*

Your experiences in class are the greatest guidance you will have in inspiring yourself to understand the difference between questions and statements. You know, we all are tempted to ask questions as we defend judgments. Ofttimes we're tempted in life to ask questions in order that we may feel secure in the judgments we've already made. I think we've discussed that long ago as prejudgment or prejudice.

To be open and to be receptive to anything, it requires that one pause for a few moments and be grateful for the questions that one asks, for the experiences reveal some of the hidden things in our minds that we've not been aware of for some time. And also, it's instrumental in freeing us from the temptation of attachment to the fruits of action. You know, a person thinks ofttimes in life they are only attached to the fruits of action by doing a job and then getting upset if everyone doesn't say it's perfect. And yet we ask questions and we reveal quickly how attached we are to the fruits of our action for our question is our fruit, isn't it?

Yes.

Go ahead with your question. You wouldn't want me to judge how you are to best ask a question. I just share with you the benefit of the experiences or the return of the question. You know, an answer is only a return of a question.

Thank you. When I am listening to good music, the world seems a better place, a brighter place. In addition, I have more energy and am more aware of my surroundings. How is it that good music diminishes the mist of my judgment?

How is it that good music does that for you?

Yes.

That's the question?

Yes.

Why, you did it for yourself. First of all, you see, God or goodness enter[s] our life in keeping with the judgments that we have made in our life of how we will feel good. So a person has experiences; they judge that it is good. And when those experiences repeat themselves in similar or identical ways, as identical as possible, they once again experience what they understand as goodness. Would you not agree?

Yes.

And so if you listen to music, you see, and your mind, you say, "Now that's good music. I love this guitar music." Or this is a piano or the flute. And they're playing a song that recalls in your consciousness experiences that you judged were good. So for you, you feel good whenever that is repeated. Do you understand that?

Yes.

All right. Now you can go in—as we evolve in life on the evolutionary path, we go to the next step where we are in tune within our being with the perfect balance and harmony. And so any music—no matter what instrument plays it—that is in balance and in harmony, we experience that goodness. But that is something that takes place within our own consciousness first. Yes.

Thank you.

You're welcome.

The history of modern Spiritualism has gone through many stages. From its beginnings of spirit rappings with messages of hope and encouragement to the illumination of the laws which govern all life. Would you please share with us the future course and direction of Spiritualism?

The universality of consciousness. It has been and continues to be an instrument through which the consciousness of man is being broadened and expanded, that the barriers of prejudice and limits are being overcome. Yes.

Thank you.

You're welcome.

Why is it possible that the veil may be pierced more readily at certain times of the day than others?

Because at certain times of the day man is less receptive to the realm of consciousness that has denied the eternal Light.

Thank you. At the present time it seems evident that the laws of nature are moving to reestablish a balance in our world. On the one hand there is an increase in geological activity and the widespread expression of disease, while on the other hand, Halley's Comet, representing the light of wisdom, is approaching. Both of these avenues are used to bring about a balance. The laws of nature must express in principle. Would you please speak on how the laws are established which manifest in such seeming different methods to achieve the same end?

The law is no respecter of different forms or methods. The law just is. Now in reference to your referral to the various imbalances and discords of nature—and the pollution of your atmosphere should be included—[and] the diseases of mankind, you see, whenever an imbalance on a planet and in the universe becomes so imbalanced that it is about to go on to a course contrary to its original design, then the divine laws of the universe of balance bring about a counterbalance.

And so your Halley's Comet that has come to your planet every so many years on its regular journey—although it will not be as close in proximity physically to what it has been in past times—it is a messenger, so to speak, a messenger to your world, to your people, and to your planet that balance, the law, shall be fulfilled. And the Earth planet is no exception of that divine law. And so balance will be brought about. It is in the process of being brought about. As a continued epidemic of immune deficiency is flooding over your land, your country, and many countries of your planet, as it moment by moment increases, it will bring about changes in the mental world of the human being, which, through those changes, less denial of what they are and, therefore, less need, the effect of denial, shall be brought about. For man on your planet is already, in his thinking, being forced, in his thinking, to make changes in the ways he will deny what he is and experience need.

So that is the positive thing to look at: that when in evolution the masses will not make changes guided by the light of reason, they do experience making those same changes, forced by the Law of Survival [or] so-called circumstances beyond their control. And so the masses of your planet are beginning to think of their survival, for as they believe that they are the limit, they are concerned with the limit that they believe that they are. And this disease is attacking what they believe that they are. Therefore, they are literally being forced to find other avenues of expressing their denial of that which they are, for they are yet to evolve to the Light of truth that they are not the flesh and bone and the limits of their belief. Thank you.

Thank you. What are the steps we should take to strengthen our vital body?

In reference to strengthening the vital body—vital, meaning exactly what it is, vital—one should make great effort to have more harmonious thoughts, to see more good in themselves. And that is expressed by seeing more good in others. For we see others through the mist of how we see our self. And so if we see only the failures, so-called, the discouragements, and the depressions, then that's how we see others. If we do not trust ourselves, we cannot trust others. And so if you want to strengthen your vital body, then start on the daily effort to see the good within yourself and be not concerned if anyone else sees it or don't [doesn't] see it.

Thank you. What levels do our questions reflect when we have difficulty answering them?

When you have difficulty answering them? They reflect a censorship that's trying to protect you from the possibility of thinking about changes.

Thank you. After reviewing questions we ask of ourselves, why does the mind want to revert to past experiences instead of allowing our spirit freedom to express itself?

Because we insist on believing we are the emotional center of consciousness, where we spend so much time. We insist on believing that we are the emotional body, where we spend so much of our expression. Yes. You see, a person says, "Well, I can say I'm not an emotional person. I try to be reasonable, logical, sensible, etc." Whoever insists on believing that they experience need is identified with the emotional water center of consciousness.

Thank you.

You're welcome.

When the price tag of self-will—I'm sorry. When the price tag of self-will levels is so high, why do we continue to pay it and grow older, when in surrendering and accepting the will of God we become free?

Because, my students, we insist on believing we are the water center of consciousness.

Thank you.

We insist on believing we are the hand and foot. We insist on believing we are the limit, the form. That's the emotional center of consciousness. That's where we find security, for we spend so much time there.

Thank you.

You're welcome.

Please expand on how to be honest in one's heart to encourage ourselves.

Well, first of all, start off when you awaken in the consciousness of expressing gratitude for the good that you feel. When you first become aware in the morning, start with the Divine Law of Supply: "Thank you, God," that's the Principle of Good, "for this wonderful good feeling that I'm experiencing." Yes.

Thank you. What is natural flow of frequencies of the universe?

What is the natural flow of frequencies of the universe?

Yes.

Well, the natural flow is balance.

Thank you.

You're welcome.

Does the constant exposure to the highest quality of video films enhance one's physical sight, as well as their spiritual awareness?

Well, it certainly enhances one's physical sight.

Thank you.

Well, you know, from the question, it's not limited to spirituality, so how could I possibly fall into the trap that it enhances your spirituality when I see other kinds of video and quality, too, as far as video, on subjects that I'm no longer interested in? *[Several students laugh.]*

Thank you.

As a person, let alone a teacher.

Please speak on the origin of the phrases left-handed and right-handed and also the spiritual significance, if any.

The origin of left-handed or right-handed?

Correct.

Well, the origin of anything that is a pair, left hand or right hand, is the beginning of serving the limit. That is the creation. That's the split. When you no longer have a left eye or a right eye, you'll begin to see. *[A few students laugh.]* Same with the hand.

Is total saturation of any frequency possible on earth?

Well, total saturation, yes, I look and see total saturation of varying frequencies. They may not be in harmony with what I'm interested in. But, yes, I've seen many people temporarily totally saturated, yes. It's known as an auric pollution.

Thank you.

Yes, we can become—as sure as the mind can drown the limited form, man can saturate himself with anything. In fact, the truth is revealed that man saturates himself with a lot of things because there are varying times he's absolutely convinced himself that he is a certain saturation of a certain frequency. That shows a true saturation, yes. However, it doesn't last, you note. We can only be infatuated for a time. Infatuation reveals a total saturation of a frequency. Did that help with your question?

Yes. Thank you.

Yes. Why, a person's even willing to cut off their right arm when they're totally saturated. Pardon?

Yes.

Or their left foot. But I've never once heard anyone willing to cut off their neck. *[A few students laugh.]* The hands? Yes. The foot? Yes. Even the ankle, they'll cut off, but not their neck. I always find that interesting. My students are never willing to cut off their neck. I don't know why. *[After a short pause, the teacher continues.]* I do, but I won't say. *[More students laugh.]* Go ahead with your questions.

Is it truth to state that there is no such thing as an original thought or ideal that is conceived or perceived on earth?

Why, it's absolutely correct. Yes. We're not the beginning; that's why we're not going to be the end. Yes. But we are, however, excellent copiers. We copy many things and, hopefully, are receptive to do a good job in our copying.

Thank you. It was stated that belief is something we first judge we can control.

The what we can control? The fig leaf is—What did you say about the leaf? *[Many students laugh.]*

It was stated that belief—

Oh! I'm terribly sorry I thought you said fig leaf. All right, go ahead. It was stated that belief—I was wondering what you got to fig leaf on such a cool day. *[Many students and the teacher laugh.]* Yes? It was stated that belief . . .

Yes.

Please speak right into the microphone.

It was stated that belief is something we first judge we can control and faith is something that we know we cannot achieve. Is—

Faith is something we can't achieve?!

That's what it says.

I was right when I thought I heard you say fig leaf! *[Many students laugh again.]* Go ahead. Now someone is teaching me something new that faith is something—oh, I see. Faith is something, well, faith is something that you are! Yes. Correct. All right, in that—yes, all right, go ahead, please. My!

And that was their final statement. Is that because we already are faith?

That's—yes. Was that a question or a statement?

It has a question mark after it, but . . .

Go ahead with the next question, please. *[The teacher laughs joyously.]* Yes, please go ahead with the questions and the statements.

Do our physical bodies emanate more or less light depending upon our attitudes of mind?

Well, yes, depending on our attitude of mind, sometimes it's most difficult to see a person, there's so little light. In fact, they absorb the light that the poor little camera and the lens is supposed to be receiving. Yes.

Thank you.

You're welcome.

I finally realized—

They're known as—excuse me. They're known as sponges. Sponges, they call them. Yes. They're found at the bottom of some of the oceans. Go ahead, please.

Thank you.

They drown themselves. It's called saturation. Yes, go ahead with your question, please.

I finally realized that want is a form. Is the form of want separate for each desire or is it general and all-consuming?

Well, is the form of want separate for each desire? It's general and all-consuming. And any desire can call it up. It's just waiting to do its number. Yes, it is all-consuming. However, you choose the desire. Now some people may choose an ice-cream cone, and some others may choose a fig leaf. In that respect, the choices are separate, but the same principle of want is all-consuming. It's just waiting to serve. Yes.

Thank you.

You're welcome.

You have asked us to keep our minds free, free like the wind, to be free in thought. You have also asked us to think and think more deeply.

Yes.

What is a thought that is free?

One that has wings. *[Many students laugh, and then the teacher continues.]* I do hope that's helped with the question.

Yes. Thank you. Is the solar plexus located in the stomach area of our body?

Well, if you call this area up here the stomach, yes, that's—can you see me out there? *[The teacher points to an area of his chest just below his xiphisternum.]*

Yes. [The secretary and several students who are seated in an adjacent room respond.]

That's my solar plexus. I don't feel that my channel is abnormal. It's in the [same] general location on everyone. But I wouldn't consider that way up there the stomach. Some people, however, consider that, I guess they consider it the pit of the stomach. Ah, yes, go ahead with your question.

If so, would the four functions be located below the solar plexus and the five faculties located above the solar plexus?

Do you mean earth, fire, and water?

I think that's what they mean.

Well, yes, the solar plexus is right here. See, there's earth. And then you know where fire is located. And water, the stomach. So fire, you see, has to be located below the stomach and above the feet. *[A few students laugh.]* So you have earth, fire, water, and then air. Yes, that's correct. Air is above the stomach, you see, the lung area. Hmm?

Thank you.

Was that the question?

Yes.

So there aren't four centers below the stomach. There's only two below the stomach. *[After a short pause, the teacher continues.]* Hello?

Yes.

You understand?

Yes.

Oh, good. Thank you.

What is happening when there is a disturbance in the solar plexus?

What is happening?

Yes.

There's a problem between the earth, fire, and water centers. They're not harmonious. Probably the fire center is overheated. *[Some students laugh.]* Usually. Not always. Usually it's the fire center's overheated and there's a lot of steam. There's a disturbance in the solar plexus. Yes.

Thank you.

You're welcome.

How does a person learn to talk a lot without saying anything?

By being aware of what they're saying before they say it. *[Some students laugh again.]* If you wish to talk a lot and not say anything, then make sure that you know what you're saying before you say it. You see, you have—you form the thought, then you open the mouth after. Don't open the mouth as the thought is being formed. You do understand that, don't you?

Yes.

You see. Like you say, "It's a lovely day." I said that to myself first to hear how it sounds in my consciousness. Do you understand?

Yes.

Well, yes, yes. That's how a person talks a lot and says only what they want to say.

Thank you.

You're welcome.

During our class after the chandelier fell, Mr. Goodwin asked each of us students what was the last scene we remembered from the movie.

Correct.

What does this tell us about ourselves and what can we learn from this?

What does it tell you that you don't already know? Well, you should already know that belief is what you direct identification to. The bondage of belief. When you look at something with your eyes and you hear something with your ears and you sense something with your senses, do you believe it? If the judgments want to believe it, they believe it. That's bondage. Yes.

Thank you. When we become familiar with something or someone, how can we avoid becoming dependent or finding security upon the forms we have created with what is familiar?

One, in becoming familiar with anything, becomes dependent upon it because one believes that they are it. Now you want to be free from the dependence of the Law of Familiarity?

Yes.

Move from the water center to the light of reason.

Thank you.

You're welcome.

When we do the Living Light exercise in reference to the Law of Identity—

Yes.

—of coming in rapport with a person, place, or circumstance that we find intolerable, is this a method of understanding a thing and being granted the opportunity of forgiving it?

Within ourselves, yes. Yes, I find the questions most interesting. Don't you find the questions enlightening?

Yes.

Yes.

[After a pause, the secretary continues.] *Shall I go on?*

Yes, can you see me there?

Yes.

Good.

As the mouth represents truth, the lips, aspiration; and the teeth, determination, do the gums represent decisiveness or resolution?

Well, depends on what you mean by the word *resolution*. If you mean you're resolved to what your determination has done, then yes.

Thank you.

Most gums are resolved to what their teeth have done, aren't they?

Yes.

Well, aren't they the little bits of sod that hold the trees [by] the root?

Yes.

Of the little teeth? If you don't take care of your teeth, what do your gums do? Do they resolve themselves?

Yes.

Pardon?

Yes.

All right.

Thank you.

I answer your questions in ways that you may understand.

Is it of greater spiritual benefit to do physical work or mental work?

You can't do physical without mental first. You see, if you, you know—that's such a strange understanding here. Read the question again.

Is it of greater spiritual benefit to do physical work or mental work?

Is that a physical or a mental worker asking the question?

I think it's a physical worker.

I see. It's a nice temptation, yes, indeed, indeed. Well, no, I want to answer the question. You must first—in order to move a physical body, you must first move a mental body. And so for me to say that there's more spiritual value with a mental worker than there is with a physical worker is ridiculous because there's first a mental worker to be a physical worker. Do you understand that?

Yes.

So the value is in the worker. Now if the worker is directing all of the work in a mental world in a mental body, they get just as tired as if they only directed part of it to a mental world and the other part to a physical. Yes. Work is work.

Thank you.

Of course, it's dependent on the motivation, you know. And who's to judge if it's spiritual. Hmm?

How do we know when a law is fulfilled?

Experience. Experience. When a, when the experience ends, the law is fulfilled. Say, for example, you know, the class started off with—what was it? Meaningful relationships today?

Yes.

Yes. Meaningful relationships. Well, now a person knows when the law is fulfilled when the meaningful relationship is no longer meaningful and they forgot it. Pardon?

Thank you.

Then they can say, "Oh, isn't that nice. The law is fulfilled. I can't remember what that experience was because the law is so fulfilled." *[The teacher and many students laugh.]* Yes, I know. Thank you. *[The teacher acknowledges the cameraman's signal.]* Go right ahead.

What—

Time passes quickly, you know. An hour and a half has already gone by in your world.

What does the—

One and a half minutes in mine. Yes?

What does the saying from the Bible mean? Those who wait upon the Lord will soar on wings like eagles.

Oh, that's beautiful! The lord is the law! And those who wait upon the law, their thoughts shall fly like wings of angels: free. Didn't we just discuss—give those thoughts wings? Wasn't that our discussion, [Student R]?

Yes. [Student R responds.]

Yes. You have time for one more question in your world.

If we superimposed our circular chart of the centers upon the Earth planet—

Yes?

—would the intersection of all but the earth-odic centers below the equator be in Africa? And above the equator in Alaska?

Well, if you superimposed them in that respect, I would suggest you stay in Alaska. Thank you. And have a very good day and a nice—Oops, mustn't forget this. *[The teacher refers to his microphone.]* And a nice week, too. Thank you. Good day.

NOVEMBER 10, 1985

A/V Class Private 23

Good morning, class.

And another beautiful day here for our little class. And today, in our discussion, [we will] continue on with whatever in life we have earned responsibility for and do not take that responsibility or control, there is always someone waiting to do it for us.

Now we seem to have a little technical problem here. So we'll be patient a few moments. *[After a pause, the teacher continues.]* I think, perhaps, something didn't get connected. Is something connected now?

Something is definitely connected now. [The cameraman responds.]

Yes. Is everything all right?

Yes.

Well, good morning, class.

Now what we have in life earned responsibility for and we do not take charge of that responsibility we have earned, we soon find there's always someone waiting to take control of it.

And so it is that my channel was advised to watch a certain newscast in your world. And I'm going to share that with you, for it is only one of the many indicators of the advanced technology that is taking place in your world. And those advanced technologies are revealing the rise and the fall of the civilizations on the planet Earth.

Many, many, many centuries ago the continents which are now under the, 'neath your oceans of your world as you know it today, rose in great advanced technology. And when they rise so high with the refinement of the mental world, the mental world is always tempted to improve on anything that comes within its sphere of action. And so it is that in times long past on your planet, civilization[s] rose and became extremely refined and advanced in a mental world. And once again the pattern is repeating itself, for the lessons to be learned that we do not learn, by the law, return unto us.

And so today in your world you are at a point of advanced technology whereas the masses of human beings of your world can be controlled by electromagnetic frequencies from technological equipment already developed, already tested, and already proven to be 85 percent accurate in the sense of controlling the minds of 85 percent of the human beings. The government of your particular country has this technology and has been testing it for several years. You are only [now becoming aware], as of, in your world, this past week—and you will hear more of it—of [the] electromagnetic equipment that has been developed that can be broadcast into the atmosphere and program your minds [to do] what whoever the operator of the equipment is wants you to do at any given moment.

You have also noted in the past two years, you have also noted that there is much disturbance with what you call nature or the nature spirits. There are volcanic eruptions. Thousands of people dying. There are earthquakes, hurricanes, tornadoes, cyclones. All of these disturbances shall increase. They shall increase as the mental world, limited in its understanding, lacking consideration for the whole—for the mental world believes it is the whole. And so more of these seeming disasters of nature shall take place. They are forewarnings to civilization to make changes in the course they are on or face what civilizations before your present one have faced many times, known as self-annihilation.

Now from this discussion I do not wish you to understand that, in any way, we are against the advancement of technology. It isn't a matter of being for or against technology. It is a matter of understanding and applying the responsibility that a person has when they direct intelligent energy to the mental world and refine the vibrations and frequencies of a mental world to such a degree and such an extent that they believe beyond [a] shadow of [a] doubt that they are that refined, mental world, for whatever we set into motion always returns to us, and we have this responsibility. We can do much with our self. And by doing much with our self, we in truth become instruments for much to be done in the world.

Now a person who makes the effort to free themselves from those realms is not concerned; nor need one should be concerned. Having freed themselves from those realms, concern does not exist. And so a person having freed themselves from those realms, even for a few moments, in those moments is an instrument for more good to be done than any thought of good they could ever entertain in their mind.

And so now we'll go to the questions that have been submitted. And let us not forget: whoever sees good in all things, including advancing technology, can only experience the joy of living. For the joy of living is subject to and dependent upon seeing good in all things. Yes, now if you'll go ahead with the questions, please.

Thank you. In relating the creative principle, love, to the centers in our universe, would love correspond to the air and belief to the ethereal centers and desire to the fire and will between the electric and air centers?

Well, now in speaking on that question and the creative principle, let us understand that fire, as you have stated, corresponds to the desire, for desire is the divine expression, and fire is a manifestation of the Light. Now the other statement that you have there, the question on the centers: [does] love correspond to the air center? That is what you've stated.

Yes, that is correct.

Well, now, divine love, divine love is the air center. Divine love. So if you're speaking of divine love, that is correct. Now the other question there?

Belief to the ethereal center?

Well—belief to the ethereal center? Now I think you're going to find, if you will study a little bit further, that the ethereal is not a binding or a bondage center, and you will find that belief is more closely related to the water center. Now, will, the lord of the universe?

Yes, was between the electric and air.

Yes. Yes, for without will, there is no reason. You can't reach that faculty. That is correct.

Thank you.

You're welcome.

Would the circles move in opposite directions as they connect to form the figure eight, the sign of infinity?

Ahh, that is a question of advanced students. And yes, they would.

Thank you. It is stated [in Discourse 24], "To the power that is, all things are possible to those who believe."

Correct.

Do we become the belief and then let faith move it?

Yes, we have become the belief through identification. Now after becoming the belief, we can move in one of two directions. After becoming the belief—belief in that respect, as stated in that teaching, the teaching that question is taken from, belief in that respect is a whole and complete acceptance in the consciousness. Once that has taken place, then one must let go. And it's that letting go where faith, the power, moves it. Yes.

Thank you. How would a person serve the Light while working at their jobs or job in daily life in the jungle?

By putting the form of good in it. You see, first of all, you, in order to do that work in a mental world, you must identify with mental substance within the self. Now in—our little friend is going up those stairs, and we'll pause just a moment. And you might want to go right up there and let him out for a few moments. *[The teacher addresses the cameraman and the friend referred to is Reddy, the church's dog. In this class the cameraman read the questions, not the secretary.]*

All right. [The cameraman attends to Reddy and is unable to read the submitted questions until his return.]

Yes. Now I'll just keep right on talking here. I have to consider everything, students, you know. Well, it certainly is a beautiful day. Can you hear me out there all right? If you can, speak up, but if you can't don't say anything.

Yes. [Several students answer. All students are seated in an adjacent room.]

Well, then I think that you can hear me. Now you—isn't this an interesting time for us to have a break for you to take care of your necessities that weren't taken care of? *[The teacher addresses Reddy.]* Now why don't you take him right out front there and I'll continue on with the class. You just walk right out that front door there. *[The teacher now addresses the cameraman.]*

Reddy.

Yes, you go right ahead. No, no, no, no, no. My friend.

This way.

Yes, go ahead. No, no, no, no, no, that's not the way. That's not the way. You go right out and open the door. There. You see? It's amazing how much more you can get from a person with a little understanding than force. You go right outside there. I'll continue on with this class here.

Now we were speaking on belief, and that is so important. You do still see me out there, don't you? And hear me?

Yes. [Many students again respond.]

Oh, that's fine. You see, we demonstrate this creative principle, of course, moment by moment. We believe that we need something. We then believe that we find it. And then we believe that without it we cannot exist. So what we are doing, ofttimes in limited and, unfortunately, negative ways, what we are doing is demonstrating, of course, the creative principle. And we have released this in the total belief that it is us, and we can't live without it. And we move this great power of faith and ofttimes suffer in such needless and ridiculous ways.

It's like a person who, who believes that, you know, they're, like, they're living with someone or in love with someone and everything is negative, negative, negative. And they just cannot continue to live that way. Well, they are seeing themselves in another (the person they're living with), and they don't like it at all. Well, nothing changes until they change themselves, but once they've changed their thinking and their attitude, especially their attitude, then they will find negativity cannot exist in a person who is making great effort to be positive and to enjoy living. So if you find yourself with negative people around you [and] you find yourself in those seeming circumstances and conditions, declare the truth in your consciousness: "I am whole, complete, and perfect. I am a positive person. I am a happy person. And that that is around me that, in errors of ignorance, emanates negativity will not long endure in my vibration." And then we just move right along in life.

Now did my student [Reddy] get a chance to go to, ah, take care—

He got the chance, but he didn't take much advantage of it.

Why didn't he?

I'm not sure.

Well, all right. Go ahead with the questions, please.

Thank you. At the end of the day I sometimes feel pressure on the top of my head, and sometimes during the day. What would this be from?

Well, the pressure could be from many things. First of all, one should ask themselves the question, "I sense pressure on the top of my head. Why this and why now? What am I thinking about? Where am I? What have I exposed myself to? Is this a pattern that is repeating itself? Does it happen every day? How many times a day? And where am I in consciousness?"

So we should consider all of those factors first. And we should make the effort to understand ourselves. And after we have done that, I'm sure that we're going to find that answer that why we are feeling pressure at certain times of the day. And we'll begin to relate to the experiences that we are having in consciousness that we have not related to consciously. And we'll gain understanding and we'll be amazed about the pressure: how quickly it'll disappear once the Light shines upon it. Yes.

Thank you. Is it true that one can actually travel in a dream state to other real dimensions?

Well, now in reference to that, "Dreamer, dream a life of beauty before your dream starts dreaming you." And your days and nights are called nightmares. Now reality—tell me, what is reality? Are you reality? That's the question you must ask. Is your foot reality? Is the room that you are viewing, is that reality? What you see and what you hear, are they reality or are they subject to and dependent upon your judgments? That's the question we must ask.

Of course, many people travel to *real* dimensions. The thing is that usually when they sleep, ofttimes that's where they are, in *real* dimensions. It's when they think they are awake that they're having their dreams and their nightmares. So let us understand what we mean by reality. You talk to a person and if what you have to say, they do not have a judgment well-established in consciousness for reference, they will quickly tell you, "Well, that's not real. That's not reality." So reality is a very limited thing, to say the least, for what is real to one is not real to another for they have different experiences, they have different judgments, and they believe they are mental substance. And in keeping with their belief and identification with their mind, reality is, indeed, extremely varied.

Now if you mean what is and what is not, well, what is, is *you*. You are what is. You are Light. You are the Power. And you are formless and you are free. When I state that to anyone that they are in truth intelligent Energy, known as Light, Life, Love and that everything else is subject to belief, judgment, formation, and limit, that is not reality to them. So, you see, our realities—to people who truly believe that they are the limit and the form in which they are, that is their reality. That is not reality. What I state is reality: formless, free Spirit. But as long as you insist on believing you are the opposite of reality, then, of course, that is, temporarily, your reality.

Thank you. Do we have a natural sound or note within us that's particular to an individual?

Well, of course, indeed, we do. We are a natural sound. We are a natural frequency and a natural note. If you want to come into balance—because you are balance; that's what you are. You are the perfect balance and truth in consciousness. And if you want to come close to that, then you take the sound with which you are familiar, such as your keyboard, and you sound middle C. And because that is the balance—that is the balance of those sounds. And that's the closest, at this stage of evolution in these private classes, that you should be concerning yourself with, is the balance of the frequency. Yes.

Thank you. Are nature spirits intelligent, reasoning beings?

They are extremely intelligent. And by reasonable, if you mean express total consideration, indeed, they do. And—reasonable in the sense that they are true to the purpose of their original design. Yes, indeed, most intelligent, most reasonable.

Thank you. Why does anxiety enter into the mind? Is it the mind drifting into shadows?

The mind drifts into unfulfilled desires, which you may call shadows—indeed, they are many shadows—and expresses what is known as anxiousness, anxiety. They can't wait (the forms) to get, to get themselves filled. Yes.

Thank you. Are those of us from the Allsoul, who chose human form to express through, part of a particular tribe of beings?

Well, I know that a lot of people would like to call the human beings tribes or tribal. However, it isn't a matter of choice. It's a matter that along the evolution of the species, you have evolved and earned expressing, from the Light, in the particular forms that you are. Of course, each step along the way a choice is being made. But one does not stand there in the Light, as the Light, and say, "Well, let's see, I choose to be an ant this time around. Or I choose to be a human being." It works in keeping with the laws of evolution and what man does individually with the evolution that he has earned in keeping with the divine law.

Thank you. Why do our judgments sleep when our senses are satisfied?

You've fed the form. You see, try to understand when you feed the form, then the form gives you a little break for a time, a short time anyway. And then when it decides it's hungry again, it rises up. And if you insist on identifying with limit, with yourself, then they have greater control in the sense that you really believe that that is you. And, of course, without this *prana* and life energy, intelligent energy directed to them, then they cannot survive. They are dependent upon your life force, upon your vitality. And they siphon that off by your attention. Whenever you put your attention to yourself, they're all waiting there and they get fed. And then you walk around life and you don't experience the joy of living; everything seems negative. You see everything wrong outside and nothing wrong inside; and that's how they get fed. Instead of having a good attitude, which would place you into balance and into the laws of harmony and health and wealth and abundant good.

I can always tell when the forms are in control because a person believes they are the negativity that they express. And if you look out and see what a beautiful day it is, they have to find something wrong with it. By so doing, energy is directed by the person, through that type of negative thinking, to the forms of their judgments. And they thrive and siphon the vitality of others by an expression of their own negativity.

It has been my experiences, along life's paths, that a person who is, what you would call in your world, a sponge, in that respect, if you locked them in a room by themselves, you ignore them, in other words, you do not give them any vitality through giving them any attention, they very soon move from feeding their judgment forms, which is an expression of negativity, to smiling like an angel. I didn't say an angel, but like an angel. Go ahead, please.

Thank you.

For a time. Yes.

Thank you. In recent classes there seems to have been very similar questions on a number of topics written by different students. What does this reveal about the student's level of consciousness?

Could reveal many things about the student's level of consciousness. It could reveal that they are very attentive to the vibrations and the frequencies of the Light, and they are gaining in that respect a rapport, not by conscious choice, but, however, by attention to the teachings that they are receiving. And their energy is being directed in that way, and there is a similarity of the type of questions being asked. Yes.

Thank you.

It could be something else, but see the good in all things. Experience the joy of living. Yes.

Thank you. At the end of the rhythmic cleansing breath exercise, when I hold my breath without air in my lungs, I experience what seems to be an increase in vibration. At first it seemed natural, though now it feels positive. Although a fear rises as this increase occurs, it quickly passes. Would you please share with us what is occurring both with the fear and the change in vibration?

Well, first of all, that which is positive is that which is natural. That takes care of that question. Now as a person places more attention upon what's happening inside of them, they are tempted to gain control over any new experience within the consciousness. And how one gains control over a new experience in the consciousness from the animal levels of evolution is to experience fear, directing the power to the totality of mental substance or self-interest in that respect. That's not an intelligent way of cultivating a new experience in the consciousness. The intelligent way is to demonstrate in consciousness the Law of Gratitude, which would increase the supply of the experience and direct the faith, the power within, to which the experience is dependent for its own continuity, to the Principle of Good or to God. Yes.

Thank you. In an earlier class reference was made to clusters of great painters, musicians, singers, and scientists who appeared every 150 years, approximately. The number in this cluster was six, the number of divine love. Would you please share more of the laws governing this manifestation and does this hold true for spiritual teachers as well?

Yes, it does. You see, so often a person does not understand that a great composer of music is a spiritual teacher. He's just using a different language. Language that many are receptive to and that some are not receptive to. So the cycle, the 150-year cycle of great composers and great artists, they are spiritual bearers of the Light. In order to be a spiritual bearer of the Light, it doesn't mean that you have to go around speaking about your worship of God or etc. A person expresses their soul through a direction and control of the mind, an acceptance that they are the receiver of the inspiration and responsible for letting it flow unobstructed.

Thank you. When I doze off, that is, when I do not consciously choose to sleep, I sometimes hear the demanding voices of my own forms.

Yes.

Why is it necessary that my eyes be closed before I hear them and what is the relationship between our eyes and our ears?

Well, first of all, you're not in control. You see, you are responsible to control when you sleep and when you wake. However, as the questioner has stated, they are not in control. They go to sleep without a conscious choice of going to sleep, and they hear their forms. Their forms are in control. And those particular forms don't want you to hear or to see with your eyes open. That's their judgment, and they don't allow you. It only reveals that they are in control and you are not. You are out to lunch or dinner or supper or a whole weekend feast in that respect. And so if you do not make the conscious choice to close your eyes and to, what you say, go to sleep, something else makes it for you. And when something else makes it for you, then that something else controls you. And if you do not care about your form and your responsibility, they're going to do whatever they want to do with you. So that is a matter of conscious choice and a matter of facing personal responsibility.

What you—what, as I stated in the beginning of the class today, what by divine law you have earned responsibility for and do not take control of, someone is always waiting to do it for you. And so that—I'm very happy and grateful for that question. That is a fine demonstration of something taking control of what we are responsible for because we did not take care of our responsibilities. Yes.

Thank you.

You're welcome.

Since Earth is the fifth planet, known as faith, what are the names of the prior planets and the lessons that were learned on those planets?

Well, first of all, that student, I understand, has not yet had the destiny diagrams and does not understand the nine planets and the sun and the moon. And so what we will do in the future, in the near future, perhaps after the turn of your year, I will instruct my channel to bring to you some of the diagrams in that respect so you can have a little more understanding of the lessons that came before the earth experience and the ones that are yet to be. Go ahead, please.

Thank you. At what stage of man's evolution was reason introduced?

At what stage of man's evolution?

Yes.

Well, the question is implying that reason was introduced as a part of man's evolution from something. Well, now, I'm sure that the questioner is speaking about the form. The question also implies that other species, or appears to imply that other species do not have reason. That is quite untrue. Quite untrue.

When we study other species and we study other forms, we very quickly see that they express the faculty of reason. The tree uses reason in keeping with its cycles of its trees—of its leaves and of its growth. The flower uses reason. The tiger, the elephant, the dog, the cat, the mouse, the eagle, the birds, the blue jays, they use reason. However, to our minds it is such a primitive state of the faculty of reason that few of us ever recognize how reasonable the other species are. The animals do not kill for the thrill of killing. The animals and their predators, of course, [kill] for their survival. And if we will make effort to study nature and to study the other species, we will, indeed, be impressed with their expression of the faculty of reason.

Thank you. You have taught that the only thing worth working for is the soul. How can one tell whether we are working for the soul?

From the absence of the question. The absence of the question, my good students. You see, the moment the concern and the interest of mental substance enters, you can be rest assured the work is not for the soul. The work is now for mental substance which is interested in how much energy and time and etc. is going to the soul when they're not sure a soul's there. So, you see, when the question no longer rises in the consciousness, you may be rest assured God's work, that which you are, is being done. Yes.

Thank you.

You're welcome.

Why is there a lull before a storm or, as this philosophy states: When all seems well, beware. Disaster is about to strike?

Satisfaction. Satisfaction. Man always becomes satisfied with how good he's doing only to see in the next blinking of the eye the divinity of disaster. You see, we have a tendency to be tempted to puff our self up. It's the, what I spoke to you long ago about puffivation, you see. We don't have to worry about someone else doing the job for us. We spend much time doing it for our self. We get puffed up, you see, [thinking] how good we were able to get this done or how we got that done or etc. And so I have taught you over the years beware when all seems well because you're off-guard at that time in that respect. You are not preparing yourself, you see, and you're not directing the attention to the Source that works things out in balance and in harmony in your life. And so the great storm comes as it never comes before, you see. We become satisfied with ourselves. And when we become satisfied with ourselves, we no longer make any effort, and we're not alert and awake and aware. And whoever isn't aware, awake, and alert is destined to experience the surprises of what you call creation. Yes.

Thank you.

You're welcome.

Does each generation of man have a predominate lesson to learn that differs from the lessons of other generations? If so, what is the predominate lesson of people, say, in the generation of up to twenty-five years of age, their parent's generation, and their grandparent's generation?

All generations have one thing to learn. They learn it in different ways and different manifestations. You're on a planet Earth, the planet of faith. You all have the responsibility to learn the Law of Personal Responsibility. You all have that lesson in common. Every generation and every age has that lesson. You are responsible for everything that takes place in your life for you are the creators of everything that takes place in your life. Yes.

Thank you. Are earthquakes the effect of man's collective imbalance in the earth center; volcanic eruptions, imbalance in the fire center; floods, the water center; and hurricanes, the air center? If so, is 51 percent of the population out of balance?

That is correct. They *are* 51 percent out of balance. And the correlation is absolutely correct. And I am happy to see that my students are making some effort to perceive.

Thank you.

You're welcome.

Will man ever evolve to the stage of working collectively on balance of the centers for the good of the whole?

Yes, the time will come, [in] eons yet to be, when man will know; through an acceptance of personal responsibility, man will awaken to the whole and completeness that he is. He will not experience denial and, there[fore], will not have the effect of needs. Yes.

Thank you.

You're welcome.

It has been stated that, "The climb is never higher than the fall," [which is a saying from The Serenity Game]. Would the fall be prevented as long as man kept his attention on what he is— correction—what it is he wanted to become?

Well, the moment man accepts what he is, then he doesn't experience the fall. However, when man accepts what he is, he doesn't experience the climb. So, you see, when man no longer insists on believing he is limit, then he won't have the highs and he won't have the lows, for there are no highs and lows to whoever is in balance for that is the Law of Nature. Yes.

Thank you. When indecision leads to confusion, are we then placed on the wheel of delusion because the many forms we have created are blocking the Light of truth?

Yes, indeed, they're blocking the Light of truth. They're blocking—we have permitted them to take control through our lack of effort to make a decision. And so from the lack of making a decision, indecision rises up. They all come in with their judgments for us to follow their particular judgments. Because they are so varied, the judgments in our mind, we experience what is known as a state of confusion. And that is absolutely correct.

Thank you. If a person [who] has a longtime pattern of being a people-pleaser, where—correction—were to declare the truth that the pattern is not him, what would be the next step to apply in order to free himself from the need to please others?

Well, first of all, a person cannot experience the need to please others until a person has first denied responsibility for their life. You see, a person who experiences a need to please others is a person who has not accepted responsibility for their life. A person in that state of consciousness has given others control over them. Therefore, they are constantly in need of pleasing those people whom they have given control over their life. I would suggest that the student spend time each day, frequently, thanking God for the wonderful, good life that they have; that they are whole, complete, and perfect. That which is, [which] they truly are, formless and free; therefore, being formless, free, whole, complete, and perfect, they do not experience need and, therefore, not experiencing need, are not dependent on what somebody else may smile or frown at them. Yes.

Thank you. Do plants and trees have an awareness of the amount of soil and room in which they have to grow? If so, does this awareness govern their size and rate of growth?

It most certainly does. They're very intelligent and they have reason. Most intelligent. They take a look in their, with their sensing and they say, "Well now, there's not much room here for me to grow." And some of them are more aggressive than others. Some of them will take their little roots and just spin them around in a circle at the bottom of a pot and others will just take their roots and go right straight through a crack and right down in to get to more soil. They have their own personalities in that respect. Just like people. Some are reticent and depending on pleasing others. While others are most aggressive and are like steamrollers, rolling over everyone. Yes.

Thank you. Would you please clarify: when we face east, do we receive from the north and give to the south?

Yes. That's a perceptive student. Face east.

Thank you. What do the north and south represent?

If you wish to preserve something that is worthwhile, tell me something, do you put it in an oven and bake it or do you freeze it? That's a question for you, cameraman.

Freeze it.

Fine.

Thank you. What is the recommended temperature of a room for sleeping?

For sleeping? Well— *[The teacher laughs.]* I smiled because I look out at my students with so many different thoughts the moment the question began to be asked. But that's not important. I'm not governed by their judgments. I would be if I were governed by my own, be it in divine order that I keep myself free from that. In speaking of the human being, not the—you're speaking of the two-legged animals, not the four. I understand that, yes. Well, if you want to find the best possible—you see, oxygen, without oxygen, you know, you no longer have a form to identify with. So oxygen is, of course, extremely important. The producers of oxygen are important. The live plants and the trees, you see, without them, there's no oxygen. And I'm sure you all understand that.

Forty-five degrees is the proper sleeping temperature. Forty-five degrees. Now whoever sleeps in temperature higher than that usually finds a condition *[As an example of a condition, the teacher sniffs.]* of [a] little difficulty with their breathing, etc. Forty-five degrees. Yes.

Thank you.

Well, sometimes in the summer it's not 45. Well, then sometimes you don't sleep as well either. Yes, go ahead.

Thank you. Some philosophies encourage the burning of incense. Does our philosophy recommend any particular smell of a flower or incense to encourage the rising of one's vibration?

Well, in reference to the question dealing with scent, of course, and some philosophies that require, what you call, incense, it has been my experiences that students of mine seem to have no problem at all entrancing themselves without going to incense. I find they can go right off into entrancement in the slightest little thing. *[Many students laugh.]* So it's not really necessary to waste the time, money, and energy to be buying incense when all you [have] got to do is expand your universe, in reference to entrancement. If you have difficulty doing your concentration and meditation, it's just because you haven't pushed the right desire button. And I can understand that. No, you don't need incense. Not in this philosophy. Thank you. Yes.

Thank you. How can we discern if we are acting in reason or have become grounded in self and have let in armies of forms making our actions the results of denial and need?

Well, first of all, you can't experience denial and need when you are in the light of reason. It is not possible. *[A clock begins to chime.]* Yes?

Thank you. I'll wait for the clock.

[As the chiming ceases, the teacher continues.] Yes, go ahead, please.

Thank you. Many old philosophies teach energy is released during the healing process through the palms of the hands. Is this true?

Well, that is one of the places that energy is released. Unfortunately, it's not the only place. Sometimes I have considered that it would be nice if that was the only place it could be released, but man would be so much healthier. But, yes. *[Several students laugh.]*

Thank you. What do the palms of the hands represent?

Action. The hands represent action. And when you turn your action, you open your action, then you are receptive to that which is to come.

Thank you.

First you act, then you receive. But whoever receives without conscious act has got problems in life. Yes.

Thank you. Does our aura spiral out around us if we do not know how to contain it? Should we contain it in a certain area? How do we do that?

First of all, by becoming aware of all your thoughts and activities in your mind, you gain control over your aura or emanation of your life-giving energy, which is being released through your body. Yes. So first become aware of these thoughts that you have in your mind and consciously aware and alert of your, your attitude. Your attitude is what is critical. Because if you want to change your experiences and you want to change your day and you want something more pleasant and harmonious in your life, then you will have to make the effort to change your attitude. Your attitude is revealing what you're thinking and what you're feeling and believing. It's your attitude. Your attitude is what's so critical. However, if you have evolved from early childhood with the attitude that if you walk around feeling miserable and you look miserable enough and you're negative enough that you will receive the energy and that you can get something for nothing, then you're going to have what is known as a very poor attitude and are in need of attitude correction. Attitude is where life's experiences are dependent. Dependent on your attitude. Yes.

Thank you. If the universe within and without reflect each other, what do the other planetary people visiting us represent in our inner universe?

Well, the intelligences in the universe, they look at your planet Earth as the fifth planet. They see what you are doing with the planet and the laws of nature and balance, how you are interfering with them from a lack of effort to understand those laws and to apply them. And because your planet affects the atmosphere in what you call outer space, which in turn affects their planets—many of them much more evolved than your own—they monitor your planet because to be forewarned is to be forearmed. And therefore, they have a responsibility, before you advance too far with your technological advancements, they have a responsibility to protect themselves. And so they have monitored your planet for some time in that respect. Yes.

Thank you. Do the dancing ecstasy, the whirling dervishes, gain a spiritual experience?

Well, indeed, they do because they totally wear out their sensual experiences in their dancing and they finally collapse. And when they—when you collapse from without, you're destined to go within. In that respect, many of them do. Yes.

Thank you. How may we become more receptive to the Law of Harmony?

To become more receptive to the Law of Harmony, that which you truly are, is to make conscious effort to change your attitude and stop all this negativity that you seem to love so much. Yes. And I don't mean just the questioner. I'm talking about everyone. The attitude. Attitude correction. If you pray for anything in life, pray to be inspired to make the effort with attitude correction. Move from the negative, which is so detrimental, not only to yourself—I find that people with suicidal tendencies are extremely negative people. Yes.

Thank you. How may we love our judgments in life, so we may experience the fullness in life?

By the question of loving one's judgments, I don't think there's any problem with the love of them. I think there may be a problem with the expression of the love of them. You see, to love oneself one must consider what they are. If one believes that they are their judgments and then one loves themselves, then they've got a serious problem because when they go to express their love, their judgments don't agree with other people's judgments very often. And therefore, there's a real serious problem in that respect.

Thank—

Love what you are and forget what you believe you are. Just love what you are. Forget what you believe you are.

Thank you.

For at least a while.

Now I'll read the correct question correctly.

Oh.

How may one bow our judgments in life so we may experience the fullness in life?

Oh, you just got such a personal message. *[The cameraman, who is reading the questions, laughs loudly, as do many students.]* I don't usually give personal messages. Isn't that interesting. Yes, that's lovely. I'm so happy for you. You know, exposure frees the soul, and it's always best for the soul that exposes itself. I think it's just wonderful. Now what is the question that the questioner asked before you put your question on top of it? Yes, go ahead. Try to read that—

The question on the paper says, "How may we bow our judgments in life so we may experience the fullness in life?"

By doing the opposite of what the other questioner— *[The teacher and many students laugh.]* Just the opposite.

Thank you.

Just come right here, my friend. *[The teacher addresses Reddy, the church's dog.]* You want to go to the bathroom. I know. You can have a little bit there. Just a little bit. It's water. *[The teacher offers Reddy a drink from a glass of water.]* Go ahead with your questions, please.

How may we free ourselves from the illusion of creation?

Well, one best frees themselves from the illusion of creation by pausing to think. Because whoever pauses to think is bound to open their eyes and be a little free from what they believe is their reality. Yes, go right ahead.

Thank you. When we ask ourselves, What we are doing with the law that we are? and there is no answer, what action should we take?

Well, it's quite obvious when you ask yourself what you are doing with the law that you are and there's no answer, that's quite obvious: you're doing nothing. *[Many students laugh.]*

But on that little note, I think it's time for us to conclude this lovely class. After all, we have the holidays coming up and time does pass quickly. Are you about finished with your questions?

I have quite a few more.

Well, we can have them for next week then, can't we?

Yes, sir.

Oh, my. Well, thank you, students, very much. It's a lovely class. And it's nice to make changes. No law says class will always be fifty minutes or ninety. Just because we have—what—ninety-minute tapes? *[Classes were made available to private students on ninety-minute audio cassette tapes.]* No, no, no. It's a nice class. Have a beautiful day. And be sure that my friend goes out to the bathroom, please. Thank you.

Yes, sir.

Good day.

NOVEMBER 17, 1985

A/V Class Private 24

Good morning, class, on such a nice, dramatic day as today. *[A rain storm was happening that morning.]*

Today's class, a bit of a discussion on the demonstrable truth: "I am not what others think that I am, for I am not the reflection of my thought. I am the creator of my thought. Therefore, I do not believe that I am the thought of I, for I know that I am the I." Whoever makes effort to declare that truth each day frees themselves from the dependence and control on what other people think of them and, therefore, are freed from the frustrations and the turmoil of what a reflection of what is has to offer.

And so the lesser light reflects the true Light. But let us never forget: it is the reflector. It is not what we are. However, it is in truth a responsibility that we have to guide it. So each thought, let us remember, we are the originator and creator of; therefore, it is our responsibility to guide and to control it before it tempts and guides and controls what we truly are.

Now these classes here are coming along in a most beautiful and harmonious way. Moving from the reflection, as far as the student body is concerned, to an awakening of what we truly are that we may fully enjoy our time on the planet Earth. And in that enjoyment, be freed from the dependence of how others react to the way that we act, for whoever acts with an awakening of what they are, and not what they think they are, is freed from the need to depend on how others react to what they do or do not do.

And so I'm going to go on now with our little classes to the many questions that you have prepared. And just before getting to that, I want to say to you that we will continue on, this December 1985, with what you would consider our tradition of an annual forecast. And we will set aside the last Sunday of the month of December for that Annual World Forecast for your benefit. And therefore, you should consider the many thoughts and questions that you have and your interest in world events and submit them. And prepare them, of course, prior to that date.

Now if our cameraman here will go ahead and read the questions this morning that you have submitted.

Thank you. What is the difference between disciplining the mind and stilling the mind?

First of all, the mind cannot be stilled until the mind is controlled. And the mind cannot be controlled without the effort that you know as discipline.

Thank you. Are the minor planets in the solar system on which we will or have evolved—Let me start again. [The cameraman misreads a question and begins again.] *Are there minor planets in the solar system on which we will or have evolved other than the nine planets of this system?*

Yes, there are.

I am attracted to the constellation Orion as though I have once been a part of it. Is there or has there ever been life on stars as well as on planets?

Life as you know it, if you consider life the limited form in which you find yourself presently encased, in that respect, no. To the questioner who has an interest in Orion, they should consider the element iron.

Thank you. What is there about—

The mineral iron. Yes.

Thank you. What is there about Halley's Comet that causes man to make changes when it comes nearer to Earth?

Its influence upon the planets that it comes close to. For example, a person who believes they are the limit is a person who is controlled by what you understand as gravity. Now gravity is dependent upon identification. And so a person who is overly identified with anything is a person not only who is grounded [but also] is a person who is under the strong influence of a gravitational, what you would call gravitational pull. And, for example, you perhaps can best relate to that: when you judge that you have a lack of anything, you experience a need. You find yourself almost driven to what you judge is the fulfillment of that need or that vacuum, for nature abhors a vacuum. You are under the influence of a gravitational pull. So when what you understand as Halley's Comet comes close to the planet, everything that is over-identified has an experience which is beneficial in the sense of helping them to free themselves from their over-identification or the gravitational pull that they have found themselves under. And in that respect, there is an awakening and a change within the consciousness of the planet which is being affected as the comet comes closer to the particular planet.

Thank you. I recognize the necessity to keep mice out of our home. But I have trouble with the dichotomy of caring about how animals are treated and feeding poison to others. What is the spiritual responsibility involved?

Yes, there is a great spiritual responsibility for we spend most of our—your earthly lives in poisoning yourselves. And so in that respect, to be overly concerned or to be concerned with the poisoning of a small, little creature or sending him on to another world should not be of great interest in the sense that one must first make greater effort to refrain from poisoning the bodies in which they are presently encased, for the law reveals that like attracts like. And whenever one spends so much of their time in poisoning themselves with thoughts which change their chemistry in a most detrimental way, then one should understand and, therefore, make changes within the consciousness so that they could speak to the little creatures, known as mice, and tell them, "There's a nice warm home over there for you. This is my home. And you would find a better home over there." So you must first make the change in consciousness to refrain from poisoning yourself, to accept the mice as the brother creatures on the planet on which you presently reside, then you would be able to communicate with them intelligently, and you would not attract them into your beds and private quarters. Yes.

Thank you. In my studies I have found that the same soul faculty pertains to more than one part of the physical anatomy. Why is this so? And what correlation do these two parts have?

Soul faculties are all triune in expression. And in reference to that question, if you will continue on with your studies, you will find that the trinity of the faculties and the trinity of the functions are interrelated.

Thank you. Is my understanding correct? There are nine expressions of each state of consciousness. The first one being self. Is that then located in the first center or earth center? And the second, being slave, correlate to the fire center, and so on?

The student is correct in their understanding in reference to that. Yes.

Thank you. Are both soul faculties and functions expressed in the lower four centers or just the functions? Do—correction— To create the balance when we are expressing in one of the lower centers, do we have to move over all—correction—do we have to move our will up the river of life to one of the higher centers for balance? Or does each center, even the lower centers, contain within the nine expressions, the balance or neutral point?

Yes. Well, each center, including the so-called lower centers, contain what you say as the balance point. Now, for example, fire illumines or consumes. It is constructive or destructive depending upon the guidance of the lord of the universe, which is known as your will power.

And I do think that we should adjust our volume so we don't have this echo.

Thank you.

Yes.

Thank you. How is it more beneficial for us to learn our lessons here before we leave this form? What is the process if we do not learn a particular lesson here and we pass on to the next realm?

Well, for example, these many lessons that you have to learn, it's like going to any of your regular educational schools on your planet. You have the opportunity in the first, second, third, and fourth grades, and all of the various grades, to learn what those grades of school, or evolution, what they have to offer. Now you have that opportunity. It is much more difficult to learn basic mathematics in college than it is in what you call grammar school. Not only does your mind and the uneducated ego find it embarrassing and humiliating to begin to learn that two and two equals four after you're in the third state in college—or when you are ready to graduate from college and start to learn basic mathematics—[but also] it is much more difficult for you. For example, you have earned in evolution these grades of school. Now the planet Earth offers those grades to you. If you do not take advantage of that opportunity, you have much more difficulty in changing the patterns and learning the lessons that you have to learn after you have left the grade of school or the stage of evolution in which, by the design of your own merit system, you have earned the opportunity to learn that lesson.

Thank you. Please share your understanding of the saying [in The Living Light *textbook], "Idle thought, like idle talk, is the greatest enemy in your camp." How does the enemy work?*

That which is idle in the consciousness of man is that which is not controlled by what man truly is. And therefore, if man permits it to continue, then he becomes the victim of the slave of the idle control of what he truly is. Idle is not constructive in the consciousness. That which is idle is not guided. That which is not guided is not controlled. That which is not controlled is not constructive.

Thank you. How can we create bridges—correction—When we create bridges of rapport with someone and do not feel so great afterwards, how can we better keep our bridge of rapport clean?

Motive. First of all, when a person establishes a bridge of rapport with anything outside of themselves, in other words, what they are doing in truth [is] they are sharing a level of consciousness. And so when a person establishes a bridge of rapport, they are in truth sharing a level of consciousness. Now one shares that level of consciousness without a conscious understanding of what they are doing and usually wake up—and that's known as hindsight—and are not very happy about it. The cleaning up or cleaning the house is something that one would have to work on with their own mind by first accepting the personal responsibility that without conscious awareness they had shared a level of consciousness which they believe that they are.

Thank you. If our adversities are our unrecognizable desires, how can we become more aware of them? Why are they unrecognizable, while most of our desires are so blatant?

The teaching is that our adversities become our attachments. Now when a person finds themselves adverse to anything, they direct intelligent energy to the creating of the form of adversity. By directing that intelligent energy to their form of adversity, they are in truth, they are in truth creating an attitude of mind of superiority from a lack of understanding the laws which are governing the condition. They are in truth denying that that potential or possibility exists in their own life. Therefore, by that denial they are destined to experience the attachment to their own adversity for it is self-created.

Now perhaps we can put it in a little clearer terms. First of all, the adversity is created by a mind which has convinced itself that it is the thought and not the creator of the thought. Therefore, whenever a person, through identification with the reflection of what they are, instead of what they are, enters that realm, that is waiting for them. Anyone therefore experiencing self-identification never knows the moment nor the day when they will face their adversity from a different perspective in keeping with their own denial or need. And therefore, it becomes for them an attachment. It is guaranteed in keeping with the Law of Self-Identification.

Thank you. Health is the effect of our subconscious, which is magnetic. Does that mean that the learning process takes place in the magnetic center of consciousness? Also, The Living Light book says that through the faculty of humility is where healing takes place. I am a little confused as to how each faculty and function expresses in the various centers. Could you please help me to understand more how this works?

In reference to how it works that the faculty of humility is the soul faculty through which the healing vibration flows, and also the faculty of gratitude, through the faculty of humility one bows to the light of reason, which reveals beyond a shadow of any doubt that they are the creator of their thought. Therefore, they are not their thought. They are not the reflection. They are the Light. And when they permit themselves to believe they are the reflection of the Light by what is known as over-identification with the reflection, which is known as self, then they experience what that limit or denial of what they are has to offer. It offers discord. It offers disturbance, which is the Law of Disease or poor health. So when a person awakens within themselves the faculty of humility, therefore, in that awakening, in the light of reason they flow in the principle of the will of God, known as total acceptance. They therefore are able, in that respect, to experience an improvement in the Law of Harmony, which is known as health.

In other words, stop identifying with the discord. Start identifying with what you are and you will experience the healing vibration that is ever available to you.

Thank you. When looking at our videos, we see things clearer through the eye of the camera because the camera is not clouded by judgments. Is there a way that this same principle can help us in listening and learning what is truly being said?

Yes, indeed, there is. And that effort has to be made repeatedly, daily, to declare the truth: "I am the creator of the thought. I am not the thought." For it is from the belief that you are the thought that the thought patterns become solidified and you experience what is known as judgments. Judgments are the censors, the mist that stands between your sight and what is, between your hearing and what is. This is why it is so difficult for people to hear, to listen, to truly understand, for the censorship of past experiences, known as judgments, adversities, prejudgments, which you understand as prejudice, is ever present unless the effort is made. At the moment you wish to see something, close your eyes. [If] you want to see something physically, first close your eyes and accept what you are. Gain control over the temptation of believing what you are. Accept what you are. You are the pure, intelligent, eternal Light. That is what you are. Declare that truth. Open your eyes and for a moment at least you will see clearly, as the eye of the camera sees clearly when it is not obstructed by dust on its lenses or dirt.

So, you see, when you want to hear, to hear without censorship, then you must clean the dust and the dirt that is over your consciousness. The dust and the dirt being the judgments and the forms of past experiences.

Thank you. Because we are both formless, free spirits expressing through form, does that mean that form always has the denial of that which he truly is until we educate our minds? Trees and plants are form and they do not appear to be in denial, like man. Why do we do that to ourselves?

When it is stated that trees and plants do not appear to be in denial, it is from a lack of understanding what denial is. You look at the plant, but you do not understand nor communicate with the plant. One plant growing next to another plant may be happy or unhappy. It likes the other plant; it doesn't like the other plant. You justify that there—of course, you use some justification that the soil in that area is a little different than that; the two plants don't like that. And that's one level of consciousness of understanding. However, when you look at the plants and the trees, they have their own personality. They have their own limit. They have their own denial. You see, that's what limit is. Limit is denial. In order to experience form, you must have the principle of denial of what is, for without the principle of denial, you cannot experience limit. And when you do not experience limit, you do not experience form. When you do not experience form, then you do not serve the purpose of the Formless, which is to enter limit and expand or evolve the consciousness of limit.

You see, limit has consciousness as an expression of the Limitlessness that sustains it. And so to look at form and to think that it does not appear to have denial is not correct at all. All limit is denial of the Limitless. It is an expression of the Limitless in a particular form. I do hope that's helped with your question.

Thank you. What happens to the ectoplasm when we are in faith?

When we are in faith, this electromagnetic energy, this ectoplasm, is used to express the Limitlessness or the true being that we are. We say, in your world, you do not fly; you do not walk upon water. Well, it is not possible for you to do so when the ectoplasm necessary to create such phenomenon is not available to one who is dissipating it in such foolish ways.

Thank you. What is the most beneficial way or ways to train a young child that he is not the forms of his mind, but what he truly is, is a formless, free Spirit?

Well, the best thing that one could possibly do for a child is to speak with the child, to offer the child constructive guidance, known as discipline, [and] never to permit oneself to believe that they are offering a child corrective guidance for their good when the person who is doing the discipline is demonstrating the direct opposite or the lack of control of their own emotions.

Therefore, in guiding a child, it is necessary to council with the child, to speak with the child and to refrain from believing that the child does not understand because of its limited age on your planet.

When you make the effort to understand yourself, when you then speak, you offer that understanding to a child, to an adult, to a dog, or to a bird. And the only thing is that a person insists on believing, because a bird doesn't react a certain way in keeping with the judgments they've already made, that the bird does not understand. The bird understands, the child understands, the dog understands, the tree understands, if you have made the effort first to understand.

Thank you. How does form act as a buffer here on earth? When we make our transition, it is said to be more difficult. How does that work?

Well, first of all, form, as a buffer, the physical being, through over-identification and belief that one is that flesh and bone, they have a buffer in that sense. They are not experiencing what they truly are. They are not aware of their finer bodies of expression, such as their mental bodies, their astral bodies, their celestial bodies. And by not being aware of those bodies and by being over-identified with the flesh body, when they leave the flesh body, it's like a child going to school. They don't have the control over it through conscious awareness because they have been over-identified with one of the grosser bodies.

Thank you. Is the interaction—no—the intersection of the fire-electric, water-magnetic, and air-ethereal centers the basis of a pyramid?

You may repeat the question for it is so important for the benefit of all my students.

Thank you. Is the intersection of the fire-electric, water-magnetic, and air-ethereal centers the basis of a pyramid?

If you are speaking of the pyramid of which I am considering, yes, it is.

Thank you. Does the prince of darkness have anything to do with the energy that surrounds the moon during certain phases of the moon?

Yes. Certainly does. And you should consider taking control over the water center. And you should understand at which point of the triangle the water center is located. Yes.

Thank you. Can one be participating in the jungle and still be growing and expanding spiritually?

Oh, absolutely. Certainly. It depends on the consciousness of the individual and whether or not they insist on believing they are the limit and, therefore, continually experiencing the need of its expression and fulfillment. Yes.

Thank you. When one has a pattern so deeply ingrained in one's being that one finds oneself continually going into the pattern, at what moment does one have a chance of pausing before the movement begins into the pattern again?

At the very beginning. At the first conscious awareness that they are beginning to experience an addiction. Yes.

Thank you. Was man meant to be principle, the divine principle, but continually reversing himself in ignorance?

Man *is* the divine principle. He wasn't meant to be. That's what he is, and still is, if you understand that man is not flesh and bone.

Thank you. Does chocolate have a calming effect on the nervous system? Is there some beneficial ingredient?

Well, chocolate contains chemicals that have an effect upon the chemistry of the body, yes. Is it beneficial or detrimental? It depends on the user.

Thank you. With reference to the circles that form the figure eight of infinity, does the upper circle, containing the electric, magnetic, odic, and ethereal centers, flow in a clockwise direction and the lower circle, containing earth, fire, water, and air centers, move in a counterclockwise direction?

It's the reverse.

Thank you. Divine will is located between the air and electric centers. To go to the electric from the air center you have to pass through the equator, where truth is. Is divine will and truth one and the same?

Divine will is the expression of Truth. The equator is perfect balance. That which is perfectly balanced is neutralized. That which is neutralized *is*.

Thank you. It was mentioned that attitude is a vibration. Is a vibration composed of atoms and molecules or is the energy, which moves atoms—or is it the energy which moves atoms and molecules?

Well, atoms, electrons, and molecules are the expression of intelligent Energy and, in that respect, are the carriers of the intelligence, yes. You see, that is what you are. Atoms, electrons, and molecules. That is what everything is. And you see difference, you see forms, varied, for you are viewing from that level of consciousness in evolution. As you make effort to refrain from over-identification with self, you expand in consciousness and, in so doing, begin to view what is and not what appears to be.

Thank you. It seems that every atom contains within it all centers and spheres that we have. Is that correct?

That is correct. The atoms, electrons, and molecules that compose what you understand as your being have been used before throughout eons of time. Some of them were part of composing what you understand as a rock or a drop of water on other planets in other times. And so that awareness, that history is available to you. And that is, of course, one of the natural benefits of evolution from refraining from limit by refraining from self-thought, which *is* limit.

Thank you. Is there a pressure point that can relieve difficulty in breathing?

Yes, there are pressure points that are used, that are beneficial for a more harmonious movement of the lungs in helping to physically correct some of those conditions. One should, however, consider that in using physical pressure points, which we are scheduled to come up with our classes within the coming year, that one cannot be using these pressure points, that are [a] very ancient, ancient method of correcting conditions in the physical body and mental body, without also working mentally with these things, for you are a physical, mental, and spiritual body. And so attitude correction is essential to the beneficial use of the pressure point philosophy and practice.

Thank you.

You're welcome.

I still have a question in relation to the water center and solar plexus. Does the water center have the same location in the body as the solar plexus?

No.

Or does it have its own?

It has its own.

If it has its own, is it just below the solar plexus?

Yes, indeed, it is. And that's where all the steam comes from. Thank you.

Thank you. When thoughts are passing through the mind and you identify with one for a split second, does that thought form go into action immediately?

Yes, thought forms have never been known for their patience.

Thank you. Is there a way to recognize it, if it is one that is not beneficial or does it have to take its course?

Well, there's certainly a way to recognize a thought form by being aware of what's taking place within your own mind, certainly. And you then make an intelligent decision whether or not you want to permit the form to remain in your consciousness and is it willing to do what you tell it to do or is it going to tell you what to do. You'll know very quickly whether or not it's beneficial to you or detrimental.

Thank you. Are the electromagnetic transmissions that you spoke of last week subliminal programming? If so, is there any definite—correction—any defense, other than being captain of our own ship?

The only defense, in that respect, is awareness. To be aware. You see, when you move along in this world of creation and you feel that you have an experience that you're not feeling too well, you're irritated, you're angry, and you do not have a conscious awareness of why you are angry, that's when you want to really make great effort, great effort. For, you see, that is permitting your consciousness to be open and receptive to whatever flows in the atmosphere. It reveals to you that you're not on guard; you're not on duty. And you have a responsibility or to pay the price.

In other words, ofttimes with a person, they will suddenly become aware, seeming suddenly become, that they don't feel too good. Well, what has truly happened, usually, in those experiences, they've been out to lunch or out to dinner in what you know in your world as fascination. They've been playing with one of their levels of consciousness and suddenly they came back home. They got back inside their little house, and their little house is in terrible shape and they're not happy at all and they feel very angry. Well, it's their own fault for leaving their house unattended while they were out playing. You see, they went out playing; they didn't put anybody in charge or on duty and they left their doors open. And when they got back, someone was in there and had made a terrible mess of their house. And they're irritated because now they [have] got to work and clean it up. But, you see, what truly happens in those experiences is they drifted out to what you might call a daydream or, you know, were tempted to go out playing and didn't take care of the responsibilities they have to their own house. Yes.

Thank you.

You're welcome.

Since we receive subliminally, do we also send subliminally—

Yes, yes.

—with individuals?

Oh, yes, yes. Yes, indeed, we do. Indeed, we do. And whoever allows themselves the pleasure, so-called, of daydreaming or fascinating must pay the price when they get back home. Yes.

Thank you. By man's removal of layers of earth in mining and cutting off mountain tops, is man releasing vibrations of eons ago that have been dormant for centuries?

Yes.

If so, how will this affect the planet Earth?

Well, it can affect it in many different ways. You have to study the civilizations that preceded you and those vibrations are being released into the atmosphere. Their atoms, electrons, and molecules, they contain, of course, intelligence. And people, being out to lunch so often, not taking care of their own mind and their thoughts, you see, they become willing[ly], though not consciously, receptive to all of those vibrations in the atmosphere.

Thank you.

Yes.

Does Greek architecture and replicas thereof reveal the religious beliefs of that civilization? If so, is there a parallel between their gods and goddesses and our centers of consciousness?

Yes, there is a parallel. And much of the architecture of that particular country, that particular race, reveals their religious convictions. But let us not be so foolhardy as to believe that all of their architecture reveals their religious beliefs, unless you consider the function of the fire center to be a religion.

Thank you. This Serenity house has been referred to as the Academy. Is that because of the similarity between the Greek Academy established by Aristotle and his philosophy teachings and Serenity?

Yes, you could say that, in principle, of the type of teachings, yes.

Thank you. Are respiratory ailments caused by a conflict of desires that lack reason and consideration for the person, other persons, and other desires?

They most certainly are. It affects the air center. Upsets the balance.

Thank you. Is the need to retreat from responsibility due to the desire of the senses to be master over one's own little world?

Well, the desire of the senses is not what a person is. And when they want to have their way, they can convince you of most anything, yes.

Thank you. Do the various branches on the tree of life correspond to our various bodies?

That depends on which tree of life you are viewing.

Thank you.

Yes.

Why is the self-accomplishment so important when a person isolates frequencies—I'm sorry, that's a separate question. Why is the self-accomplishment so important?

That is the design of living. You have entered the Earth planet in order to accomplish what you have to accomplish. And if you do not accomplish that, which some do not—in fact, many do not—then you accomplish it in the earth-bound realms, for you have a responsibility in keeping with your evolution.

Thank you. When a person isolates frequencies, is he purifying those frequencies?

Not unless he has control of his mind. First of all, there's some degree of control in order to isolate the frequencies; however, it goes beyond that. And it is necessary for the faculty of reason, the light, to be unobstructed in one's efforts. Yes.

Thank you. Is our spiritual consciousness—no. Is our spiritual conscience located in the odic center?

Yes, it is located in the higher center or what you understand as the odic center.

Thank you. As students of the Living Light, what is our role as the laws of nature bring about a balance?

What is our role as the laws of nature bring about a balance? The question shall not be asked when balance is attained. You see, the question is only asked from a lack of attaining the balance. Once the balance is attained, there is no longer a question, for the answer is the application. One need not be concerned. When one is balanced, one is not concerned of imbalance for one is just balanced.

Thank you. Please explain what happens to us when we daydream and do not control our own reality.

Yes, I spoke on that a few minutes ago. You leave the house that you're responsible for without proper corrective measures; then you come back and you wonder why you're irritated and you're angry and you're emotionally upset and why you're not happy. Yes, that was covered a few moments ago.

Thank you.

You're welcome.

Please explain the divine Law of Return and how to keep mental interference from blocking the flow of this law.

Refrain from servicing thought patterns that have been solidified, known as judgments, and you'll have no problem whatsoever.

Thank you. What should we do to make every moment in life count and stop wasting our energy on past experiences?

What should we do to make every moment count? Well, every moment counts, if you believe you are your judgments, for they're getting plenty of the counting. What we should do is to enjoy life. But you cannot enjoy life as long as you insist on believing you are something that has passed, that you no longer have control of. You see, that which has entered your consciousness by your own choice and has served its purpose, when you no longer use it, you experience the abuse from it, in the sense that if you do not make conscious effort to control that which has passed, then that which has passed you will soon experience is controlling you.

So, you see, how does one control that which has passed in their life? They have an experience a few years or ten or fifteen years ago and they say, "Well, that experience is over. Oh, I'm so grateful that that's over." The question is, Is the experience over? Well, if the experience is over and it's fulfilled itself, then it won't repeat itself. If it is not over, it will repeat itself. Depending on how much you believe that you were the need or the denial that created the experience is how much it will control your life when you no longer consciously experience it. But it subconsciously, through your magnetic field, affects your life.

Now if you let it go in an understanding that it was something that you alone created, that you have experienced what it had to offer, it is over and you convince that part of you that created it that it is over in your consciousness, it will not plague you anymore. But if you don't, it will continue to rise every time you enter this self-thought.

Thank you. How may we free ourselves from the mental law and expand our consciousness and accept our right to all the goodness that life has to offer?

By stop thinking of yourself. Each time you think of yourself, you have the problem, for each time you think of self, you believe you are the reflection of what you are and do not accept what you are. And by that law, you have those type of experiences.

Thank you. Please explain the saying [from The Serenity Game], "The essence of dreaming is the law of life, and the law of life is Divine will or God's expression."

Yes, the essence of dreaming is the law of life. The very essence is what you are. And what you are is this power that creates. It directs energy, intelligent energy, and it creates the form. You are the creator. You are not what you have created. You see, that's the fine line of distinction: you are responsible for what you have created; you are not what you have created. And the big step, the *big* step to make in evolution is, you are responsible for what you have created; you are not what you have created. You see, if you will accept responsibility that you, in evolution, as an intelligent being, have created the form that you are in—stop believing in the illusion that someone else created you. Stop believing, whether you want to call it God or this or that, stop believing in that illusion. Through the laws of evolution, you have created the form that you presently experience. That form is not you. That form is what you have created. Because you have created it, you are responsible for guiding, disciplining, and directing it. It is not what you are. It is only what you have created. Yes.

Thank you. When I inhale during the rhythmic cleansing breath, my mind is clear. When I pause, it balances. When I exhale, it bombards me with thoughts. [The teacher laughs joyfully.] *Why does it happen on the exhale?*

[The teacher continues to laugh.] That's when you lose control. And if you will be honest with yourself, you will find that when you exhale, it is not as harmonious, it is not as rhythmic in any sense of the word, as when you inhale.

And I thank you very much for this lovely class today. And I look forward to seeing you again next Sunday. Have a nice week. And remember, you are not what you think you are. You are what you are. And good day, students.

NOVEMBER 24, 1985

A/V Class Private 25

Good morning, students.

This morning we'll have a little preview, in the sense, of the coming year, not our forecast, which is scheduled for the last Sunday of this year. But after many years of effort in bringing this philosophy to you, we have finally moved in your world with equipment necessary in order to bring to you the science of this philosophy presented in a way that you may better understand it. And so in the coming year of 1986, we have this scheduled to bring to you, and you will find it a great aid in understanding the laws that have been and will continue to be revealed to you.

Now we'll begin this morning's class with the questions that we stopped with at our last class. And if the cameraman here will be so kind as to read these questions one at a time so that none are missed, then we'll go on with that.

Thank you. When I do the rhythmic cleansing breath, my breathing is much deeper and there are less thoughts. Is this because the desires have been satisfied?

When you do the cleansing breath properly, you will find that there are less thoughts with which you are identifying, for the cleansing breath, properly applied—without the breath, the thought forms are not registered in the consciousness, those that have been, those that are, and those that are hoped for. So by controlling your breath, you take control of your mind. By controlling your mind, you take control over your experiences. It does not mean that desires or thoughts that have already registered are satisfied. It simply means that you have gained control of your mind and are therefore no longer identified with them at that time.

Thank you. Does biting the fingernails come from insecurity, which is self-pity and judgment? Why does it take that form, if it is?

Well, in reference to biting the fingernails or to playing with the toes or to itching a person's nose or any of those things that are self-identified, it is an over-identification with the form that is not being satisfied with the energy that it demands for its many experiences and expressions.

Thank you. If one has a tendency to be in rapport with others and works with many people and the rapport is beyond conscious thought, and the persons speak of an illness they have, how can one keep themselves from absorbing and matching the illness? Is saying, "I am not the form," over and over the best way?

That is one of the many ways, by declaring the truth that you are not the limit; therefore, you are not the form. However, one must understand that a rapport established is first established within one's own consciousness in order to be established with another. So when a person, working in rapport with other people, will first make the effort to be consciously aware that in order to establish a rapport with others they must first establish a rapport with the level within themselves—and at the time of establishing the rapport with the level within oneself; that is the time for one to declare the truth: "I am not the level. I am that which is using the level. The level is subject to my orders, to my dictates, and to no longer express itself when I choose it is not to do so." Yes.

Thank you. After death, how do you know when you have reached the highest level you can go to and how can you tell if other forms are masquerading as higher levels in order to draw you into their level?

By not knowing. You see, knowledge knows much and wisdom knows better. It is when you know something that you become assured and convinced of your own self-importance. And it is when you do not know—for knowledge is subject to the control of mental substance, which is controlled by the king of creation. So it is when you do not know, that that is when you have awakened. That's known as wisdom.

Thank you. Would you please explain the process by which faces of people or animals appear in objects that are weathered or manufactured, such as tile?

Well, in reference to faces appearing in various objects in creation, try to understand and to remember that your eyes, they are the lenses and you are the camera. And depending, of course, upon your level of consciousness at any time, you may perceive and, therefore, see superimposed images upon physical objects or images in your world. That is usually an indication of a person who is moving through the doorway of imaging, imagination, and they are in the doorway; they've not made the step over. And they are not fully identified with the material world of what you call substance. Yes.

Thank you. Who are these people and are they from higher or lower realms?

Usually they are from realms that are very closely identified with the earth realm, and that is ever revealed in the state of consciousness and the experience of the viewer.

Thank you. In a previous class, you said that we refer to Halley's Comet as a comet. What is it really? Is it composed of ice, as earth scientists have stated?

Well, in reference to Halley's Comet or any comet, that you call a comet, try to understand that all things are composed of atoms—atoms, electrons, and molecules. Try to understand that atoms are not something that are new or old. They are something that is. Your body, your own physical body is composed of the same atoms that have expressed in other forms at other times in other worlds in other universes in other planets. And so when you understand that that which is form or limit is composed of atoms, electrons, and molecules, that you are the very Light that can and does control those atoms, electrons, and molecules, [so] that when you wish to experience something, anything than what you have already experienced, you have to refrain from identification from whatever you think has been. By refraining from identifying with what you think has been, which is known as reference, that is when you are in a position to gather these atoms, electrons, and molecules to serve you in keeping with your conscious, intelligent choice. Therefore, a comet is only a comet in keeping with your reference or identification with knowledge. And knowledge is only a reference of what has been. Therefore, it knows much; and therefore, wisdom knows better.

Thank you. In photography is there a recommended relationship between the shadows and the light, for example, the placement and proportions of light to shadow? And what are the spiritual principles involved?

Well, in reference to photography, that is, the capturing of image on to magnetic film, in reference to what you call photography, try to understand that the best possible photography or capturing of an image is ever to face the light. Now I realize that this is contrary to your education. However, if you will do your filming from the borderline of the shadow world and capture the light, not directly, but indirectly—for, you see, you're dealing with what is known as illusion. You are actually capturing a reflection, an illusion. And so you, or the camera, if it is properly placed at the proper angle to the light, which is the very sustenance through which the capturing of illusion is made possible, then you will have the finest possible effects and experiences from what you know as photography. Remember that you are working to capture reflection or illusion. And therefore, it is your angle to the light from the shadow of belief that is critically important in order for the best possible images of illusion to be captured onto magnetic film.

Thank you. What is the spiritual significance of the elephant?

The spiritual significance of the elephant is quite clear in reference to its long, long record of work. The elephant is, on your planet, is one of the few beings remaining that is capable of and demonstrates intelligent thought and consideration in reference to its work on your planet Earth. Now the elephant not only has demonstrated but does have one of the finest memories and recall of any beings on your planet, far exceeding the human species. The elephant from its many ages of evolution is in a position and demonstrates the spiritual value of its purpose of being on Earth. It is used by those teachers who have awakened to the benefits of freeing the souls from realms, [trapped] through over-identification with limit. And having found themselves trapped in those conditions, the elephant is ofttimes and frequently used to help them because of the elephants' evolution as a being on your planet.

Thank you. The intelligences from other planets are watching our Earth slowly self-destruct. It was said that they are watching in order to protect themselves as they, too, are affected by our transgressions. How do they protect themselves in their realms from being affected?

Well, in reference to protecting themselves as the planet Earth has been monitored for eons of time, how they protect themselves is by taking corrective measures in reference to their own technological advancement in evolution.

Now speaking on that—and I was going to speak to you on that at the annual forecast—speaking on that, let us go to the law that clearly reveals itself: as man finds, through his ever-advancing and expanding intellect, as he finds that he is capable of creating forms that will do jobs for him and accomplish things that he wants done that he does not, for varying justifications, do for himself, man becomes dependent upon the forms that he creates through his own ever-expanding and advancing intellect. Now as man becomes more dependent on that which he creates, man becomes more bound by the forms that he has created. And so in keeping with the Law of Evolution, man is becoming more and more dependent upon the forms that man creates.

Man is offering to those forms, though he calls them mechanical, he is offering to them his ever-expanding intelligence. He is imbuing the minerals with the intelligence that he has himself. Now by so doing, he does not consciously create computers to be selfish; he only demonstrates the law in the very creating of this advancing technology. He does that without a conscious thought for he does it by what is known as the Law of Motivation. He is motivated to create forms to serve him to free him so he may do other things of his choice.

Now there is a balance with advancing technology. And the balancing is—as it is in anything that is created by mental substance—to look at it frequently and to demonstrate being with it or being without it. It is critically important in anything that one finds beneficial to their mind to make the conscious effort daily to be with it or to be without it. Without that effort being made, man someday awakens that he is dependent on the very forms that he has created. And by being dependent upon them, he gives to them the power over his life. Consequently, he lives to experience the bondage that he has created through his errors of ignorance, for he is abusing, not using, the forms, the technology that he has brought about by his advancing intellect.

Thank you. The name of Summer Land was used to describe a higher realm of consciousness. Does this correspond with the summer or south in consciousness, which receives as we face the east and the light? Do all the realms have names? And where do their names come from?

In reference to Summer Land, the student is correct in its position of south as you face the east. Now as you face the east, which side of you is on the right and which side is on the left? *[After a short pause, the teacher continues.]* Yes, I'm asking you, cameraman. Face the east. Tell me—

South is to the right.

South is to the right as you face the east.

Yes.

Is that what you're telling me?

Yes.

South is to your right.

Yes.

Is that what you're saying?

Yes.

What's to your left?

North.

So when you refer to, when we refer to Summer Land, when it is clearly demonstrated by facing east, its position of south, then you understand that a Summer Land is a land that is freed from what you would understand as aggressive act. It is more or less in keeping with what you would understand as a vacation. It is a land that is pleasant. It is not a place that one would stay for an extended period of time, for one is not accomplishing in evolution. It is a plane of what you might consider rest.

So whenever you make a change, whenever you have learned various lessons, you get what is known as a rest, a rest time, that you may enjoy the fruits of your labor, that you may experience a relaxation from the great effort that has been made. And so from plane to plane, as the changes are made, you will experience what is known as a Summer Land. How long it lasts is ever in keeping with your evolution. And the longer you remain in a Summer Land, the more difficult and greater is the work you have to do when you finally leave the Summer Land. It is similar to a person in your world going on a vacation: it never seems long enough, and you dread the return back to work.

Thank you.

You're welcome.

The summit that was held in Geneva with our president and Russia's secretary general, did this meeting bring any lasting good for the world? [The Geneva Summit with President Reagan and Soviet General Secretary Gorbachev was held on November 19 and 20, 1985.]

Well, whenever there is any effort made and there is sincerity in the effort, then only good can come from it. As I stated to some of my students months ago in reference to that summit meeting, that it was in the best interests of the planet Earth for the president of the United States and for the premier of the Union of Soviet Socialist Republics to have a meeting and to visit each other's country in the very near future; that it was the wisdom of the angel monitors, who monitor the planet Earth. And therefore, I can only assure you that only good can come from it, regardless of appearances.

Thank you. There are nine expressions of each center of consciousness. The first expression being slave. Is that an expression of the earth center and, if so, are there eight more expressions to the earth center? The second one is slave. Is that—and I can't read the next word—of the fire center?

Speaking on that question there, yes, that is correct. There are nine. And that teaching will be fully covered in our coming year with our science of diagrams.

Thank you. How may we allow harmony to have a higher priority in our lives?

Identification is the key. We alone choose what we identify with until we enter the realm where we believe that we are those experiences of the past. Reference is our greatest burden to bear on the Earth planet. We refer. And what we refer to in consciousness is a judgment we have made. And so reference is, indeed, a heavy cross to bear, a true burden, for those who are self-identified on the planet Earth. When one has an experience and there is no reference, one reacts in keeping with a wild animal who is, whose instinct is survival. Reference is the burden.

Thank you. When we bind ourselves in thought, can we feel this as a constriction within our physical bodies?

Yes, indeed, we can. Our problem is we know too much. And whoever knows too much is filled with reference. And as I just stated, reference is, indeed, our burden. And so we're burdened with a, with a cross of mental substance. You see, my friends, that which benefits us is that which removes the burdens from our mind that our little soul may rise and that we may experience the joy of living.

So you have classes; these classes are given to you to help you to unload that which you are burdened down with. And so when you pause and you look around the world and if you don't have reference for something, then experience the joy, for you don't have reference for it. And not having reference, you're not controlled by that burden.

Thank you. How can we release this constriction?

Refrain from reference. I just covered that.

Thank you. How can we remove the thought of I from our consciousness?

Well, how can you remove the thought of I from the consciousness? By taking control of the mind, for it exists within the mind. It doesn't exist anyplace else. You see, with so many choices that a person has in their life to think about so many things, the I is one of the last things one would want to bother with and have an intelligent and joyful life. So the only thing—you have been given the cleansing breath. Through the cleansing breath, properly applied, and through the various other exercises that you have already been given, if you will apply what you have been given, you won't have any problem being burdened down with the thought of I, for the moment that the thought of I begins to register in your consciousness, you do your cleansing breath and some of the other various exercises you have been given, and then the next thing you know, you're not plagued with that great burden known as the thought of I.

Thank you. Why is it so difficult to let go and accept total consideration of everything in the universe?

Well, the more practice one has in thinking of themselves, the thought of I, and the more practice one has in believing that they are the thing that they are thinking about and the more reference that they have, then, of course, the more difficulty they have in changing the pattern. But it is not impossible. My students are already demonstrating moments of that.

Thank you. Though I tell myself and continually remind myself that I am not limit, I find myself repeatedly becoming limit. In this the nat—Is this the natural process that goes through . . . ah . . .

I understand. The thought that we create with our mind, once gaining control from a lack of the creator's effort to keep it under control, it does not easily give up the position that it has gained. [A clock begins to chime.] And so in that respect, it is a natural process, yes, in that respect.

I'll wait for the clock. [After the chiming stops, the cameraman continues reading the questions.] *OK. Do the triune points join together to form a diamond shape within the sphere of one's true being and does it extend outward as well as crossing within?*

Yes, it does. Very perceptive of that student. Yes, it does.

Thank you. When we think of our questions for discussion, are those thoughts that become questions given to us, at times, as revelations from the higher realms that we are receptive to at the time?

A few.

Thank you. Does the spinal column hold light energy? Is the energy stored there?

Well, if you could consider a flowing river as a warehouse, a storage, in that respect, yes. Try to understand that this life-energy known as *prana*, it flows from the base of your spine up over the base of your brain; that it flushes over the brain [and] it goes back down through the spine.

Now in the coming year, as I have already stated, with the equipment that we are finally gathering up in order to bring this to you, we will come and give to you in our classes the science of diagrams. We will also give you the demonstrations with our new equipment on video and audio of the actual pressure points and what they are able to accomplish through living demonstration.

Now I want to speak to you a moment on that. There are many books for untold ages available on your planet that give various, what you call, acupressure. Now as things have passed down throughout the ages, they get changed and what is known as contaminated by the falsifying hands of the copyists. We will give to you various pressure points to bring about control of this river of life. Now your breath is critically important and the various exercises that you've already received. And when this is brought about in your coming year, it is, remember, it is given to you in keeping with your own soul evolution. And those who cast their pearls before the swine, the uninitiated, soon find they have no pearls left to cast. I think all, all men would agree with that great truth, yes. I think they call it senility in your world. Or does it have a different name? Go ahead with your questions, please.

Thank you. If one has reached the stage of total obedience to the Light, would this be considered a large spiritual step to take?

Well, not to many students that I have, it wouldn't be considered a large spiritual step. It depends on who is viewing. Now if you're asking me, as a teacher and the work that I have to do, it is the natural progressive step. What the mind calls total obedience, it already demonstrates. I find many of my students who demonstrate absolute obedience: absolute obedience to the forms they have created that are now controlling them. You see, a person who believes they have to have this or have to have that, a person who denies that which they are and experiences this insatiable need and believes that they are the need, which is the effect of their own denial of what they are, now there's a person that has absolute obedience. The only thing is in the direction of this absolute obedience.

Now many people demand absolute obedience. Well, it is absolute obedience that they are serving that is demanding absolute obedience of another who is demonstrating absolute obedience to something else. You see, oil and water doesn't mix. And either the water or the oil is going to have the absolute obedience in time. I do hope that's helped with your question.

Thank you. You have stated that through the power of concentration or will, we will be able to clothe ourselves in any form that we are able to imagine that we may—

Pardon me. We already have. Thank you. Go ahead.

—that we may serve the purpose and intent of the Divine within us. Do you mean after we have left physical form or while we are in form?

Well, it's totally dependence on, dependent on the direction of your absolute obedience. I mean that you have already done that through the power of your will and the laws you have established. And you may change that at any time and any moment. Yes.

Thank you.

If that's what you want to do.

Would this apply to all? To being like an actor, to where our physical body would be the same and yet we would emanate a different character accordingly to the situation?

No, you would, having evolved through your absolute obedience to the Light that you truly are, you would change the atoms, electrons, and molecules of your present form and would wear a different cloak. Yes.

Thank you. What is the effect of someone talking in their sleep? How can it be corrected?

Well, one speaking in their sleep, it is obviously a demonstration that the forms they have created have taken such control there's no longer any censorship and they just are little blabbermouths and give away all the secrets to anyone with a listening ear.

Thank you. Does dancing always express itself through the fire center? Can it be an expression from the higher centers as well?

Dancing is not restricted to an expression of the fire center, though that is the most frequent and common use for the expression, yes. It doesn't have to be. It isn't always. Yes.

Thank you. Why would an endeavor in life and just—no—yes. Why would an endeavor in life end just when it has been expanding and growing to become something different?

Well, it is our perception. I know from looking into that question from that questioner, that student, that it is definitely, in that particular respect, it is perception of the perceiver.

Thank you. Is the energy of the crystal electromagnetic or is it a different form of energy?

The energy that is captured and directed by what you know as the crystal is an electromagnetic energy of the finest and highest possible vibrations known to man.

Thank you. Would it behoove us to study mathematics in preparation for our classes on diagramology?

Why, well, indeed, it would behoove one to know that two and two doesn't add to five. Yes, some basic knowledge would, indeed, be most helpful in that respect.

Thank you. In a recent class it was given that we can become aware of past civilizations and planets by becoming aware of the intelligence and vibrations of the atoms, electrons, and molecules which compose our physical bodies, for they once were part of these past civilizations and planets. Would you please speak on the process by which these particles are so indelibly marked with the vibration that lasts for eons?

An atom contains within it the possibility of recording all experiences of which it is a part of. For example—and it is demonstrably true and scientifically true—an atom that is a part of the composing of your little finger was once contained in the little finger or the temple of very, very ancient, ancient times. Now the intelligence of that, the awareness of that experience still exists within the atom. It is indelibly imprinted. No matter how many eons pass, those experiences do not change; they are indelibly recorded within the atom [as] the atom, having been a part, in its evolution, [of] expressing in a person's finger of thousands of years ago or the building or the brick of a temple. Now a person has access to all this information within the house in which they live. It is up to the individual to gain sufficient control and to awaken to what they are in order that they may clearly read the various atoms. As long as they believe that they are the finger, therefore, they cannot see nor hear clearly what that finger truly is. They are over-identified with the form, and they have reference, judgments, that it is what it is not. And so by believing that the finger is what the finger is not, man is blinded to what it truly is and, therefore, unable to read and let alone to study and to understand the atoms that are there that contain recorded history of eons of time, far beyond the planet Earth, the atoms that compose your body today. Yes.

Thank you. Is it possible to purify the vibration of atoms, electrons, and molecules? Is this part of the purpose of the soul expressing in form?

It is not a matter of purifying the atoms, electrons, and molecules. It is a matter of taking control that you may arrange them in such a harmonious way that you are no longer obstructed by them. You see, the evolution or refinement of something is everything in its place and a place for everything in keeping with the divine plan. Yes.

Thank you. Do the vibrations of atoms, electrons, and molecules of past civilizations pose a threat to archeologists at the excavation sites and the visitors to museums where these artifacts are exhibited?

They could. It depends upon the viewer. It depends upon their state of evolution. It depends on various factors. Some people are more easily affected by these vibrations than others. It is ever in keeping with their Law of Identification. For example, if you take a person to view a computer show, for example, and their identification is with plants and flowers, they will not be as readily nor as easily affected by the various demonstrations of electronic technology. And so, of course, that factor of identification of the viewer is critically important.

Thank you. You have said that atoms, electrons, and molecules have been used before on other planets and other times. Do some of these atoms, electrons, and molecules remain with us through each expression?

Some of them do in keeping with the law. Yes.

Thank you. If one has expressed elsewhere, as a mineral, such as iron, and there is no time in truth, would they not still be expressing on that star or planet as well as in human form on Earth?

In that respect, yes.

Thank you. Is memory par excellence composed of atoms, electrons, and molecules?

It is your perceptive [perception] of them that is known as memory par excellence. It is your perception. Yes.

Thank you. You have spoken before of the observers who are here to see over our planet inhabitants and to see that we do not cause problems in the universe. Would they destroy us for the good of the universe if we went too far? Has this happened to other civilizations or has that been due only to severe imbalances?

They assist us in keeping with the Law of Imbalance. And in that respect, in answer to your question, would they destroy us? They are not the doers. They assist us in destroying ourselves if that is the choice that we have made. Yes.

Thank you. What is the cause of so many mother and adolescent daughter conflicts?

Competition, child, competition.

Thank you. Is the traditional family unit disappearing? If so, what will take its place? [A clock begins to chime.]

Promiscuity and license. It already has.

I'll wait for the clock. [After a pause, the cameraman

continues.] *Thank you. Were the Egyptians a spiritually advanced society before the birth of Christ? If so, what laws were set into motion or broken that caused them to decline as a group of people?*

The belief in glory. And in reference, were they an advance civilization prior to the birth of your Christ, in that respect, yes, indeed, they were highly advanced long before your Christian era.

Thank you. In—

Glory, try to understand, is an expression of pride. Go ahead, please.

Thank you. In music is a flat note a magnetic or negative direction and a sharp note an electric or positive direction of the same note? For example, C sharp is also D flat. If so, does this principle apply to our centers of consciousness so that we are electric when ascending the something and magnetic when descending? [It seems the cameraman was unable to read one or more words of this question and replaced those words with "something."]

Yes, I am smiling there with my student there. And I have shared with some of my students the flat-heads and the sharp-heads. And yes, indeed, indeed, it is. You're either flat or you're sharp. And I find many times, yes, flat-heads are magnetic; and sharp-heads are electric. Yes, that is absolutely true. In fact, that is a preview that I was discussing with some of you in reference to our teachings coming up in the forthcoming year that you move up the scale, which is also color, which is also, of course, one and the same as sound. And as you step up, you take control and that's known as a sharp. And as you fall back and you go into reference, and therefore step on your own judgment, that's known as a flat. And so those who are evolving are sharp, and those who are falling back are flat. Yes.

Thank you. It seems that the jungle is getting to be more of a jungle today than even a year ago. Is this true or am I perceiving through a cloud of judgments?

Read the last sentence, please, again.
It seems that the jungle is get—
The last sentence.
Last sentence. Is this true or am I perceiving through a cloud of judgments?

Well, I'm very interested in the word *perception*. You see, we do not perceive through a cloud of judgments. We conceive by our judgments. And so one sees things ever in keeping with their own evolution. And when one sees the jungle, the way—what you call the jungle—[it] really is, it's like an awakening. We must not allow our self to awaken and to be the expression of reformists, for there is nothing more detrimental to the peace and harmony of one's mind than to enter the realm of reformation, to reform. It is one thing to have an expression of relief from having passed on through a lesson of life. It's something else to try to convert everyone else after one has done so, for one does that only to gain unto themselves the strength necessary to keep on with their changes.

So it is in the student's, and all students', best interest to be grateful for the crumb of change. And to stop giving life-giving energy to the delusion that they've made no change in 20 or 40 or 14 centuries or whatever time they've been exposed to the Light. Of course, that's just a device, a little ploy by the human mind, you understand? It's what you call in your world kind of a con game, you know, to gain a little bit of pity and a lot of energy. One who's able and smart enough, cunning enough and clever enough to express sorrow and pity and sigh and exhaustion and helplessness, you see, is one who, usually from a little expression of helplessness, gains a phenomenal amount of someone else's energy, you know. And one should ever be on the alert with that type of cunningness and try to understand that we all have this wonderful ability to use it constructively and wisely. It is no longer necessary for us to use these ploys and games of life to gain energy or to try to get people off the track of what they're trying to discuss. And when we make a little effort to grow up like that, we'll get right down to the cause of things and, therefore, in so doing, have the demonstrable cure right before us. I do hope that's helped everyone with those questions, you know. Yes.

Just, just keep moving right along. Don't worry about the jungle. There's enough to take care of without the jungle. I'm going to bring in a few machetes. I told my channel the other day, I was going to have some machetes made for him to hand out to the students and then to turn them around and show them which way the jungle is. *[Many students laugh.]* Thank you. Go ahead with the questions, please.

Thank you. Is patience the only path to truth because we give ourselves the opportunity to see what we have created, are bound to, and may free ourselves from?

Yes, very excellent perception in that respect. Definitely. Excellent. That reveals a little effort to study and hopefully to apply. They're on the right track and continue on with it. You won't find a dead end from that.

Thank you. In reference to he who hesitates is lost, when we demonstrate the sense to pause, how do we stay free from hesitating and becoming lost?

Well, the sense to pause is not hesitation. One hesitates—you see, he who hesitates is lost. Hesitation reveals that there are several contrary desire forms trying to get their way in the consciousness and that the light of reason is not present. Now the sense to pause is one who calmly takes control of their mind, pauses, and views all of the varying desire forms that want to be expressed; that casts the light of reason upon them. And by casting the light of reason upon them, one has the lion's sense to pause and has the strength and control over the forms. However, he who hesitates is lost for the hesitation—hesitation is these various forms that are still in control, and there's a hesitation because who's going to get the control. So there's a vast difference between he who hesitates is lost and the intelligent path of the pause is the strength of your soul for it has within it the light of reason. Yes.

Thank you. I have difficulty seeing things in clouds, but I see forms in wood, water, foam, rocks, etc. Is that because, possibly, the rocks—correction—the others are lower center physical forms?

Indeed, it reveals an identification with the other centers of consciousness that exceeds identification with the air center. And so that's a lovely, wonderful perception there of that student. Yes.

Thank you. Why do we experience cold? What causes the experience besides the physical? Is it distance from light, which is warmth?

Fine perception. Indeed, it is. Now remember, it is the light of the consciousness. So, you see, when you experience cold—you must remember that the body has certain varying degrees that the body can tolerate without any ill effect. And it far exceeds this 70 degrees that so many believe that they've got to be in. Yes, please go ahead.

Thank you. Why are many creative people inspired at the darkest period of our earth night, when the greater light is furthest away?

The desire for the Light is far greater. You see, the darker the night, the brighter the Light. And so when you're in the depths of the darkness, there is a greater drive. When the decision is finally made to awaken and you find yourself in the darkest night, your drive for the Light is far greater than if you were closer to the Light. Man values what he makes great effort to attain.

Thank you. As Halley's Comet helps us have less need, will that extend to world hunger? Will there be ways to solve it?

You already have the solution to what you know as world hunger. However, those in control of your planet at this time have made their choices and those choices, having been made, they do not change readily or easily. What you know as world hunger is an error in the thinking of the people of your planet. World hunger only exists because of an error in thinking. There is sufficient food supply on your planet to care for all people and all species. It is an error in thinking. It is not a lack of supply of your planet. Yes.

Thank you. When I am listening to my audio rhythmic cleansing tones and doing the breath and visualizing the sky, it seems the sky encourages thought. Can this happen? Why does it seem it is so?

It isn't the sky that is encouraging the thought. It is you that are encouraging the thought, but you don't have to. It's a matter of controlling your mind. It's a matter of making an intelligent decision. You look at the sky and you decide that you want to see a beautiful landscape and a beautiful landscape, for you, you have created. Now for anyone else who enters that level of consciousness, they will see the same landscape that you have created. Yes.

Thank you. After we have answered the question "What have we accomplished?" in the Rotunda, what determines the next realm where we go to?

The answer to the question determines the next realm.

Thank you. Could you please speak on your understanding of the oracles of Delphi?

Well, in reference to the oracles of Delphi before they were totally abused by the greed and the errors of ignorance of mankind, [they] were used by the prophecy schools for their students' purpose of expression, like you would send anyone to a music school. They are given the opportunity, of course, to demonstrate their ability. And so the oracles of Delphi was a school of prophecy. And if you will study history, your history, you will find that those people with the wealth of your world and those people in high position requested a certain oracle to speak to them at Delphi. Now what [that] history is telling you [is] that the students work[ed], as student prophets, and answered the questions through the oracle. And there were those in position, in political, financial position, who, of course, knew this, and they requested the teachers, the various teachers or the more advanced prophets to be the ones to answer their questions. And the oracles of Delphi [were] not only very popular in that time but there were many, many, many, many oracles. Some of them, of course, more accurate than others. Yes.

Thank you. When we emit a thought, being a color, a sound, and a vibration, does each thought have also a shape, like in the kaleidoscope?

Yes, each thought does have a shape. And I would like to say that the shape is like the lovely, beautiful diagrams and geometric patterns of the kaleidoscope that you have been viewing, but I cannot say that. However, someday you will get to see the color, the sound, and the odor of the form that is the effect of your thought. You may not like the smell. I don't know how much you will appreciate the color or the sound, but that will, of course, be dependent on what you enjoy in creation. Yes.

We have time for one more question here.

Thank you. White is middle C on the musical scale. There are three primary colors: red, blue, and yellow. They each correlate with a soul faculty. Red, action and healing; blue, spiritual; and yellow, wisdom.

Yes.

Do all soul faculties stem from the primary colors and branch out?

The Light of spirit, the Light, the intelligent Light, that which you are, is what you would understand as pure white or [middle] C. From that there is the division, the effect of expansion, and those teachings will fully be covered in our coming classes.

Thank you very much and good day.

DECEMBER 1, 1985

A/V Class Private 26

Good morning, class. Another beautiful day here today.

And I think you will note, [I am] speaking to you through the mist of creation, so to speak. *[The teacher refers to the video filter that was used on this video that obscured the edges of the frame with a white haze, but left the center of the frame clear and unobscured.]* We're going to continue on here, first, with the questions from last week and also the ones that have been submitted for today's class.

Thank you. Since atoms and molecules are recycled and there is really no time, are the Akashic records recorded inside of each of us or are they actual records kept in a particular realm?

They are actual records recorded inside of each of us in a particular realm within our consciousness. Yes.

Thank you. Since there is no time, can crystal record what we call the future as well as the past?

Indeed, it does.

Thank you. Did Jesus dematerialize his body after his so-called death or did the angels assist in this matter?

The angel within assisted in the matter, and in keeping with the law that like attracts like, in that respect he had assistance, yes, of course.

Thank you. Does the possibility of dematerializing one's body stop after seventy-two hours after passing on?

It has to take place in keeping with the Law of Identification within the period of seventy-two hours. That is correct.

Thank you. What form is the closest living form on Earth now that is a relative of the birds?

The form on your planet, on your present planet that is the closest to what you call the birds on your planet, is that the question?

Yes.

And you want to know what the closest relative to the birds are?

The closest living form.

The closest living form, then it would be what you know as the lizard.

Thank you. Are there birds on other planets besides Earth?

Birds, in respect to the judgment of what you understand birds are, no. Birds as birds, yes.

Thank you. What form did the birds evolve from to its present evolution?

Well, the birds, you understand birds with wings; of course, you understand birds [with] wings who live, basically, in the element air. [They] use it as their avenue of movement or transport. All life form comes from—life form as you know it—from the water center. So in that respect, all life is from your oceans of your planet. Yes.

Thank you. Why do churches use bells as part of their structures and in some religious ceremonies?

Well, in reference to churches in your world using bells as part of their structure, it is basically, the bell is for the frequency that the bell emanates or sounds. And consequently, because it is capable and has been used as the balance frequency, it is still used in your world today for religious or spiritual purposes, yes.

Thank you. Is the firmament spoken of in the Bible the ozone layer or was there once another layer around the Earth?

No, the firmament is the ozone layer.

Thank you. Is the science part of the Living Light based upon laws of physics and other sciences?

It is based upon laws of physics. It is definitely. The key to the universe is mathematics and is based upon it. Yes.

Thank you. Do computers have thought forms? If so, is man receptive to them?

Man is receptive to that which man creates. And in that respect, all computers have thought forms, for man has created them with thought forms.

And in speaking on computers, I think we'll pause for a few moments because it is so important to your present evolution in your world. Computers, as you understand computers, [are] something that your mental world has created in keeping with denial, which offers need. And in keeping with those laws of judgment of mental substance, man has created a machine to do work more efficiently, to do it more quickly than he himself is capable of doing it in keeping with his own thinking, his own beliefs, and his own obstructions.

Now man has created something to serve him. It is not the first time that man has done so. It is a repetition of history in your worlds. And so man has created this fine technological equipment to be a servant to him. However, man shall awaken to realize that whatever he creates to serve him, he is not only responsible for, he becomes, in time, the servant of. For example, a computer, as you know computers, will do what you want them to do as long as you demonstrate the law that it demands. And the law that that which you create with your mind demands is absolute obedience. So that which you have created, known as a computer, demands absolute obedience in order to serve you in keeping with your needs and your own demands. However, man presently believes that the computer is serving him. Someday he will awaken, as he has awakened in eons past, that he is serving the computer: that it will only do what he wants it to do when he first does what it wants him to do.

So if you understand in your advancing technology that you are the servant of whatever you create—whatever you create in consciousness, you become the servant of ever in keeping with your denial, which is your need. So if you understand that and you accept the demonstrable truth of how advancing technology really works, then you will not have such a rude awakening down the path so to speak.

Thank you. What caused the sudden extinction of dinosaurs from the planet Earth?

The change of the poles. They've changed several times. Each time they change [there is] a rapid change in the movement and the evolution of the planet. For example, you can relate the growth of the planet, or the growth of any planet, to the changes and growth of a human being. You take a child from just a little baby; [when] it reaches a state of early puberty, it goes through a drastic change, the ages of twelve to fourteen. The planets go through these same or similar changes in keeping with their growth through childhood, adolescence, through adult and aging. And so the planets reveal to you, as your Earth planet reveals to you, the law that governs all creation, including your own form.

And you might adjust the volume control, so we don't have the echo for our students this morning. Thank you. Yes.

Thank you. What is credulity?

Well, credulity will be—of course, we have a diagram on that, which we'll go into our diagramology in this coming year of '86. Credulity is a demonstration of a person who is easily imposed upon. One who is credulous is one who is absolutely convinced that they are their needs, which are effect[s] of their denials of what they are. Yes.

Thank you. From within can resentment be directed from one level to another instead of it being a cause from the outside?

Well, all causes are within. And it is in keeping with our own reaction within our own consciousness whether or not we express or demonstrate resentment. For example, a person experiences resentment whenever they judge they are being rejected. Now many people have many experiences, and I have found throughout these years that people who are easily rejected—they reject themselves easily in their consciousness—are people who are over-identified with themselves and the belief in their judgments. And they are so over-identified, it's known in your world as a person who is completely in love with themselves. And so anyone who is over-identified with themselves is a person who experiences, in the course of a day, many rejections and, therefore, fills themselves with its demonstrable effect, which is known as resentment. It chemically poisons the system. It poisons the atmosphere. And it is certainly the opposite of the joy and goodness of living.

Thank you. Why is it hard to tell oneself the truth?

Well, first of all, one is the truth. And for one to declare what they are, that which they believe they are is threatened. And in that respect, a person who, at any moment, believes that they are the thoughts of their mind, the judgments, and all of the past experiences is a person who finds difficulty in accepting what they are, but that is something that slowly and surely, through evolution, changes. And a person, in time, expresses what they truly are and is a person who fulfills their purpose of being in form.

Thank you. When you feel you have, and you get mental and emotional conflict, does that mean you really haven't told the truth? Is there another explanation?

Kindly read the question again in reference to when you feel emotional conflict.

It's relating to the question prior to that about telling the truth to oneself. And it says, "When you feel you have, and you get mental and emotional conflict, does that mean you really haven't told the truth? Is there another explanation?"

Well, mental and emotional conflict is an identification with judgments that one believes that they are. And because judgments are not in accord or harmonious with each other, when they rise up in the consciousness, then a person experiences a mental turmoil or a mental conflict. That's in keeping with what was given to you so, so very long ago: we always get what we really want. It's a matter of honesty to accept what it is we really want. Ofttimes we believe we want something, and when we merit the opportunity of working and receiving that which we believe we want, we find that we are not about to make that effort, which only reveals to us that there is another priority within the consciousness; that we believe we want one thing and when it comes up against another judgment in our consciousness, we very soon find out we never really wanted that anyway. We want the other priority and the other judgment, which is the obstruction to what we think we want or believe that we want at any time. Yes.

Thank you. Is it the soul that makes commitments always or do our levels make commitments for us also?

Well, our levels are very happy to make commitments whenever they judge that by making the commitment they're going to have their own way. And so we find ourselves ofttimes making commitments. From lack of control we've entered a certain level of consciousness, and those judgments want to have control for a time. And so we commit our self only to experience a little later on that another level of consciousness and judgments have risen and they demand that they have their way. And so we make a contrary commitment. And then we find in time that our spoken word has lost its power for we have transgressed the Law of Commitment.

There are commitments that are of our soul, of what we truly are. And then there are the tempted commitments of the various levels. And a person becomes known, sooner or later in life, as a person who is not reliable; their word is not their bond for it does not contain the power of their heart. Yes.

Thank you. You spoke of casting pearls before the swine. What does this saying mean and how does it relate to Serenity?

Well, in reference to casting the pearls of wisdom before the swine of ignorance, one should try to understand that which is instrumental in being the element through which intelligence may express itself, and to cast that contrary to the purpose of its design is to transgress the Law of Wisdom. And therefore, a person must pay the price for that foolishness.

Now a person in their evolution, speaking in reference to Serenity and this school, a person in their evolution and through their own individual efforts, they establish laws through which they receive what you would understand as pearls of wisdom. And for them to demonstrate by being a blabbermouth in reference to them, only reveals that they do not value what they have received. And from a lack of valuing whatever we receive in life, we guarantee the loss of it, for the law demonstrates for us repeatedly that whatever we have no value for in life we guarantee to lose.

Thank you. I was in error on reading that last question. The word was senility *and not* Serenity. *So the question was in relation to senility.*

Well, I've answered the question that you asked in relation to Serenity. And so we will move on. And you can make the corrections for our next class in reference to the student who asked that question. I'm sure they'd be most grateful for your apology. Go ahead, please.

Thank you. Are we going to self-destruct as a race of beings on this planet?

Well, we self-destruct moment by moment. Are we going to self-destruct as an entire race? Well, because individuals compose societies and races, in reference to that, if you call a complete change of form from what you presently know as self-destruct, then in that respect, yes. Try to understand that your form on your planet, which you understand as your human body, is of very recent time in respect to the universes. It's perhaps calculated in matters of hours, not even days. So your form, as you know it today, is just a speck in the universe of so-called time. And it will serve its purpose. It is presently in a stage of adolescence, what you would consider a teenager, as far as the form is concerned. It will go through its maturity and its aging process, and another form shall rise, in keeping with the laws of creation and the Law of Evolution that governs form.

Thank you. Could you kindly speak on competition, why and how it takes root in our minds and is it, as some think, necessary for growth?

Well, challenge is necessary for a mental world for it is the stimulation of the human ego. Now without the incentive to compete, one does not experience the stimulation to the human ego. Now the human ego is designed to serve a very good purpose: to ever refine and to progress. And so if you don't have a stimulation of what you understand as the human ego and you don't have competition to benefit it, from which cometh challenge, then the purpose of the design of the human ego is not being served. And it is not a matter of the person having an ego. Ego is part of the design of the form of the mental world. And so we all have ego. The benefit of it is to recognize it's a vehicle we use and never to permit our self to believe that it is us.

Thank you. If the sphere of our true being—

May we pause for just a moment, cameraman. I think it is an important lesson which you have granted the opportunity to us, to all of us this morning that you would use the word *Serenity* to express the function known as senility. And I think, you see, these are always important things. I have taught you over these many years to question yourself, "Why this and why now?" Now, so we'll take these few moments to bring about some light and understanding of our students and specifically this morning with [Student R, the cameraman]. In what way do you understand the word *Serenity* to mean senility or best, perhaps, you could grant us an understanding of the word *senility*?

Well, when I read the question—

No. What does the word mean to you, please?

Senility?

Yes.

One who is very old and loses touch with reality.

Oh, yes. Now that's what senility means, is that correct, to you?

That's my understanding.

Your understanding of senility. One who is very old and loses touch with reality.

That's—

Would you not say, then, if one who is very old and has lost touch with reality, that they are not serving the purpose of their design in reality?

I don't know.

Well, if you were very old and what you call senile and you were losing touch with reality, what would be your purpose for being in reality?

I have no idea.

Do you feel you would have a purpose?

I'm sure there must be a purpose or it wouldn't be.

I see. Well, I'm interested for you all, as students, why you would think Serenity—why you would speak "Serenity" and think senility.

Well—

Don't you find that interesting?

Yes.

Don't you find it interesting to speak "Serenity" and think senility?

Yeah, well, at the time I wasn't thinking senility when I spoke "Serenity." It was . . .

Did you read "senility?"

I did.

Well—

I read "Serenity." And then I had to go back and study it and interpret it and finally I realized that I had read it wrong.

Oh, I see. Well, I think it's important for this class that we think how interesting it can be what we relate to what, wouldn't you say?

Yes.

Yes. And to relate senility to Serenity is a most interesting revelation, wouldn't you say?

Yes.

Because, after all, spirituality begins with an *s* also.

Yes, it does.

Go to the next question, please. I may be old, but I don't quite accept that I'm senile. Go ahead with the question, please.

Thank you. If the sphere of our true being creates a diamond shape through the triune points, does that then mean that each individual sphere joins together in the Allsoul to form a larger diamond-shaped structure as in the molecular structure of atom?

I'm happy to see that the class, as a whole, is progressing so beautifully. Ofttimes a person—in reference—yes, that is affirmative. It is absolutely true. Ofttimes we think that we are not changing. Ofttimes we think that we are not growing. For so many times, so often we stumble and we fall. And it is at those times, when we stumble and fall, that we permit our self the luxury of discouragement and to permit our self to be used by the forms and to state that there is no change; nothing's happening; been around for many years and there's no change whatsoever. It is only those times when we can realize that there is something using our mouth, and we'd best take control of our mouth, let alone our whole being.

I want you to know, as students, that there has and is continuing excellent progress being made in these past few months. It has not been easy, I would not say, for some of you. But that that comes easy goes easy, for it does not have the value within our consciousness. And the changes are taking place within your being spiritually, and when you make a little more effort to identify, through your thought processes, with the universal consciousness rather than so much of the mundane, so much of the limited consciousness, you will see more clearly the changes that are taking place.

And when a person permits themselves to identify with the obstruction, sooner or later they are going to experience the luxury of discouragement. And it is, indeed, encouraging when you will take a few moments each day and look at the whole perspective. You've long been identified in evolution with form and with limit. And so you must not permit your limited minds to expect miraculous changes in your world of limit in the way you want them. Oh, these changes, sometimes seemingly miraculous, are taking place in your limited consciousness. And they are not pleasing to your limited consciousness ofttimes. But it is absolutely necessary for the breakdown of the old, which is used as atoms and electrons and molecules, to create the formation of the new, whether it's a new thought or a new physical form, which you'll all be entering in time. It is a matter of what you permit yourself to identify [with], whether or not you see clearly the progress that has been made over this time.

Now many of you have been with me for a number of earth years. And ofttimes you think—I don't—you think that you're making no changes and you're making—there's no growth. And you wonder, your minds, you say, what you're doing even being. Well, that's when you can be assured that the forms that are still trying to hold you to their service, those masters of the old, are using their last-ditch efforts to hold on to you as you're moving through and evolving through these various realms of consciousness. Go ahead with your next question, please.

Thank you. Is it possible to hear what another is going to say before they speak and is this a bad habit, a habit of not listening?

Well, now, first of all, it has nothing to do with not listening because you're listening to something. Of course, it is possible to hear what a person has to say before they physically say it because before it is physically said it is formed in a mental world and a thought form is created. And so, many people are receptive to thought forms through an inner awakening of being aware of their own. And therefore, through that effort in life, they become qualified to be receptive to the thought forms of their own. And therefore, in keeping with that law in principle, they are aware of the thought forms of others and that registers within their consciousness before they physically speak the word.

Is it a good habit or a bad habit? It depends on what you do with it.

Thank you. Is Mercury the ninth planet and Jupiter the first?
No.

Thank you. When the camera is recording physical forms, particularly human forms, is it possible—correction—is it also recording mental, astral, and other forms as well?

Indeed, the magnetic, electromagnetic process is capturing all of those forms. Your developments in your present stages of evolution rarely reveal the other forms. That is correct.

Thank you. Is the cause of father and son conflicts competition as well?

Yes, yes, that's a part of the conflict is competition. Yes. Father and a son, and a mother and a daughter. And it has served as an instrument to stimulate the ego and hopefully, through honesty and the light of reason, to educate the human ego. Yes.

Thank you. In a recent class reference was made to contamination due to predominant vibration in the atmosphere. How may we discern whether the cause for our emotional upset is a predominant vibration outside of us or the expression of a subconscious type—or tape?

Well, first of all, a person certainly realizes that exposing themselves to contamination, they first have to identify with self in order to experience it. So we are not left helpless. We are not left without the light of reason to be in the midst of the Philistines, where the Divine Spirit, known as God, shall deliver us. It is a matter of making the effort within our consciousness to be with a person, place, or thing and to not be a part of a person, place, or thing.

Thank you. When we become aware that an experience triggers our emotional security tapes, how can we best use that information to become more aware of the subconscious judgments governing our emotional security and broaden our horizons?

By a declaration of demonstrable truth that our security is not dependent upon forms created in the past or forms created at any time. That is not where our security is. We must first make that declaration in consciousness many times, whenever we feel we're getting close to our security being threatened.

Thank you. What is the cause of severe, wrenching leg cramps and what can be done about them?

A nerve condition. Now, for example, these, what you call severe, wrenching leg cramps is a condition of the nervous system. It reveals that the nervous system of the individual, which is governed and controlled by the water center, by what you understand as the emotions, is greatly disturbed. So through effort to take control over that realm of consciousness, to accept the possibility of something better, to make effort to refrain from dependence on people for your emotional security, then you will start on the path of bringing about the necessary changes in the mental realm. And in time, the physical realm, which includes the nervous system, shall respond.

Now I spoke to you several times in reference to pressure points, which will be coming up as a part of our ever-advancing and expanding teachings here in these private classes. And I want you to understand, like the questions asked about cramps and the nervous system, when a pressure is applied to certain pressure points of the human body, there is an opening up [of] an obstruction that has been created.

Now I'll speak for a moment on that. I spoke to you about the river of life, the little boat of identification on that river of life. Now this river of life flows in your being. It flows up, and it flows across and washes what you understand as the brain. And it flows back down the sides of the spine. So you have this continuous flowing process, coming up through the neck of your anatomy, which represents the will, and you have the head, which represents your intellect.

And so when there is an inharmonious condition, a conflict, and a contrast between the lord of your universe, which is your will, and the human intellect, which houses all of your judgments, when this is in conflict and contrary, you create in consciousness an obstruction to the flow of the river of life. Now in your physical body this river flows up from the base of your spine, this *prana*. And it flows up through the will, through the neck, comes over and washes over the brain, the intellect, and returns back down, only to continue its constant flow. *[As the teacher speaks the previous sentence, he moves his hand to depict the flow of the river of life. First, he places his right hand on the back of his neck, then moves it to the top of his head, then moves it around the top of his head, and finally moves his hand down to the back of his neck.]* When this conflict is deep in consciousness, you create a condition which causes a physical obstruction or dam on your river of life.

Now pressure applied in a certain way, very specific and definite ways, temporarily remove[s] this dam that you've built up unconsciously. It physically removes it so that this river can flow harmoniously once again. Now it will last as long as effort is made to bring about the changes. And they do not come suddenly overnight. So it is not advisable, with these teachings that are coming up to you in the turn of the year in reference to—and there are two major pressure points in the human body. Very specific. Very definite. They have an effect upon your entire body. It is not in the best interest to become dependent upon constant pressure upon these points in the physical body without the effort being made in consciousness to bring about the necessary changes in your thinking and judgments. Otherwise, designed to serve a most useful purpose, it would only become a crutch in the sense, a person not making the effort to make changes in the consciousness would simply become more reliable [reliant] upon physical pressure (application upon the pressure points) and that would not serve a good or beneficial purpose over a long period of time.

Go ahead with the rest of your questions, please.

Thank you. I have heard the term apport *used with reference to transfer of an object or person from one place to another. Does that deal with the breaking down of atoms, electrons, and molecules of a form and rearranging them in another location? How does it work?*

Well, it certainly does. I wouldn't consider it breaking down. I would consider it a changing of their molecular structure. Now how does it work? You know, a picture's worth a thousand words. And so take, for example, you can relate best to—say that you have a judgment. And I don't think we, any of us, are in short supply of that substance. We have a judgment in the mind. And you want that judgment out of your consciousness. So you go to work to remove that judgment, that form from your consciousness. Now try to understand that form is a composition of atoms, electrons, and molecules in a certain molecular structure. And so a judgment, a thought form solidified, is the same basic structure as what you say a physical or chair structure is. Now many of you are aware of the difficulty and the effort that it takes on your part to change the molecular structure of a judgment that you believe that you are. So as you make the effort to separate truth from creation, to look at the judgment that you have been servicing and to declare the truth and finally awaken that it is something that you have created, however, you are not it, when that day comes, you find that you are able to change the molecular structure and release it from your consciousness.

Try to understand any judgment that you have within your domain in your consciousness you have created and has a certain molecular structure. You are responsible, and only you can remove that from your mind. And that is ofttimes very difficult for a person. It is as difficult as one believing that the judgment is them. So the first step in creating what you understand as [an] apport, the changing of the molecular structure, the releasing of it from your being or from your view and permitting its reconstruction at a distance, is a process that you are already doing whenever you remove from your consciousness a judgment that you have believed that you are.

Now you have other awakening[s] of that process happening. For example, you make the effort to counsel an individual and you finish counseling them, you've gone into their realm of where those judgments exist, you've gone into that within your own consciousness, and you have established a bridge of rapport. And then you're through with your counseling and helping the individual; they walk away. [They are] just walking on air feeling so good, and you crawl away for days or weeks after, for in this philosophy it's often been stated that you've picked up the package. And so that process is taking place all the time. Yes. Go ahead.

Thank you. Years ago, the term surrender *was used in the teaching of this philosophy, but it is rarely used at present. Why is that?*

Well, it is rarely used at present [because] at the time it was brought through to you to surrender, the basic student body was on a certain level of consciousness. And when that was brought to the students at that time, it was instrumental in bringing to the human ego greater incentive to do something. For the human ego in its uneducated expression, the last thing it wants to entertain is to surrender anything, for it possesses whatever comes within its domain. And so the word *surrender* has not been used in our teachings for a long time. It was designed and brought through to be used to help the student body at that time. It has served its purpose. And now you have moved more into the word of *acceptance*, absolute obedience, just like the computer, and total acceptance. And that's the reason: it's known as evolution.

Thank you. What are the states of consciousness? The first self and the second slave. Would you speak on this?

Well, whoever permits themselves to think of self has established the Law of Slavery because, you see, when a person thinks of self, then of course they believe they are these various forms that they have created. And so when you think of self, the forms rise up, and you start serving them and become a slave to your creations. So self and slave is, in that respect, daily, moment by moment demonstrable to all people. Think of self and be the slave. And a person who does not think of self is free from slavery, is free from bondage. Whoever permits themselves to think of self immediately steps into the chains of slavery. Yes.

Thank you. What are the states of—no. Fire illuminates and consumes. Does earth cover or nourish, water drown or save (water being necessary for life), air blow away or cleanse? If these are not correct, will you please reveal what is?

In reference to your understanding, it is very well put.

Thank you. Why does there seem to be more suicides [on] Mondays? Is there more self-pity? If so, why is that?

Well, I would think in your world of creation it's most understandable. Most of you people have established laws through which you play on the weekend and have to face personal responsibility on Mondays. And so it is understandable that you would establish in your world what you have for some time, known as blue Mondays, because you have to get up and get out of bed and you're not playing. The two days of playing have passed. That is something you have created.

Thank you. The Earth has been cleansed several times in mythology. Noah, by water. Atlantis by explosion or fire, then water. Are there—are the cleansings moving through the centers and is the next one by air? Will we eventually move on to spiritual centers?

Oh, yes, indeed, we will. And the next one is the element air. Yes, indeed, that is absolutely correct. I'm happy to see some homework is being done. And some thinking, some initiative thinking. Yes.

Thank you. If we students, who have much exposure to the teachings, are so slow to learn and change, how can the greater world be helped? It takes so long. It seems there isn't much time for anyone else.

What do you mean by anyone else? What do you mean by that? "There isn't much time for anyone else." What does "anyone else" mean?

I believe he's relating to the world outside this organization who has not had the benefit of the exposures and teachings.

Well, they're all in a process of changing. And it is, indeed, a slow change, but it is taking place. It's taking place through pain and suffering. You know, people make changes when things become most distasteful. So it is happening.

Thank you. How can we determine whether our thoughts are magnetic or electric?

Your experiences tell you constantly whether they're electric or magnetic. Your experiences always tell you whether or not you are electric or magnetic.

Thank you. How can we learn to encourage ourselves?

Oh, yes, indeed. That's an excellent question. And there's one simple answer: stop thinking of yourself. And when you stop thinking of yourself, you'll be amazed how encouraged you are.

Thank you. How can we keep our thoughts in the moment of now and not in the past or the future?

We just answered that. Stop thinking of yourself.

Thank you.

Be encouraged. Now I'll speak to you more about being encouraged and you'll understand that means stop thinking of yourself. Yes.

Thank you. How can we keep ourselves from being short-circuited?

Well, I don't want to answer every single question you have there by [saying] stop thinking of yourself and be encouraged. *[The teacher and many students laugh.]* Well, the thing is a person always shorts themselves out in respect, you know, they ground themselves; it's their thinking.

Why is it so difficult to change one's thinking? It's difficult to change one's thinking only to a person who believes they are their thoughts. And when we make the effort to stop that foolhardy way of thinking, believing we are all these thoughts and all these forms, then we won't have such a struggle and we won't find ourselves so grounded and so much in little childish rejection just because—you know, a person—it's interesting—a person who has something that they want presents themselves to someone. And the other person says, "Well, I'll be with you in a moment." Or "I'll take care of that later," because the person who brought the request never once considered anyone or anything but themselves. And so they go to the person with their request and the person who has other responsibilities says, "Well, I'll take care of that later," they walk away in total rejection, which only reveals how much they're in love with themselves. And so that's a matter of when you think less of yourself, you'll find out how encouraged you'll be about life. Go ahead, please.

Thank you. How can we become more receptive to change?

Well, the way to become more receptive to change is to get thoroughly disgusted with the way things are. And when you get thoroughly disgusted with the way things are and when you've reached the bottom of the barrel of the way you've made things, then you become more receptive to the possibility of change. And so, you see, when things are really what you consider tough, when they're really, you've just about had it the way things are in your life, be grateful for you are in the process of becoming receptive to making a change within your consciousness.

Thank you. When we have allowed our self to be under the control of self-pity, what is that we can say or do to self-pity in order to free our self? Is there anything that self-pity respects which would cause it to back down?

Yes, self-pity fully respects the Law to Ignore. And when you think and feel you're in the pity of self, which is the over-identification to self, immediately get to work. Immediately go to work and do some hard work, which will redirect the energy, and you'll be amazed how quickly self-pity will respond to that. It just can't bear to be ignored. And so it'll race around the universe to try to get in someone else's little house. Go to work. That's all you need to do. Yes.

Thank you. In giving from the heart, is it possible to give without the mind's awareness of it and its asking for something in return?

Well, I'll tell you, I've never known—I'll finish this, our class, here this morning—but I've never known in your world anyone who gave from the heart that the mind wasn't aware of it.

Thank you for such a lovely class today. [I] suppose there could be some people that give while they're in a state of sleep and then, in that respect, the mind there consciously wouldn't be aware.

Thank you and have a nice day.

DECEMBER 8, 1985

A/V Class Private 27

Good morning, friends, and welcome once again to our classes.

And I do hope with our bit of evolution here that you are not only able to see us but you're clearly able to hear us. If not, you'll please speak up. And we'll begin this morning with these many questions here that you have prepared. And I find it, well, you might say quite comfortable here in this new location for these classes. *[In the previous indoor classes in this series, the teacher was seated in the library of the temple while the students were in the adjacent room. In this class, however, the teacher is seated in the east wing of the temple, which were the living quarters of Mr. Goodwin, while the students are seated in the dining room and watch the class on a large monitor.]* So you go ahead, please, with your questions.

Thank you. If one discovers that one is poor at competing, what steps can one take to become better at meeting the challenge?

One will find in life there is no problem in meeting a challenge if the challenge has great value to the person who desires to challenge. So if one finds themselves what they say as poor in meeting a challenge, then one should view what they are very good at, in their thinking, in meeting any challenge and direct their attention in that area of consciousness and gradually, slowly but surely, gain what is known as sufficient self-confidence to meet any challenge.

Thank you. Why would one create a form that tends toward the sensuous and then choose to follow a spiritual path? Is this a contradiction?

It's a revelation of the various steps of evolution. One chooses what one over-identifies with; and in so doing, time and evolution, through the many experiences that they have, they are inspired to make changes. And so in that respect, one has the functions or the faculties, and sooner or later one awakens that one without the other is certainly not a balanced life.

Thank you. In the Allsoul, are we part of the same energy and power that is present in nature here on earth, both the benevolent and the destructive side?

Why, yes, we are an inseparable part of the whole. And we choose, moment by moment, whether or not to identify with the destructive or the constructive. So in that respect, of course, that is absolutely true.

Thank you. Is the strength in nature, nature being the trees, mountains, and planets—plants, the same molecular structure as we are in the Allsoul?

Well, in respect of comparing the trees and the mountains, the plants and the flowers, if your understanding is limited to the form which you are aware of with your senses and with your functions, then in that respect, no, for it is far more involved than just limit or form. The molecular structure is identical.

Thank you. Does the strength lie in the grow—correction—in the joining together of light force in all living things to make one divine, neutral, intelligent Energy?

Well, the divine, neutral, intelligent Energy is an intelligent power. That's what Light is; Light is power. Now I don't want to give the impression or be an instrument to create confusion. Mental force is not the spiritual power. It is not identical. It is a lesser vibration, controlled and limited by formation or form.

Thank you. In a Hopi Indian prophecy, it was predicted that a container of ashes might, one day, be thrown from the sky that would burn the land and boil the seas. What did they mean?

In reference to that particular prophecy, they're speaking of ashes spread across the sky and burning the lands and etc. From the destruction of one thing is the birth of another. And so we see these steps in evolution as one thought form disintegrates into ashes, so to speak, it is the essential ingredient for the birth of a more evolved form. And so any civilization, identified with their world as they know it, viewing its ending, its change or destruction, would refer to, to the experience and the prophecy as a change in the world. And so in reference to the Hopi Indian prophecy, they prophesied an ending to the world as they knew it at that time. And they prophesied that from the ashes of their civilization would come this great change in the world, which you on Earth are presently experiencing.

Thank you. Is the Earth going through the same purification process that man goes through to return to its source? If so, does this mean that the surface will become uninhabitable and the interior of Earth habitable, just as man eventually looks within?

Indeed, that has already happened with other planets in the solar systems, yes.

Thank you.

That is the natural, progressive step of evolution. We first evolve from the core and expand outward. When we reach the limits of our state of evolution, we begin to contract and to return to the source from whence we have sprung. That is the process in creation of humans, of all forms, including planets.

Thank you. Is exposure the only way for man to be purified?

Exposure helps man in the sense of an expansion of the consciousness. Now that which is hidden, once revealed, grants, by the Law of Revelation, understanding. From understanding springeth wisdom. Yes.

Thank you. What does the following part of the 23rd Psalm in the Bible mean, "Thou preparest a table before me in the presence of mine enemies; thou anointest my head with oil; my cup runneth over"?

"My cup runneth over." "Thou preparest a table before me in the presence of my enemies." So in reference to those statements and the same in reference to the statements, "In the midst of the Philistines I shall deliver thee," is to help to guide man to strengthen his faith that that which is his is within him, that it is sustained and maintained by a Divine Power that no enemy created by the mental substance can ever destroy.

Thank you. What does the Bible mean, "The meek shall inherit the earth; and shall delight themselves in the abundance of peace"?

"The meek shall inherit the earth and delight themselves in the abundance of peace." The path of nonresistance serves man well in many ways, for the battle with anything or anyone is a battle with a created form within one's own consciousness. When one no longer battles something within their consciousness, one no longer directs intelligent energy to feed it. When one no longer directs intelligent energy to feed it, it cannot long survive. And so in that respect, wisdom reveals ofttimes the wisest path is the path in consciousness of nonresistance. By accepting the demonstrable truth, "This is a form created by my mental substance. I alone am responsible. It has no power over me except the power I give to it through a direction of intelligent energy by the Law of Identification."

Thank you. If one changes the forms which have caused the hands to be crippled, would the hands heal themselves and become normal once again?

Hands, feet, knees, legs, backs, all respond to the created form that sustains them. As the form is changed in the higher levels of consciousness, the lower or more gross forms respond accordingly.

Thank you. Did some tribes of the American Indians pattern their headdresses after the spectrum of colors found in light? If so, was one of their reasons to signify their oneness with the Light?

Yes, in that respect, for when one works to design anything that covers what man believes is his glory—for the head to your civilizations represents the glory, the glory of the temple of God, the glory of the form—and when one adorns it with all of the frequencies and vibrations contained within the white

Light, which is the Light of Life, then one is showing respect and making effort to become in harmony with the purity of the white Light of Eternal Truth, which they know in their heart that they are.

Thank you. What is the best procedure to follow in fulfilling a promise or commitment?

In fulfilling a promise or commitment, one must first make the effort to be fully aware of the various levels of their own mind. For if one does not do so, one is frequently tempted not to fulfill the commitments that they have made. So often a person makes a promise and a commitment without the total consideration of all of the levels of consciousness which they service. And because man is quickly tempted by various levels of their mind to commit themselves for the purpose of self-gain, man finds great difficulty in his life for he breaks his promises, he breaks his commitments for he has moved in consciousness in service to another level of the mind which has no interest nor desire for the commitments and the promises that another level of his mind has made. Total consideration of all the levels of our mind prior to making a commitment or promise is absolutely essential to a man of character.

Thank you. How would you take control of forms that are talking while you sleep?

First of all, by talking to the forms before you ever go to sleep and by granting them the kindness, the kindness and consideration of guidance when you awaken. So if the effort is not made by an individual to take control of their mind, then they must pay the price of their mind taking control of them while they sleep.

Thank you. Would it be possible to recognize it while you're awake? And how would I go about it?

Well, to recognize the various forms created by one's mind, one must first make effort to declare the truth: that they are not the mind; that the mind tells them many things. They must make the effort to separate truth from creation by daily making the effort through their cleansing breath and the various exercises that they have already been given—and affirmations—to separate themselves from the thoughts of their mind. And in making that effort, then they become qualified to place those forms in proper perspective, as they are the children that a man has created.

Thank you. What does a person choose instead of force in a situation they may be tempted to use force in?

What does a person choose instead of force when they are tempted to use force in a particular situation? First of all, by taking control of their mind and not allowing themselves the temptation. Now once they have been tempted, they must declare the truth: that that experience, that's taking place in their mind, which they understand as temptation, will bring no benefit to them. For example, a person who is tempted is a person who is not only weak in character but is a person who has no control. A person who is tempted is a person who willingly desires to become the victim and the servant of another person. So one must first be honest with themselves and find out what within their thinking [tempts them to] have a desire to have someone else control them and to serve someone else.

Thank you. If competition is good, could you speak on what is its balance so that it doesn't become intense aggression?

Competition becomes intense aggression when man refuses the wisdom of total acceptance. Now if man accepts the wisdom of total acceptance, which is the will of God and the flow of goodness, then man, knowing that his mind is designed to serve him, that his ego is designed to serve him, knowing that his ego is stimulated or exercised by a challenge, with the total acceptance, man therefore is not attached to victory each and every time his ego is challenged.

Thank you. If diamonds are a crystal and are an emanation of balance, is that the reason a man gives a woman, traditionally, a diamond ring? Why doesn't the man also get a diamond?

Diamonds, jewelry, is an ancient symbol of deception. An ancient symbol. Diamonds are not the crystal of which we speak, which is the perfect reflection of the balance of frequencies and vibrations. Diamonds, for eons of time, have been given, like other so-called precious gems, when a person is tempted to fulfill what they judge is a need, a desire that they have created in their mind, the effect of denying what they are. Now in order to fulfill that need, man, his mind, judges he must offer something. And so the luster of certain gems, especially diamonds, have been used for they have a tendency to deceive from their brilliance. You know, in your world one often says that you dazzle them with brilliance and baffle them with something else. And so what is the finest thing you can give but a ring of slavery or bondage that has a little stone on which they may be dazzled with brilliance as they're bound with, I think you call it, something that begins with bull. Yes.

Thank you. I have better concentration and breath control in the morning. Is that because desires have been fed during sleep?

Well, it could be an effect of the exhaustion of one's expressing their desires while they're sleeping. Many people have various types of dreams, an expression of their desires. Some of them almost drown during that time. In that respect, it could be. Yes.

Thank you. How does one keep from slipping into satisfaction and keep a good feeling about a job done while moving on?

By knowing that they are a channel through which the Divine Energy is flowing and that if they were not there to do the good job, there's a hundred thousand others very capable of doing it.

Thank you. It was said in one class that the planet Mars, ah, corroborates—I think is what it says; I'm not sure—with the fire center. Does that mean that Mars is one of the nine expressions of the fire center?

Well, Mars represents an expression of the aggression of the fire center. And, you see, when you—well, in reference to that question, it's a bit complex in reference to the statement contained within the question. If my hearing is correct, it says one of the nine fire centers?

Ah—

That's new to my understanding. This is why I'd like that—
Nine expressions of the one fire center.

Well, I see, you want to express the totality of the fire center. Well, let's try to get a little simpler understanding of that. Mars represents aggression. Aggression is a part of the purification of the fire center. And in that respect, yes.

Thank you. Is my understanding correct in that when our faith in God is greater than our love of demons, our merit system improves, and therefore our transgressions are lessened than if we believe we are the forms?

Well, yes, I would like to clarify one thing: that when our faith in God is greater than our love of self. There's a tendency, you see, for us to forget about the word *self* when it comes to demons. And if we leave out that most important word and create a sin, an error of omission, then we're back to what you would call square one. So let us understand that when our love of God is greater than our love of self, for self being the house in which we allow the demons to play, then in that respect, yes.

Thank you. Are the planets that are closer to the Earth, such as Mars and Venus, a more predominant influence within our fire and water centers—

Yes, just a moment. To those who are identified with self and to that degree only. Please continue with the question-statement.

Thank you. And does the water center correlate with the planet Venus and the planet the moon?

The water center is directly related to the moon. Now in reference to Venus, the ancient symbol of love—such an important thing. When you speak of conjugal love, the love of the human mind, you cannot speak of it without the brilliance of deception, for it is a mental expression. And the mental expression, created by the mind, is an effect of denial. So when you have denial, you have deception, for whoever denies deceives first themselves and becomes the instrument and qualified to deceive another.

Now it is very important here that we understand—I think I'll use this little, this little, block here. There. That's very comfortable for my channel. *[The teacher places a small, rectangular pillow, which has a u-shaped cutout to accommodate his neck, on the chair to support the nape of his neck. The dimensions of the small, roughly-rectangular pillow are 7.5 inches long, 3 inches wide, and 3 inches tall, with a u-shaped area removed from one side.]* You cannot experience denial without becoming an instrument of deception. For to deny the truth, the inevitable path, is to express deception. So denial and deception are hand in hand.

God, good, the principle that you are is total acceptance. To move from that truth, you have falsehood, the effect of deception. So deny and deceive. Accept and experience in consciousness the freedom and the goodness that you are.

Now, for example, when a person permits themselves the type of thinking, oh, they were just doing fine until someone else said something, what they are doing is demonstrating denial and deception. So whoever refrains from denial in consciousness does not deceive themselves, does not experience need, and does not become the victim of their own thought form creations.

Thank you. Are all the planets at various stages of evolution and growing pains? And how does this affect our centers of consciousness, if at all?

It affects us, definitely, in keeping with our identification with those centers. And yes, they're all going through their growth and growing pains.

Thank you. What is the purpose of all the rings around Saturn? Are they representative of the nine expressions of that particular planet?

That is a planet of great wisdom and truth. That is a planet of knowledge. That is the planet where the schools of the universes that are governing your solar system meet and work for the wise course of evolution of all forms. And that planet is protected by the nine frequencies that are necessary for any, any teaching of great value to the universes.

Thank you. What is the most beneficial way to teach gratitude to a child?

Demonstrating it is the best possible way of teaching it. A picture is worth more than a thousand words.

Thank you. The time is approaching in our world when we celebrate a virgin or odic birth. Would you please share with us something of the lives and duties of the other people who were so conceived?

First of all, because I think we'll all agree that we, as individual forms, are not virgin or odic conceived in that respect, that's certainly not in our expression, that those who bear that great weight of responsibility are doing quite well with it. And we really need not be concerned for I think we'll find it sometime in evolution before we reach that state of consciousness. Yes.

Thank you. Is pride the will directed to the lower centers of consciousness?

Pride is the very glory of the house of the ego. If the ego is educated, then it becomes a servant for a wise man—can become a servant. But when it is from the uneducated ego, then it constantly trips us up on the path of evolution.

Thank you. How may we learn the purpose of the design of a thing?

By making the effort to learn the purpose of our own design. Whereas we are so familiar with our form, it behooves us to study and make the effort to become aware of the purpose of the design of the parts of our house that we use so often. That's all right, there, my little friend, Mr. Red. *[The teacher addresses Serenity's dog, Reddy, who was often called Mr. Red.]* Cameraman, close the window. I guess he got chilly. I'm not. Go ahead, please.

There is a lot of racket out there.

Yes?

Thank you. Would you please expand on the statement you cannot mix oil and water?

Well, in reference to the ability to mix oil with water, if you've tried to mix it, and so many people have tried, they do not mix, for one always rises to the surface. So in reference to truth crushed to earth shall rise again, you cannot mix oil and water. It is very foolhardy to speak forth one thing while you demonstrate another. That is an effort of a foolhardy person trying to mix oil with water. There's no way possible that you can speak one thing while you demonstrate the opposite.

Thank you. Please speak on celibacy and how much attention should be directed in one's effort to disassociate from old established patterns in our sexual behavior.

Well, first of all, when one accepts what they are, they will not experience the denial of that. And in accepting what they truly are, they will not experience the need and will not have these so-called sexual behavioral problems. A person has, what you say there, sexual behavioral problems because they have over-identified with it. And in the over-identification with a function, one can only experience an ever-increasing need for its fulfillment because it is in keeping with the law of denying what one is and trying to become what one is not.

It's only important to a person who over-identifies with it. For example, if a person over-identifies with their big toe or their ankle, sooner or later their big toe or their ankle will constantly demand energy from the person. And if a person doesn't continue to feed it energy by directing thought, intelligent energy through thought form to it, then the toe begins to bother them and disturb them. However, that which disturbs us in time does awaken us. And when we wear out from an over-identification with our sexual behavioral problems, we, sooner or later, we will grow and awaken that it's not as important as we used to think it was. And we may even move, as some of my students have, fortunately, when they, at times, have demonstrated that they'd rather have the cash. Yes.

Thank you. Could you please share your understanding of our solar plexus?

Our solar plexus? Well, if you'd like to look out at your solar system and you would like to see that there is a sun and there is a moon. And that if you will visualize the sun, in the center there of the universe, from whence cometh the light, physical light and its radiations, your solar plexus could be described in that way.

Thank you. Could you please share your understanding of how creation and faith or balance are brought together? You have the great, so-called unseen power that moves all situations.

Well, it moves any situation that you are responsible for creating and, therefore, a part of, and, by the divine law, have the right, the divine right, to be an instrument through which it may be changed. And so in that respect, whatever you are involved in, in any way, you are therefore a part of. And being a part of, you, of course, have not only the responsibility but you have the right to be an instrument, in being a part of something, to be an instrument through which you may evolve and grow.

Thank you. It has been said that the brighter the Light, the darker the darkness. Is this—

No. May I, may I speak up a moment here, please? The brighter the Light, the darker the night. Now I think you're going to find it most important, someday coming up, to understand that the only difference between *light* and *night*, in reference to your world, are two letters. One of those letters is *l* and one of those letters is *n*. Now letters in your language, as you know them today, are an effect of the evolution of symbols or signs over a period of many, many, many, many centuries. And so the understanding of words long ago lost to your civilization, the understanding of letters long ago lost—they are the evolution of signs and symbols. And so the statement given to you some time ago is, was, continues to be: The brighter the Light, the darker the night. Now there is a difference between the word *night* and the word *darkness*. Please, now, repeat your question.

Thank you. I'll repeat it with the correction made. It has been said that the brighter the Light, the darker the night. Is this process always present throughout each realm into the higher realms?

There is no night in the higher realms. Now, for example, darkness moves in the night. Night is a vehicle that darkness uses. Now if you understand that, then you'll understand and—clearly with the statement, the darker the night, the brighter the Light—the brighter the Light, the darker the night. Darkness moves in the night. Without the night, it does not move. Now what is this night of which we speak? You look out and see, "Well, I can't see the tree. It's nighttime." The tree is there. There's lesser light, and in lesser light, forms, darkness, move. It is the movement of those forms that is the darkness. They move in the night. So you experience what you understand: you see clearly for it is light; you do not see as clearly for it is night. And so this is going on at all times in the consciousness. When you evolve to higher realms of consciousness, there is no darkness for there is no night in which the forms can move. Yes.

Thank you. What happens to the forms while we are resting, as compared to when we sleep and the forms have their so-called heyday and get their feeding?

Whoever rests is in the light. Whoever sleeps is in the night. So the difference between the light and the night is the difference between rest and sleep. One rests and one rejuvenates in the light, for you rest in the light; you sleep in the night. So those who sleep enter the night and feed the forms of their own denials of what they are. It's known as the sleep of satisfaction. Service to the functions is the experience that you know as satisfaction. You see, when you permit yourself to believe that you are your form, then you guarantee your service to the forms of your denials.

Thank you. Are the colors of the soul faculties and their corresponding sense functions of a similar color?

Yes.

Thank you. In the past two movies we have viewed here at Serenity School, "The Emerald Forest" and "Baby," they have such a devastating effect because of what man is doing, doing to himself and his planet. Is there realms where we can live in peace without the self-destructiveness? Also, will we be able to communicate through vibration, sound, and color with all species of all the universes?

Yes, that is in truth our destiny. And yes, there are planets where that is taking place and has for eons of time. Man can only offer his environment what he offers himself. So as man on Earth looks at his environment and he looks around him and he sees the destruction and the sorrow, then man can relate: that is what he's doing inside himself. Whoever over-identifies with limit is destined to destroy it.

Thank you. Is our Law of Identification that which moves our will in all realms as to what we merit and our environment?

Yes, indeed, it is.

Thank you. In all cultures color is more predominant and vibrant. Is that a demonstration of a more natural affinity with their purpose of what they truly are?

Yes, it is.

Thank you. What is the correct angle to the light in photography?

Forty-five.

Thank you. That is all the questions I have.

Well, isn't that lovely here. Here, at this lovely holiday season, I'll take a few moments before we conclude our class here today. I know that most of you are aware that my channel had a, oh, I guess you would call it a highway experience or a roadway experience. And so today I did speak with his doctor and said that we would make the class, perhaps, a little bit shorter today for he did overdo there yesterday. *[A few days before this class, Mr. Goodwin was a passenger in a motor vehicle that was struck by another motor vehicle that was traveling at a significant speed.]*

However, I'm looking here at all of you, you know. I know it's, perhaps, sometimes, you think, difficult for you that I can't see you, but I see you all very clearly there. And I don't think that you're up or down, or in or out because I see you right here before me. And I do want to take these few moments to really share with you my encouragement that I experience over the efforts that are being made by you as a student body. Now we look back a short six months and time and again I've had to reprimand you—some of you—and it doesn't mean that I won't have to do it again, but I know it is just not the holiday season that there's a greater awakening taking place within your consciousness, because it is taking place. And that's very, very important. Ofttimes, you know, when those levels you sometimes over-identify with, you think that there's no change at all. I can tell—anyone who listens can tell—when it's you that's using your mouth or it's some of those other things temporarily using your mouth. There has been, there continues to be, a fine growth process taking place spiritually.

My job is, and has been, to share with you laws and demonstrations that are affecting your spiritual growth and awakening. You all know that I have not come to take care of your pocketbooks or your wallets or any of that other foolishness. That belongs to that fellow down there, you see. My job is to share with you the Light. And once you are moving along in the Light, you no longer have any concern or interest in that other stuff for it just flows in keeping with the law that you are flowing. When you don't build a dam across the river of life, you don't get drowned in the flood. And it's really quite that simple. So as you build less dams—dams, of course, you know are obstructions to the flow of the river of life which you are. And, you know—I'm sure you're all aware, maybe some of you are smart enough to guess what a judgment is: it's a log, you know. It's a log. You use it to build a dam across your own river of life.

And I'm happy to see that the majority of you no longer have such a need to self-destruct. It's encouraging. Because this suicidal tendency, you know, this *hara-kiri* stuff going on, it's not as prevalent as it was. And I am aware that this experience that some of you have had, the majority of you, to commit suicide, the slow process, the slow way, you're not as interested in that self-destruction as you were. And because you're not as interested in self-destructing as you were, you're going to experience, and are experiencing, more abundant good and a happier day.

Now I'm instructing my channel, when he comes back from where he's gone, to take a few moments to see all of you and then he's to take a rest and you're to have a fine day. And I know it's the holidays, but I think you could have made a little more effort to prepare a few more questions; however, it worked out just fine.

Thank you and good day.

DECEMBER 15, 1985

A/V Class Private 28

Good morning, class.

And a very joyous season to all of my students in celebration of the ancient and the modern celebrations and activities. This morning we're going to begin our class with the questions that you have prepared.

Thank you. Is my spiritual—in my spiritual notes, I've found the number seven is the great mystic, the trinity, seven, seven, seven. What does that mean?

Yes, the number seven is an ancient number of the psychic, so-called, and the occult and the mystery or the mysterious. You will notice that the so-called number seven is a horizontal and a vertical line. You will also notice that it is a number throughout the ages that, through ignorance, people have believed is some type of a magic or special number.

The meaning of numbers is very important for they reveal the mathematics and the key to the universe. However, one should not, should not depend upon a particular number as some magic wand to make changes or transformations in their life, for they would, in so doing, do a great disservice to themselves. Therefore, the number seven, tripled or otherwise, is only a mist to those who see the mist. And we see mist in our lives when we allow the shadows of the past, the servants of the judgments, to place the mist before us.

Thank you. Since we are composed of atoms, electrons, and molecules, does our attitude affect the universe of each atom, electron, and molecule of which we are composed?

Yes, indeed, our attitude has a very definite effect. For, you see, our attitude is composed of electrons, atoms, and molecules. So often we think of form as something that is in a gross expression. We rarely think of form in its composition of atoms, electrons, and molecules in reference to what is known in this philosophy as a thought form. Well, a thought form is created from atoms, electrons, and molecules. And because it is created of the same substance as your physical body, naturally, in that respect, it has an effect upon all physical as well as all mental expression.

Thank you. In physics, the electron is said to contain the unit of negative electricity, the proton, the positive charge of electricity, and the neutron, the neutral particle. Does this represent the magnetic, electric, and odic parts of an atom?

It represents the electric, the magnetic, and the neutral. You see, do not be confused with the odic, which is not the celestial realm of consciousness nor the celestial center. The odic is a formation. Now if you in, for example, in the forming or creation of anything move from the celestial realm, through the centers, to the odic center, then you carry with you the higher rates of vibration. However, that is not the usual process for the masses of the Earth planet. For the descent is down into the earth center, rises through the fire center and on upward. Your planet, Earth, is a fire center of consciousness covered with the physical substance, as you know it, of an earth center. Yes.

Thank you. Are there nine centers to each atom?

There are nine centers to each atom, electron, and molecule. Nine is not only the totality, it is the completion of the design of the purpose of any form. Yes.

Thank you. Is the spirit of Christmas a soul expression?

To those who have entered soul consciousness, what you understand as the spirit of Christmas is, indeed, a spiritual expression.

Thank you. Do microwaves that travel from satellites made by man to space stations, called dishes, have an effect on atmosphere, weather, nature spirits?

The transmission of microwaves in and of themselves, the microwave, does not have a detrimental effect upon atmospheric or environmental conditions. However, that which is transmitted over the microwaves has varying effects for the so-called positive and the so-called negative. So in that respect, it is dependent not upon the carrier, but upon the information that it is carrying.

Thank you. What is the law or laws that are being established with the earth station at Serenity? [The earth station referred to in this question was a satellite dish set up at the temple to receive satellite transmissions.]

The laws that are being established are rather evident and obvious to all of my students: it is a broadening of the horizon of communication. And from a lack of communication, there is not possible the expression of understanding. And without the expression of understanding, of course, there is not harmony, there is not peace, and certainly wisdom does not prevail.

Thank you. On a spectrum of electromagnetic waves, where does thought fit in? A higher or lower frequency than visible light?

The highest frequency of the mental world is below what you understand as middle C. Quite flat.

Thank you. The armillary spheres used in classical astronomy during the seventeenth and eighteenth centuries looked very much like our globe with the centers of consciousness that you taught us about. Is there any connection between them?

Yes, there is.

Thank you. If we choose to be the servant of God, is it true, then, that leadership is becoming a servant to your own God and path in life? Could you expand on this, please?

First of all, a leader first learns duty, gratitude, and tolerance. And a leader learns the awakening of that triune soul faculty by becoming the best follower. And so it is the best follower that becomes the greatest leader, for a leader must be willing, under all seeming circumstances and conditions, to follow that which the leader, as a follower, dedicates his life.

Thank you. When you have an inspiration and you know it is good, is it right to act and bring it into manifestation?

First of all, inspiration is not dependent upon a mental function for its expression. The human mind knows much. Wisdom is in the realm of inspiration. And so a person, so inspired, is guided by the faculty of wisdom to express and bring into manifestation their inspiration in keeping with the realm of consciousness that they first attuned themselves to, to receive and to experience the inspiration. It is a handmaiden of wisdom. One need not concern themselves in a mental realm of consciousness, for whoever is truly inspired and has entered that realm is freed from the dependence or need of the mental realm of consciousness.

Thank you. What would cause a person to hesitate?

Well, there are many things that cause a person to hesitate. One of the most common things, in reference to a person hesitating, is the whispering, the so-called echoes of the past in their consciousness: experiences. For example, a person has many experiences, and when a person hesitates, they are listening—there's a difference between hesitation and pause. When a person hesitates in something that they want to do, the hesitation reveals to them that the various judgments in control at the time are making sure in the mental realm that it will in no way interfere with their own selfish needs. And so a wise person pauses to contemplate, and a person controlled by their mental realm and their emotion hesitates and becomes extremely frustrated.

Thank you. What is the cause and effect of sarcasm?

Well, first of all, sarcasm is defined by each individual in various ways of definition. And to one person, someone is, appears to them at a certain time to be extremely sarcastic. That could, or could not, be the so-called facts of the matter. However, in reference to what is truly sarcasm, it reveals a person who is extremely insecure. It reveals a person who is often frustrated. It reveals a person who is extremely defensive and one who is a servant to absolute faith in the mental world and, therefore, expresses fear.

Thank you. Does receptivity and creating happen at the same moment? Would it be like breathing in (receptivity) and breathing out (creating)?

Yes. Try to understand that a person's receptivity is dependent upon what they have previously created. Now, for example, a person desires to enter a state of consciousness of peace and harmony and abundant good. That is the desire that they are aware of. However, have they made the effort to expand their awareness to the eighty-one levels of consciousness that they, as beings, are serving? If not, then there is a problem for the individual. For you believe that you've come into peace, that you desire to experience better experiences in your life, to have more good in your life and more abundance of health and happiness; however, which level is speaking at that moment? Is it the majority of the levels of consciousness that you are obedient to? If it is the majority of the levels of consciousness, then the demonstration will reveal what is known as majority rule. However, if it is not the majority of the realms of consciousness that you are serving and you are, at that time, not aware of those other realms of consciousness, then, indeed, there is difficulty in reference to speaking forth one thing and receiving the same.

Thank you. In what way is honesty our security?

Well, whoever is honest with themselves is freed from fear, for through honesty and this light of reason of the soul faculty, one then is not dependent on something they cannot control. For being honest with themselves, they know what they've made the effort in their own consciousness to control and to awaken and to educate. And they also, through honesty, know which of the realms of consciousness that they've made no effort, as far as their own responsibility inside themselves is concerned, they've made no effort or little effort to control those realms.

And when a person is honest with themselves, then they have a clear perspective of exactly what they want to do and what they're going to do and what they *do* do. So in that respect, honesty is not only the best policy for good living, honesty with oneself, but it frees oneself from the dependence of the mental realm of consciousness, which so many people fear because, not having made the effort to understand those realms, the effort has not therefore been made to control those realms. And so, therefore, what you do not control and you are responsible for, you very soon awaken someday to find out because you are responsible for it and you made no effort to understand or to control it, it is now controlling you.

Thank you. Would you please share with us the spiritual meaning of pearls and in what way are they living?

Well, in reference to pearls, a seed, all seeds are living. Now if you wish to limit your understanding to whatever is living for you is something that has to be within the boundaries of what you have judged living is, then in that respect they are not living. They are living, and they are moving. So many people look at a stone and they judge, ignorantly, that the stone and the various atoms, electrons, and molecules of which it is composed, of course, is something that is not moving. All form is moving. It is man's perception that deceives him.

Thank you. Do we not see the tree at night because of the night or because of the darkness moving through the night? Or because of our own judgments?

That's what the darkness is: limit, judgments. That's what judgments are: limits, boundaries. And so we do not see the tree in what you call the night for the darkness is moving at that time. Now when it isn't moving in your consciousness, then it's moving in someone else's consciousness. So, you see, it is the viewer. You see, the darkness is moving. The Light is ever present; the darkness is ever moving in that respect. And so a person, if they choose, through lack of effort, to view the world through the movement of their judgments in consciousness, then, of course, the day for them is a dreary day, a darkened day, or for many it is, indeed, a night.

And so you hear throughout all of the many religions, throughout all of the centuries upon centuries and centuries, that the realms of the angels, where there's peace and harmony, good and the joy of living, is a realm of consciousness that has no night. Well, they speak to you in that way that you may understand that it is a realm of consciousness free from limit, free from boundaries. And by being freed from limit and boundary, there is no expression of judgment, which is limit and boundary. And therefore, realms of Light are realms of understanding. That's why the people who enter those realms in their efforts in evolution experience the joy of living, which is the effect of the wisdom of expression.

Thank you. Is there a correlation between the orbital patterns of electrons around the atom and the levels of consciousness?

Well, yes, indeed, there are because, you see, man is the creator. And so man creates. Though he is sadly limited in his awareness of what he is creating, man on your planet is aware of taking a piece of wood and some tools and making a stool. That he is aware [of]—that he has created that. And yet when it comes to the creation of forms which have an effect and are his experiences—for that's what experiences are. I stated and spoke to you some time ago in reference to outward manifestations, which are experiences in your life, are revelations of inner, inner attitudes of mind. And so attitude correction is the path of the wise man that he may choose the various forms that he is creating that they may be servants of what he truly is, the Light, and not be the servants of limit. For that which you limit in consciousness, you limit in your experiences in life for you are the creator. Each day, each moment you are creating.

Now the process of the creating, so rarely is a person conscious of that. They are very conscious, very conscious of much of their thinking, but they are not conscious, from lack of effort, of the process that moves from their thought to the formation, to the limit, to the judgment, and especially to the experiences that they encounter each day.

Thank you. After we have received an answer to the question, "What inside of me desires me to be the servant and victim of another?" what is the next step?

Well, first of all, if one finds themselves in desire to be the servant, the victim, and the slave of another, it, of course, reveals that—one thing—they are very weary of making effort to bring about changes in their life. They want changes in their life; however, they quit before the victory in making those changes. And so it's a lazy man's way to present oneself to another and establish the law to be the victim, to suffer, in hopes that someone else will make the changes for us in our life. It is a foolish path. And any student of mine that finds themselves temporarily trapped in the need to be someone else's slave and someone else's servant, in that respect, will not always be there, not as long as they're in my school here. I can assure you of that. So it's only a matter of laziness in consciousness. It reveals a pattern of experiences for anyone who has tried many things [and] never stuck with anything long enough to experience the victory. And here in this little school, for those of you who stick, for those of you who have the right kind of glue, you will move through that level of consciousness. I can assure you of that.

Thank you. In reference to the class on denial and deception, if man stopped denying the truth that he is, would he stop deceiving himself by how good the good old days were?

Why, certainly. There would not even be a thought of the good old days. Once man stops deceiving himself, he's no longer tempted by what has passed. And as I've said before, if the good old days were so good, then why didn't we stay there? I have to go a long ways back, myself, but I am not tempted for the good old days when I see the good times in the now. Yes, go ahead, please.

Thank you. If we no longer wanted for things or registered need, would we no longer be so concerned with the passage of time or growing old?

Well, the thing is, it isn't a matter of things; it is a matter of denying that you are a part of them. Once you accept what you truly are, you're freed from the need, for that which you are is the whole. So when you accept what you are—you are the whole—this, this denial no longer exists for you.

And so let us stop and pause for a few moments here. You are the universe. You are the universe. That's what you are. Now when you permit yourself to deny that you are this universe through which all of these things express, ever subject to your will—you see, I have never in my life—and I don't wish to say never, but to relate to you I will say I have not and meaning never in your understanding—I have not met a person in my experiences in these universes that is weak-willed. I have not met a person that's weak in will. I have met many, many people, many, many people, but I have not met a person, yet, that has a weak will. Now I have met many persons, many people who choose not to direct their will in certain areas and make no effort in those areas of consciousness. But I look at all of the 81 levels and I find phenomenal will. It's only been limited to a few things, a few areas of expression. So there's no such thing in truth as a weak-willed person. There are many people who have used their phenomenal will perhaps to 1 or 2 or 3 or 4 levels of consciousness, but that in no way guarantees a weakness in their will power. It only reveals they chose not to direct that phenomenal will to areas of consciousness that others feel are absolutely necessary for what they call good living. Yes.

Thank you. One of our earth dictionaries defines justice *in theological terms as one of God's attributes by virtue of which He wills equal laws and makes just awards. How would the Living Light define* justice?

Justice is a process that each individual is going through moment by moment. Now in reference to our spiritual conscious-conscience that knows right from wrong, we also have this educated conscience that tells us what's right and what's wrong. And remember that an educated conscience serves the functions of your being, and a spiritual conscience serves what you truly are. And so we have this process in our mental world that says that this is justice and that is not justice. Now let us look at it in another way. When we accept justice in our mind, as an expression of our mind, freed, totally freed from dependence on what someone else does or doesn't do, when we accept justice from that vantage point, then we will find how just we really are to ourselves. Yes.

Thank you. When we register pain, what portion of the pain is due to fear?

All portions of pain are due to fear, the dependence on the mental world. For a person to remain in the mental world, they must spend a certain percentage of their identification in a mental world or they do not long remain in the world. That is the law in the mental world. And so a person registers pain when they are identified with a mental world. When they free themselves, at least temporarily, from identification with the mental world, then they will find there is no registration of pain.

Thank you.

And therefore, in that respect suffering is, indeed, great to those who are over-identified with their mind and their mental world.

Thank you. Is fear governed by the expansion-contraction principle, that is, does it grow or expand in proportion to the amount of denial and deception in control and contract in proportion to the awareness of truth?

Yes, in that respect in the mental world, it, indeed, does because it is the absolute faith that we direct to mental formations that create the fear.

Thank you. It is said that there are 9 spheres and 9 planes of consciousness through which we pass before reaching the Allsoul. What is the difference between a plane of consciousness and a sphere?

Well, there are 9 planes to 1 sphere. And so in that respect, there's quite a difference. For example, there are 9 planes to 1 sphere of consciousness, and there are 9 spheres, which is the totality. And so therefore, in that respect you have the 81 levels of consciousness.

Thank—

Now I would like to speak on this a bit here, a little bit more, on your prior question there on fear. If the judgments of the mind, which are the solidification of the thought forms that we have created from our thought patterns, did not have the ability to register within the mental world what you understand as fear, they could not gain control over your life.

Now go ahead with your questions, please.

Thank you. Are the soul faculties and sense functions representative of the spheres and planes of consciousness?

The spheres and planes of consciousness. Why, yes, indeed, there are. Indeed, they are. Now read the question once again, for I find some of you students down there a bit perplexed.

Are the soul faculties and sense functions representative of the spheres and planes of consciousness?

Yes, yes. They're representative of the planes. There's 40 functions and there are 40 faculties. Now, try to understand: 40 functions, 40 faculties and there's the one, divine, neutral Power that holds them together. And so there you have your 81 levels of consciousness. So 9 planes to 9 spheres is the 81 levels of consciousness. Yes.

Thank you. Is our goal on each planet to return to the Source only on a different awareness and plane of consciousness?

Yes, that's known as the Law of Evolution, which governs all form or limit. And good morning, my student. Mr. Red is here. *[Mr. Red, the church's dog, may have just awakened from a nap.]* Yes.

Thank you. What are the nine frequencies that are protecting Saturn and are they the same frequencies that protect all great teachers or teachings of value to the universes?

Yes.

Thank you. Words are made up of syllables and it appears that night and light are so-called opposites. The letter L appears to be similar to the 45-degree angle, and [the capital letter] N appears to be two pyramids facing in opposite directions. Is my understanding correct?

Reread the question. And my student, here, late out of bed, wishes to go in that chair. *[The teacher again refers to Mr. Red.]* So I think that you should make some arrangements for that lamp here. Well, how's he going to get up there without breaking that lamp—like that right now? We'll just pause for a moment here. We have a responsibility with two of my students here. Next time you'll have to get out of bed at the proper time. I—no. I think—sit. There. Well, I, I will let him sit up here. *[The teacher slides over in his chair to make room for Mr. Red, who was a good-sized dog, and the chair was not that big.]* Here! Just a moment, class, please. All right. Here! You can sit there. There. All right. Yes, go right ahead. Can you hear me over there? Yes, I think we'll be fine now. Now please reread this question here for a moment there.

The question was, "Words are made up of syllables and it appears that night and light are so-called opposites. The letter L appears to be similar to a 45-degree angle, and [the capital letter] N appears to be two pyramids facing in opposite directions. Is my understanding correct?"

Yes, in that respect, I would say yes. Now, however, you want to try to understand not to confuse the simplicity of truth with the complexity of intellectualizing. Yes.

Thank you. What is the purpose of the moment of the forms—
Here. *[The teacher addresses Mr. Red.]* Yes.

What is the purpose of the movement of the forms in the night?

What is the purpose of the movement of the forms in the night? The movement of forms *is* the night. And so if you are identified with forms, you have a lot of night.

Thank you.

I do hope that that's helped with your question. Yes.

Thank you.

Yes.

Our earth station here at Serenity school is facing south for efficiency.

Correct.

Is that because the south is the receiving direction?

Well, it's because your minds have placed them, [the broadcasting satellites,] in such a way that we must face south in order to receive the finest possible transmission from this geographical area on Earth in which we find our self. Now if they had been placed where they should have been placed in your sky up there, then—and your understanding and technological advancement was sufficient—then we'd all look east and get a fine transmission. Yes.

Thank you. Which direction does the river of life flow, clockwise or counterclockwise?

Which direction does the river of life flow? Clockwise or counterclockwise? Well, let us answer the question with a question in [that] respect. Awakening is a process that is, by the laws of responsibility and by the laws of physics, within. Do you know of anyone that can get within anything by going clockwise?

No, I don't.

All right. Now I want my students to understand that counterclockwise is the way to go inside. And the way to understand anything is to get into it and not to be deceived by the covering and the appearance that form gives. So please reread the question.

The question was, "Which direction does the river of life flow, clockwise or counterclockwise?"

If it's a river of life, it's counterclockwise.

Thank you.

Now if the river, you have a different understanding of it, then it's clockwise and goes out and wastes all over the universes. Yes.

Thank you. Does it flow in the same direction in all of our nine bodies?

Yes. Everything flows within and is experienced without.

Thank you. What type of crystal is the most pure for recording?

Well, the most pure crystal is pure crystal; crystal that comes from your planet Earth. That's pure crystal. Yes.

Thank you. Is the most accurate molecular structure for crystal [a] triangular arrangement?

Yes.

Thank you. In the Garden of Eden myth, was the consumption of the apple a transgression or a progression?

Well, try to under—if you are interested in the myth, which is really in truth a story revealing what takes place moment by moment for humanity on your planet, you have to ask yourself the question, Was Adam given a lemon or an apple? Yes, I'm asking you as a student. *[The teacher addresses the cameraman, who is reading the questions that were submitted by the students.]*

He was not given either. He was—they were placed near him.

And what did he taste? Who bit the apple or did they bite the lemon?

No, they bit the apple.
Well, who bit the apple first?
Eve.
She bit the apple.
Yes.
And when she bit the apple, she tempted Adam, correct?
Yes.
Well, it's too bad it wasn't a lemon. Because, you see, first of all, you cannot grant to another what you have not already granted to yourself. And so if you will understand what the story is revealing: she offered to another what she first offered to herself. You see, it's a wonderful myth. It's a wonderful teaching, when you understand these were handed down from many teachings—here, we're—my student here, we're going to have to, going to have to have a little more counseling here in class. *[Mr. Red, who had been sleeping on the teacher's lap, moves his leg in a way that pokes the teacher, who readjusts the position of Mr. Red's leg.]*

Now the teaching is, there's no way to get something for nothing. So Eve bites an apple. She offered it to herself. Now after she offered it to herself, she offered it to another. And so when someone offers you something, try to understand they have first taken it themselves, in speaking on a mental world, you understand. So you cannot grant or offer to another what you have not first granted or offered to yourself. And so you hear in your world, you know, you hear these, well, I guess they would call them rather smart or cocky little statements, "Well, I got another hooked!" I think that's the statement that's used in your world. Well, there you are, you see. And if you understand what anyone is supposedly giving to you, they first gave it to themselves and having given to themselves, they feel, "Well now, I'll give this to another. But what is it that I am giving?" So often we confuse loans with gifts, and that's something we should be always alert to.

And, you see, the apple, it doesn't mean that it's a bad tree in any sense of the word. All trees have some kind of seed, you know. And so it depends on what you do with them. So you can use them wisely or you can be wasteful with them, yes. I do hope that's helped with the question there.

Thank you. Why do many humans pass over at late winter or early spring?

That's when they fall.

Is it because of the transitional nature of that time? Is there a deeper spiritual significance?

No, no. It's the weaker time. It's the—weaker in the sense of the vibrations of the universes. Fall, winter, and very early spring. You see, the rejuvenation process comes in the latter spring and in the summer. Try to understand, people who are over-identified with their form are people who are very subject to the changes of weather. They are people who are subject to the flux and flows of the tides of old creation because they've already identified with the flux and flows and tides of creation. Now if you want to understand people and understand yourself, if you find yourself a person who is easily affected by changing weather conditions, easily affected whether the sun is shining or it's misty outside, if you're a person like that, then that's good that you understand that is brought about by your over-identifying with the form that you're wearing, which is a part of nature, of course, in that respect. Yes.

Thank you. Why do many hum—No. Could you speak on the spiritual significance of Christmas beyond Christianity? Ancient religions celebrate this time for different reasons. Is there deeper significance than what we usually perceive?

Why, there's much deeper significance to the winter solstice and all these things. There's, certainly, there's deep significance to this time of year. And you will find throughout the ages and the various religions that it's a time of year of hope. It is a time of year when one is taking stock, so to speak, of what they've accomplished and especially of what they have not accomplished. And so what you call your Christmastime is a time of hope. And after a week or so after the hope, usually about a week, I think that's about what your calendar reveals, there's determination. And you call that resolutions. You're making New Year resolutions, for, you see, you have been, you think, inspired with new hope. And so that time of year, throughout the ages, has represented to that realm of consciousness, the mental realm, a hope for something better, a hope for something different, a hope for something bigger, a hope for something greater. I've yet to find anyone hope for less. They always hope for more, and then they make all these foolish resolutions and then live in the rest of the year in guilt because it was nothing but, like you say in your world, puffing in the wind. Yes.

Thank you. Are there certain periods of time in our twenty-four-hour earth day when the veil is thinner than other times?

Indeed, indeed, there is.

Is one of those times early hours of the morning?

Indeed, indeed, it is. And in reference to the seasons, you see, there are seasons everywhere, though some places you say, "Well, there's no season change here." No. You only mean that it is not as revealing. You go over to the warmer climates and you don't see a change, but there is change. Of course, there's seasons all over your planet. And so if you want to *move* with a vibration, then you want to move in the early spring. You see, that's the time to really move ahead, you see. You will find that because of over-identification with your form that you have the energy of the universes of form with you at that time. And so for new endeavors and new projects, for those who are over-identified with their little form, that's the time to do it.

Thank you. Is the ego less active in the early morning hours? There seems—

Yes. Excuse me [for interrupting you]. It's exhausted. Yes. Early morning hours, the uneducated ego has to have a nap. That's the best time, yes.

Thank you. There seems to be less earth things for it to react to during those hours.

Well, during those hours there are less people to fight with. Most people are sleeping. Their uneducated ego demands it. It's exhausted. Yes.

Thank you.

You're welcome.

What is the meaning of reason *in regard to the intellect?*

What is the meaning of *reason* in regard to the intellect? Reason is in an entirely different domain. You know, you can intellectualize all you want; that's the domain of logic. You see, reason is the wonderful, beautiful, cherished thing that humans have access to. It's known as the faculty of reason. You can't build anything that expresses reason, but you have built many things that express logic. So you have something that's greater than the machines that you build and the androids that you've made: you have reason. You have made things that have logic. Don't confuse the two.

Thank you. Should we spend some time each day on the questions from Sunday's class?

Well, I would spend some time, out of twenty-four hours. But then again, you know, I have tried to consider myself a bit practical in evolution that each movement that a person makes is affecting everything around it. Because when you move your hand, you are moving it through substance that you don't see or feel, but by that process and by that movement, you are affecting the forms that are in those realms of consciousness, of course.

Thank you. There is a discourse in The Living Light *[textbook] about Mars, the planet of war or action, and Venus, planet of love. And they are part of us and we are part of them. Would Mars be located in our earth center and Venus in the fire center?*

Well, for those who still have the need of believing in conjugal love, in that respect, yes. It's always, you know, love and war, war and love. But that's not the love of which we teach.

Thank you. It also states in the same discourse that when Venus and Mars are in harmony, we will gravitate to another area of consciousness where harmony reigns supreme. How does this occur?

Well, it's quite simple: it occurs when the fire center destroys the earth, for the fire is greater than the earth center. You see, the reason that the fire center is greater than the earth center is because the fire center is the cause and the earth center is the effect, not the other way around. And so the earth center, being the cause, and the fire center—the fire center, being the cause, and the earth center, being the effect, of course, the father's greater than the son; the cause is greater than the effect.

Thank you.

Why is the cause greater than the effect, cameraman?

Why is it greater?

Why is the cause—why is cause greater than effect?

Because cause has the power.

The power to what?

To create.

To repeat the effect.

Yes.

Correct. That is—you're absolutely correct. Definitely. Yes.

Would you please explain how we become receptive to the Law of Gratitude?

How we become receptive to the Law of Gratitude? By not being concerned about it. It is the concern that keeps us from it.

Thank you. When sudden changes occur, what happens that causes the nervous system to react? Is it shock to the mental body and why does it make the heart so sore?

Kindly reread the question.

The question was, "When sudden changes occur—

Sudden changes, yes. Do we mean, by sudden ones, ones that we are not forewarned about and, therefore, have not made the judgment we can control them? Reread the question, yes. When sudden . . .

When sudden changes occur—

Yes.

—what happens that causes the nervous system to react? Is it shock to the mental body and why does it make the heart so sore?

Lack of control. The awakening [that] we don't have control. The greatest Light we experience when we're off-guard mentally.

Thank you. If one finds oneself becoming attached to another and it seems to be a subtle effect that one is halfway into before they wake up to the fact, what can be done with such a condition?

Be honest with themselves and make the effort to come out of the need, which is the denial of what you are.

Thank you.

And stop playing the thrilling games of temptation, also, would help, too. Absolutely necessary.

Thank you.

You're welcome.

Is it the human condition, so to speak, that causes us to be subjected to all the various experiences in the jungle while we are here in form?

Well now, that question implies many other things that should be covered. Reread the question, please.

The question was, "Is it the human condition, so to speak, that causes us to be subjected to all the various experiences in the jungle while we are in human form?"

Well, the human condition, let us not deny that we make the human condition. It is a matter of making the effort. We make our human condition. We are not limited by our human body until we convince our self that we are our human body. That's why I wanted you to reread the question because it implies other things. Let us not deny personal responsibility.

[The] human body is an effect; it's not a cause. And a cause can repeat any effect that it is designed to repeat. So, you see, let us not confuse our self and believe we are the human body and, therefore, subject to the human frailties. We are the user of the human body; we are not the human body. I want that absolutely clarified in the class.

Thank you. Since we have triune points that form triangles in our true being, does that mean that there are other possibilities of angles, points, and degrees within us, just as we see in the night sky?

Well, yes. Absolutely. We are a composition of the atoms, electrons, and molecules which mathematically are governed by the key of the universe, numbers. And when you reduce numbers to what their true essence is, then you have symbols. And that's what you should be interested in, is the meaning of symbols.

Now, for example, you have three basic symbols, three basic symbols. You have the triangle; you have the square; and you have the circle. Now those are three basic symbols that you should make effort to understand. The mathematics and key to the universe is not the numbers 1, 2, 3, 4, 5. That's not the mathematics of which I am speaking. The true mathematics is symbols. And the basic, primary symbols of creation are the triangle, the circle, and the square. Yes.

Thank you. This is the last question. Are stars, planets, and galaxies in other places also what we call nature here on Earth and are there nature spirits everywhere in the universe?

Everywhere there is form there are nature spirits. There does not exist in universes known and unknown, in galaxies distant and far, there does not exist any place, anywhere where there is not form. Your eyes are designed to serve the purpose of the body that you are using and wearing at this time. Therefore, they have been designed to perceive forms in the universes of like composition. And so when you look at the atmosphere, you do not see the forms of what you understand as empty air. When you enter in consciousness the air center that is within you in what you truly are, then when you look at the air, the element air, you will perceive with the eyes of the element air. And when you perceive with the eyes of the elements of which the various centers are composed, that's when you will see.

As long as you insist on identifying with the earth center, then you can only see with earthly sight. And when you make that effort, which you are doing, in ways that your minds do not yet conceive, you will perceive with the eyes of the various centers that your consciousness is gradually, surely moving up through.

And now I will say a very good day, a very happy day. I know that life is filled with the spirit of joy when you allow yourselves as students, as people, as individuals, to identify with the spirit of joy that you are and not be so concerned with the many things that you see, but you in truth can never be.

Thank you and good day.

DECEMBER 22, 1985

A/V Class Private 29

Good morning, class.

Welcome to this new year in your world. And I see that some of you have been working diligently to benefit from these pressure points that have been given to you. However, I do want to say one thing: the opening of the pressure points is through the awareness. And the removal of the obstruction to the natural flow of divine energy is, of course, through the power. *[Please see the appendix for additional information regarding the pressure points.]*

And so I'm going to begin our classes this morning with some of the questions that you have prepared. And our cameraman here will begin with those questions.

Thank you. I was one with a vision of world brotherhood of humanity. Knowing that will not come to pass on earth makes me feel sadness. How can I help myself beyond that?

Yes. One should not permit themselves the luxury of what you know as sadness, which is based upon a lack of understanding of the various realms of consciousness. One would not expect animals to do the various achievements that human animals do, for one, in understanding the various stages of evolution and the expression of the Divine Spirit, would not permit themselves the luxury of judging the divine laws. And so in understanding that the so-called brotherhood of man is expressed in a level of consciousness of full understanding, granting others their right to their evolutionary steps, then one would not be saddened with the judgment that what they desire will not happen in the time and realm of consciousness they desire it to happen, especially when it is contrary to the natural, divine laws of evolution.

Thank you. Since we are only effective when praying when we are in a good place mentally, is it possible for us to visualize a person we know who could be helped, as being surrounded by and receptive to the Light?

Well, first of all, we are instruments to help others by first helping our self. We are therefore qualified and in a position to be effective. Now for a person to desire to help another who insists on actions contrary to natural law, who insists upon believing they are the level of consciousness that they are presently identified with, when a person is ready to make a change—and people are ready to make changes in their life when they reach the bottom, the bottom of their own judgments of how things should be—you find that they are encouraged and begin the upward path when they have reached their bottom.

Now the bottom for any person is ever dependent upon their over-identification with a form they have created, known as a judgment. And so when the judgment they have created and believe that they are fails them sufficiently, they will make the changes and begin to rise. Therefore, to help a person, one must use wisdom and understanding, of course, that the person is not yet ready. When they are ready, the changes will be evident. And to tempt oneself to force change upon another is detrimental to the person they are tempting to force change upon and extremely detrimental to the person who has made the judgment to do so. God helps those who help themselves by helping others. Let us not demand that others make changes in their lives. Let us be more interested in the changes that are necessary for ourselves.

Thank you. Why must the family structure be destroyed? What is it that makes it not good at this time?

Well, in reference to family structure, in reference to relationships, in reference to any form, any limit that a person permits themselves, through over-identification and attachment, to believe that they are, whatever they place in front of that which they are shall be removed. Whether you call that destructive or constructive has no bearing whatsoever upon its removal from the true being that you are. Therefore, when you permit yourself to become dependent upon limit, limit shall be removed and not always so graciously as you would like to have it.

Thank you. If a person is not very good at mathematics, and you have said it is very important, relating to the universe, what can a person do to help themselves relate better? Is there a certain field of mathematics it would be beneficial to invest time in?

Yes. When you understand that mathematics is the expression of pure organization, which is the effect of a disciplined mind, you will have no problem in understanding, for mathematics is the key to the universe, your universe. So through your efforts of discipline, you will benefit from organization, pure organization, which is in truth mathematics.

Thank you. Is there a musical instrument for each center and will you reveal any or all? Is the drum for the earth and the flute for the air?

I will reveal to you the most important instrument that you are aware of in your world today: you know it as the flute.

Thank you. In The Living Light *[in Discourse 15], it says, "In one moment we create the good only; in the next, through experiences, create the opposite." What do you mean through experiences we create the opposite?*

Through experiences we create the opposite of what we are for we believe that we are controlled by that which is beyond our control. Contrary to what we would like to believe, we do insist upon believing that the cause of our condition and our state in life is an effect, an effect of something beyond our control. That is what the statement means.

Thank you. What causes a person to have so much resistance?

Well, I find that people have phenomenal resistance to things that they don't want to do, and they are absolutely almost completely absent of resistance in things that they do want to do.

Thank you. Is resistance the opposite of acceptance?

Resistance is an effort on a person's part to express what they believe is their way in reference to their so-called rights. However, that type of thinking does not contain total consideration and, therefore, is not beneficial to any evolving soul.

Thank you. Is it ever beneficial to listen to what your levels have to say or should they be silenced?

First of all, when you try to silence that which you believe you are, you end up quite frustrated. And so the wise path is to allow a few moments of expression of your levels and to be very careful in your thinking to refrain from believing that you are them. Accepting that you have created them is one thing. That is the path of reason and light. Believing that you are them is the path of darkness and destruction to oneself.

Thank you. Why do I feel that I need to protect myself from part of me? That is—is that childlike? What is stopping me from coming out to play?

It is childish, not childlike. To fear a part of oneself only reveals an insistence on believing that one is the effect and refraining from accepting that one is the cause. For when we accept that we are the cause of our experiences, we grow by an awakening of personal responsibility and, once again, become the captain of our ship and the master of our destiny.

Thank you. You have shared with us the spiritual meaning of both the circle and the triangle. Would you please share with us the spiritual meaning of the square?

The circle, the triangle and the square, and all the various diagrams, and the mathematics are forthcoming in your year here of 1986. They are not being presented today for in your world they are not quite yet ready. And they will be brought to you through the science of diagrams and mathematics in this year. I cannot tell you the exact date because I am working with minds on an earth realm, and therefore they are most unpredictable. They can be forecast, but as far as an absolute, accurate prediction, you must understand that one has individual choices in life. And therefore, I am working with people on the earth realm in order to bring that science to you through an expression of the video and audio that you receive. And I will say, however, that it shall not go past the twenty-second day of the month of February, for that is when the change shall come. Be it in divine order, much, much sooner. Definitely it shall not go past that date.

Thank you. When we are confronted with a disaster of our own making, we frequently become emotional with those who are nearest to us and not, for example, the clerk at the corner store. Is this due to our over-identification with those who are nearest to us and our ego need to be perfect?

Well, of course, it has to do with those who we judge we can take advantage of, and we in life, of course, judge we can take advantage of those who we judge are attached to us or who have been kind to us. And so it is understandable that we would take advantage of those we judge that we can take advantage of without the fear of reprisal. And so one does not go to the corner grocery store and tempt to take advantage of the clerk, for [one] might be likely, you would say in your world, [to be] slugged in the mouth, I think is the term.

Thank you. In a recent class it was revealed that our perception is ever dependent upon our identification, and as our identification expands, so too does our perception. Would you please share with us more of your understanding of this process of identification?

Yes, it is the nature of the human mind to identify, to analyze, and, therefore, to judge and to possess. And so we find in the mental world this expression of identifying, of controlling, of possessing. For by over-identifying with mental substance—in order to do that, we have first made the step of denying what we are. And so we find that whenever a person has permitted themselves to become over-identified with what is known as mental substance, with the human mind, they are ever in need. For anyone who denies what they are shall, as long as they deny what they are, they shall experience what they are not. And we experience what we are not by over-identifying, over-identifying with our mind.

To broaden one's horizon is to awaken one's perception. To accept the right of expression of all form is to free oneself from the limit of any form. Therefore, a person who wishes to be freed from those constant needs, from the emotional upheavals that accompany them, from the frustrations of a little effort and judging there is no gain, which is contrary to the natural law, a person who has fallen into that trap in evolution can free themselves when they hit the bottom. It's when we hit the bottom of our judgments that we begin to broaden our horizons as we climb up and accept the possibility of something better. To accept the possibility of something better is one step. To accept our divine right to it is the intelligent step.

Thank you. Why is it that the uneducated ego ever seeks to destroy what it cannot control?

It is the very nature of its own need to destroy what it cannot control, for, you see, the uneducated ego is ever in need by denying what it truly is: a servant, a vehicle of what you are, an eternal being. And so it is its very nature to control everything that it conceives and everything that you identify with. That is its very nature, for it is born from denial of the true Source.

Thank you. In an earlier class you made reference to other breathing exercises that would be beneficial for us. Have we demonstrated sufficient value for what has been given that we may learn of these other exercises?

They are forthcoming.

Thank you. When we make a decision to rest during the night, rather than sleep, should this be done gradually or all at once?

Gradually. I've yet to find a change that is lasting or enduring that was not based upon the principle of evolution, which is gradual, consistent change.

Thank you. If we should rest at gradual intervals, should we wake up each hour or go within to awaken when impressed?

One goes within to awaken when impressed.

Thank you. What steps should be taken in our nutrition to require less sleep?

First of all, in reference to nutrition, let us concern ourselves in reference to this question on nutrition and inner awakening, to the nutrition of the human mind. We find a lacking [of] proper nutrition of mental substance. The control of mental substance is the nutrition of mental substance. And so effort made in controlling one's thoughts is the first step in the proper nutrition of the human mind. And so when the human mind receives proper nutrition, it is inevitable that its outer expression, known as a physical body, shall benefit therefrom.

Thank you. What steps should be—no—How many, or how may one cooperate with the higher power within to allow God to guide our lives more fully?

By refraining from dictating to the Divine Source. By refraining from the insistence of having what you believe is your way. By accepting, we refrain from believing, for there is nothing to believe when we accept. When one accepts the goodness that they are and makes the next step to accept their divine right to it and the third step, through faith, the absolute conviction of mental substance, they are experiencing it, then one frees themselves from the bondage of belief and enters the path of faith, where the power of the Principle of Goodness, known as God, flows unobstructed.

One of the great benefits in proper application of the pressure points, to which my cameraman is lacking in application—and I have instructed my channel to see that that is corrected—one of the great benefits is a restoration of balance in the emotional-mental realms of consciousness. And when that is properly done, through awareness and power, when it is properly done, there is a freedom from the upset and the frustration. And rather than to make it a regulation for my students at this time, I'm going to continue on to allow it to be done on a voluntary basis. If I do not find an increase in the application of it, then it shall be compulsory for the attendance of my private classes.

Thank you. What is the difference between cheerfulness and joy?

One is cheered from an encouragement of the fulfillment of the desires of their mind. One is joyous in the acceptance of what they truly are. So in that respect, there is a vast difference between being cheerful and being joyful. Joyful is what you are, as a true being. Cheerful is what you can become when you have your desires filled the way you want them filled, when you want them filled. And so one thing is what you are, and the other thing is what you can become by your own beliefs. Yes.

Thank you. We speak of an ozone layer, and I think of it as being around the outside of our atmosphere. Does ozone also exist in the air we breathe?

Why, certainly it exists in the air we breathe. It is a layer in the atmosphere, and you inhale the atmosphere. And so it isn't a matter of so many thousands or millions of miles away; it penetrates the very atmosphere that you breathe.

Thank you. I believe it was once stated that life as we know it cannot be without the ozone layer. What is the ozone layer and does identification take place as the soul passes through it?

Yes. As far as your ozone layer, life as you know it does not exist, for it protects you from destructive rays from the source itself. You see, for example, if the light is too bright, it is not only best that you see it not now, for if you see it now and the light is too bright, then it shall destroy you. It shall destroy what you believe you are.

The Light of eternal truth frees what you are, destroys what you believe you are, for what you believe you are is based upon a denial of what you truly are. So in that respect, one finds struggle and difficulty in a mental world for anyone who has chosen an awakening spiritual path of consciousness, for the spiritual path of consciousness offers to you the guidance and discipline and organization necessary to awaken to what you are.

In order to gain, you must give. You must give up what you are not, what you believe that you are, in order to experience what you truly are. You cannot experience nor be consciously aware of what you are until you let go of what you are not, yet insist on believing that you are. For by letting go of what you are not, you no longer use divine, intelligent Energy to sustain and to maintain limit and delusion. So when you let go of the delusion you have created (your belief in it), then you will experience what you truly are: the Light that is. And everything that you could possibly desire of the Principle of God, freed from dependence on any type of mental gymnastics, is yours to experience. But that is the step that everyone has to make sooner or later who remains on the path of awakening of what they truly are. It is not an easy path for the mind and for the realm of consciousness that you believe you are. For that realm, it is most difficult because the forms that you have created in that realm know, from your own intelligence in your own mind, that if they are not sustained by the Light, they shall return to the source of mental substance from whence they have been drawn and created.

Thank you. Once I was privileged to see a spirit baby, and it was the happiest baby I've ever seen. Are all spirit babies that happy? If so, is it because they haven't been contaminated in form?

That is absolutely correct. For they are what they are and are not dependent upon need and, therefore, are freed from the frustration and the discord, which is disease, known to the mental world.

Thank you. Do space probes pierce the ozone layer and, if so, can it heal itself and close again?

The ozone layer has been pierced many times. It can and it does heal itself for it is the Law of Balance, the Law of Nature.

You may adjust the shade behind you, please. *[The cameraman pauses his reading of the questions as he adjusts the window shade.]* That's fine. Thank you.

Thank you. Does the succession of middle C notes, which are arranged at the beginning of class number 4 serve to break down the molecular structure of negative forms? [A few of the beginning classes in this series included a sequence of musical notes, which are an essential part of the rhythmic cleansing breath spiritual exercise. The audio cassettes of those classes had about three minutes of those tones, while the videotapes had about eighteen minutes of audio tones and also depicted a sunrise as seen from the east wing balcony of the Serenity temple.]

Yes, they do, for they are a positive structure and that which is positive is superior to that which is negative when they come into contact with each other.

Thank you. Does an aborted fetus become a spirit baby or does it return to the Allsoul?

An aborted fetus does not become a spirit body. It already *is* a spirit body. It simply loses its shell of earthly substance.

Thank you. In the [Twenty-Second] Annual Forecast last week, you said California would break off from the continent caused from an earthquake. Will it float like an island?

Yes, it will float like many islands.

Thank you. When one desires to replace fear—

If you call an island something that floats. Yes.

Thank you.

I don't, but some do.

[While many of the classes in this series of classes were given with the students in the presence of the teacher, in this class, as in the last few classes, the teacher was seated in the east wing

of the temple while the students watched the class on a large monitor in the dining room, which was located one floor below the east wing. When the students were in close proximity to the teacher, their laughter was often recorded on the tape of the class and could be noted on these transcriptions. However, when the students were remote to the recording equipment, as in this class, none of their laughter could be recorded or noted.]

Thank you. When one desires to replace fear with faith, what can one say to oneself that begins the process?

When one desires to replace fear with fate?

Yes. Faith!

Oh, what a difference. Now please restate the question.

Yes, sir. When one desires to replace fear with faith, what can one say to oneself that begins the process?

"I accept the possibility of something good happening in my life. I accept the experience thereof. I'm freed from dependence of my mind, which is so impatient."

Thank you. Is feeling something or one's feelings the truest sense we have, and can it be trusted?

Well, it can be trusted if it's feeling and not sensation, but one first, however, must discern the difference between sensation and feeling. Now many people mistake sensation as a feeling. You take a needle and you prick them with it, and they say that's a feeling. Well, it's actually a sensation. So one must discern the difference.

Thank you. Should one have a balance, literally, between the faculties and the functions, as both operating in oneself simultaneously?

Yes, absolutely. The balance is required in order that you may experience the freedom and the truth that you are.

Thank you. When you speak of numbers being the symbols of the squares and circles and triangles, do you mean the actual shape in points and degrees?

That's a part of it, yes.

Thank you. It appears that there is an increase in people's interest in the metaphysical, psychic phenomena, hypnosis, crystal power, etc., particularly in Marin county. Why here and why now?

They've tried everything else.

Thank you. Are highly advanced science and spiritual understanding the same thing?

Highly advanced scientific?

It says, "Are highly advanced science and spiritual understanding the same thing?"

Yes. Not in the respect of the technological advancements, but highly advanced science and spirituality are handmaidens.

Thank you. Why are some people slow to anger and while others are quick to anger?

Some have more control.

Thank you. This religion by—correction. Is religion by TV the way that religions of the world will go in the future or are the present experiences with it a passing phase?

Oh, in your country they are not a passing phase. And for your world, for your particular country in which you now reside, it is the wave of the present; it is the flood of the future.

Thank you. What is it in us that wants others to think like we think and gets upset when they don't?

Need, born from denial.

Thank you. I have noticed a big difference this week. Could you please share with us how the energy flows when we use these new pressure points? I have noticed when I'm not concerned with what I can't have, my energy goes to what I do have. Could you please share how this works spiritually?

Well, first of all, the energy, when the obstruction is removed through proper application of the major pressure points of the human body, there is an increase in the flow of energy. Now that which is diseased and discordant in the vehicle is that part of the vehicle that is not receiving sufficient energy to maintain and to sustain it in a proper way, sufficient to its own need. Now, for example, if you do not use the hand for a time, then you find difficulty when, once again, you choose to use the hand; you find difficulty in moving the fingers and moving the hand. It is because it has not had use of the divine Energy which sustains it. Now you call that exercise. When you exercise, there is a flow of energy to the part of the body that is in movement and to the part of the mind that is in movement.

When you have, from various experiences, created an obstruction to any part of your vehicle, that obstruction does not allow sufficient energy, intelligent energy, to flow to that area of your body. And you begin to experience problems that it doesn't function properly. It doesn't work the way it used to; it doesn't work the way it used to when sufficient energy was getting to that part of your body.

Now the major pressure points that have been given to you is not something that is new. It is something that comes from very ancient, ancient ages long, long ago. It is the proper application of it. It cannot be properly applied by one tempting to do it to themselves, for the very movement of the hands and the arms to do it to oneself creates an obstruction, an added obstruction, and you do not benefit as you should.

Now when this energy flows and you note, those of you who have had the teachings and most of you at least are aware that the neck represents the will. Now the will power is the lord or the law of your universe. When this intelligence is permitted to flow through the lord, the law of your universe, without interference, your health is restored. Physically. Mentally. Emotionally. However, its application, because of obstructions created and believed in for so many years, requires a continuous application of pressure in order to remove the obstructions. You will note that pressure properly applied, there is a benefit, an immediate, noticeable benefit. Then you will also notice that the obstruction seems to build up again. And that is true. You have old-time obstructions that you [have] believe[d] that you are for a long, long time. They're not going to stay out of the way in just one or two applications upon these major pressure points. *[Again, please see the appendix for more information.]*

So as I said in the beginning of the class, because of its great benefit, psychologically and physiologically, unless greater effort is made by some of my students and my cameraman for application on this pressure point, I shall require it as a requirement for being in the private classes.

Now rather than to place our attention, at this phase of application, upon how it works, let us more wisely place our attention upon whether it works or not. I can only tell you that it works. I should know something about it. And it works for me. It works for my channel. It works for millions of people I've known through eons of time. And it certainly works for you because you are not greater than any of us. And therefore, you are not different or special; so it will work for you, properly applied. I just want to be sure that you are opening the pressure point through awareness and that you are moving the obstruction through the power of the Divine Intelligence itself.

Thank you. What are the guidelines for being a helpful neighbor in a community while maintaining one's own privacy?

Yes, a high fence.

Thank you. How does one serve—

Well, you might say—excuse me, Mr. Cameraman. You might say minding one's own business; taking care of their own nose. You know, the nose is very important. Do you know what it represents? The nostrils and the nose?

Well—

You have a large enough nose there, you ought to know what it represents.

Reason. [The cameraman laughs as he responds.]

Reason and what? *[After a short pause, the teacher continues.]* The thing that you've strived for, for so many years.

[After another short pause, the teacher again continues.] Could it possibly be consideration?

Yes.

Well, I think you ought to do a little study. Go ahead with the question.

Thank you. How does one serve a cause loyally, while remaining free from the pitfalls of belief and judgment?

By the original motivation. By reminding oneself of their true motive. If they want to serve a cause, they must remind themselves; and therefore, through that reminder, they won't step into the pitfalls of personality and go against their true motivation.

Thank you. Why are some people tempted to over-identify with their jobs?

Well, they have great need, and that's one of the ways they've chosen to express that need. Need to control. And so they have problems with any job, because, you see, the job represents to them an opportunity to control something. And that creates a lot of problems for people, I note, in your world.

Thank you. What should one advise someone who is interested in Spiritualism, but is highly skeptical of the science of communication? Where should they start their investigation?

In the natural laws of life. And, for example, it is foolhardy, a waste of energy and a waste of time to work to convince anyone of anything. One does the work they have to do and cares less what the world does with it. One is therefore free to do the work that they have to do.

Thank you. Would one be more receptive to spiritual inspiration while in outer space, avoiding some of the mental contamination of Earth?

Yes, one would have an increased opportunity, as one has when they cross the equator of your Earth planet.

Thank you. Could you please tell us the meaning of the three primary symbols: the triangle, the square, and the circle.

That's coming up, as I've promised you, in this year of 1986. And it shall not go past the month of February and the twenty-second day.

Thank you. Do these primary symbols correlate to certain colors? And if so, what are they?

They certainly do, and that is being revealed in the science of diagrams, which is coming up shortly.

Thank you. As we learn our lessons on earth, which is the effect of the fire center, do we evolve to the number six of divine love, which is representative of the next planet in evolution and the next center, being a water center?

Yes. Let us not forget that six, the ancient, eternal number of divine love, once taken by mental substance is also the symbol of what you call the devil or satanic forces. So let us remember that which is spiritual is the domain of the spirit, which is your soul. And that cannot be taken by mental substance without experiencing what mental substance has to offer. Mental substance is not spiritual substance. You cannot mix oil and water. To tempt to do so is to invite so-called disaster.

Thank you. We are composed of electrons, atoms, and molecules, and they are composed of symbols. Are each of the nine centers associated with one of the three primary symbols?

Yes, they are.

Here's a further part of that question, "As the air center, being associated to the circle and so forth?"

Yes.

Thank you. From the primary colors, other colors are formed and represent certain parts of the body. Do the symbols also represent different parts of the body?

They do.

Thank you. This is the last question. How many other symbols are derived from the primary symbols and what are they?

That's coming up in the science of diagrams. You should already know that there are eighty-one. Go ahead.

Thank you. That was the last question.

That's fine. So I will say good day to you. You have a fine week. I'm sure that you will and continue on. Some of you are doing very well with your application on the pressure points. And some of you are not doing at all, well or otherwise. However, that will be corrected. And my cameraman will have the opportunity to choose which of my students that he would like to work on his neck, because he has not been having it done as he should. And I know that with all you lovely ladies there that one of you would be gracious enough to volunteer.

Thank you and good day.

JANUARY 5, 1986

A/V Class Private 30

And let us begin with our questions this day, please. *[The recording of this class may have begun after the teacher said "Good morning, class." It was customary for the teacher to begin each class with a greeting.]*

Thank you. In view of our country's problems with security information leaks, how would the Living Light Philosophy address the issue of the individual's right of privacy versus a nation's security?

Whereas an individual's rights of privacy have already been given forth to the rights of the whole, in a society, then, of course, how would they be affected or how would this philosophy apply? It would apply in keeping with the Law of Personal Responsibility and of individual choice.

Whenever one makes a decision to become a part of a whole, a part of a society, of a nation, or of an organization of any type, then one accepts in making that decision the good and the continuity of the whole for the purpose for which it was founded. And so this philosophy would teach, and does teach, the responsibility in keeping with the choice that has been made by the individual.

Thank you. How does one know if one is voting responsibly?

One votes, in reference to these political questions, one votes in keeping with what they understand is in, of course, their own best interest based upon their experiences in any society. And how does one know if they are voting intelligently? By thorough investigation, and from that investigation making a decision, based upon the investigation they have made, what would be in their best interest, for that which is in their best interest, of course, is what they have to offer to those around them.

Thank you. What is the most effective way to being receptive in learning a foreign language?

Well, in learning anything, one is most receptive between the so-called states of conscious awareness and so-called sleep. And one is most receptive at that time, and that, of course, is the best time for learning anything.

Thank you. Does our subconscious control our health through our obstructions to the flow of the river of life?

Yes, indeed, our so-called subconscious does control our health in that respect. And if the divine energy is not flowing in an unobstructed way, then there're certain parts of our anatomy that do not receive the necessary energy to maintain and to sustain those parts and, in that respect, discord and disease becomes established. And you know it as poor health.

Thank you. As planets age and mature, do they evolve through the centers of consciousness or do they remain associated with one particular center throughout their incarnation?

No. All things formed do evolve through the various changes and centers of consciousness.

Thank you. Do we experience a greater receptivity to the spiritual at the North Pole?

Yes, we are more receptive, of course, when we are in the magnetic field.

Thank you. Humor is the salvation of the soul. Is the energy that laughter produces the effect of disassociating from judgments we have over-identified with and thus allow the river to flow more freely and restores our health?

Well, would it be true that laughter is only an expression of humor at no one's expense. However, so often we find that humor, what so many understand as humor and laughter, is at the expense of another individual through a lack of understanding the evolution of that person. Now when we are able to laugh at our self, then we are in keeping with the Law of Personal Responsibility and humor in that respect does free our soul. So by beginning with oneself and finding the humor in the various situations that one finds themselves involved in, that come and go in their world of creation, then, indeed, one is instrumental in saving their soul through humor, for it is at no one else's expense. It is only at the so-called expense of the one who is personally responsible for it.

Thank you. Would you please share with us your understanding of the purposes of the left and right hemispheres of the brain?

Well, yes, indeed. The so-called left and right hemispheres of the brain have been designed to serve a particular purpose. And to the questioner, I am sure that you are familiar with the function of logic being in one of the hemispheres and that the emotions, that which controls the emotions is in the other hemisphere. And so you also, I'm sure, are aware that the artistic and creative functions, there, of the human mind are in the hemisphere where the emotions are in control. And I'm sure you're also aware that in the other hemisphere, which is reserved for facts and figures and for logic, ofttimes a person believes that that is reason. Well, each hemisphere is designed by the Divine Architect to bring about a balance in the human expression, so-called; and so it is when a person makes effort to move from the left hemisphere of receptivity to the right hemisphere of creativity in application.

Now so often a person will find ideas or think they have found an idea in their mind and nothing happens with it; it never gets to leave their mind. In fact, in time it becomes almost a possession. And that is revealing a condition of imbalance, for the will is not being used to move the idea or the thought into constructive application. We find people who have made little or no effort to gain control over their emotions are locked in the hemisphere which is not designed to put into application that which it receives.

Thank you. When the Earth passes on, what form does it take?

Well, the Earth, just like—is a physical expression. I accept you are speaking of the physical expression of the planet Earth.

When it passes on through its aging process, it returns to the source from whence it was created. Now the physical body returns to the planet from which it has been raised up or created as a physical substance. And so planets demonstrate the same law, and they return to the source from whence they have been created.

Now all things, like a great spring of water, flow from the Divine Light. The closest thing in understanding, perhaps, you can accept at this time is that as a planet has come from the light of sun and is physically a part thereof in its birth and evolution, so man returns to the Light which he is. And the planets, as they age and evolve, they begin to go through drastic changes over a period of untold hundreds of millions of years. And they return to the light that gave them birth.

Thank you. What is the origin of symbols?

The origin of symbols, as you know symbols, is something that is very ancient, that has evolved from basic mathematics. Unfortunately, in your world today your understanding of mathematics is quite confusing. The mathematics, which is the pure expression of organization, is best understood in your world today in a better understanding of what you know as ancient symbols, for they were designed in times long past to reveal the basic organization or mathematics, which is the key to the universe.

Thank you. Do the primary colors originate from the sounds of the universe and the effect, being color and vibration? What are the Earth's?

The Earth's vibration and color is brown.

Thank you. Does each universe have its own predominant sound, color, and vibration?

Yes, it does.

Thank you. Does one withdraw a law already established once we have moved from belief to faith? On this earth, do we automatically go to the next place, being six, or what does happen?

Well, a person who has freed themselves from the bondage of belief has moved or evolved into the realms of faith and, therefore, is not limited by form or creation. And in the withdrawing or establishing of a law, that is only possible when one's consciousness has evolved into that realm of faith, which is the freedom of limit or belief.

Now what happens to a person? It's happening at this very moment. We are all moving through these various realms of consciousness. Now, as I said here so many times, the darker the night, the brighter the Light. And so whenever you make effort to evolve—and it is an eternal, progressive thing, as long as there is form and as long as there is identity, form, being the effect thereof—then it is the law of form or limit or creation to obstruct and to absorb the free flow of Light or Energy, for it does not feed off of itself. It is dependent upon that which sustains it.

And so when you create a thought form, then the thought form, if you do not make effort to, through identification, to direct energy to it, then it rises up and creates in your mind difficulties and frustrations and various other obstructions to your peace and harmony, for it is your child. And without your effort to educate your child, it shall continue to call out in its hunger.

Thank you. Because the Earth is a fire center, is it through fire that the Earth will be transformed back to the Allsoul?

Yes, it will. That is its evolutionary stage. It is a fireball. And it shall return to what you may call the source of fire in that way. Yes, it is.

Thank you. After my pressure points are done, I have felt a pins-and-needles sensation in my neck. What is this?

You will find many and various sensations throughout your body or your neck. And in this respect the student is speaking of a pins-and-needles sensation. Energy has been released as you would open up the floodgates of a dam. Energy is being released, and one of the many sensations of flow of energy to a part of the anatomy that has been lacking in proper sustenance could be described as a sensation of pins and needles, as you say. *[Please see the appendix for more information on the pressure point exercise.]*

Thank you. Why are intimidation forces effective on some people and ineffective on others?

Yes. And that's a very good question, of course. If we have spent our life intimidating our self through over-identification with our self, then we are very susceptible to someone's effort to intimidate us, for we have established the Law of Intimidation by first spending so much of our time in intimidating ourselves. Some people do not spend their lives in intimidating themselves, and therefore they are not as receptive to the forces of intimidation.

Thank you. We are taught to accept the right of every thought to express itself so that, through acceptance, we are freed from it. What happens to the thought forms when they are accepted?

Well, when you, first of all, when you accept a thought form that you have created, then you recognize its divine right of expression as a part of something that you have created. You, in so doing, establish the Law of Responsibility, personal responsibility for what you have created. Now once having established that law, that places you in a position and qualifies you to direct that which you have created. However, if you refuse to accept and refuse to recognize that it is a creation of your own mind, although it could well have been created in your days of ignorance, if you refuse to accept what you have created, then it shall, in time, take possession of you by the very law that you have established. Therefore, a wise person accepts that which they have created in order that they may qualify themselves to take control of their creation.

Thank you. As the gap between technological advancements and the masses of people in the world widens, will there be a spiritual awakening of the masses or will it mean they're falling further behind in their spiritual development?

First of all, as the great technological advancement continues, it will reach a point when man will awaken to the facts that he is not in control as he thought he was. And when that day dawns in your world, which it is dawning presently, then man shall begin to go inward, for he will awaken to the demonstrable facts in his world that what he thought he was controlling and that was giving him so much pleasure is in truth controlling him. And that is the next step in which man will go within to a greater spiritual awakening, for no one likes to be under the control of something that they are not in charge of. And therefore, that very experience will help man along his spiritual journey.

Thank you. In the pause spoken of in the lion's strength is the ability to pause, is the pause a pause in breathing or thinking or moving or all three? [A saying from The Serenity Game states, "The sense to pause is the lion's strength."]

All three, for you cannot pause your thinking, and therefore you cannot pause your moving, until you have first paused the breath of life, which is the very sustenance of the forming of the thought and the moving of the form.

Thank you. The philosophy teaches that every knock is a boost. Does this work both when we knock someone else and also when someone else knocks us? And what is the boost?

Well, in keeping with every knock is a boost, when you believe that you are knocked, in the knocking process you are inspired to make changes. And the boost [of] which I speak is your experience, the effect of that: the experience of your making those changes is known as a boost. So when you, by the laws you have established, begin to experience knock after knock after knock, you will note, in hindsight, that from those knocks you have made changes in your mind, and the effect of the changes that you have made are known as a boost.

Thank you. Does a person have to identify with levels to experience awareness or can you have awareness without identification?

Well, a person, once having qualified themselves in the various levels of consciousness, can, through the Law of Disassociation, recall and be aware of various levels of consciousness without becoming attached to those levels through an over-identification with them. Now, for example, many people read a book, and through lack of effort of disassociation, they experience many emotions in keeping with the story of the book and the novelette that they are reading. And therefore, that type of a person, you see, has made little, obviously, effort to disassociate from their fruits of action. And so if you are one who has made effort to disassociate and not to be trapped by belief through attachment to your fruits of action, then when you read your novelettes, you will not experience all of the emotions that are written between the pages, and that is, of course, an intelligent person.

Thank you. When you continually feed a weakness and you know what you are and the pull is so strong, where do you start to neutralize or to begin to have some sort of control?

The beginning of all control, of course, is in your awakening and, therefore, acceptance of, that the forms you have created in ignorance are instruments in your believing that you have need. And that denial of what you are creates, for you, experiences of ever searching outside for the goodness that you are. For you have, through errors of ignorance, left home in order to find home. Well, no one will ever find home by leaving home. And so you're all on the path of returning to home, your home. Now many experience a return to their home, a true return, for a true return to one's home is never ever dependent upon what someone else does or does not do. A returning to your home is ever dependent on what efforts that you alone are making in your own consciousness.

Now when you have created a form in your mind and you have fed it for many years of your life a great deal of energy, then only through your declaration frequently in the course of a day or night that it is what you have created, it is not you, [that you free yourself from it]. You must speak to your creation and declare the truth: you are responsible for it. You are not it. You are the creator of it. You are not it. And so when that effort is truly made daily with those forms that have, in your experiences of past times and days, risen up and possessed your minds and done so many things to your body, that will no longer have control of you.

It is through a lack of effort that the forms you have created in your experiences in the past are able to possess your mind, to use your body, and to bring into your life so much frustration and so much discord. It is only through your lack of effort. If you allow these forms, from lack of effort, these forms that you have created in your errors of ignorance, if you allow them an inch, they will take a thousand miles in your life. And when you are first aware of them, if you do not work diligently to take control of them, through a lack of effort, you see, they'll tell you, "Well, what's the use?" You see.

It's just like a person that's trying to make a change in their life in anything. When you try to make a change, the forms that you have created in your days of ignorance, they rise up and convince you that they are you. They convince you they are you because you are not making the effort to disassociate and to demonstrate daily in your life the truth and to disassociate yourself from what you have created. Now we disassociate ourselves from what we have created not by turning our back and avoiding what we have created. We disassociate by facing the forms we have created for what they really are. They do not have soul. They only have movement when we direct our intelligent energy that flows through us, this great power flowing through us, whenever we, through identification, direct that energy to them.

Now when we declare the truth, "Yes, you are what I have created in my ignorance. You are not me," that is something that each of my students should use, along with the pressure points that are of such great benefit to you. [You] should use that declaration. "This thought in my mind is what I have created. It is not me. There is no way that it can convince me if I continue to make the effort." I do hope now that's helped with your question.

Thank you. When you have a question to ask and you ask it in your own mind and an answer comes, is it still important to ask the question here in class?

Well, I have always said that the purpose of being in class is to share your efforts in a greater understanding. Now when you have a question in reference to a spiritual path and you believe that you have received the answer to your question and you believe that the question of a spiritual nature was important enough for you to make the effort to ask yourself the question and then, as you say, to receive the answer and not to share such an important question with co-students and the class could only, of course, reveal a little temptation to selfishness.

It is true the secrets of the universe are never given to blabbermouths. And if you judge that the question you have and the answer you have received is a great secret and, therefore, should not be shared with others on the spiritual path, then of course it is most understandable. However, only time, the great healer in a world of illusion, will be able to show you the wisdom of how perfect each of us are.

Thank you. In the text, you talked about how someday the mind and its many thoughts will be outside and I will be within. When does this shift take place?

The shift takes place when we accept that we are the peace and the power, that everything else is brought into being as a temporary vehicle through which that which we are may express in worlds of limit, which offer, of course, all the functions and the deception of the denial of the truth. It is our true purpose, through disassociation, through effort, to express this pure intelligent harmony that we are through the vehicles that we have created. The only way we can do that is by frequently declaring the truth: "This vehicle I have created. I'm responsible for its education."

You, as human beings on the planet Earth, have a grave responsibility. You have entered the planet Earth as instruments of the Light to evolve forms, to evolve limits. Therefore, when you do not make that effort daily, through the Law of Disassociation, through the Law of Personal Responsibility, to declare the truth in your consciousness, "I have created this feeling. I alone am responsible for I alone create it. I have created this thought form for I alone have established the law of its creation," [you do not evolve those forms]. You have a responsibility, a grave responsibility to educate and to evolve the forms that you have and you do create. Now a form does not evolve when we permit that which we have created to control its creator. We are the creator of our thoughts, which are forms. We alone have created them. By the law of creating them, we are responsible to guide them, to educate them, to discipline them to serve the purpose of good. We have failed miserably in that effort when we do not educate the forms that we have created. I do hope that's helped with that question.

Thank you. Why does the mind like to delude you in the thinking that things are different instead of seeing how things truly are?

As long as forms or thoughts of your mind can find a way for no effort to be made, then there is no change. As long as you insist on believing all is well, then there's nothing to inspire you to make any changes. The forms you have created are very satisfied with that which you are feeding them. And being satisfied, you sleep. You see, you can always tell a person who is very satisfied with the way things are going: their forms are having a real heyday in their life. It is when you are working and making effort to make changes that your forms become very upset. It is when you are lazy in consciousness and make no daily effort to educate what you have created that you take a free ride on someone else's life. At least you are tempted to be a free-rider. I think in your world they call them freeloaders. And more appropriate is the word *freeloading* for it is, indeed, a great load for anyone to bear.

Everyone has their own cross to carry to the heights with the return to their home. And one must choose wisely who they permit in their universe. And you choose wisely by looking at your experiences and looking inside and making an intelligent decision of what changes will be necessary for you to have outward manifestations that are harmonious to you. So that which you find that is not harmonious in your consciousness, make effort to change it. And that which is around you which is an expression of that disharmony, an expression of that discord, from laziness in consciousness, will, indeed, disappear in your life.

Thank you. Does our birth number correspond to the predominating frequency we emanate through our earth life?

Yes. Yes, indeed, it does.

Thank you. Does that birth number take place in the Rotunda?

Well, you are the number. You are the number, and you're known by a name. And if you will understand that—you are number, known, identified by name.

Thank you. You spoke of having an opportunity to be more receptive to spiritual inspiration while crossing the equator. Will you please explain that?

Well, first of all, the equator of your planet, what you understand as the equator—and tell me what you do understand as the equator, considering now I just have one physical student here and I'm talking to all of the others of you there in that lovely room. *[During this class the teacher was seated in the east wing on the second floor along with the cameraman, who read the submitted questions. All the other students were watching the class on a large monitor in the dining room on the first floor of the Serenity Temple.]* You, tell me what you understand as an equator for your world.

My understanding of the equator is the, is an imaginary band around the center, which is an equal north-south meeting point.

The north-south from what?

From top and bottom.

Based upon the poles as you understand them.

Yes.

I see. And you understand that that is a measurement, that so-called equator, based upon your mental understanding in your world. Is that correct?

That's correct.

I see. Well, then you understand that you are faculties and functions. And that there is a point at which they come together. Is that correct?

Yes.

I see. And you understand you are positive. And you are negative. And there is a point at which that comes together, also, in your universe.

Yes.

Or do you feel you're only positive?

No, not at all.

I see. Well, wherever there is a meeting of opposites, there is an equator or boundary line. And at that point, a person who is evolved spiritually passes through the door. And I think you should understand that.

Thank you. Would that apply to someone living on the equator or is it the change of location when crossing it that makes one more receptive?

Well, one is more receptive when the two poles meet than when they are in either one pole or the other. Yes.

Thank you. Is there something to the distance and space inside the triangle, square, and circle that relates to numbers being symbols?

Yes, there is.

Thank you. What can parents do to keep children who grind their teeth while sleeping?

What can parents do with children who grind their teeth while sleeping?

Yes.

Yes. Well, now there are certain points which can be very gently massaged to help alleviate a condition of suppressed desire, which is the true cause of the expression of determination or grinding of the teeth while a person is, as you say, asleep. Now if you are working with a child, then it behooves you to very gently, to take this finger and the thumb, and to massage—and I'll show you here, gently—to massage in a clockwise position, not too deeply however, to massage in a clockwise position for fourteen clockwise rotations and then to massage in a counterclockwise [for] thirteen [rotations].

[With his right hand, the teacher places his thumb on the right side of his throat and his middle finger on the left side of this throat, again, just below his jaw and on either side of his trachea. Using the distal phalanx of his thumb and finger, he moves his hand in small circles in a clockwise direction as his thumb and middle finger transcribe small circles. After several rotations (use fourteen for the complete exercise), he then changes his middle finger for his index finger. Using his thumb and index finger, he again moves his right hand in small circles in a counterclockwise direction so that the thumb and index finger transcribe small circles. Complete thirteen rotations for the entire exercise.]

Now what this does—there are two particular points here. And you'll have to be careful not to apply too much pressure. That helps to release a buildup of tension underneath of the muscles under the jawbone area. But I would use it wisely. And you will see a change.

You know, it's like a little animal here, like my student over there, this lovely, little, red-headed student of mine there in the chair there. *[The teacher refers to Mr. Red, the church's dog.]* You see, when he's grinding his teeth, which my channel has registered strong complaints, so to speak, to our friends over here, for he has this grinding process himself, we have instructed my channel to massage him in that area. It stops right away.

Now if you have people bothering you from what you understand as snoring, then do the same thing in this part of the area, right into here, and it will reveal, you see, what will happen within a few moments, very few moments, you'll find that that snoring has stopped, you see.

[The teacher uses his right hand to perform that same massage on either side of his nose where it meets his face just a little below his eyes.]

And so it's a matter of the flow of energy going to the obstruction that's been created by these various suppressed desires, and the aggression and this energy being blocked and it causes these various problems. Yes.

Thank you. Do each of the triune points have dimension into another dimensions?

Yes, they do. Yes, they do. And, you see, as I stated to you at one of our other classes here just, I think it was the last class, that we are working diligently to bring about our diagramology onto the video-audio [tape] there. And I have had reports that you've got to take in your little electronic equipment; [it] seems to have a little bug in it. And I have checked on that, and it's being taken care of. And we should be moving along within a few weeks on that.

Thank you. When you use the terms hothead *and* cool head, *are you referring to the temperature of one's thoughts?*

Oh, yes, I'm referring to the temperature not only of one's thoughts but of one's body. You see, you will find people who are very emotional and people who are very frustrated that they're very hotheaded. Their temperature in their being is, is—some people would think they should be hospitalized at that time. Yes.

Thank you.

Those are hotheads.

Does to disassociate mean to be indifferent to that which surrounds one?

One shouldn't—no, no, no. Disassociation does not mean to be indifferent, for to be indifferent is a denial of personal responsibility. It certainly, absolutely does not mean indifferent. What it does mean, clearly, for a person to disassociate, is to be with a responsibility and not attached to the fruits of action by judgments of how it should be fulfilled. I do hope that's helped you.

Thank you. Is man the only species of animal kingdom which often has conflict between the individual and the group or society?

No. All form is limit. And when man identifies with his flesh and bone, he's identifying with limit. And, why, packs of wolves, they have problems. You see, there's one captain of the ship and even the dogs know that. And any dog that's tempted to try to make two captains for the ship, one always rises supreme. You can only have one captain to a ship. All animals of your planet know that. Even the birds know that.

Thank you. In historical terms, why did man, above all other animals, develop the greatest needs for love of self and self-pity?

For man has the greatest denial. Whoever has the greatest denial of what they are is destined to have the greatest need. Whoever has the greatest need is destined to have the greatest pity. Whoever has the greatest pity is destined to have the greatest love of it.

Thank you. In [Discourse 37 of] The Living Light it is stated that credulity and suspicion are the balancing points of logic, and when they are out of balance, we express anger from the function of resentment.

Correct.

How would this imbalance lead to man's establishing the Law of Denial for himself?

Well, first of all, in reference to that credulity and suspicion, which is one of the diagrams that's coming up very soon, as soon as our video and everything and our computers are all set, we will cover that fully under that particular diagram. Yes.

Thank you. What is the proper angle for crystal to be cut in order for it to have the most accurate reflection?

Fifty-four degrees.

Thank you. Is it advisable for us to wash our hands before and after the acupressure procedure, as was done in our healing chapel?

[Part of the devotional services of the Serenity Spiritualist Church, which were held at the American Legion Log Cabin in San Anselmo, California, were for healing. Those individuals who wished to participate in the healing process entered the healing chapel and sat at one of the four available chairs. Healers would then endeavor to be receptive to the Power that sustains and heals all life and serve as a clear and open channel for the Power to the recipient. There was no physical contact. After the healing process was completed for one person and before the next was seated, the healers rinsed their hands in water.]

Always. You have a fine little sink in that room downstairs, a fine little—running, cold water. *[The teacher refers to a multipurpose room on the lower floor of the temple where the students often performed this acupressure exercise on each other. Please see the appendix.]* Just turn it on a little bit. Don't be wasteful.

Be conservative. And just rinse and wipe your hands. If you need to wash them, go to the bathroom, but they shouldn't be dirty anyway when you're doing that. You just rinse the hands off before, and you rinse them off after. And you have a nice little running water tap there.

Thank you. Are there equal numbers of positive molecules and negative molecules in the universe?

Are there equal numbers?

Yes.

In order for form to be, there are equal numbers. [In] some form you call distorted, there's an imbalance in the equal, yes. They're not equalized.

Thank you. By what process do the positive molecules overcome the negative, as mentioned in our last class? And how does this effect the overall balance?

Well, how do the positive molecules overtake the negative ones? Is that the question?

Yes.

Well, when the negative ones are lazy, they are overtaken. And, you see, any molecule, including man, who does not make the effort to serve the purpose of his original design, by knowing himself and understanding the original design, is taken over. Yes. And people are taken over each day. But the only way they're taken over is a lack of effort and laziness on the part of the person who is taken. Yes.

Thank you. In—

You know—Excuse me. In your world you say, "Oh, I sure got took on that one," or "I sure got took on something else." Well, of course, you got took. You made no effort, and therefore you were a shining light in the universe waiting to be taken. Yes. I know a lot of people in your world just waiting to be taken. Taken of what? It varies. Or taken for what? That varies. Yes.

Thank you. In Buddhism the chant is similar. They use the square, triangle, and circle in their visualization of man. Is that religious structure in its basic form more pure than the other religious structures on earth at this time?

Well, I just smiled in reference to your question. Yes, it is affirmative. It is certainly more accurate. Because so long ago, you know, I was accused, from some people in your physical world, of just being an old Buddhist monk. Well, you know, they have a great deal of good to offer to the world. And there's a great deal of truth in it. And because you find some similarity, perhaps, to the Living Light Philosophy and Buddhism or Taoism or some of the others—those are name tags that people give.

I assured people at that time that I'm not a Buddhist monk. I'm not a Catholic monk. I'm not a monk, period. For it is my understanding of your word *monk* that you never get married and fall into that institution. Well, I fell in and crawled out eons ago. It's so long ago—although it is vivid in my memory at times when I hear so much from my students on relationships and needs, you know. But, no, I've never been a Buddhist monk or any monk, period. I may look like one because I don't overly dress, but then again, [in] these warm climates that I have to work in, I don't find too many cool heads in my classes either on earth or in some of the other classes that I have to give daily, as you would say.

And so in that respect, let us remember that the Light, there's only one Light, [which] expresses in different ways. You're going to see some similarities in all philosophies and religions. And if you don't see some similarities, then they're not philosophies and they're not religions. They're just some kind of a business. Yes.

Thank you. As the Earth evolves in its maturing process, is it moving out of the number five or will it always stay five until it dies?

No, for the universe moves through the various states of consciousness. And something that moves from one state to another changes its number and, therefore, changes its identity and, therefore, changes its expression. Yes.

Thank you. If a person finds that they seem to give in to what is called a cold at regular intervals, what does that reveal and what can one do to change that cycle?

Make an effort to awaken to what your need is. You see, every expression and experience you have is a reflection: it reflects a need in your consciousness. And so if you have a need for energy, [if] you have a need for attention, you'd be amazed what the human mind and its created forms will bring about in order that your need that you believe that you are may be fulfilled. Yes.

Thank you. I have noted that at times what I have called gratitude has much relief in it. Could you speak on gratitude and relief, and how they relate, if they do?

Well, relief from tension, relief from pressure, etc., yes, they certainly do relate. I don't know of anyone in any universe that can't relate gratitude to relief because, you see, when you're grateful for what you have, you are relieved from what you thought you didn't have. And so that's a relief. Now when a person counts the blessings of the few little crumbs that they have, in the process of doing that, they are not thinking of what they don't have. And when they're not thinking of what they don't have, they find how relieved they are with what they've got. And I'm sure that everyone can understand that in a simple way. Yes.

Thank you. It seems that functions try to masquerade as faculties often in my life. How does one become aware of the difference?

One becomes aware of the difference by [making the effort to] stop thinking of oneself so often, and then one will be able to discern which is a function and which is a faculty in their life. It's an over-identification with the mental world that causes the concern and the confusion.

Thank you. How many dimensions are man receptive to on Earth?

Eighty-one.

Thank you. Are there more than four dimensions that man has heard about on Earth?

There's 77 more. Wouldn't that make 81? Yes, there's 77 more.

Thank you. Are numbers—

Well, some men have heard about 81. Yes.

Thank you. Are men—no. Try again. Are numbers of figures as we see them a configuration of a circle, a square, and a triangle that we see only a portion of because of our limited dimensional viewing on the earth plane?

That's true, for all straight lines are circles. What you see as a straight line is a circle.

Thank you. Is sound, color, symbols, and forms could be considered as different stages of the evolvement of man to his present state from what he really is? If the statement is correct, please state the order beginning with man as a form.

Well, now let's read that word by word, please, because we want to get to—we have a few minutes left and that's many questions in one.

Yes. It starts out, "Is sound, color, symbols, and forms could be considered as different stages of the evolvement of man to—"

Well, first of all, read the first sentence, and we'll answer that.

Is sound—

Sound.

—color—

Color.

—symbols—

Symbols.

—and forms—

Well, sound, color, symbols is the very ingredient [of] what you understand as form. So that is, yes. That's affirmative.

Could be considered as different stages of the evolvement of man to his present state—

Just a minute. Could be considered as different stages of the evolvement of man?

Yes.

Well, there is only one composition of form, and it's what is stated in the first question. And our time has run out. Please hold the question for our next class.

Thank you very much, students. Have a very good week. I know that you will. Through the Law of Effort and personal responsibility we, indeed, have the joy of living.

JANUARY 12, 1986

A/V Class Private 31

Good morning, students, and welcome to our continuing classes on the Living Light Philosophy. *[A clock begins to chime.]*

We will begin today with your questions that you have submitted.

May I wait for the clock to finish?

That'll be fine.

Thank you. Are numbers or figures as we see them a configuration of a circle, a square, and a triangle that we see only a portion of because of our limited dimensional viewing on this earth plane?

That is correct.

Thank you. Is sound, color, symbols, and forms could be considered as different stages of the evolvement of man to his present state from what he really is? If the statement is correct, please state the order, beginning with man as a form.

Well, there are several questions combined there in that question. And so we will take those several questions one at a time. Read the first question of that series, please.

Is sound, color, symbols, and forms could be considered as different stages of evolvement of man—

They are.

—to his present form, what he really is?

To his present form as you see and know it, yes.

If the statement is correct, please state the order, beginning with man as a form.

Well, first of all, we must see beyond the form that we presently see form in order to give the order; otherwise, it would not be relevant to you.

Thank you. There are times when I find it difficult to write down the questions for class. Why does this happen and how can I correct it?

Well, first of all, we find ourselves in various levels of consciousness at any time, and usually, of course, from a lack of understanding, the effect of lack of effort, we do not know which level of consciousness we are in. And you should, as students, know that there are forty levels of consciousness which are in service to creation or the functions, and forty levels of consciousness in service to the faculties and the Light which you are. Therefore, if you are, at any time, in levels of consciousness that are in service to creation, then, of course, you would experience what you understand as difficulty in asking questions that are of the faculties and of that which you are. And in order to overcome that difficulty, one should make effort to be consciously aware of which level of consciousness they are in, whether they are in service to the functions [and understand] that they are not prepared, while in service to the functions, to ask questions which are in the domain of the faculties.

Thank you. Will we be given more understanding of the colors and their relationships to our attitudes when we study the diagrams?

Oh, yes, indeed, you shall.

Thank you. Harmonious music is uplifting. How can we become more receptive to its spiritual meaning?

Well, that which is harmonious is that which is in balance. And that which is in balance is that which is healthy. And that which is healthy is, of course, that which is the Principle of Good. And therefore, a person, through control of their mind, can at any time of their choice become receptive to that which is good by bringing themselves into a balance between their faculties and their functions.

Thank you. What is the difference between motive and credulity?

What is the difference between motive and credulity? Well now, for example, if you understand that credulity is that—a person in a state of credulity is one who is easily imposed upon, for they have established the Law of Laziness in consciousness. And whoever establishes the Law of Laziness in consciousness, in the area in which they have established that law they are easily imposed upon, for they make no effort on their own part and they expect something for nothing. So there is a vast difference between motive, motivation, and our credulous state at any given time. For example, a person, as I have stated, who is credulous is one who is demonstrating getting something for nothing by making no effort and [demonstrating] laziness in consciousness. A person who is motivated is a person who is acting and, therefore, is a person who is demonstrating some degree of responsibility.

Thank you. Is it advisable for students to have discussions regarding personal matters and or the philosophy either before or after the pressure point exercise?

Well, certainly any type of discussion, in reference to the pressure points that you have been given, any type of discussion would be best suited after twenty minutes from the pressure point work that has been done. It is not in the best interest to whirl in the mental realms prior to a spiritual exercise; nor is it beneficial to whirl in the mental realms prior to twenty minutes after. The best thing, of course, is not to whirl in those mental realms at all. If you permit the mind to interfere, then you are not receiving, of course, the full benefits of the spiritual exercise. For example, the application of pressure, which has been well-discussed with you, to free this divine Energy—and I have stated to you, in freeing that Energy, one should be considerate of where they are directing that Energy by their mind. And so if you choose to direct that energy that you have now become receptive to, to mental substance, then you can only expect the experiences that the Law of Duality, which controls mental substance, has to offer.

Thank you. What advice can you give us as students on what we can do for there to be peace, harmony, and unity among us?

Peace, harmony, and unity among us—it is something that is established by an individual. What each person can do is to look inside for the peace and harmony that they have been seeking outside and demonstrate the Law of Personal Responsibility by applying that law and being the peace and harmony amongst themselves, for that is what the student, I accept, is asking: How can they experience peace and harmony amongst the many levels of consciousness that a person serves in any given moment?

Thank you. How can we know whether we are helping someone by reminding them of their duties or being a crutch that they are dependent upon?

Well, first of all, let's read the first part of the question once again.

How can we know whether we are helping someone—

Thank you. How can we know whether we are helping someone? How we can know is by not knowing at all. Knowledge knows much and wisdom knows better. The human mind has absolutely nothing to do in question or dictate of spiritual work. And so by separating truth from creation, by separating the spiritual from the mental, then one will walk a path of wisdom and will not be tempted by their mind to judge whether or not they are making another a crutch or whether or not they are serving the divine Light that they are. For whoever makes effort to serve the true Light that they are is not concerned whether that true Light, which they are, is doing its work, for it does its work absent of concern.

Thank you. What is it that, following some of these classes, there is such a variety of reactions among students? Some are peaceful and quiet. Others are belligerent and verbose. What is happening and what should we be doing to show our appreciation?

Taking control over oneself. Whoever knows themselves has qualified themselves to know another, for there is only one Light, one Truth, one Being. The creation of the human mind deceives us, and we believe many things. So what we can do in observing the variety of expression, which we are observing with mental eyes, is to take control of our self and to be the living demonstration of peace and harmony. To enter the world of creation and not to be a part of it is the spiritual work that we are all responsible for.

Thank you. What should we be doing following a class with exposure of forms looking for a new home? And during such a class, what is advised when our own forms rise up?

Take control of our own mind, and we will not have to fear the forms of another.

Thank you. Mathematics, the pure expression of organization and the key to the universe. Are there other keys to the universe or is organization the key to all universes? If so, what are they?

Mathematics is the key to the universe which includes all universes.

Thank you. The Earth color, being brown, does that not mean confusion in the Living Light Philosophy and why? What are the lessons we, as a whole, are here to learn in the confusion?

We are here on the planet Earth, the fifth planet in your solar system, to learn the lesson of faith: to rely upon that which we are and to refrain from directing that which we are, faith, into the mental world. Whenever we direct our faith to the mind, into the mental world, then we become the slaves of belief. That is the bondage. And so we have this wonderful opportunity here in life to be the living demonstration, to be what we are, to make a little more effort in understanding that we don't need, we don't need to create forms with our mind in order to be fulfilled. That is one of the great deceptions of mental substance. That not accepting what we are, we demonstrate what we are not. And by demonstrating what we are not, we fill our universes with need for we have denied that truth of what we are.

And so accepting what we are, what we truly are, frees us from this constant panorama of forms and trying to fill a vacuum that cannot be filled. For the vacuum is created by the denial of what we are. Know thyself and you shall free; you shall free that which you are. But until you make the effort to know beyond a shadow of all doubt what you are, then you will continue to experience need. You will continue to create, with the human mind, many devices and forms to fill what cannot be filled. You cannot fill a cup that is full, for what you pour in runneth over. And so to tempt oneself to fill the full vessel which they are is only a path of struggle, a path of upset and discord, a path of disease, [which is] certainly the opposite from the harmony and the balance which you are.

Thank you. What center is compassion located in?

What center is the faculty of compassion located in? Well, first of all, I'd like to ask that questioner, What is compassion? What are the remaining triune faculties of that faculty of compassion? Has that been stated?

No, it has not.

It has not. Very well. For if you understood the two faculties that are inseparable from compassion, then you would understand that it could only be located in the higher centers of consciousness, that it could only be located in the odic center.

Thank you. If a level has gone underground and is using deceptive tactics, what is the best way of educating it and growing through it?

Well, of course, I accept that the questioner is speaking of themselves and, therefore, is in a position to take corrective measures. And there's only one faculty that would be advisable to use and that is the faculty of honesty.

Thank you. In accepting one's levels, are you saying that one simply accepts them or is it a more involved process?

Well, first of all, people say they accept things with their conscious mind, but when it comes to the inner mind, where forms are created in the water center, known as judgments, then it is a more involved process because many people say, "Yes, I accept that," but when it comes to what they understand as their emotions and the water center of consciousness, we find the direct opposite to be true. So in that respect, it is much more involved than just saying that, "I accept." Of course, if a person repeats that declaration ("I accept") frequently and sufficiently to the created forms that obstruct it in the water center, then the "I accept" form will then gain a foothold in that center of consciousness.

Thank you. Can one, through a deep need for attention, create a situation where one takes that which does not belong to one, or are all persons involved participating in a way to bring this situation about?

Well, first of all, read the first part of the question again.

Can one, through a deep need for attention, create a situation—

Thank you. Can one through a deep need for attention create a situation? Like attracts like [and] becomes the Law of Attachment. And therefore, one can and one does, through so-called deep need, through attention, create these various experiences. And those of like kind are gathered from the universe to assist them in their effort.

Thank you. I'm having a struggle with an addiction from my past that has a social amenity, as alcohol is in other circles.

Yes.

And I find myself unable to free myself from the addiction and those involved with it.

Yes. *[After a short pause, the teacher continues.]* That's the question? The addiction? Yes. Well, now first of all, we have to begin by refraining from the statement that you find yourself unable to free yourself from this addiction, which is having severe social consequences for you. And so you must refrain, first, from ever again thinking or speaking forth the inability to grow through this addiction, for by thinking and speaking that forth is a denial of the very Light and Truth that can and will free you from it through your constant, daily, daily efforts.

Now one turns to the Light within and accepts the possibility of freedom from the obstruction they have created, which has been stated as an addiction.

Now what is, first, an addiction? An addiction is the final state of a judgment created by the mind, sustained by directed energy to it over a period of time. When the created form, through directed energy, becomes, within the consciousness of a human being, greater than the human being who has created the form—and that happens when you permit your mind to believe that it is you. Therefore, the law of separating truth from creation must be applied. It must be applied religiously. Now you have been given, all of my students, a way, many ways, in which to make that effort. "This is a form that I have created. I experience the sensations, the thrills that it offers to me. It is a device that the form uses in my mind in order that I may serve it as often as it desires to be served."

Try to understand when you first created the form, which you call, now, an addiction with severe social consequences, try to understand that at the time of your conception or conceiving this form, known as a judgment in your mind, it was conceived during a time of ignorance, of denial of what you are. So the original form, the judgment form, which you now know as an addiction, contains within it this ingredient of insatiable need and greed. And therefore, it offers that to your mind whenever it chooses to take control over you. Now through understanding of what it really is, you make the first step in gaining control over what you have created.

But you cannot permit your mind to be used by the judgment form and to tell you that you've tried everything; you're helpless; you're not able to control it. Because at those moments, when your mouth speaks forth those words, that is the form that is using your mind and mouth. And that is not you.

So if you will first understand how you created the judgment form, which you know today as an addiction, if you will first understand that and you will then understand that when your mind tells you and your mouth speaks forth that you cannot overcome it, it is the form that is in control. You are not in control at those moments. You can be in control by not permitting the form to use your mind and your mouth. It has been designed by your mind for a very specific, very selfish, and very greedy purpose in days of ignorance. It is not interested nor does it have any consideration of the social consequences that you are faced with and are suffering through. It was not created for consideration or interest of social consequences. It was created for the sole purpose of giving to you what you had denied at the time of its creation.

Thank you. How can one know if what one sees and feels is real or merely a fantasy?

Well, first of all, "Dreamer, dream of life of beauty before your dream starts dreaming you." And your dream starts dreaming you through what you know as experience. And so in that respect, everyone is dreaming a dream. We are dreaming a dream, and—but I think what your question is, How can you know whether it is a dream through which you have control and are creating in a physical world the experience of that dream or is it what we would understand as a daydream, which does not have the lord of the universe or your conscious, directed will power, in order to bring it into physical manifestation in the world in which you identify? And so one knows, of course, from their own experiences whether or not they are creating a fantasy, for their experiences show them clearly whether it was a dream of life or it was a fantasy, for the dream of life has the lord of the universe or the will power in it. Experience reveals what the true dream was. And fantasy just goes and has no substance in the physical world which you experience.

Thank you. Is it so that when others are critical of a responsibility another holds, that they really are criticizing the breakdown in the system and not the individual who has the responsibility?

Well, now I don't like you to have to reread so many of the questions, but I do feel for the benefit of my students we should read this a bit more slowly so that they can understand that many questions, [which are] seemingly one question, contain about twenty. So let's take this step by step, please, some of these questions.

Is it so that when others are critical of a responsibility another holds, that they—

Another what?

That another person holds.

I see. That another person—I see.

—that they really are criticizing the breakdown in the system—

Which system are you referring to?

The system which bestowed the responsibility.

I see.

Evidently. And not the individual who has the responsibility.

Well, first of all, are you telling me with this question that a person who is critical of what another person thinks in reference to something is really critical of the system that they are serving and not of the person themselves? Is that what the question is about?

That's my understanding.

That is what the question is about. Well, you'd have to ask the person that is critical. I mean, you know, after all, some people use those devices to criticize the system by picking on an individual, and some people criticize an individual by using it as a device of a system that they are serving. So in a thing of that nature, you see, you would have to ask the criticizer. Yes.

Thank you.

Yes.

We stated—correction. You stated . . .

I did?

. . . that we are our birth number. Are we the same number throughout the eons?

Well, you are numbered, yes, of course. Everyone is a number. I know they don't like it. People don't like a number because, you see, it doesn't seem to be quite unique enough, and yet numbers, mathematics is the key to the universe. And without numbers, without mathematics, you would not even be. And therefore, not being, you couldn't be named. And so let's not look so despairingly on numbers. I think that many numbers are unique. I think all numbers are unique. I think each number is unique no matter how many other millions of people have a similar number. They can have any number they want.

Now in reference to numbers, yes, you're a number. And you have a purpose to serve in keeping with the number of your incarnation. So in that respect, your number, your identification on your planet Earth—there's one planet Earth. And that number serves that planet and, hopefully, well, be that in divine order. And you move on in evolution, and you have a number, your identity and your number, for the next planet of expression. And so in that respect, the number that you are, of course, changes in keeping with the planet on which you express at any given time in evolution.

And when you understand what you truly are (a part of a whole), if you want to call the whole a number five, then everyone's number five. But we're speaking of identity, the indentation in the consciousness, to dent the I, and that gives you what you understand as a name. Well, the denting of the I is a number that did the job in the first place. And so, yes, you have a number for Earth, and you [have] got a number for someplace else because you have different jobs to do on different planets. And you [have] got to clean up the act that you didn't clean up when you had the opportunity, of course, to clean it up.

Thank you. Does the name we have in spirit correspond to our accomplishments and, if so, does the name change as we continue to grow?

The name that you are known [by] in the realms of Light—and there you have [a] name in order to express, and you are known by your name, and it reveals the record. Now if you want to call your record a hundred percent accomplishment, well, that's fine. It does reveal the record, yes. And, of course, one accomplishes by doing nothing. But by so-called doing nothing, what is accomplished is not of benefit to the universes. On the contrary, it's a detriment.

Thank you. Cells are made up of atoms, which are made of protons, electrons, and neutrons, which are made up of subatomic particles.

Correct.

One of the subatomic particles, called photons, are vibrational energy which have consciousness. Would each cell then have memory which could be tapped into for past life recall?

Why, certainly. They all have a record, a memory par excellence. Why, certainly they do. This is like your cloning that—they all have that intelligence. For example, your personality and your entire record on earth can be known by just a fraction of a piece of your skin, as long as there's a cell there to be read.

Thank you. Does crystal, worn on the body, help to amplify the higher consciousness?

It helps to amplify whatever consciousness you make the effort to be in. Yes. You know, it's like a magnifying glass. If you want—if you choose to put it on a magazine that isn't worth being on the public newsstands, it doesn't matter to the magnifying glass; it will still magnify it. And so if you want to wear a crystal and you want to think certain ways, well, everyone will get to see. Yes.

Thank you. Can a crystal pyramid have anything to do with weather and atmospheric control?

Yes, it can because it is the purest of reflection.

Thank you. What is happening when a person has multiple personalities? Is it our identification with levels or could it be earth-bound souls expressing through them?

Well, first of all, it's an absolute lack of effort in the responsibility that we all have, known as personal responsibility. And there are souls that enter your planet, as they enter many planets, who, as part of their lessons, having flunked them so many times, they experience what you understand as multiple personalities. They're not taking care of the house that they have earned. They're not securing [it] when they leave it, and they leave it frequently. They are not facing their responsibility to see that the windows and the doors, they're all secured. So some passing stranger just doesn't waltz or walk on in. And so that's a lack of effort on a person's personal responsibility. And you understand it as multiple personality, and there are many earth-bound, so-called earth-bound spirits still attached to the flesh and bone.

You see, when a person is attached to the form and to the limit, then they haven't broadened their horizons; no effort's being made to broaden their horizons. Now there's a sure way, if you want to be earth-bound, you want to remain on earth, fearful of what you call death and you don't want to leave—there are many untold millions of people who have left their flesh and bone who remain on the Earth planet and who periodically get to experience the sensations of the fleshy body by using someone else's body, whenever they can and however long that they are able to remain in there, because it does take a concentrated will and desire. The only thing is that you have no guarantee if you're going to be able to get in one of those bodies, though there are many around that people aren't responsible for. And those earth-bound spirits are able to get in there and take possession for a time and get a little charge. And, of course, the more often they're able to use your body that way, then the more often they're going to, and the easier it is going to be for them.

I have stated before, and I will state again, that if you don't take care of what you're responsible for and what you have earned in evolution, there's someone waiting to take care of it for you. Now how they will take care of it remains to be seen, but I can assure you they will not do the job that you think that they should be doing. And there is no way that you can control them for you've given up control of what you're responsible for. So whoever gives up control of what they're responsible for is in no position to control that that is around them for they've given up that right, you see.

And so, my students, all of you should consider making greater effort to remember when you don't make effort to control your mind and control your body, someone else is making great effort to do it. And it happens more often than you, as students, realize at this time.

Thank you. Why would the original person not remember the other personalities expressing?

Because they're not at home. You know, if something takes place in your house and you're out to lunch someplace, who knows how far away, and you're not on duty and on guard, and someone goes in and does all kinds of things in your house, how can you expect to remember what you're not aware of? You're not aware. You're not there. So, you see, when your body can be anyplace, your house, and if you're out to lunch, out to dinner, and who knows where else you're out to, you can't expect to remember what somebody else, who came in and used your house, the one you're responsible for—well, you don't know what they did with it. The only thing you could possibly experience is that they abused your foot or did something else with some other part of your anatomy. And when you get back in you say, "Well, this isn't where I left this. What happened here?" Now you may have that experience, if they've not been too kind to your house and been a bit abusive with it. Yes.

Thank you. It was said to me that it is better to stay in the background. Why is it better?

Well, if you have a problem in placing yourself in the foreground and you are not yet sufficiently evolved to do so, then wisdom reveals, until you're able to strengthen yourself, that you remain in the background.

Thank you. And how about the people who did and do speak up and out, like Martin Luther King, Jr.? What causes a person to feel they need to do that? What are the benefits and drawbacks?

Well, they're certainly a lot of benefits. Detriments or drawbacks, if you want to call it, it depends on your own evolution and the work that you have to do. You will know from within yourself if you have a particular job to do. And the longer you procrastinate on that job that you have to do, the more difficult it's going to be for you to do the job that you know you have to do. You all [are] evolving and have certain work to do. And if you say, "Well, I don't know what my job is," it's because you haven't made the effort to be honest with yourself to find out in the first place. Otherwise, you would know. And you've probably, many times, faced the job that you have to do, and you just refuse to accept what it is. And you don't like your merit system. Well, it doesn't matter whether a person likes their merit system in evolution or not. They're not going to escape it by not liking it. They're only going to make it more difficult to face when, finally, it's faced when all the chickens come home to roost. And it doesn't matter whether you like the chickens when they come home to roost; it's guaranteed by the very law that you created them.

Thank you. How can I best express my soul talent and stop stifling it? How do you find your way—Let me try again. How do you find your own way of expressing?

Well, are you referring to the cameraman or are you referring to, to my channel or to me? Do you know? *[After a short pause, the teacher continues.]* Well, it doesn't matter, because there's only one simple answer: stop being so concerned. You see, concern is the cloud that keeps you from finding and doing what you're supposed to do. You have a soul talent. There's no problem. Get it out of the mental world and it will do its work.

Thank you. What is the single most important thing we can do to maintain good physical health on the earth realm?

The single most important thing we can do to maintain good health, physical health on the earth realm?

Yes.

The single most important thing you can do is to think correctly. *To think correctly.* To think right. To stop all this other foolishness. Whoever thinks right has the right attitude. It's a matter of maintaining the right attitude; attitude being thought patterns; thought patterns being created by thoughts. So right thinking is right action, and right action is the right body, the right health, the right wealth, and the right joy of living.

Thank you.

Change your attitude. It's the single most important thing you can do.

Thank you. If the Earth is of the fire realm, why is there so much water on it? And what does it mean to us?

Well, when you take the water and you put it on the fire, you have expression. And no one can deny that your planet Earth is not a planet of expression. I find limitless expression on your planet Earth. And so with the fire and water you have what you understand as life form. You must have heat and you must have moisture in order to have life form as you know it. And, as

I said, no one can possibly deny that your planet does not have many life forms and certainly a fullness of expression.

Thank you. Our body is made up of much water and also salt. Does the salt tend to preserve the water or emotions? If this is so, what can we do to counterbalance that influence? And does sweating, which temporarily releases water and salt, help?

Well, first of all, one who perspires does find a little release from some of their conditions. But I have taught you that work is God's love made manifest, the manifestation of goodness.

And in reference to the question of salt, the preserver, does it preserve water? Well, it preserves that which is created in water; of course, it does. That's where your judgments are created. They're created in water, in the water center. They're preserved by the salt, the salt that you are. And what can you do to root out some of those little things you've created there in that water center? Well, turn up the fire. Turn up the fire. The fire inside. Because, you see, you have this water center and you have this fire. Now if you want a new expression, well, you [have] got to build up the fire inside and make some thrust, you know. Without some fire, you don't make changes.

You [have] got to use the fire center in an intelligent way. Now I'm not speaking of using the fire center by no effort and let it go drain down into you know what. I'm talking about the fire center and rising it up so it becomes a light of your world, you see. You see, you take control of your mind and then all that energy and that burner down there will go up and illumine your mind. And so that's the effort to be made. You want changes in these judgments of yours that are binding you and everything? Well, you go right down there and you build up that fire that's just lying there from lack of care and effort and send that heat up to where it needs to be sent up there. And get a little illumination in the mental world here, up at the top, right there, you see. *[The teacher touches the left side of his head, near his temple, with the fingers of his left hand.]* Go ahead, please.

Thank you. If the good old days that are now don't feel as good as those of the past, is it our judgments which keep us from the feeling of present good? And how can we shake off the hand of those judgments?

Well, it certainly is, because, you see, for example, the judgments that you are presently servicing are telling you it isn't like it used to be [in] the good old days, that today is not as good as the good old days because they're not having their heyday in your consciousness. They're shadows of the past. They want to be fed. And if they can get the feeding from you, the energy and the attention, then they, of course, feel good, and you experience what that feeling is—and mistake that for what you are—as a satisfaction, you see. They're pleased and they're happy. And if you want to make changes in your life, you are going to have to learn to separate truth from creation. Until you make the effort to separate truth from creation, the past from the present, and the future from the present, and work with what is, then the change will not come about.

Thank you. When we go to other realms after death, do we have to experience death there in order to be free of the pain caused by fear?

One experiences death as long as one believes, for one believes as an expression of the created forms, which are the effects of denial of what you are. So as long as one believes they are the flesh and bone, as long as one, through identification, is addicted to it, then one shall experience death and one shall experience birth. Death and birth do not exist to one who has not denied what they are. Death and birth exist only to those who have denied what they are and believe what they are not.

Thank you. What effect does the astral world have on us if it's the ozone layer and if we breathe and live in its atmosphere?

Well, it has much effect upon all people who, from lack of effort and understanding, are not in control consciously of their astral and mental bodies. Then it has an effect of whatever we permit as an attitude of mind. We come into those realms of consciousness, and not having control of our astral and mental bodies, then they go off and go out to lunch and are used by the other astral forms to do their bidding for them. And then people wake up from a sleep and say how exhausted they are to themselves. They are not rejuvenated because they've gone off into an unconscious state; their mental and astral bodies have gone out and been used by others to do the slave work of the senses.

Thank you. What dimension does one enter when they are in a true meditative state of mind?

Well, if you're in a true meditative state of mind and your state of consciousness is above the lower centers, so to speak, then you can only enter spiritual realms of consciousness.

Thank you. What is the difference between organizing our thoughts and disciplining our thoughts?

Well, first of all, no thought is organized until it's first disciplined. For example, you must take control of a thought before you can get it organized. And in order to take control of a thought, a form that you have created, you have to first get it to respond to you. And you don't get anything to respond to you until you take control of it through discipline or guidance. See, discipline in truth is guidance. So if you don't discipline a thought, then you are not guiding a thought. And if you don't guide a thought, there's no way possible you can control a thought. And if you don't control a thought, then don't even consider organization.

Thank you. What is the molecular composition of a positive thought?

Well, the molecular composition of a positive thought can be well stated in this one statement: a molecular composition is a composition that is completely free from concern. It is one that is filled with acceptance. Not the possibility of acceptance, [but] absolute acceptance. For that creation guarantees the law. For example, when you create that condition in consciousness, it isn't a matter of accepting and doubting and accepting. It is the absolute acceptance. Now that absolute acceptance is known as the power of faith. The power of faith. That is the power. And when all of your bodies, through your own discipline and guidance, are united for the sole purpose of absolute, *absolute* acceptance, you will have the manifestation. And you will speak your word forth into the universe. It shall not return to you void. It shall accomplish what you have sent it to do.

Thank you. What effect does weather have on the ozone layer?

Well, weather, of course, has varying effects upon the ozone layer. The most beneficial effect of weather, if you're speaking of weather, dry climates or etc., moisture, moisture is the most beneficial.

Thank you. How many facets are there in a perfect crystal?

How many facets are there in a perfect crystal? Well, I can tell you this, if you want it as perfect as your world of creation can make it, then you should consider fifty-four.

Thank you. Does to spin in mental substance mean that one is grounded in the left hemisphere?

Indeed, it does. Indeed, it does. Let's say more likely they are satisfied in the hemisphere.

Thank you.

Whatever you're satisfied in, you're grounded in. I'm sure you'll all agree.

Thank you. In what way is the river of life related to our will?

Well, in what way is the river of life related to our will? Without our will, it doesn't flow. Therefore, it's very related.

Thank you. What occurs to the river of life when we deny possibility and hope?

Then the flow of the river slows down.

Thank you. Would you please share with us an example of what you meant when you said, "You get inside of a thing by going counterclockwise"?

Well, yes. This here is a very involved study, and I want to answer it in as simple a way as I possibly can. To get into something, you must go out of it. Now I know that sounds contradictory to you. Say, for example, you are tempted to get into something by getting involved with someone. Well, how do you get involved with a person? You get involved with a person by working counterclockwise of getting uninvolved with a person.

Now, for example, you have a temptation, a desire: you'd like to be involved with that person over there. Now what you actually start to do [is] you start to dissect that person; you start to see what you judge is their good points, their bad points, their strong points, their weaknesses. You start an analysis, an investigative process. Now what you are actually doing in consciousness is you are going counterclockwise, taking them apart, dissecting them, like you would under a microscope, a little bug, you see, and seeing if they fit into all of the judgments that you have made. Now if they fit, if you are able to squeeze them into the limits of your judgments, then what happens is once that judgment has been made, "Yes, they do fit," you find yourself on the clockwise movement, and you understand that as now being involved.

Well, the truth of the matter is you were getting involved when you were working, going through the dissecting process to see if they would fit in your consciousness into your judgments and were [a] sufficient number of your judgments satisfied. In other words, you have the generals of your judgments, you have the colonels, and down at the bottom there you have the buck privates. You're not too concerned with the buck private judgments, but the generals and the five-star generals and the colonels and the majors, now they carry some weight.

So that's what actually goes on, you see. We're talking about the counterspin and the spin of the consciousness, yes.

Thank you. The planet Uranus has nine rings. Does it also, then, have schools of Light? [The cameraman pronounced "Uranus" as "yu-'rā-nes."]

The planet Uranus has nine, and it does have schools of Light. However, it does not have the light of Saturn. There are different schools between those two planets. Yes. *[The teacher pronounced "Uranus" as "'yur-e-nes."]*

Thank you.

Yes, you call that planet what?

Uranus. [The cameraman again pronounced "Uranus" as "yu-'rā-nes."]

Oh, you call it Uranus. All right. Fine. Call it what you will.

Yes, sir.

We understand what you are talking about.

Well, that was my ignorant understanding.

Well, no, that's fine. I do think that's what your planet calls it. Anyway, go ahead.

Thank you. "Love all life and know the Light." Is this the effect of the perception that all life is an individual river of life and at some time an inseparable part of a greater river of life?

Well, it is the greater river of life. You are the river of life. You are inseparable. You are an inseparable part of that river. And so, "Love all life and know the Light."

Now, as we're closing up—we only have a couple of minutes left—I did want to speak to you a little bit, with so much interest in [it], on Halley's Comet. If you'll try to understand you have been witnessing for eons of time now, as this Halley's Comet passes by once in a lifetime, so to speak, on your planet, once in your lifetime, you're actually witnessing the birth of a planet. Now that's what it is. But, you see, because your span of time and your identification with limit or form is so, so intense, then it is most difficult to conceive that a planet is born, is being born. You're witnessing the actual birth of a planet.

Now I know that your scientists and things may describe this so-called Halley's Comet as the garbage can of the universe. Well, if you want to consider yourself as a form [of] the garbage can of the planet Earth, then that is fine. We do not consider the birth of a planet or a planet a garbage can. What it does, as it passes through, it gathers unto itself, through its own force and movement, it attracts unto itself particles in space. And that's how a planet is born. And someday your scientists will accept that a planet is born; it is sent out from what you understand [as] a sun, a great fireball, and this little fireball is spit out into the universe. It travels through space, gathers up, through its own attractive force and gravitational pull, it gathers unto itself various, what they now say in your world, is garbage. And in eons yet to be there is a new planet in the sky.

Now because it passes over your planet Earth at approximately every seventy-some years, it is gathering elements and things from the universe that are a part of the planet Earth. So you are witnessing the birth of a planet on which life as you know it shall reside at some time in the future.

Thank you and good day.

JANUARY 19, 1986

A/V Class Private 32

Good morning, class.

This morning we'll continue on with the questions from our previous class and the ones that were submitted for today.

Thank you. Could you please share with us your understanding of this saying [from Discourse 62], "I am only the vehicle of the Light and it is the Light that doeth the work and that is all that is eternal"?

Yes. Speaking on that, I am only the vehicle of the Light for it is the Light that doeth. If we understand that the mind is a creating process and that Light, or pure energy, is the mover, the creating is done in a mental world. The movement of the creation, the energy that sustains that which is created, is the Light. Now it is the same as you are the creator of form. You are the effect of that creation of form when you choose to be. However, you are not the form that you have created. You are the Light which sustains it. You are the Light which makes it possible for the mind to create forms. So in that respect, you are not what you think you are, unless you believe that you are.

Now in these teachings and in these classes, we have evolved from the bondage of believing to the freedom of faith. And so each moment we are faced with bondage of what we have created or freedom through responsibility of what we have created. So our choice is simple at any moment. We move either in faith and freedom or we move in belief and bondage. So when you have an experience, if you believe that you are the experience that you have created, you are bound to its effects. When you accept that you are the power which is moving the form you have created— you are responsible for the creation; you are not the creation. You are responsible for the experiences which are the effect of what you have created. However, you are not the experience and you are not the effect. You are responsible for it; however, you are not it and can never ever be.

Thank you. As one of our earth dictionaries defines security *as freedom from danger, risk, poverty, or apprehension, would the Living Light's definition of* security *be akin to freedom from the mind's control over the eternal soul? What would the definition be?*

Well, of course, it is freedom from limit. It is freedom from the vehicle controlling the power that you are. And so that is the definition. It is freedom from the limits, which are a mental world and which create these various forms which we often are tempted to believe, for a time, that we are.

Thank you. Why are we tempted sometimes to have the last word in an argument?

Well, of course, we are often tempted to have, what you say, the last word in an argument for that is where our security has been placed. That is the false security. Now whenever we place our security in our mind and what it is able to accomplish, and we do not, as you say, get the last word in an argument, then, of course, we feel very insecure for we do not have that false feeling of perfection in what we believe that we are.

Thank you. What methods are used in helping animals on the other side to be free of temptation?

You will find that animals are tempted as domesticated or educated animals. Now the animal kingdom does not experience what you know as temptation until they become over-identified with human beings. So it is a transference of the weakness to the animal that you experience that animals are tempted. It is something they have been educated to. It is not a part of their natural expression. An animal fights only to survive, goes by his basic instincts, and is not tempted in the ways you understand temptation until man domesticates them. And then, unfortunately, they are frequently tempted.

Thank you. What would one's responsibility be in the following situation? An animal, when its owner moves away, chooses to remain in its neighborhood and accepts food handouts, but does not get too near to people. The animal's owner returns several times to try to find it. You know where to find it. Would it be in the animal's best interest to help the owner find it or let it remain free?

Well, first of all, if the animal has been taken from its freedom by domestication, then the person who has domesticated the animal has a responsibility that must be fulfilled. Once you domesticate what you understand as a wild animal, you have a responsibility for the survival and the health and care of that animal. So it isn't a matter of domesticating an animal and then setting it free, for once it has been domesticated, it is not again free in its form.

Thank you. Do what we call the Ides of March correspond at all to the time of Tower of Babel, when God assembled man's— no—I can't read the word. Something about man's language. It has been written that this occurred at the full moon of March. Is this correct or accurate?

That is accurate. It is correct.

Thank you. Please discuss the Mason's part in building the Tower of Babel and how does the Masonic Order stand today in the Light?

Well, in reference to the Masonic Order, it is based upon a spiritual foundation of long, long ago in your world. And as far as its standing in the Light, it's very purpose of being was, and is, in service to the Light. Now you must try to understand there are various societies or degrees in what you understand as the Masonic Order. And so ofttimes that's what you see, [and that] is very questionable about its spirituality or its spiritual motivation. However, it does remain to this day in your world as a moving force in freeing many souls from the bondage and realms of belief.

Thank you. How did such an order with high initiate teachings ever become involved with such a project as the Tower of Babel?

It has what you understand as members or people to support its organization. And so in reference to the Tower of Babel, if you will understand whenever a person becomes dependent upon their mind, they are in the process of creating for themselves a tower of Babel.

Thank you. When the Earth was becoming a planet, did the so-called missing link occur after man was here and walking upon the Earth or did it happen like Halley's Comet, as it moved through space collecting matter and information?

Well, I've spoken many times on this so-called missing link, which you will not find on your planet. If you will try to understand that your planet, the planet Earth, has been visited, eons ago, by intelligent beings from other planetary systems, if you will try to understand the evolution on your planet of the animal form, if you will try to understand what you know in your world as a hybrid, then you won't have any problem in understanding the so-called missing link. Now if you understand that a missing link is a visitor who has come and gone, then you have no problem—and has left what the visitor has left.

Thank you. Is being electric in attitude the same as being tough in attitude?

Well, I wouldn't consider being, expressing the electrical part of your being as one of being tough. So often the word *tough* is an expression of the magnetic field and extremely emotional and does not carry with it any light of reason or constructive good as a final result. So I would not consider the word *tough* as being electrical when so often in your world I find so-called toughness an expression of a very negative and feminine emotional being.

Thank you. Is there a hierarchy among birds, and, if so, what bird is the highest?

The Golden Eagle. There's a hierarchy in all species. Yes.

Thank you. Did Martin Luther King, Jr. accept, through a contract in the Great Rotunda, that he would be assassinated while in form here on earth?

Well, in speaking of that person or speaking of anyone who has their, what you would understand as, destiny to fulfill, they are aware most of their life at various times of their responsibility and what they have to do. And being aware of that from the time of entering the planet, it is something that does not come to them as a shock. And those who are dedicated in that way are willing, of course, to accept that as part of the necessary payment of the work that they have to accomplish. Not being overly attached to limit and to form, they do not suffer as one who is overly attached to limit and form would suffer.

Thank you. Why does the mind find irritation to be so painful? Is its survival of all it perceives at stake?

Well, irritation, the awakening of the soul, of course, represents to the human mind that [it] is losing control. And whenever the human mind judges that it is losing control, it expresses what it feels as an annihilation of its own continuity.

Thank you. Earth scientists understand that Halley's Comet is composed primarily of ice. If this is correct, is this comet to become a water center planet?

Yes, all planets go through the various phases in evolution, and that is correct.

Thank you. In earlier classes reference was made to transition being determined by separation of the Isle of Hist.

Yes.

Would you please share with us more of this process?

Well, I can share with you in reference to the separation of the Isle of Hist, without which what you understand as transition is not possible—for example, you have been given the teachings of the boat upon the river of life. Now if you will try to relate those teachings that you have already been given to the Isle of Hist, then you will understand what is taking place on this river of life and this boat or identity that you are upon it. So I would recommend those interested in the process of transition do further study on the classes that were given to you on the river of life and the little ship that you really are sailing upon it. Then you will be prepared to understand, through further questioning, when the diagrams are given to you in the forthcoming days, this separation process, and will certainly have greater understanding of what happens whenever you permit your identity to become grounded along the river of life.

Thank you. Is the brain the instrument through which the Power that we are is transformed into physical force, which then manifests itself as experience?

Yes, the physical brain is the instrument that is used. And in speaking on the physical brain, let us further understand and spend a little study in the electrodes that control the forms created by the human mind. You see, in your world today your science has evolved, in respect to electromagnetic fields, to the point where, through charge of electricity, various thought forms that you have created by your mind can be changed and transformed into thought forms, judgments that are more constructive. Now this is demonstrated in your medical field by certain charges of electricity and electrodes placed upon the physical, human brain.

The spiritual path that you have been studying and are studying accomplishes these changes through proper concentration and breathing in a slower, but more sure and secure way. However, it does require dedication to the various exercises that you have been given. Now we have spoken on that in many ways over the years. For example, we have stated to you that when you wish to bring about a change in your attitude, when you wish to bring about a change in the various forms that you have created, that it does require an equal amount of energy directed to the new form that you are working to create. Now when an equal amount of energy, through attention and identification, is directed to the new form that you wish to create, you will neutralize the other form. Now this is an actual electrical process taking place within your physical, human brain.

So when a person wishes to bring about new experiences in their life, experiences that they are sure will bring them into what they are seeking—now we're speaking now, of course, on a realm that most people identify with, a mental realm. That's what you're working with until you evolve on through that. And so what happens, when you work to make a change in your thinking, a change in the solidified thoughts, which are judgments, then you experience a discouragement. You are tempted to not continue with the effort, and that is always the indicator that you are about to bring about a neutralization between the new form that you are creating and the old one that has been created.

And so in your world today, your scientists and doctors are able to place an electrical charge into certain areas of the brain. The difficulty with that is that, by so doing, the individual is not evolving. The individual is becoming dependent upon a crutch that something beyond his control is making the changes in his mind. Consequently, when the person leaves your physical world, they have those forms that they have created waiting for them. Because only the change has been brought about in the vehicle. The changing of the higher bodies has not taken place yet, for the electrical charges and electrodes are working upon the physical expression of the human brain and not the changes where they truly should be made.

Thank you. When we have been guided that we would experience greater harmony through acceptance, how may we grow in acceptance?

Well, the question of how may we grow in acceptance—for example, when you are concerned or interested in growing in acceptance, try to understand that it reveals to you how you can find a way to control acceptance. So that actually is not acceptance at all. One accepts and that's what's done. One does not question how they can grow in acceptance, for it isn't a matter of question. It is a matter of demonstration. For example, a person has opportunities thousands of times daily to accept or to battle. And therefore, one should not concern themselves with the mental activity of growing in acceptance. One should simply demonstrate, through declaration, "I accept personal responsibility. My thought is in my mind. I put it there. I can take it out. By the law of putting it there, I have the right to take it out. I think this is a beautiful day. I alone put that form there. I alone can take that form out. No one can take from me what I do not first, through my error of ignorance, give to them."

So if you permit yourself to believe that someone has made your day miserable, if you permit yourself to think in that way, then you are demonstrating, through a lack of accepting personal responsibility, that whatever someone else does is how you live. Surely a person in that attitude and frame of mind is ever lost in not knowing who they are, why they are, and not even knowing what they truly are.

And so let us not be concerned in how to grow in acceptance. Let's just be acceptance and growth will take care of itself, freed from the mental concern.

And remember, whenever you do not make the effort to declare the truth, "This is a thought in my mind. I put it there. I put it there by my belief that someone else is greater than I. And I demonstrate they are greater than I when I permit myself to be miserable and judge that it is because [of] what someone else is doing to me," remember that no one can do anything to you that you do not want, first, done unto you, for you alone allow the form to enter your mind and only you alone can move the form out of your mind.

Thank you. Why are our judgments created in the water center?

Judgments are created in the water center for that is the realm of consciousness through which birth is given forth. That is the creating center of consciousness. So [if] you find a person who is very creative, you will find a great identification with the water center. You will also find what you understand as emotional dependence. You will also find in that creating, creative type of person, you will find great difficulty in an expression of the continuity of the faculty of reason.

Thank you. Does separating truth from creation mean separating now (truth) from past and future (creation)? If so, is the now the river of life and the shores the past and future?

Oh, yes, yes, indeed, it is. I'm pleased with the students in their study and investigation. Now is the eternal present. It is the only place where you will find freedom. It is the only place to direct your consciousness, is in the eternity which you are. You see, when you permit yourself to identify with the eternal moment, what you are doing [is] you are declaring and expressing what you are. You are eternal. Everything else is what your mind has and does create. What you are is eternity. You are the river of life. Your form, your identification is the little ship sailing upon it. The shores are what is to be and what has been. That is under the domain of the mental realms of consciousness. What has been, what will be, is ever in a constant process of change. You see, the waters eternally wash the thirsty shore, for they sustain form. They sustain the *maya*. They sustain the illusion.

And if you permit yourself to identify with what has passed, you will suffer through concern of what is to be, for you have over-identified with *maya* or illusion at the expense of the freedom of what you are. Eternity is what you are. Identify with what you are [and] experience the abundant good and freedom of what you are. Refrain from the temptation to look back, and when so doing, you will not be filled with worry or concern of what is to be. Whoever identifies with what he is, is free and shall be what he is. So identify with the eternity that you are by looking to the moment in which you are conscious and aware. For in the moment that you are conscious and aware, that *is* what you are.

Thank you. How does one lock up their doors and windows when leaving their house of clay?

Yes. When leaving one's house of clay, when going out to lunch or to dinner or breakfast, as I've stated, to secure the form that you are leaving, one must use the faculty of reason. One must look at all of the weak areas of their little house and their mind, one must look at their weak areas by simply accepting the demonstrable fact that they are tempted in certain things. For it is only through a weakness in the house of clay that temptation is able to come in and rob you of what is justly and rightfully yours.

Now we are robbed in the night. That means in the moments of ignorance in the darkness. And that is because we are not securing these areas of our little house that we understand as weakness or temptation. So when you want to leave your house, take stock of your weaknesses, the weaknesses of your house, secure them with the light of reason and honesty, and when you return, you won't have any foreigners in your house who have taken control and now you're the tenant, instead of the owner.

Thank you. Why do we spend so much energy to protect our self-images?

Because we believe that we are that which we have created. Whoever believes that they are what they have created works diligently to protect what they have created for they are attached unto themselves. And that's known as attachment to the fruits of action. You see, the fruit of a person is what a person believes that they are. So if you believe that you are a certain part of your house and a piece of fruit falls from that part of your house, then that piece of fruit, that is what you are.

And this is why parents have such great difficulty in trying to guide their own children objectively and in the light of reason: because they believe that they are the fruit, that they are the child. And there is not separation from truth and creation.

And so when we no longer spend so much of our time and our energy in believing that we are the fruits of our action—and just take a look at the past if you want to see how much has gone rotten—and move on to the eternal moment and you won't have any problems with this self-image foolishness.

Thank you. Does our soul evolve in the same way that a planet does, as was discussed last week in the description of Halley's Comet and its growth process?

Yes. Yes, all forms are governed by the laws of form, and they all evolve and progress in a similar way in keeping with their formations, of course. Yes.

Thank you. If we do not have to create forms with our minds, what happens to our mind? Does not nature abhor a vacuum?

That is correct. And so you become most unstable. The thing is, is not to tempt to restrain the human mind from creating. It's its very nature to create, to gather, and to garner. The thing is, is to understand it for what it is and not to be attached to it to the point of believing that you are it. You see, the problem is, is what you understand as the self-image: you're trying to protect what you have created. The self-image is something you have created. You have created it. And therefore, because you have created it, you believe that you are it. As I gave the example a few moments ago, so many parents believe that they, being the creator of their child, that they are their child and they act accordingly. That's not intelligent. It is not reasonable and it certainly is not beneficial.

So your mind creates many things. The question is, Will you stop and pause and say, "I am creating this. I am not this that I have created"? You know, and then you will not suffer through the various changes that your creation is going to go through. You see, people, they create a marriage. They create the conditions through which they have the experience, all right? We create the conditions through which all experiences we encounter. And so if you believe that you are what you have created and you create a marriage, it involves another human being. They believe they are what they have created. And so you have two individuals that have created, that is, in their belief, the same thing, when it doesn't work out at all. Because, you see, there are no two forms identical. And so you have two forms coming together; they have created a marriage. The law pulls them together in keeping with what they have created, but they're not identical. And there's no way possible that they can be. And so you have problems.

Stop believing that you are what you have created. Stop believing that you're the finger at the sacrifice of the eyes. Stop believing you're the tooth at the sacrifice of the foot. Stop believing that foolishness and you won't have any problem with self-image. You won't even have any problem with marriage. There won't even be any. Thank you. Go ahead.

Thank you. I feel I caught a glimpse of myself in another lifetime wearing renaissance clothing amidst architecture found in the Mediterranean area. We are taught that we do not reincarnate back to Earth. Is there similar architecture and life styles on another planet? Please help me to understand whether it was a spiritual or mental experience.

Well, first of all, you see, you want to try to understand that we are ofttimes, in our mind, attracted to various experiences, historically, throughout history. There are many factors involved.

Now let's go beyond all of this reincarnation and everything, and let's go to what I've been discussing. You are eternity. That's what you are. You're not form; therefore, you're not limit. You are not past; therefore, you are not future. You are. The most difficult thing for the human mind to accept is that you are. That's all. You are eternity. That is what you are.

Now, being eternity, you are not controlled by or the victim of illusion and delusion, which is known as time and space. Time and space does not exist in eternity. Time and space are created and are the domain of a mental world consciousness. They do not exist in truth. Distance exists as a relative in your consciousness. Without your consciousness, you do not have reference. Without your mental consciousness, you do not have relative. And so if you will only try to understand—and you must move from identity to limit and form to understand—you are everywhere, everything at all times because you are that which moves time. You are the power through which mind creates this illusion of time and space. You are that which sustains mental substance, that creates forms that become shadows. So without reference, you are no longer controlled by the illusion.

For example, a person wants to know themselves and to be free. To know oneself goes beyond the process of thinking about what oneself is. You are not self, for self is restriction; self is limit; self is that which is created by the mind. You are not the mind.

Now in these private classes we are working to help you to evolve to go beyond the limits, for you are that which is beyond limit. To go beyond limit, you must make the effort to accept the possibility that time and space and form are the domain of creation. You are not creation. God is not a creator. Creation is an effect. It is in the domain of limit or form or denial. That which is form is limit; that which is limit is denial; that which is denial is that which has fallen from what it is. You are not an effect; you are cause. So when you begin to make these changes in consciousness to go beyond the illusion of time and space, you are returning to cause, that which you are. Thank you.

Thank you. Sometimes I hear high frequency noise. What causes that?

Well, first of all—high frequency noise, you say? Well, as far as that is concerned, it's an interpretation of the mind, for what is noise to one is music to another. Now the cause of a high frequency sound could be from many different things. I would personally have to investigate your state of consciousness at the time. It could possibly be an awakening into other dimensions. It could also possibly be caused from an irritation or a judgment being disturbed in the consciousness. So there are many possibilities of a high frequency noise registration in the consciousness. Yes.

Thank you. It seems to me that all numbers, no matter how large, reduce to the number one through nine. Is that correct?

Yes. There are only nine. That is correct.

Thank you. If that is true, does that relate to [in] any way to the nine centers of consciousness?

Yes, it does. You cannot add or subtract and have totality. Nine is totality and nine, also, is eternity and infinity.

Thank you. In the Catholic religion there is known as so-called saints. What are they really and what purpose did they serve?

Well, they certainly served a purpose to many people to help inspire them to walk upon a different path than what they were trodding. And they were human beings on your planet that gained the reputation of being very spiritual and dedicated to something beyond the realms of creation.

Thank you. If a comet gathers particles from other planets in the universe for its own formation, then we are also made up of particles from other planets.

Why, yes. Yes, my good students, we demonstrate that constantly. We're constantly trying to gather from that that we get close to. We're always seeking to gather and to garner. You see, that's in keeping—you see, if you watch the planet and the comets as they pass on through what you know as space and time, you will see they attract unto themselves, through centrifugal force, many different things. They're always gathering unto themselves. Now people do many things in centrifugal force to gather unto themselves all kinds of things. And some people call that the cosmic garbage can. But call it what you will, it does not change the principle of gathering and garnering. That's the process of old creation, my friends, that which you are not. So don't identify with creation and have to face the sadness in reality of being a garbage can. Yes.

Thank you. What planets was the Earth formed from?

What planets was the Earth formed from? Well, your planet, your planet Earth here, the fifth planet, as you might say, was sent out from the main solar system, from the sun as—try to understand the father and mother of the universe. You know, it's mother nature and so-called father God. Well, it's the electrical thrust that sends out from itself into the universe. And all of these elements as it moves out, into the atmosphere, it attracts unto itself what you, some people call a cosmic garbage can. And there you have creation. And so the planet Earth, your little, young, adolescent planet here, has come out from its parent, from the father, out into the so-called universe and space, spinning, as you understand it, gathering and garnering unto itself for eons and eons of time and growing in the process. Yes.

Thank you. It was said that the schools of Saturn are different from the schools of Uranus. In what ways are they different? [Do] the lessons that are learned at these schools originate from a different center of consciousness?

Yes, they do. And I can say this to you, Saturn, the planet of understanding and the planet of wisdom, that is the planet through which, as time, eons pass in the universes, you will know is the planet of awakening.

Thank you. When we have merited being in the higher spiritual realms of consciousness, we are known by our name, which reveals who we really are. [Does] the communication, as we know it now, become obsolete and we are freer to just be demonstrations and carrying on our work?

Carrying on our work. Well, yes. Communication in these other realms, when you speak forth a word, the form that your mind has created goes with the word. And so in that respect, if you tell a person, you say, "Oh, I love you," and you are thinking, "I wonder when she'll get out of my life," or vice versa, you see, the person gets to see the form your mind has created, as well as the words that you speak. And there the light of honesty shines so beautifully.

Thank you. Why is it that after being in the jungle with so many people and vibrations, an overwhelming sense of fear almost paralyzes me at times? It feels like the walls are closing in and [I feel a] need for complete solitude with no distractions or noise.

Yes, that's most understandable because one is experiencing the fear of their own weaknesses, you see, and their temptations. And so they want to go hide in a closet. And I think that your world is quite familiar with people going in and out of closets. And if you try to understand it's just a false sense of security to go hide in the closet, you see—but remember that through effort on your part, you be with the world and not a part of the it; you be in that world and never a part of it. And so in that respect, you have no problem as long as you make the effort to declare the truth that you're in this jungle; you're not a part of the jungle. You become a part of a jungle when you believe that you are the jungle. So all you [have] got to do is remind yourself that you're in it, but you're not a part of it. Because you don't believe that's you. You know better. You know that's not you. Then you have no problem there. And you won't have to, through so-called fear, which is faith in mental substance, go hide in the closet and lock the door and turn the key. Yes.

Thank you. From what other planets in our solar system is Halley's Comet attracting elements in its formation as a planet?

Well, it's attracting elements, it's attracting from all the planets that it passes by. And it certainly has attracted plenty already from the Earth planet. And it will be attracting more very, very soon.

Thank you. Is Earth the primary source of such elements attracted by Halley's Comet?

No, Earth is not the primary source.

Thank you. Will any of the planets in our solar system be in existence at the time of Halley's formation as a planet? If so, which will they be?

All the planets that you presently know, plus ones you don't know.

Thank you. Having attracted many of Earth's elements, will Halley's Comet have the lessons of faith to experience?

As part of its lessons it will have, yes, but it will not be the primary one.

Thank you. After doing the pressure point for a time, does it help to strengthen one's immune system?

Yes, it helps to strengthen all systems, including the immune system. But remember, the strengthening of one's immune system is also dependent upon immunity to certain cushions of judgment that one has been entertaining for a lifetime. Yes, I do hope that's helped there.

Thank you. If so, what would cause a person to become very sick then? Would it be the judgments and the forms being so long in control retaliating?

Yes. I think we just answered that. Absolutely. Yes. Definitely.

Now look at this, the time has passed so quickly. We'll have to reserve the rest of our questions for our next class. And I know that you'll have a nice day. It's been a beautiful morning and so nice to be here with you.

Thank you and good day.

JANUARY 26, 1986

A/V Class Private 33

Good morning, students.

I see that you have already had a very fine class from Isa, my student. And this morning I would, perhaps, like to continue on with some of that and, be it in order, take care of some of your questions. *[Isa Goodwin is Mr. Goodwin's mother. She would regularly instruct, guide, and correct the students through Mr. Goodwin's mediumship.]*

It is so important to understand the balance of the electric and magnetic vibration or frequency. So often in your experiences you find yourself what you call and understand as emotionally upset, which, of course, is the experiencing of the return of the creatures that you, of course, have created.

Whoever makes the conscious, daily effort to separate truth from creation, whoever makes the conscious, daily effort to declare, "I am what is. There is no past until I choose to service that which I have created. And because there is no past in truth, therefore, there is no future. Past and future are relative. They are dependent upon the created forms which the human mind chooses to identify with. Because in truth there is no past, and therefore there is no future, I am free. I am that eternity. That is what I am. Being that eternity, there is no magnetic; there is no electric." For by bringing the electric and the magnetic into a perfect balanced frequency, you overcome what you understand as gravity or grounding. Therefore, freedom is dependent upon your effort to bring into balance frequencies of electric (future), magnetic (past), until those frequencies, from a perfect balance, are neutralized. This is a law of physics. An understanding of this law is based upon the number five.

Now you have been given, in these classes over a period of time, the meaning and the understanding of this number five. Two is creation. The creation of the electric. Two, the creation of the magnetic. The future exists because there is a past.

The past exists and, therefore, creates a future. That is what you understand as time, the great illusion. That is what you understand, and yet you are the one that is. You are in truth that one. You are in truth the eternal and the infinite. It is when the infinite in its expression (eternal) becomes the nine of totality. And so when the line joins the circle, you have what you understand as fulfillment or totality, for you have identified, and from the infinite, which you are, have joined the eternal circle of what you are not. Now the circle of eternity is dependent upon the line of infinity in order to experience.

To free yourself from this totality, the totality of creation, requires the removal of the circle from the line that has joined it. Now at the joining of the line of infinity to the circle of eternity requires an indentation. This indentation takes place in what you understand as a division; a division being the individualization, the moving from what you are to what you are not.

So let us apply this law of physics. Let us apply this demonstrable truth to a thought of our mind. Let us look at this nine and let us see. With separation, we have the infinity. We have what we understand is a straight line. However, we also know that a straight line is only straight to the viewer, for infinity is in truth the circle of eternity. And when we separate the completed circle from what we view as the straight line or one, then we have the truth as we see it individually perceived in the eternal moment of which you are.

To bring about changes in the gravitational pull of which you find yourself bound to your planet Earth, you must understand the mathematic principle of totality: that it is in truth not electric and magnetic. It is in truth the separation of the neutrality.

Now when in your world you moved with your science in what you understand as a split or separation of the atom and the experiences from the split of the atom released a force that was a great shock to your mind, then try to understand: that which you are has been separated to what you believe you are. And when you once again unite in consciousness, by first a separation and then a reuniting, you will experience not what you know as experience, for you will be what you are: whole and complete in consciousness. As sure as the atom was split, you, an atom, have been split through the Law of Identification. Therefore, you must consciously split or separate what you are and what you are responsible for creating. Once having done that, reunite that which you have created to that which you are and you will return home. And you will no longer be controlled by the force of mental substance, which is in truth a separation and an attempted reunion in an unbalanced way.

So let us now, as we're moving on to [a] more advanced understanding of these basic principles and teachings, let us look at mathematics; let us look at the numbers in an intelligent way. Let us look at the five. Let us look at the nine. Let us add unto the five and then let us add unto the nine. And let us understand from that addition what is the total or sum that we identify with.

For some time, for many, many, many eons of time your world has been in darkness in reference to the laws governing what you understand as nature on your planet. And the day has dawned, when, through mathematics and physics, man is beginning slowly, stumbling along the path, to understand himself. For as man moves in a greater understanding of himself, he understands the universe for man is a universe. Man's form is in the image of a universe. And when, through proper perspective, man looks to what he understands in his world as the sky and man views the planets revolving, man will see beyond a shadow of all doubt that the position of the planets in a solar system, viewed from the proper perspective and dimension, reveals to him the form that he is on the planet of his identification. For example, the planet Earth is the fifth planet. Man is in form the number nine. You must move, through more effort, to an understanding of dimension, the dimension that you are. Move to a greater understanding through a little effort.

"What is the number of this thought form that I am creating at this moment? For once I understand the spiritual meaning of numbers, I will have the mathematics necessary for the key to open the universe, the universe which I am, for that is what I am." Limit is ever in keeping with the mathematical configuration that you have created in moments and times of ignorance. You are the effect, through identification and lack of conscious choice, of the mathematical combinations you have created.

You are not without the way.

Everything in all universes are frequencies, vibration. They act and that which they act upon reacts. Some time ago I spoke to you on being the actor, not the reactor. Act by understanding what frequency the thoughts you think are being created on, for only on that frequency, when you enter it, can you experience or react to the act of creating.

You cannot be affected by anything that you are not on its original frequency of creating. Therefore, you can look at your life and grow in understanding that this particular feeling is on frequency number such and such and, through that gradual understanding and application of the law, choose the moments intelligently when you shall enter that frequency.

You are held to your planet in physical substance from the ignorance of understanding the Law of Balance. Whoever balances one thought, whoever brings into balance one form, from what you understand as counterbalance, shall neutralize that which they have created. We bind our self through an error of ignorance. Understand belief binds; faith frees. This is a basic mathematical formula, for belief is a frequency of adhesion, and faith is a frequency of freedom or release. Freedom is an effect of faith, and bondage is an effect of belief.

Accept what you are and you will start upon the path of freedom from bondage. Accept what you are by separating what you are from what you are not and then reuniting in a perfect balanced frequency you and what you have created.

And now we'll take a few moments here to take care of some of your questions.

Thank you. Is karate designed to bring all of our bodies into alignment and balance?

Karate, its spiritual purpose, is designed to bring harmony to the mental and physical body. When you establish the Law of Harmony, you unite all its parts, in speaking of limit or body. Therefore, the spiritual purpose of that wonderful exercise, for exercise is what it truly is, the spiritual purpose of it is instrumental in helping a person to unite the various parts of limit, the effect of which is harmony. And through harmony, like attracts like. And whoever establishes that law in a realm of consciousness to which they are identified, such as a mental world and its effect, a physical world, through the Law of Attraction, attracts the harmonious bodies in a united whole. And this is why those who are dutiful and religious to exercises of guidance from the light of reason can only benefit therefrom.

Now karate and all of these different, ancient, very, very ancient exercises, what they are in truth—though I know in your world they are taught as defense mechanisms, which they certainly do serve beautifully. And they are designed so that you will act and not react. For example, in such exercises when you are receiving the force of a blow, they are designed that instead of using your vital life energy to react to the blow, you do not react; you act. And because you do not react, you act instead of reacting, the person who is using the force of the blow, it is turned against them by not reacting.

Now this has to deal, in that question, with the Law of Gravity. And someday these things will be more fully discussed. For example, whoever uses force to overcome or counteract another force becomes the victim of their own force. The spiritual design of the exercise of karate is to use intelligently an exercise or movement of the form with the light of reason and the power of faith. Therefore, a person who is truly dedicated to those type of exercises is not the victim of their own force. Whenever you use force to overcome force, you become controlled by the Law of Force and, therefore, are grounded by the Law of Gravity.

Thank you. Would it depend on the teacher at all?

First of all, in reference to that question, let us not deny the demonstrable truth of personal responsibility. Number one: the teacher that we merit is the teacher that we have earned. Good, bad, or indifferent. So I hope you stay around for a little while until I finish this sentence. Therefore, it depends upon you in the final analysis. If that's the teacher you merited, that's where you were when you merited the teacher. And if you still have that teacher, then that's what you continue to merit. And so it depends upon you. The teacher is an effect of the Law of Value that you have established. A teacher is an effect of the Law of Value that you continue to establish. Yes. *[A clock begins to strike.]*

Thank you. Why is it more difficult at times to discern right action? And what is the spiritual definition of discernment?

First of all, concern is the difficulty. And the spiritual definition of?

Discernment.

Discernment is self-evident: the lack of concern is the awakening of discernment. For discernment is a spiritual faculty and cannot be controlled by a sense function.

Thank you. What is the spiritual, symbolic meaning of the owl and the cat?

Well, in reference to the wisdom of the wise old owl, [it] is ever in keeping with the intelligence of the suspicious cat. Now a person must use suspicion not as an expression of the shadows of has-beens. A person more wisely evolves from the function of suspicion to the faculty of caution. And so you will find a great similarity between the cat and the wise old owl. The owl is not wise without the caution of the cat. And if you see similarity in the forms of the owl and the cat, then you are beginning to perceive: the branches have come from the same root.

Thank you. The next question was, "What is the interrelationship between these two animals spiritually?"

I think that has just been covered.

Thank you. "Truth is like a river for it continually flows from the Mountain of Aspiration," [is a saying from The Living Light *textbook.] Is the Mountain of Aspiration the celestial center from which the river of life flows from in its purity?*

Yes, for example, I think you should spend a little time on understanding totality or the figure nine. And as I said to you earlier, we are working with you in order to bring into your physical world the diagramology, which [for] many of you students who have been with me [for] some time, it will be like a fresh spring of water as you will have a much greater and broader understanding of the mathematics and the diagrams and the colors and things. And those students who are with me of recent time will surely benefit in the broadening of your horizons.

Thank you. What is the primary lesson of Halley's Comet and what number and color is it?

Well, first of all, if you will take a look at what you understand as the Halley's Comet, you will notice that it gathers unto itself from the planets that it comes close to. It gathers up all [these] different materials, and some of your people say it's a great cosmic garbage can. Well, if the formation and birth of a planet is to be considered a garbage can, then, of course, all planets are garbage cans. And I'm sure that many of you will agree at sometimes in your life on any planet. However, you will note one thing about the comet, as it passes through the solar system:

you will notice that it comes close enough to a planet to gather unto itself a part of the planet. You will also notice, however, it does not get trapped in the gravitational pull. Now that should tell you a great deal about what number it is. And it should also, with a little thought, definitely reveal to you its color.

Thank you. Judgments are created in the water center. What is the process that these judgments get grounded on the shores and enter the fire center? Do these judgments, then, just move from center to center, once created, until we move them up the river of life to one of the higher centers?

Excellent question. It's very important. Very, very important. To understand, to understand the water center is the gravitational pull on which things become solidified and grounded. Now if you will understand that and will consciously make effort to balance the water center, the field of gravity, with the electric center, you will have no problem in being bound, grounded in slavery to limit and form. Do not tempt to overcome grounding or gravitational pull by a counterthrust or force, for in so doing you have not learned the lesson that [you are] on your planet to learn. You have simply used force to overcome force and are still controlled in your consciousness and experiences by force.

Thank you. The functions form and deform our astral body. Is that the same as our mental body?

No. No, for example, the physical body contains your mental body and all the other bodies. And the physical body is an effect of your mental body; and your mental body is an effect of your astral body.

Thank you. Pure thought, purity being white and thought being action, we express a color known as pink, a blending of action and purity that is divine love. How are thoughts considered to be action?

Thought—when you, as a being, being the Power—for that's what you truly are—when you constrict or contain the Power, you become the creator of limit. Man is the creator. Man takes what is and tempts to contain it. By man's effort to contain what he is, he identifies with what he is not. When you tempt to control the air, for example, you may contain a portion of the air, and the portion that you contain or limit, to some degree, you control. However, the principle, the air itself, you cannot control. You can only control that which can contain. And because your cup runneth over, your container being full, you experience this constant need, the effect of denial.

Thank you. Why is time, the great illusion, a healer in a world of illusion?

Time, the great illusion, is a healer to a world of illusion for by man's belief that he is time, he can only be healed by what he believes, through over-identification with what he has created. As long as man insists on believing what he has created, then by his belief that he is what he has created, he can only be affected by that which he believes that he is. Man cannot be affected by what he does not believe that he is. Man can only be affected by what he believes that he is.

Now, for example, people will say, "I am not that. I fear becoming that." By the very expression of the fear of becoming that, you have recognized that you are that in potential, and you fear the potential rising beyond your control. That's how man fears: first man must believe that he is the potential in order to fear what he compares with others that they are.

Thank you. The Living Light Philosophy teaches that God is not a creator. How then did creation come to be?

Is there sound when the tree falls, unless you are present? Unless there is an ear to hear the sound, does the sound exist? *[After a short pause, the teacher continues.]* Now I'm not going to tell you which came first, the chicken or the egg, for we all know without the egg, there is no chicken. So we all know that the design of the chicken is microscopic in the egg or the seed. Now you are the seed, through the Law of Identification.

How did creation come to be? What creation? Is there a green tree to a man who has no sight? Is there a whisper of a wind to [a] man who has no ears? Is there movement to man who has no feeling?

And so, my friends, when you ask, How did creation come to be? you must first ask, "What is identity? What am I? And how did I come to be?" When the tree asks how it comes to be, by knowing that it be, through the law of comparison and experience, effect of its own creation, then you must answer by asking the question, "How did I come to be?" For you believe you are creation. And because you have convinced yourself that you are flesh and bone, limit and form, you cannot, you cannot experience anything differently. One cannot experience that which is beyond their belief, for when one tempts to experience what is beyond their belief, they go first through the so-called trauma of reeducation, which is nothing more and nothing less than a replacement of their judgments in the priorities and values of their consciousness.

So first to understand creation, you must separate yourself from creation. One cannot, cannot understand what they believe that they are. One can only play with what they believe that they are. They have not objectivity. You cannot have objectivity through over-identification. For when you over-identify, you are bound by belief. So first separate truth from creation; separate what you are from what you believe you are in order to begin the process of understanding what you are.

Now when you understand what you are, you will have no problem understanding how creation came to be, for you will have freed yourself from what you believe you are (creation) to what you are (that which is the Power that is). So do not tempt yourself to understand limit, when you insist on believing that you are limit.

Thank you. Would you please share with us your understanding the principle of addition?

The principle of addition? Well, first of all, I want to look into the question and the interest on the principle of addition. Many people add many things and come up with a sum total or even a subtotal that they are very unhappy with. What does that have to do with the principle of addition? It has everything to do with the principle of addition. So let us place the principle of addition in the center of consciousness from whence it has total control. And what center controls the principle of addition? Do you know?

[The teacher addressed the cameraman. Although it is likely the cameraman responded, his response was not discernible on the recording.]

No. What does addition offer? *[After a short pause, the teacher continues.]* If you have one apple and you add one apple, how many apples do you have? Pardon?

Two.

Two apples. And if you have two apples and you add two more apples, how many apples do you have?

Four.

And if you add four to the four that you have, how many apples do you have?

Eight.

And if add another eight to the eight that you have, how many apples do you have?

Sixteen.

And if add another sixteen to the sixteen you have, how many apples do you have?

Thirty-two.

Do you have more than when you made the step into the principle of addition?

Do you have more than when you made the step into the principle of addition?

Yes, before you made the step into the principle of addition, do you have more?

Yes.

You have more. You have more of what you first had?

Yes.

Is that correct?

Yes.

Now you tell me what center of consciousness offers to you more of what you already have. Well, I'll give you a clue: it begins with *w*.

Water center.

Thank you very much. Now we've had a wonderful class today. I look forward to seeing you again next week.

Thank you, friends.

FEBRUARY 2, 1986

A/V Class Private 34

Good morning, class.

On this morning we'll go right into the questions that you have, especially the questions you have on our last class.

Thank you. Would you please speak on the process through which functions develop to become faculties?

Yes. Speaking on that question of how functions evolve and express as faculties, when you understand, as we were discussing at our last class, what you know as the Law of Gravity and you study and understand that resistance creates friction, and friction is in truth an adhesion, then you will have a broader perspective and a greater understanding of how functions evolve and become faculties.

Yes, next question, please.

Thank you. What percentage of man's present diseases are functional disorders?

Well, functional disorders, try to understand there's a vast difference between what is known as a psychosomatic disease and a functional disorder or functional disease. The functional disorders and the percentage of functional disorders—you can attribute 90 percent are functional. That is the root cause of disease. Now as far as understanding a functional disorder, which is, of course, created by the mental realm of consciousness and, understanding what you say is a physical disorder, please try to realize that the vibration created by the forms created by the mind are known as a functional disorder, having a direct effect upon the chemical balance of the physical body. Now as the chemical balance of the physical body has, also, a direct effect upon the mental body, then you will understand that 90 percent of all so-called diseases, discords, are in truth functional disorders. To work upon the effect of a physical disease without considering its root cause, which is functional, is only a band-aid effort on anyone's part.

Thank you. How does one stay out of the magnetic pull of the water center?

Well, I have spoken to you on that in reference to the balance between the fire and water centers. Now how does one stay out of a center which their true being, which their river of life, that which they are, must flow through? You don't stay out of a center. You harmoniously flow through it. There's no way of going around the centers of consciousness. You pass through the centers of consciousness.

Now I do feel that you meant to say, How do you refrain from being stuck in the water center as you're sailing through these centers of consciousness each and every moment? Well, [if you want] not to get stuck (grounded), then you've got to understand the Law of Gravity and you must apply that Law of Gravity and gain control over it. Your consciousness flows through the centers of consciousness. It flows through them, the river of life, that which you are.

Now if you permit yourself to become grounded, that is, influenced by the gravitational pull of the center, then you identify, over-identify, and you become what is known as stuck in one of the centers.

And so to move through the centers in a harmonious way is not only a moment-by-moment effort, it is a conscious awareness of the center of consciousness you are in and to remind yourself each moment you are passing through it; you are not it. So when you find that you are being tempted to be stuck, so to speak, in the water center, tell yourself the truth, "This, too, is passing. It is passing as I permit it to pass for I am the one who has tempted myself. And therefore, I am the one who is experiencing this center of consciousness." So when you remind yourself that you are the one passing through a center of consciousness—that you've tarried there too long from your temptations of mental substance, it's time to move on.

Now ofttimes in life you will have an experience that repeats itself until you find yourself becoming bored, and you say, "Well, now I've had enough." And when you say that to yourself and you are sincere, you begin to move your little ship on this river of life through that center of consciousness because you have finally made a conscious decision that you have had enough and it's not worth it to you. And in fact, you even permit yourself to enter a state of consciousness known as boredom. And when enough is enough, it's enough. But only you can make that decision and move your little boat, your little ship, and sail along the river, the river of consciousness.

You see, the river, you see, the river is what you are. The little boat is what you've dented: your identification. So it's up to you to remind yourself, "I've stayed there long enough. It's time for me to move on." To weigh these things out consciously. And when you find yourself in centers of consciousness that offer you the lack of goodness and the lack of happiness and [the lack of] the joy of living, then it's time to say, "I've had enough." And in so saying it, demonstrate the sincerity of your statement and you will find yourself moving on.

Thank you. Since judgments are born in the water center, in what center do they die?

Well, that which is born in water is always transformed in fire. And so you find that whatever you create—death is purification. It is the returning of the elements of form or limit to their base source from whence they have been drawn or pulled by the Law of Gravity.

Thank you. Since we begin life on Earth in the fire center, does this mean that we end life on Earth in the fire center or its corresponding center, the electric center?

No. Those who—you begin life on your planet Earth in formation in the fire center, expressing through the water center. Now those who tarry and remain in the earth-bound realms of consciousness after leaving the physical body are those who remain in the water center and do not return to the fire center. The way out of a thing is the way you get into a thing. You got into the form that you are now expressing through, through the fire center. And so the way that you get out is through the fire center. Now try to understand that the fire center is a center of purification.

Thank you. Are all the lower centers negatively charged and all the upper centers positively charged?

Well, I think I just covered that. Whatever is negative is in truth positive; whatever is positive is in truth negative. It is the components, the amount of the components in the positive and the negative that expresses itself, and you understand it as positive and you understand it as negative. You see, you must take apart what you have put together and rearrange its components in a more balanced way.

Thank you. Are we, as students, expected to be able to know what center we are in, be able to go to a center we decide to go to, and to leave the center when we decide to?

Well, I would refrain from using the word *expected*, for it implies a lack of personal responsibility. In other words, when we permit our mind to say, "Well, am I expected to do that?" then, don't you see, we create within the realms of darkness a form which says, "Well, I didn't want to do it anyway. I was expected to do it." You see, if you must expect, then expect from yourself, like in your own little backyard. Then you can go to your own little backyard, you have no one else [to blame]—there are no scapegoats—and you can say, "Well, I'm the one that expected this of myself. I have no one else to blame because I did not meet up to my own expectations." So, no, let's delete the word in this context here, of *expected*.

And let's state clearly: you are receiving the way in which you can grow and free yourself. Now if you do want to grow and free yourself, which you have demonstrated, to some extent, then from yourself you expect that experience, that experience of freedom, that experience of growth. And so in that respect, you can expect that from yourself for it is your divine right to expect it as an effect of your own effort. Yes, expect it from yourself, but do not delete the word *effort* in your expectations in life.

Thank you. Do the people of Atlantis share the same missing link we do?

Well, the people of Atlantis, all people as you know as human beings on your planet, of course, all stem from the same root. And in that respect, why, certainly.

Thank you. On what part of Earth was the continent of Atlantis and would you please relate its size to someplace we recognize?

Well, on what part of the Earth as you know it today—of course, you still have what is understood as the Atlantic Ocean, the lost continent of Atlantis. In reference to its size, it can be compared to the country of the Soviet Socialist Republic, a little bit larger, however. And, of course, in that time Europe, as you know it today, did not exist. Your country, the United States, as you know it today, did not exist. And so as far as its locations, you would consider the edge of it, as far as the Atlantean continent, off the coast of southern Spain and extending far over to the shores of perhaps what you understand as the Caribbean.

And try to understand that's only one of the two major continents of the time of which we are speaking.

Thank you. I read a description of Atlantis which spoke of people walking along crystal walkways, communicating telepathically, without talking, wearing clothing and headdress of a crystal-kind of fabric. Is that correct?

Well, you don't need crystal sidewalks in order to communicate. However, in reference to what you have read, there is, of course, truth in respect to the crystal as used for communication purposes. And someday you will look to the crystal not as an object that is outside of you, when you have the greatest crystal of all right inside of you.

Now I expect we should take care of its location before we have another class. I'm sure I'll be getting questions on that. The crystal of the consciousness is located where you would understand is the pineal gland. Now it has long been dormant, though it still remains there, of course, in the form. Activating of the gland is not something that a person wishes to tempt until such time as they have brought their form and being into balance and they have, by conscious choice, moved from one center of consciousness to the other, for one cannot survive, [in] your present life, in awakening to the mass of forms that are created by an undisciplined and unguided mind.

Thank you. What causes the body to go into a spasmodic stretch when waking from sleep?

Well, there are many causes. One of which, of course, is the return of the astral body. There are other causes. For example, you are, perhaps, more likely [to] view it in the animal, four-legged forms as their little bodies return and they, what you understand, awaken to the conscious earth realm. And so that happens to all forms of life: the return of the bodies that have been out into other dimensions. Hopefully, consciously in those other dimensions. So often unconscious in those other dimensions, only paying the effect of the little tour that they have just made.

Thank you. We saw a team of elephants and riders playing a kind of soccer ball on television. Do the elephants enjoy playing ball?

The elephants enjoy the, one might say, the viewing of the animals who play ball. And so it's rather a competitive thing. You know, so often you'll train an animal, including an elephant, which is a very intelligent, four-legged being on your planet and has been for eons of time, you teach them something, a game of playing ball or some other game. And they enjoy, as children do enjoy, sharing and playing and expressing how much they know in comparison to how much you know. And so there's always the competitive thrill and challenge. And having minds and [being] intelligent beings, they enjoy witnessing the antics of the humans, the two-legged beings. And sometimes they get disgusted with them and they just won't play ball at all.

Thank you. When a person knows they have sold out in their business dealings with another, would it be best to tell the other person about it or to bite the bullet, so to speak, and pay the price?

Well, first of all, you're paying the price by selling out. So the first thing to do is to accept that you have sold out. And by stating that you have sold out, you've already accepted that you have sold out. So then the next step is to ask your question to yourself in honesty, "What was it that tempted me? What is this weakness in the moral fiber of my character that has tempted me to sell out inside of myself?" And once you come up with an honest answer, then you will be guided by the light of reason and consideration to speak forth, not from a water center, for that's not reason and that's not light or consideration, but from the higher centers of consciousness in that respect, from the air center, and explain to the person your weakness and how you tempted yourself to sell out to them in a business dealing and to correct it as intelligent adult beings, so that you can both move on and grow from that point forward. Yes.

Thank you. In astrology there are certain signs that are fixed signs. What does fixed *mean?*

Well, a lot of people say that they have fixed signs and they have fixed situations. Well, that which appears to be fixed is dependent upon your own perspective. As I've stated before, everything is in motion. That which is form moves. Your perspective of it ofttimes confuses you, and you say it is not moving. Well, it's your perspective. Everything is moving. So if you mean by saying *fixed* that something is stationary and not moving, no such thing exists. What you see as fixed or stationary is a frequency that you have yet to perceive.

Now in speaking on that I'd like to say a few words this morning. Frequently is frequency as sure as friction is adhesion and as sure as resistance is friction. And so when you look at anything and you say, "That is fixed. That is stationary," you are looking with a very limited view. Now when you permit yourself to say that something is fixed, it is immobile, you reveal to yourself a certain frequency, a low frequency.

Now through your own effort, you can, and it is your right to, gain control of your mind through effort to establish a higher frequency of consciousness. You see, by identifying with the lower frequencies, you find obstructions. Those who identify with the higher frequencies, through the Law of Frequent Application, create a higher frequency [and do] not have the obstructions in consciousness. You cannot have obstruction when you, by your own effort, rise to a frequency that passes through the lower frequencies. You see, a higher frequency passes through a lower frequency. If you are on the same frequency as the object, then the object is an obstruction. You must learn to rise to higher frequencies through daily application of the laws that have been revealed to you. And through your effort [in] identifying with higher frequencies by becoming higher frequencies, then what you view as an obstruction does not exist.

An obstruction exists only to a person who is in the frequency of the object they wish to remove. You do not overcome by friction and resistance. For that which rises is destined to fall until such time, through effort, you understand and change your frequency. As long as you remain in the frequency of limit, which is a very low frequency, then you will always experience limit. For as you remain in the frequency of limit, your identity cannot move, for you believe you are limit. For example, man believes in death for man's frequency is that frequency. So man looks and sees form, not understanding the principle of movement and of constant process of changing form. Man identifies and believes in coming and going in life and death for that is the frequency that man, in his own effort, believes that he is.

Thank you. How would a person best use being a fixed sign to its best benefit?

Well, first of all, to those who choose the lower frequency, then—for example, if you choose to believe that a rabbit's foot will bring you money, then please get yourself many rabbits' feet. I am working with you as students to help you increase your frequency and, in so doing, not to have and to experience need for such things.

Thank you. Why do some people seem to thrive on complaining?

It is the child's way, the child's way of feeding. In your world you might even like it unto a vampire. They're constantly feeding on someone else for the forms created have just had their feeding to such a point that through these various devices (complaining, self-pity, and etc.) they have an increase of energy so they can move around, for the forms that they constantly create with the mental world, what you understand as judgments, have just depleted their vital bodies. And so complaining and griping and self-pity and whining and crying is a child's way of receiving vitality and energy as the child continues to feed the forms he has created in his own little mental world without consideration, without a real father and mother to guide it and to help and show it a better way of experiencing the benefits of vitality and energy.

Thank you. How will I know when I have separated from my parents? Does it mean I won't physically see them anymore or be in their lives?

Well, I would say, in such a question as that, it would probably be that you would think of them as much as you do the air that you breathe. So if you think each moment of the air that you breathe, then that is how often you would think of them.

Thank you. Was it a divine plan in another solar system that the human inhabitants of Earth be mixed with a higher intelligence and fulfill the possibility of a higher vision?

Yes, indeed, it is the divine plan.

Thank you. Does potassium act as a coolant for the temperature of the entire body and help keep it cool?

Yes, I see that someone's been making some effort to do some, a little bit of study.

Thank—

It does. Hot-tempered people can benefit, you know, greatly from becoming a raisin-head.

Thank you. What would be the best approach toward a group of people who are ignorantly holding in captivity a creature who should be set free?

What is the guidance they are requesting?

They're asking for guidance on approaching a group of people who in ignorance are holding a, some form in captivity.

Well, first of all, the question must be asked, Are they a part of that group of people? If they are not a part of the group, then unsolicited help is not only to no avail, it's quite detrimental. However, the Law of Presence is the Law of Solicitation. So one must consider whether or not they have the responsibility as a part of the group responsible for holding captive a little being.

Thank you. What triune faculties help one when referencing into the past experiences of one's life?

What triune faculties help anyone?

Yes.

Well, it takes several triune faculties to really help us. But if you just want a few, then I would begin with duty, gratitude, and tolerance, and I would study classes that have been given on that faculty and move to faith, poise, and humility.

Thank you. What does it mean when a person has a favorite color?

Well, a favorite color is the, of course, the expression of what one desires. So the question must be, Why do they desire it? So let's go beyond that and understand what one feels comfortable with and why they feel comfortable with it. Is it something of a spiritual nature? Is it something of a hereditary nature? Is it something of an environmental nature? Is it something that they have found [that] makes the best image for them through which they experience a temporary goodness? So there are several factors there involved. It's not necessarily a spiritual nature that one has a favorite color. There are many factors involved.

Thank you. What color is it best to surround oneself with? Does it change depending on the level of a person's development?

Well, first of all, balance is what we have always taught. Let us understand balance. We're now asking about color. For example, all colors is what you are, as you are all sound. A wise person wants to put into perspective all that they are. They don't want to leave anything out. That's known as balance: put in all that you are. And so because you are all colors and because balance is the path of reason and light, then it is understandable and it behooves an individual to put all their colors into proper perspective and in perfect balance. Well, when you do that, you have what is known as the color, if you can call it a color, you have what is known as white; it's a combination of all color. And so that is when it's all brought into balance. When it's brought into perfect balance, then you have white.

So what do you surround yourself with? You don't say, "O God, surround me with white." You simply bring yourself into balance, the effect of that balance is white. Many of you call that purity. Yes.

Thank you. Sometimes I don't depend on something out of ignorance, rather than faith. Could you speak on how those two things can be similar and how to recognize which you are using?

Why, I haven't found, yet, a person who doesn't depend on something, even though they may consider it themselves. You see, everything in form is dependent. Show me something in form on your planet that's not dependent upon the element air. Therefore, we find whatever has limited itself, its true being, and entered what is known as form is a dependent being. So whether we like it or not, all of us in form, while in form, are dependent. We're dependent upon our eyes to see, our ears to hear. We're dependent upon the element air in order to survive in a form, in the form as we know the form on the planet Earth. So therefore, we are all dependent beings.

However, we do not always express gratitude for that which we depend upon. How often do we say, "O element air, I am so grateful to you for without you I could not remain in this form?" How often do we say, "O ears, I am so happy that you are there for without you being there I could not hear these lovely sounds?" How often do we say, "O mouth, I'm so happy you're there?" We don't take the time to tell our mouth how happy [we are] that the mouth is there. We're so busy using it, don't you see? And so we're so busy breathing that we don't thank this wonderful element air and the divine Principle which has made it possible so that we could be in form. And so, you see, we are in truth dependent upon many things.

Now the problem here is that we are dependent on so many things that we surround our self with—and things that we hope will surround us—we're so busy with our dependence, it's rare that we express our faith in the divine Light that has made it all possible. For in truth everything is in dependence, dependent upon the divine, eternal Light that is. So when we take pride, we are dependent upon the various functions of the being; the functions of the mental world that tell us how great we are and how well we are doing, and therefore we experience what is known as pride. And so we find our self in a constant process, moment by moment, of dependence.

Now our teachings are because you identify with form, with limit, because you're bound by believing that which you identify with, that you pause a few moments in this great dependence on everything and just pause for a few moments and direct the consciousness to the divine Light that is the true source that sustains all of the things that we depend upon to have this beautiful bondage that we know as self, which is a total dependent being. You see, there is no being on your planet as dependent as the human being. The human being, more refined and evolved in many ways of form, is the most dependent being of all beings on the planet Earth. I do hope that's helped with your question this morning.

Thank you. At times I have had a vision of world peace and brotherhood of man.

Yes.

Since that is not to be on this earth plane, could you tell me what from where such visions spring?

World peace and brotherhood is a realm of consciousness that, in time, we all enter, freed from the multitudes of dependences that sustain our belief that we are separate beings, you see. You see, there's a part of us that knows how dependent we are. And that part of us knows that and would like to be less dependent. Well, to be less dependent, you must return to the Source and with this dependence—you see, you must have dependence in order to have limit.

So with this limit, which is dependence and offers to you this little thrill of being special, you see, then let's narrow it, all those multitudes of dependencies down to the one that sustains all of it. You see, why not go direct to the horse's mouth, so to speak, in your world? Why not go direct? Why go through all these intermediaries? Why go through all those intermediaries when you could go direct? It is your responsibility, my children, to go direct to the Source. You see, go direct, direct to the Source. And if you think that for some reason or other that you have spent such a lifetime of a mass of different dependences, well, just say, "Now look, I'm going to consolidate all of this." Like you consolidate your bills all into one, you see. All to one. Move everything to one, and you'll see what a wonderful life it is.

You feel that you're hungry? Turn to the Light, to the One. You see? You see, turn to the One. And from the oneness, you will experience, "Oh, I've got to go to work. Yes, I'm going to be hungry and more hungry than I've ever been. I must go to work. I must demonstrate the love of the Divine Principle made manifest." And experience the goodness. It's a four-letter word. It's known as work. And it's a wonderful feeling. It's a wonderful feeling to feel that you accomplished something, you see, even if it's some small thing. But to accomplish something, one feels better. Why does one feel better when they accomplish something? Because something is now depending on them. You see, that—there's a difference in feelings. You see, we're so used to depending on all these other things, when we get a breath of fresh air that something depends on us, we feel rather good, at least for the moment of the dependence, you see. Yes.

Thank you. Would you speak on the consecutive steps needed to bring a dream into reality?

Well. The consecutive steps? You want a paint-by-number series, I expect. Well, whatever it is that you dream that you want, accept that you have it. All the necessary steps, known as experiences, will be waiting for you. Choose wisely what you want, for you must pay for your denial of what you are.

Thank you. You have said that when we pause, we also pause our breath. Could you speak more on the difference between pause and hesitate and breathing?

Well, a person who makes the effort to pause is consciously aware and has done it by a conscious choice. A person who hesitates is controlled by forms and judgments that they have created. So a person is not using the faculties when they hesitate; they're using the functions. But, however, when a person makes a choice to pause, they use their faculties. And so I feel there's a vast difference between hesitation and pause. Pause contains the potential of consideration of the payment for what they are being tempted to step into. Now hesitation doesn't contain that consideration. Hesitation, controlled by the functions, permits the forms of judgments created from past experiences to see how much they're going to get out of the situation before they get into it. But pausing weighs out everything and especially the Law of Personal Responsibility.

Judgments are not concerned about personal responsibility. How could they be concerned about it? They don't have any. There's no such thing in the creating of a judgment as personal responsibility. No, no, no, that doesn't contain that ingredient in the functions and in the judgments. Yes.

Thank you. In making attitude correction, is the first step awareness of the detrimental attitude? Would you please give us the correct—correction—the consecutive steps?

Well now, you know, this paint-by-numbers is not the way we grow spiritually. It's how we grow mentally. I'm not here to feed the mental worlds and forms of consciousness. Let's stop this paint-by-number business this morning and consecutive steps. Now read the first part of the question. What is it the student desires?

In making attitude correction—

Attitude correction. Thank you. Attitude correction. Well, first of all, a person's not happy with their experiences, which are an effect of their own attitude, which is a frequency. You've identified with a frequency that is filled with obstruction. It's a low frequency. And so through an attitude correction, you have a different attitude. You look at things differently. And through an attitude correction, you not only free yourself from the gravitational pull that has you now bound, in what you understand as belief, you create a new frequency; and therefore, you pass through it. You pass through it by being a higher frequency than you were. And that comes about through an attitude correction, which, of course, is a change in your frequency.

Now I spoke to you earlier in this class this morning that frequency is frequently. Whatever you do frequently is establishing the Law of Frequency. So what you do frequently, if it is not something that you enjoy and if it isn't something that you enjoy the payment for, well, then just change the frequency frequently and you will experience something that's different. I didn't say better and I didn't say worse. That's totally dependent, of course, upon your choice. Nothing in life is something for nothing. It does not work that way. Yes.

Thank you. We have a name and our birth number, which doesn't change. Is our earth name also an unchanging name? Where did it originally come from?

Well, it came from the needs of—if you're talking about your earth name, your earth name came from the needs of the people who believed they were responsible for you entering the planet. Well, in a physiological and psychological sense, yes, they had that responsibility, but what they don't understand, they had a responsibility to have you in the first place. That was their evolution. You had a responsibility to have them. That was your evolution. So in that respect, they gave to you what they felt would fill their needs. Or perhaps a sponsor they had for you; in payment for you being sponsored, they gave you his or her name. So there's many variables there [in] how you got your earth name, you see.

Like, for example, you might have had a mother that was fond of her uncle or perhaps fond of her father. And in order to keep thinking of her daddy, she named you by your daddy. There are many factors involved in that respect, you see; and they are so many they add into the millions. And I don't think you'd want a class just on that because there's so many different causes of how a person receives their earthly name. It's part of the little payment received by the parent for their effort in allowing you to come to the planet.

Thank you. Our responsibility is to guide, educate, and discipline our forms. Could you give an example of a form and those three actions and how to apply them to a form we have created?

Yes, an example of a form? Yes, you'd like to go out into the beautiful sunshine of the day and you're locked in a house. The doors are all locked and you can't pass through them. Yes. So [if] you want to get through them, then you must unlock the door and open it. You must find the key. The key is in you.

And so when you want to have these experiences, you have to remember the forms you create are obstructions to what you want to do. You create them. Now because you create them, you've got to remove them. You've got the key. You're never left without the key. Every single door that you close and lock, you have the key to, because you're the one that made the door in the first place. And you're the one, in the second place, that closed it and locked it. So you've got to find the key because you've got it in your pocket.

Now there might be many keys. And there are for many people. They have all kinds [of keys]; they have so many keys they can hardly walk, they have so many keys. They have so many keys because they've created so many doors. And the more doors you create, the more doors that can be closed and locked. And then you forget that you locked the door, and then you can't find the key in your pocket.

So let's stop and think about—you talk about forms, you want a step-by-step understanding. Well, just understand that the human mind is always looking for something, something better, to make less effort and to get more. And so you're in a house and you only have 2 doors. The next thing you do is you make 4. And next thing is 6 doors. Then you make 8 doors. And then you want a door right next to your chair and you make 12 doors. And then when you want to get out and you don't want to walk too far, the key to the door that's just a foot from your chair, well, you can't find that key at all. See, you've made too many doors, and there are too many of them locked because you didn't want anyone to come in and steal what you got.

And therefore, you have to understand that's the way the human mind is. You keep creating all of these different doors, and you keep putting all of these different keys in your pockets. And you can't find the right key when you want the key.

Well, there's only one thing to do: move from the house that you've created. Say, "That's it. Has too many locked doors, too many keys I have to carry. I'm going to move out under the apple tree. And that's where I'm going to live from now on. No doors. No windows. I'm totally dependent upon the elements. I can't tell them that it's too cold, because they'll just do their thing. But I will adjust. I will adjust rather than to be locked in when I want to get out." Yes.

Thank you. What is the true purpose for which the United States of America was created?

Well, if you're speaking on the spiritual purpose of the country of the United States being founded, it was founded on the basic principle, the basic principle of opportunity to grow and to experience the goodness that the planet has to offer. Now it was brought into being for the purpose of expressing that spiritual awakening. In order to permit that to be, it must contain all of the various expressions of the human mind. There must ever be a flux and flow, a friction and adhesion, for without that, it comes under the influence of bondage, of grounding, of gravity. And so in the experiences that you have in your particular country, where you find dissenters and you find friction and you find adhesion, remember that without that principle, there would not be the breath of fresh air that you know as freedom. And so in order to maintain and to sustain freedom, there must be, there must be friction and adhesion in perfect balance.

Thank you. Does fear have a color? If so, does its color vary?

Oh, fear has a beautiful color. Yes, it's yellow all the way. Not gold. Sincerely now, sincerely it is yellow. It is a yellowish-green color. I think in your world you would call that, not particularly—what is that color, you call that lime-green—it's rather a slimy yellowish-green color. That is the color of fear. For what is fear an effect of? Faith in the human mind, an absolute lack of courage, a lack of effort.

You see, laziness creates fear. Lazy people are fearful people. Lazy people are people that have—well, you understand in your world—they have a yellow streak. It runs from the tip of their temple right down the spine and even passes down to the toes. It's all yellow, you see. So you've heard that in your world. Yes, it is a yellowish-green. It is controlled by mental substance, a form which has convinced an individual that they can get something for nothing. They don't have to make too much effort, and they can get all of that. That's, yes, that's what—and they live in fear, you see. Fear of, "Will someone do this for me or do that for me? Will I be able to convince someone considering how yellow I am?" Yes. It's a lack of courage.

Thank you. How does fear work through confusion?

Well, a confused mind is a mind that cannot decide what it wants to do. And by not making a conscious decision, it remains confused. And so a confused mind, of course, is a very fearful mind. And a very fearful mind, as I have just stated, is the effect of laziness and lack of conscious effort. It's the opposite of courage, you see. It's the opposite of endeavor. It's the opposite of initiative, you see.

Thank you. Why are we often tempted to place all our hopes and efforts into one endeavor in hopes that it will reward us?

Why, certainly we're often tempted that way, to get something for nothing. We all know better, but we still try, at times, to get something for nothing. Certainly. And then when it doesn't come when we judge as soon as it should come, then we dump that out to try something else that maybe we can get something for nothing there, without too much effort.

You see, there's a part of the mind—when you understand that when you're in service to these different forms and when you even think about making effort and you believe you are the judgments you've created, they immediately rise up because that means they're going to get less feeding. They're like vampires. And they're going to get less feeding. So certainly, if you believe that you are the judgments of your mind, you have great difficulty with courage; you have great difficulty with making effort. Because for you to tempt yourself to make effort to do something different, well, you're taking that energy away from those forms that you've been feeding. By the very thought of thinking of yourself, you feed your judgments. And, of course, they're going to rise up the minute that you try to create something different than them because then they won't be able to control it and won't be able to get the feeding that they're used to getting because you'll be giving it to this new baby that you have created, you see. Yes.

Thank you. What principle would you recommend for someone to follow in starting a new business?

Well, first of all, stop thinking of oneself, because the more you think of oneself the more you've got the judgments of the past that come up and create all kinds of experiences for you that are detrimental to your change of your new business. So first of all, start with a fresh start by forgetting what has been and working with what is. Now if you'll do that and take control of your mind, you won't have any problem in success of a new business. A new business is exactly what you say it is: new! So being new, you can't afford the luxury of thinking of what has been. You can only afford the practical, reasonable way of thinking of what is, because it's new. And because if you permit yourself to think of what has been, they will rise up and they'll tell you, "Well, we did it this way before, did it that way," and you have all of that foolishness to work with. Yes. Lack of concern is the success of a good businessman.

Thank you. Is the theory correct that when matter meets its own antimatter that they obliterate each other and form pure energy?

Well, if you—you see, I don't like that word *obliterate*, when it's really transformation. You see, these words here are very important in teaching because they have different meanings to different people. And so you're talking about matter and antimatter. Well, you're talking about the principle of friction and adhesion. And so there is con—there is a transformation; there's a change of frequency. The component parts remain; however, they are in different balance or perspective, you understand? I do hope you understand. So you're not really obliterating something else; you are transforming it. And just because you cannot perceive the frequency of pure energy until you permit yourself to rise to what you are, which is pure, intelligent Energy, then, of course, you say it is obliterated because you can no longer experience it. But you could experience it when you return to what you truly are, which is pure Energy. Yes.

Thank you. Is this principle related to the process of the soul melting back into the Allsoul?

Is this principle the same as the soul melting back into the Allsoul? Well, melting, yes, you know, you do have to go through purification to return to what you are. And while you're identified with the process, then one could understand it would be melting, just like you melt, you know, any kind of a metal, you see. I mean, after all, there's raisin-heads, onion-heads, and then there's metal-heads. And so in that respect, one could say, yes, they are melting. You know, if you're, if you're very solidified with your judgment, then you're an iron-head, you see. And there are a lot of iron-heads in the universe. And, of course, these things do have to be, what you say as, melted down as they pass through the fires of purification.

So when you, through conscious effort, as I have stated before, and through a few moments every day, you see, [that] establishes a frequency that is most worthwhile and beneficial to anyone. And so when you do that and if you will consider that by making that little bit of effort, just a few minutes every day, you are the one who is benefiting from an established frequency from the frequent effort, you see.

Now I see how quickly time has passed this day. And I know you will have a wonderful week. We have many questions yet to answer at [our] coming classes. And I'm happy that you're specific, but try not to be so identified with painting your world by number. The beautiful things of life are those things which are not so restricted. Mathematics, you understand, is not dull and restricted by number. It is a perfect organization in perfect flow. That which is mathematically correct is that which flows unobstructed in the universes of so-called time.

Thank you. Have a lovely day. I know you will.

FEBRUARY 9, 1986

A/V Class Private 35

[Good morning,] class.

Today, carrying on with our continuing studies and efforts, let us begin with what we all search for and seek, known as freedom.

You've had in your classes the teaching that freedom is the effect of self-control, and so it is. And self-control is the effect of personal responsibility. And personal responsibility is the effect of acceptance of the demonstrable Law of Life. And so as we trace these laws and follow them in our evolution, we begin to experience what we know as the joy of living.

Now we're waiting, in your world, for the arrival of certain equipment in order that we may bring to you, via [these] videotape sessions, the science of diagrams, known as diagramology. *[The A/V series of classes were recorded on videotape.]*

And it's important for all of you to trace these laws from the cause to the effect and how they move through our universe. It is most important to remind our self of the law for in so doing we then can flow with the law established, and we can also choose wisely which laws we wish to establish at any moment. So often in our life we begin to think about the law when we experience the effect, and the effect is not to our liking. However, each time we fall, we rise again.

So today on such a fine and beautiful day as it is, make a little effort to encourage yourself in understanding the effect, which you know as experience. And in understanding the effect, you start to move along the path of understanding so that you may bring about these changes through establishing of new laws in your life and experience this, this wonderful goodness that's all around and about you.

To resist is to be the victim. I realize that that is contrary, contrary to the thinking in your world, but let us understand more fully what resistance really is. Let us understand more fully how we ground our self and, in so doing, experience the things we desire not to experience.

Each time you pause and you declare the truth, which is acceptance, each time you do that, you free yourself from that karmic wheel of resistance and adhesion. So accept what is, and in so doing you will be in a position to change what is by intelligently establishing a law of your choice that will bring you from the experience that you may presently be involved in.

Now we have these many questions that we have prepared—you have prepared. And I accept that our cameraman has that little picture box over there rolling so that you have a full class, rather than an edited class. I never was one that was fond of editing. I don't think anyone is fond of editing, unless they can be the editor. Now we'll go ahead with the questions.

Thank you. Please discuss the principle to ignore and when to apply it.

Yes. I'm very pleased to have that question, right in keeping with the subject this morning that we are discussing. For example, you encounter an experience, an effect of law you have established; you don't like the experience. You do not want to direct intelligent energy to it to make the little molehill of experience a great mountain in your consciousness; so you accept the experience as an effect of the Law of Ignorance that you had served and are serving. Now this is the law that has been established: the Law of Ignorance. When you declare the truth, "I accept this experience for in a moment of my ignorance I established the law and experience its effect. I no longer choose to experience these effects," therefore, through an acceptance, which is the declaration of personal responsibility, you gain control over the self. And through gaining control over the self, you are in truth applying the law to ignore. You are no longer serving the law that you had established, for you have accepted that you alone established it, and by that acceptance, you are freed from it.

Thank you. What is the spiritual, symbolic meaning of lightning?

Well, the spiritual, symbolic meaning of lightning, if you are looking for an understanding of the cause of lightning—or are you looking for an understanding of the true meaning of what you would understand as uncontrolled, intermittent, or spasmodic light? Lightning, of course, is an expression of the Light. And it is true that in your world there are moments, perhaps infrequent sometimes, when there is what you might say, "I saw the Light," the lightning of an idea. The symbolic meaning of lightning, as you look in the sky and you experience what you understand as lightning, the symbolic meaning are those moments in the darkness when an awakening takes place. Now just because it may be lightning in the sky, please don't misunderstand that you saw the Light, the true Light. No, no, no. You've asked for the symbolic meaning, and I have given it to you in keeping with your understanding at this time.

Thank you. What is the spiritual, symbolic meaning of thunder?

Well, there we are. Thunder and lightning. The nature spirits are really drawing the interest of my students. And that is one of the many benefits of change. So you have these lovely little storms, you call them here on your planet, and you have the roar of thunder and you have the crackling of lightning. Well, all forms express themselves, including the nature spirits. I find many two-legged forms, human beings on your planet, that strike and roar. And they certainly do it more often than the nature spirits do it. Yes.

Thank you. Why is the river of life a fluid rather than a nerve or skeletal frame?

For example, that which flows in, as all things are in movement—but try to understand the difference between movement and flow. Now the question is, Why is the river of life a river, rather than a nerve? Well, there wouldn't be a nerve, if there wasn't the river of life. A nerve or skeletal form is an effect of the river of life. And so the river *is* life, the expression of Light. And it is the river of life. I didn't make it the river of life, and I have no intention of trying to do so. It just *is*, as Light *is*. We can ask the question, Why is there Light? Especially if we are attached to the dark. And so we can ask our self the question, Why isn't it a nerve? if our thoughts and identifications are such. However, it is the river of life. That's what it is. Truth does not need any defense. It doesn't contain need. Truth just is. And so river of life *is* river of life. And no thought and no desire can possibly change it. And so whether or not we are fond of the twilight or the darkness or the mist or the light of high noon, we're not going to change it by our desires.

And I do want all of my students to understand that when you accept life, what it is, then you won't have any disturbance of trying to make it something that it is not. Yes.

Thank you. What is the river of life when we lose our physical body?

The river of life doesn't change. Your physical body changes. Your river doesn't change; that's what you are, the river of life. So whether it is expressing through a tree or expressing through what you understand as the human being, the river itself does not change. Truth does not change. There's nothing for it to change to. You see, that which is, *is*. That which is not can be manipulated and molded. However, it does not change the basic ingredients because you mold or try to change it. The river *is* the river. That is the way that it is. And when we accept the way life is and what it is, we will not have any problem, no problem whatsoever.

Thank you. Is it true that sons more often resemble their mothers, and daughters, their fathers, than the other way around? The resemblance being not only physically and mentally but also spiritually. If so, why?

Well, I have never taught that sons resemble their mothers, spiritually, and daughters, their fathers, spiritually. So there's no "If so," in reference to that question because it is not true. There are sons who do resemble, physically, to some degree their mothers. There are daughters that resemble to some degree their fathers. However, that is not something that is an absolute law. It has to do with many, many factors, especially the factors of evolution and the attraction of the soul. Let's go into that just a little bit. For example, if a person has a certain attachment in an incarnation and the attachment that they have and have yet to grow out of is more expressed in a male form than it is in a female form, then it is understandable that a daughter would represent her father and that a son would represent his mother in that respect. But there is no set rule that that's the way that it is. No, no. You go ahead with your question.

Thank you. What should we do if we recognize that we have spiritual arrogance?

Well, the only thing that I have found in reference to arrogance: I have never been able, yet, to find a spiritual arrogance. I have found mental arrogance that identifies itself as spiritual, but arrogance does not exist in the spiritual realms of consciousness. So in that respect, the words *spiritual arrogance* [are] non-existent. Mental arrogance, cloaking itself in a deceptive garment of spirituality, yes, that is something that is expressed on many planets and the lower stages of evolution, but there is no such thing as the arrogance of spirit, only the arrogance of mental substance attempting to deceive those who are still in and identified with mental substance that it's spirituality.

Now I know that I don't please all you students, but if I did, there wouldn't be room to seat all of you, would there? Yes, go ahead, please.

Thank you. How is God's love made manifest in work?

When a person is working, they are experiencing an effect of the Law of Accomplishment, constructive accomplishment, to bring about some good in their life. And when a person works and makes the effort to bring about some good in their life, by the law [that] we grant unto others what we grant to our self, we therefore become instruments through which the environment in which we are expressing our self is evolved and benefited in a constructive, sensible, reasonable way. And so when a person is working, accomplishing some constructive good—now I didn't say total constructive good, for there's all types of work and there's all types of things we're attracted to in work. And sometimes we're all in one body when we're working, and sometimes we're only partially in the body when we're working. But work is God's love made manifest, for it is an accomplishment, a constructive accomplishment, which fulfills the purpose of our being. You see, we're on the planet Earth here and we've come here with responsibilities to fulfill. Now everything—you take a look at the lovely flowers here, you take a look at the trees, you take a look around and about you, they're all serving a constructive good. They're serving the purpose of their design.

When man refuses or refrains, through an error of ignorance, to work, he is going against the purpose of design of the form that he is encased in on the planet Earth. Now when he goes against the very purpose of the design of the vehicle that he is expressing through, then he's going contrary to the Law of Evolution and, therefore, will not and cannot experience what is known as God's love made manifest. The workers win certainly is the saying. What do they win? They win the victory over the error of ignorance which goes against the purpose of their form on the planet Earth. Yes.

Thank you. Are the rays of the sun as beneficial through a glass window as they are outdoors and, if not, what is lost through the glass?

Whatever obstructs the flow of the light, of course, has its effect upon our receiving its full benefits. So in reference to the rays of the sun and the light, being receptive to them through an obstruction which changes the rays, then of course it's not as beneficial. And that is the reason: you have placed an obstruction there. Whether you see through it or not, it's immaterial. You have made a change in the very rays themselves. Yes.

Thank you. You have taught us that numbers are the key to the universe. That seems to me to be divine neutrality. But the numbers as we know them seem to be form, not principle. Is that true?

First of all, in order to understand principle, while identified with a vehicle which is form, it must pass through form. And that which does not contain form does not enter form, for form will not allow it in. It is alien to it. So you must try to understand what you have been given: that truth is individually perceived. In other words, you receive Light and you receive truth ever in keeping with your individualization of it. In other words, ever in keeping with the form or the garment you will permit it to wear in order for you to accept it. And I do hope that's helped with your question.

And this is why we share the truth with you in so many varied forms. For example, principle to your mental world has to wear a certain garment for your mind to accept it as principle. And so we share with you the many garments in order that someday one of those garments will enter your consciousness through one of the levels of consciousness. And in accepting it, that the little seed will be planted in fertile soil and that it will grow and it will expand your consciousness and, in so doing, broaden your horizon. For when your horizon is broadened, then the forms that are able to enter your mental consciousness are nowhere's near as limited as they were before. So it is through a broadening of your horizon, through a greater understanding, that your little mind, which unfortunately so often so many believe that they are, will allow more different forms into the mental consciousness. And the more different forms that are allowed in, the greater the expansion of the consciousness, the broadening of the horizon, the acceptance of the will of the Principle of Good, which is known as the divine will.

Now you all know from your experiences of over-identification with form that there are only certain forms that you will let into your mental world. And as you grow older, slowly but surely, you let a few more different forms in. And the more different ones you let in, the broader becomes your horizon, the freer you become for you have experienced greater acceptance and are on the pathway of entering what is known as principle. Yes.

Thank you. What does "ah-oo-hm" mean and can it play a part in helping a student to spiritually awaken?

That which is given to you, as a wonderful mantra, is perceived by you through an application and use thereof. What it means to me and what it means to the Light is ever dependent upon how much censorship of the mind, through identification with mental substance, that you have in the way.

Thank you. There are stones called runes, containing ancient Viking symbols. Each one has a specific meaning. They are said to be used for spiritual guidance by the higher self. There is a recent book called, The Book of Runes, *which explains the meaning of the symbols. Is this a valid instrument through which to guide oneself?*

Well, if that question is from a student of mine, there is no time and no energy in your world of time and illusion to study anything that you are not already studying, for what you have been given is so much that it is extremely questionable that you would have time to investigate so many diverse paths.

Now, I'm not saying that you should spend your time only studying the Living Light, which you are working and paying for in your world. However, I would like to impress upon your consciousness that not only a house divided cannot stand—no man can ride two horses and reach the same goal. So, you see, you have to make an intelligent choice. There is one thing to study many things and get nowhere. There is something else to study one thing and be honest in your daily effort and experience the wisdom which comes from the so-called passage of time. And you cannot get anything out of anything that you don't put something into. So if you put your time and your effort into a study and you are consistent with it, then you're going to get something out of it.

There are many philosophies available to you and [they are] very tempting to the mind. Of course, there are. And the most popular ones are the ones that tell you in so many different ways, "No change of thought is necessary. All you have to do is depend on what I have to offer." Now those are the popular thoughts in the planet Earth, for they appeal to and tempt the forms of mental substance. Of course, they do no benefit in that respect to what you truly are, but they do tempt and they do appeal to what you are tempted to believe that you are for a time.

And so let us make effort to stick with one thing daily. If you find the philosophy you're studying boring, then please speak up. So we can understand, all of us, what happens to our mind when we experience what we know as boredom.

And so I do want to speak to all of my students in that respect. You are not restricted from studying twenty or thirty other philosophies. But in so doing it is ever at the expense of the one philosophy you are here to study: the philosophy of life. There is only one Light. It is expressed in many different ways. Once you make your choice, make effort with your intelligence to stick with it. And don't expect to graduate while you're on the planet Earth. I'm still waiting to graduate, if that's what graduation is all about. Yes.

Thank you. In dancing, all parts of the body need to work together. How can I help myself to stay relaxed and be in all of my body, especially my feet?

Well, I think that's a wonderful statement there. In dancing, all parts of the body are necessary. And so if you want to help yourself stay together, you've already answered your question: dance a little. At a proper place and a proper time. You see, you see, you've already stated that for you that all parts of you must be together in order to dance properly, isn't that correct? Pardon? Yes, did you say yes? *[In this class, the teacher and the cameraman were in the east wing of the Serenity Temple, which was one floor above the main floor, while the rest of the student body watched the class on a large monitor in the dining room, which was located on the main floor. The cameraman read the prepared questions. Given that arrangement, it was not feasible for the teacher to clarify the question.]* That's my understanding of the statement. And so I'm so happy that you have perceived the way to do that, you see. Dance a little, each day, by yourself.

Thank you. I would like to know about wearing other people's clothes. Is it vibrationally detrimental? Is there a way to neutralize the clothes before wearing them?

Well, first of all, now we don't want to get to the point that we have to be in a little cage, totally isolated from the universe, but there are many things to consider. First of all, when you go to a store and buy new clothes, you don't really know how new they are. You only presume that they are new. You never take a look at how many hands have handled it and what they've thought and what they've done. So there's many different factors involved. So what I would like to say is this: you can best benefit yourself by making a little more effort on not letting other things or things around and about you disturb you by an acceptance of personal responsibility, of course. And that path will keep you free.

And as far as if you have some particular thought about some clothes that someone has given you and you don't like the way that they act or this or that, well, of course, each time you think about those clothes, you're going to think about the person, through the Law of Association in the human mind. And in that respect, of course, it would be detrimental because you have entered the realms of personality and are therefore in service and a victim of your own thought form. And so I wouldn't be overly concerned about that. I wouldn't want to see any of my students naked for they had no clothes, but if they are applying the law, they won't have to worry about nakedness. Thank you. Go ahead, please.

Thank you. Right before a change, everything seems dark and confused. Does it always have to be this way?

Well, of course, we make it that way. We make it that way. And just before a change, everything seems dark and confused. And there seems to be a terrible struggle and everything because you must understand that your little soul, your true being, your spiritual being, is encased in a physical and mental vehicle, and that which is going on in the spiritual being, and the changes to come are being sensed, rarely accurately, but being sensed by the mental body and the mind. And it is that sensing of something foreboding—it's always foreboding to the human mind because it's a change. And if you understand, of course, and accept what controls the human mind—all those forms. And those forms are sensing there's a change; something's going to happen. Well, what's going to happen is not to their benefit because they sense that it's different. And that which is different, of course, is contrary to their survival in their thinking. And so in that respect, being in a body, a human body and a human mind, and the forms that control it, prior to any change, they rise up to, like you say in your world, protect their turf. Yes.

Thank you. What is happening when everything is going along OK and then circumstances reveal that you're being stopped or held back?

What is happening when everything seems to be going OK and then circumstances stop you, like, dead in the water, so to speak? Well, if you experience that something is stopping you dead in the water and you thought that everything was going OK, it does reveal to you, student, that there needs to be a little correction in the thinking process, for what you thought did not prove to be accurate. And so beware when all seems well. Be alert when things seem OK, all right?

Thank you. As one goes within, it is another—[I will] try again. As one goes within, is it another dimension one is going into?

Well, as one goes within, each body expresses in the dimension and the consciousness from whence it is composed. And so in that respect, of course, there are these various realms and that is true: that is where you go to when you truly go within. To which one of those realms? That, experience will reveal to you.

Thank you. Is the inner being the direction where one's guides and teachers reside on the other side?

Yes, that is, indeed, where they reside.

Thank you. Is the entire universe expanding and contracting, adding and subtracting, in a diamond-shaped molecular structure?

Well, to try to bring that into the mental world . . . *[The teacher pauses for several seconds as he considers the question.]* In order to answer that question that you may understand it, then I would say, yes.

Thank you. Why does personal attention, at times, create within oneself a thirsty, selfish need that seems to never get satisfied?

Well, first of all, you're asking about personal attention and why does it create an insatiable, selfish need, is that correct? Well, when you speak of personal attention, you're really speaking of the forms you have created, for that's what you identify with and understand as personal. And, for example, you take a look in the mirror; you look at your eyeball and you say, "That's a pretty nice-looking eyeball." You keep looking at it and you say, "Well, that's better than most eyeballs I've looked at." And then the next step you know it's the best on the planet Earth. And then the next thing you know it's the best made in the whole universe. It's very unique, you see. Of course, for you, it is. The more attention you place upon it, the more you need to feed it. And so I've taught you that the law reveals that which you place your attention upon, you have a tendency to become. And so one should be very careful in where they place their attention.

You know, you see, long ago we spoke of the body, the astral body being formed and deformed. Well, perhaps now you get a greater understanding. Now, you see, take your thumb for instance; you take your thumb here. Now, you see, if I take and place my attention each day upon my thumb, the more attention I place upon it, the more energy I direct to it in consciousness. Well, by so doing my thumb begins to get larger and begins to grow because I've given it more and more energy. Now you're looking at a physical thumb, which is a representative of a mental thumb. And therefore, by placing more and more attention upon my thumb, over a period of time, in my other body I'm mostly all thumb. Therefore, I'm not able to walk, because here's this huge thumb and very small feet, very small head, and very small body. But the thumb is extremely large. So, you see, that's the forming and deforming of that astral body.

Now placing so much attention upon my thumb is not practical because my thumb doesn't have toes and doesn't move like a foot. Therefore, I'm stationary. But I do have a thumb. It moves a little bit. But it cannot speak, it cannot see, and it cannot do the many other things of the complete body. So those people who place their attention consistently upon the—I'm just taking, for example, the thumb; it could be the big toe, you understand, just the toe—those people who place so much attention upon a limited part of their vehicle, find in the other dimension that that part of the vehicle has grown so huge, it is so big, at the sacrifice of the rest of the vehicle. It doesn't even move. It's not very practical. In fact, it's most impractical. But it is the forming and the deforming of the body. Yes.

Thank you. What is the importance of a twenty-minute period for meditation or our exercises?

Well, the importance of a daily exercise or meditation is to gain control over the many forms that you believe that you are that have such detrimental effects upon your life. And you cannot gain control over them without consistent, daily effort, considering consistent, daily effort is given, and has been given, by untold hours, and thousands of them, to the forms that you're creating. And so that's the importance of it: to be able to free yourself from that and to view objectively and not end up a huge thumb unable to move.

Thank you. Is the principle of subtraction associated with the higher realms of consciousness?

Yes, it isn't what you must add, but what you must subtract that frees you from the great cross that one insists upon bearing. Yes, in that respect, that is correct.

Thank you.

Yes.

When there is an obstruction to the river of life and the forms along the shore begin to drown, why do they drown in that which sustains them?

Well, now, that's like asking the question, Why does a person fall in love instead of rise? You know, I want you to understand, as students, that when you believe you're form, you fall. You see? That's when you fall. That's not when you rise. So when you ask your question, Why do the forms drown in that which sustains them? I must ask you the question, Why do you fall in love? Why do you drown in it? Why don't you rise? But, you see, then we have to understand that the judgments, which [are] the forms created in the water center, they drown in the very thing of their creation. Why, of course. All things return unto the source from whence they were drawn. So your judgments, drawn from the water center, the forms, you understand, why, it's understandable they return to the source. And so they drown themselves. Why do they drown themselves? Then I ask you the question, Why do you fall in love? Why don't you rise to the air center? Yes.

Thank you. In the process of counterbalancing, is the counterbalancing thought of a corresponding, yet higher realm of consciousness to the original thought?

Kindly restate the question, because there are several questions here that must be answered and we'll select one of them.

Thank you. In the process of counterbalancing, is the counterbalancing thought of a corresponding, yet higher realm of consciousness to the original thought?

Well, what—I see. I see. Prior to its contamination and censorship by the formation of mental substance to create the form from the original idea, yes, in that respect, of course. But I wanted to clarify because there are several questions there. Yes.

Thank you. Is space travel necessary for the evolution of mankind? Why, if it is so, is it true?

Well, it's necessary for the evolution of mankind as long as mankind believes he's limit and form. And then in that respect, in order to expand the limits that he has made by mental substance, he must have space travel in that respect. No, it's not true for the true being. One is not limited by the laws of gravity. One is only limited by gravity by being gravity. Yes, go ahead, please.

Thank you. If we are more advanced spiritually and we are discouraged from bearing children, will not that mean children will be incarnated into poorer situations?

Well, now just a moment. Did you say that you are discouraged from bearing children?

That's what the question says.

Is that what, is that what the—kindly restate the question because I think there may be a misunderstanding in respect to the teachings of the Living Light. If you believe that the Living Light Philosophy teaches you not to have children, then you have to understand your motivation for having children. You see, the purpose of intercourse is for the sole purpose of procreation. Now if you have a different motivation about intercourse, then it is understandable you would have a different understanding about procreation or bearing children. And so I think there's a misunderstanding about the natural process of bearing children in a physical world of the planet Earth. Kindly restate the question.

If we are more advanced spiritually and we are discouraged from bearing children—

Just a moment. First of all, it says, "If we are more advanced spiritually and we are discouraged from bearing children," we—the statement is—now let's clarify this. If we are more advanced spiritually, there's no discouragement or encouragement of bearing children for the motivation of the pleasure of the senses of intercourse no longer exists. So now I want to clarify this because we're dealing with a science, here, and philosophy, and we're dealing with the river of life, that which we are. So I think that would help clear the atmosphere. First of all, you state the person may be spiritually advanced. Well, if they're spiritually advanced, encouraging or discouraging having babies does not exist. Go ahead with the next question, please.

Thank you. I am grateful for my form as it helps me to learn and fulfill what I am here for.

Yes.

If my parents choose not to bear children, if this planet so chooses, are there—ah, I can't make out what the word is.

Go to the next word.

Something about planets, a person at my stage of evolution would go to, to learn what is needed?

Well, first of all, a most interesting question. Let's take a look at your planet Earth. You're going to find—some of you'll still be on the planet to experience it. First of all, there's a breakdown of what you understand as the family unit. Second of all, fewer and fewer children are being born on your planet. And so this needing is referring to the form. I feel here in these questions, some of these questions this morning, that there is a fear that the purpose, there, of intercourse is going to disappear. Well, of course, it disappears when you no longer believe you are what you are not, now, in the sense that you know it. So there appears here, this morning, to be a great deal of concern about the continuity of relationships in a physical way, I'm speaking.

Now when you evolve to the point, which you will, that physical relationships are not necessary, for you no longer experience the need for them—you can only experience the need for that which you have denied. And you can only deny that which you are for a time.

So you don't have to be concerned or worried about having a sexual relationship, for it is an expression and an effect of your identification with limit, which leaves you in need as a person who is only half there. So, you see, even though you temporarily may believe and identify that you are half a person, because you are in truth a whole person, you will not always experience being half a person and experiencing need through denial. So when that in your evolution takes place, as it is gradually—you know, they say that age is so beneficial in that respect, depends upon the person, of course. It's in the mind anyway. And so everyone is evolving to the awakening of what they are: a whole person, not a half a person. For you are in truth a whole and complete being. That is what you are. So whenever you accept what you are, you will not experience what you are saying: need and being half a person.

Now when you think that, you know, your desire is the greatest, that you've got to have this or that because you first judge that you're half a person and therefore the other half is someplace else, well, in that moment, tell yourself the truth: "I'm [a] whole and complete being. That which I truly am is whole, complete, and perfect, for it is the Light itself. That is what I am." Now if you go to work on that mental form, you will find that the emotional reaction that you've been having to that mental form you have created will gradually disappear as you experience what you truly are: whole, complete, and perfect. Now I know that you just don't do it, like snapping your finger. *[The teacher snaps his fingers as he speaks.]* And I know you, also—the worst thing a person can do is to suppress. Education, awakening is the way.

We have time for one more question here this morning. How quickly the time passes. My!

Thank you. We are here to evolve form and limit, which we have created.

Yes.

What happens to form when it evolves and could you speak on anything that evolves which does not have soul?

Anything that evolves which does not have soul? I can speak on many things that *change* that do not have soul. And change is the law through which evolution is made possible, of course. So there are many things—soul, as—you see, soul as you understand soul—you see, you still have soul as the individualized soul, and there's another step to go to the essence of what truly is. Now if you want to go to the essence of what is, then that which is in this lovely rose here, this right here, is what is inside of you. *[The teacher gently touches a rose in a large bouquet of red roses that is on his left.]* That's the Light itself, the Energy, the neutral, pure Energy.

But in speaking of soul—read the question once more for clarification there.

We are here to evolve form and limit, which we have created. What happens to form when it evolves and could you speak on anything—

Ah, yes. Thank you. It returns to that which it came from. You see, we always go home, whether we like it or not. Presently, don't you see, temporarily, we're all wandering around the universe and the jungles and things. Everything returns unto its source. So you are only on a little—what would you say?—a journey. You're on a trip. That's all. You're just on a trip. And in the course of a day you may take forty trips. Some of the trips you like and many of the trips you don't. So, you see, through identification of a form you have created in your mind, that's the trip you go on. Might be a short trip [or] a long trip. It may be a pleasant trip or a most unpleasant trip. That is the trip, you see.

And so when you combine all of that, you're on this journey through the planet Earth. Your responsibility is to expand the consciousness that you have, you see. You've identified, you've made that indentation; your responsibility now is to expand it. How to expand it? Well, through the Law of Acceptance, that is the Law of God, that is the divine Principle, you see, itself. Acceptance, that is the will.

You see, acceptance is what you are; denial is what you are not. So the more you resist, the more you go against what you truly are, the more experiences that you have that are unpleasant, for you are going against what you are. Stop going against what you are by accepting the wholeness that you are. Accept what you are. Be not concerned with what other people accept or don't accept. You can only live for you. Accept what you are. By accepting what you are, you will be a whole and complete person, and you will have the awareness and the experience of that wholeness and that completeness. Begin only with yourself. You can only accept yourself. Accept what you truly are. Accept your responsibility for what, in errors of ignorance, you have created.

You know, just because you create something doesn't mean you're going to live with it throughout eternity. People create many things, and they don't even last a day. They only last as long as you allow them to last. So don't be discouraged about what you've created. Create something else if you insist on being a creator. You know, people just insist on being mothers and fathers. If they can't create babies, they're going to create other kinds of babies. Those are known as forms in the mind. So we are, indeed, great creators. Probably the greatest creators that the planet Earth has ever known. We're constantly creating something.

So in the moments that we're not pausing—and hopefully we'll begin to pause more often. And in that creating process, let's create some babies that will do as they're told and stop serving those babies that we created so long ago that refuse to do anything, even though the light of reason reveals they've got to grow or go. So let's create some babies that are under good guidance. You know how you do that? You stop and think and you say, "Now let's see, I want to create a wonderful feeling." Well, you create a wonderful feeling. You don't have to rely on something past. Create what you want to create. You see, we're all creating. And while you're in that creating realm of consciousness, let's create some babies that will do what they're supposed to do and serve the purpose of their true design in the sense that we keep control of them, that is, whereas they are our creations.

Have a very good week. Thank you. It's been so nice to be with you here again today.

FEBRUARY 16, 1986

APPENDIX

Divine Abundance

Thank
(Gratitude)

You
(Principle)

God
(Divine Intelligence)

I'm
(Individualizing)

Moving
(Rhythm)

In
(Unity)

Your
(Realization)

Divine
(Total)

Flow
(Consideration)

The Controlled Spiritual Environment Affirmation

You are in a controlled spiritual environment of truth and freedom
Where peace and harmony reign supreme.
Be awake, be aware, be alert.
Your purpose of being is freedom from what has been.
Thoughts of self are foreign to this environment.
Take control of your mind and experience the joy of living.

The Laws Be

Our being is the consciousness, Truth.
Holy be the identity
The joy of Life
The totality of Acceptance
In mind as it is in heart
Grant us the Light
Our daily sustenance
And forgive us our has-beens
As we forgive those has-beens who tempt to steal our joy
Free us from the romance of self-love
Deliver us from the service to the false king of shadows
For Light is the kingdom
And the power and the glory forever
Peace be, the order of Divinity

The All That Has Been Affirmation
From a Recording of Affirmations

All that has been cannot be
That's not God and I'm not free
Until I give then I be
The joy of life that sets me free.

The All That Has Been Affirmation
From A/V Class Private 12

All that has been cannot be
That's not Good and I'm not free
Until I give then I be
The joy of life that sets me free.

The Divine Healing Prayer

I accept that the Divine Healing Power
Is removing all obstructions
From my mind and body
And is restoring me
To perfect health, wealth, and happiness.
My heart is filled with gratitude
For the Divine Law of Acceptance
That is healing both present and absent ones
Who are in need of help.
Peace, the power that healeth,
Is guiding my thoughts, acts, and deeds
As God and I go hand in hand
Living a life of joyful abundance.

The Total Consideration Affirmation

I am the manifestation of Divine Intelligence. Formless and free. Whole and complete. Peace, Poise, and Power are my birthright.

The Law of Harmony is my thought and guarantees Unity in all my acts and activities, expressing perfect Rhythm and limitless flow throughout my entire being.

Without beginning or ending, eternity is my true awareness and sees the tides of creation, as a captain sees his ship.

As the Light of Truth is sustained by the faculty of Reason, I pause to think and claim my Divine right.

    Right Thought. Right Action. Total Consideration.
               Amen. Amen. Amen.

[The following text and drawing are from the personal notes of the vice president of Serenity, a man who also served as the cameraman for these classes. This procedure is referred to in A/V Class Private 29 and 30.]

Acupressure of Circle of Logic

This procedure, as given by the Friends, is to help students restore balance in their universe, as long as effort is being made by the student who is the recipient of the procedure.

Procedure:

The student who is seeking help should sit, with back perfectly straight, on a stool or low back chair. Hands in lap, body completely relaxed.

Student to be helped, and one who will administer the pressure, should do the cleansing breath, three times. *[Note: A/V Class Private 30 also recommends that the person administering the pressure have clean hands and that their hands be rinsed with water immediately before and after the procedure.]*

The student who is to administer the pressure should stand behind the seated subject. Referring to diagram, place the index finger on top of middle finger. Be sure your finger nails are short enough so they won't dig into the other student's neck. Place the middle finger on the spot, point "A" on diagram, press firmly, and rotate tip of finger in small circle to the right, clockwise, 14 revolutions. Change fingers so that the middle finger is on top of the index finger, see diagram. Press index finger firmly, on same spot and rotate counterclockwise 13 revolutions.

Find spot "B" on diagram, and repeat procedure. Rotate middle fingertip 14 clockwise, then rotate 13 counterclockwise with the index finger. That completes the procedure.

APPENDIX

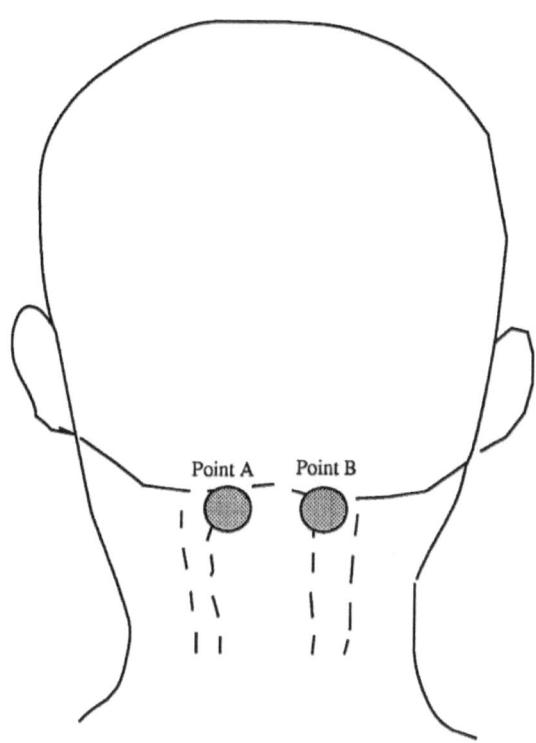

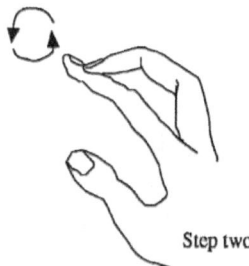

[In Seminar 33, the teacher refers to a pamphlet that was published by Serenity many years earlier. The name published on the cover of the pamphlet is "The Descent of Man," but the title page has two titles, "The Celestial Marriage" and "The Descent of Man." Here is the text of that pamphlet as it was published. An asterisk indicates a page break.]

THE CELESTIAL MARRIAGE
or
THE DESCENT OF MAN

A FABLE
FROM
THE BOOK OF LIFE

*

GIVEN IN HUMILITY
TO ALL
HUMANITY

*

One day in great **ASPIRATION GOD** sent forth from itself **WILL**, and the sons of **WILL** became. Now the sons of **WILL** were of **GOD**, yea, they were **GODS** sent into form, but knew not because of form. The sons of **WILL** roamed the universes for eons and eons of time ever seeking other forms. After much searching they met to consider what they must do. For seven days and seven nights they discussed, and at the seventh hour **ILLUMINATION** fell upon them and said, "Behold, sons of **WILL**, within thyself is **COMPASSION**, know it, and unto thee shall be given." Alas, the sons of **WILL** knew **COMPASSION** and that night the daughters of **DESTINY** became.

In the morning when the daughters of **DESTINY** awoke to the sons of **WILL**, the **GODS** and **GODESSESS** of nature danced in jubilee.

Now the sons of **WILL** married the daughters of **DESTINY** and all nature wept with joy.

One day in **TRUTH** a son was born, his name was **INEVITABLE**, and the sons of **WILL** were greatly pleased. Now the daughters of **DESTINY** were quite unhappy for they **HOPED** for a daughter, and so that night in **DESIRE** a girl was born, her name was **LUST**.

Now **INEVITABLE** grew in the warmth and sunshine of the day. Oh how he loved the sun, for to him all **LIFE** was **LIGHT**.

LUST grew up to be a beautiful and lovely woman with a great fondness for the moon and darkness, for had she not been born in the night of **DESIRE**.

Time passed on, and one day **INEVITABLE** felt he would go into the night to find **LUST**, for he had heard so much about her, and had sent her many messages asking her to come into the **LIGHT** so that they may know more of each other. **INEVITABLE** went down, down into the darkness of night, and as he descended a great **FEAR** overcame him, but he found **LUST**, her face glowing so beautiful by the reflection of the sun. From the shadows where the **LIGHT** of the moon shone not, a voice spoke unto **INEVITABLE** and said, "Behold the beauty and the glory thou hast found, is it not worth the descent into our realms?" But from within, a voice spoke to **INEVITABLE** and said, "Take her to the realms of **LIGHT** that you may see more clearly in a day of **REASON**."

The senses won, and that night in **DESPAIR** a child was born, her name was **GRIEF**. The years passed and **GRIEF** could not be comforted, for she had been born of **LUST**, in the night of **DESIRE**, by the promptings of **PASSION**, and knew not of **TRUTH**.

INEVITABLE wandered on and on with the daughter **GRIEF**, hoping to return to the realms of **LIGHT**, but no, the centuries passed and only **SORROW** did they know.

Then one day a bird from the realms of **LIGHT** landed on his shoulder and sang this song, "In **SORROW** doth thou stay for self-pity knows no way."

INEVITABLE thought and thought of the meaning of those words, then he thought of his homeland **TRUTH** where he had been so very, very happy; and in **CONCENTRATION**, he found himself leaving the realms of darkness, passing through the lands of **IGNORANCE** and **EXPERIENCE** to return to his blessed land.

LOVE ALL LIFE
AND KNOW
THE LIGHT

*

OH MAN THINK HUMBLE
YET WELL OF THYSELF
FOR IN THY THINKING
IS CREATED
THE VEHICLE OF
THE SOUL

Cover Image of 1972 Edition
of *The Living Light*

[The cover image of the 1972 edition of The Living Light *is displayed on the frontispiece of this volume. Reference to the symbolic image is discussed in excerpts from the following volumes of* The Living Light Dialogue:*]*

[Volume 2, Consciousness Class 44, pages 480-481:]
"And we'll begin with the outside of it, [The teacher refers to the cover image.] which is the snake, representative of wisdom consuming itself. Now why does the symbol of wisdom consume itself? Does anyone know? Does anyone know why wisdom is self-consuming? Because, my friends, if it's wisdom, then it can gain nothing from outside of itself: it already is wisdom. So all that wisdom is—you understand, you don't gain wisdom and neither do you give wisdom. Wisdom is self-sustaining. When you rise to a level of consciousness where wisdom expresses itself, then you will become it and it is self-sufficient unto itself. So the snake consuming itself is representative of wisdom, in comparison to what one might call knowledge. Now, knowledge is something that you gain. It's something that you put into your brain and you feed back at your discretion—but not wisdom.

"The next step is the interlaced double triangle, which is a very, very ancient symbol. It is the meeting of the spirit with matter. It is the power above that meets the forces below. And at that junction, when those two triangles meet, that's the negative and the positive poles come together in creation and the divine spark, the rays of light, life is so-called born into matter.

"Now you all know that all poles are triune. The negative pole is triune and the positive pole is triune. In fact, my friends, as we've stated before, all things that are manifest are triune and that is why three is the number of manifestation.

"Inside of the interlaced triangles you'll notice on the top of the pyramid in the rays of light is the all-seeing eye. Now the all-seeing eye is that that is not distracted, because it sees everything and so nothing gains its attention. And that is why it is the all-seeing eye. The triangle itself, the pyramid upon which all knowledge, the all-seeing eye, all wisdom, and all life rest, is the pyramid of manifestation. All things in all universes (physical, mental, or spiritual) are triune. There are three parts to all things: that is an absolute fact of physics and it is a truth of the universe."

[Volume 4, Consciousness Class 78, page 172:]

"Then, we'll be happy to share our understanding. The serpent so designed—consuming itself—is the ancient and eternal symbol of everlasting and eternal wisdom. The double triangle, with its apex downward, is the manifestation of the Divine Power and the balance of nature, its own creation. The pyramid with the all-seeing eye on the top is the eternal Light that never closes, that sees all things, that knows all things, and that ever is and ever has been."